The Jacobin Republic Under Fire

The Jacobin Republic Under Fire

THE FEDERALIST REVOLT IN THE FRENCH REVOLUTION

PAUL R. HANSON

THE PENNSYLVANIA STATE UNIVERSITY PRESS

UNIVERSITY PARK, PENNSYLVANIA

Library of Congress Cataloging-in-Publication Data

Hanson, Paul R., 1952–
The Jacobin republic under fire :
the Federalist Revolt in the French Revolution /
Paul R. Hanson.
p.   cm.
Includes bibliographical references and index.
ISBN 0-271-02281-7 (cloth : alk. paper)
1. Girondists.
2. Montagnards.
3. France—History—Revolution, 1789–1799.
I. Title.

DC179 .H36 2003
944.04'2—dc21   2003004788

It is the policy of
The Pennsylvania State University Press
to use acid-free paper. Publications on uncoated stock satisfy
the minimum requirements of American National Standard
for Information Sciences-Permanence of Paper for
Printed Library Materials, ANSI Z39.48–1992.

Contents

Maps

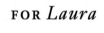
FOR *Laura*

Acknowledgments

One of the lessons I learned from Lynn Hunt, many years ago when social history was most in vogue, is that politics do matter. The political process may not always work, the views of the electorate may not always be heeded, votes may not always be accurately counted, but politics do still matter. They mattered intensely to French revolutionaries. This book is, above all, an effort to understand the debates and battles that raged from late 1792 through 1793 over how democratic politics were to be practiced. Here at the dawn of the twenty-first century most Americans seem to view politics as either irrelevant or inefficacious, even as our nation touts itself as a defender of democracy worldwide. I find that disjunction troubling. One of my hopes in writing this book, as in all of my teaching about the French Revolution, is that by studying the passion that French men and women brought to their engagement in democratic politics we might rekindle some of that passion today.

It goes without saying that books do not write themselves, nor do authors write them alone. Over the past dozen years, my research and writing has been supported by grants and fellowships from the National Endowment for the Humanities, the American Philosophical Society, the American Council of Learned Societies, and Butler University, and I am deeply appreciative of that support. In spring 1995 I spent a month at the Newberry Library in Chicago, and during that stay I first conceptualized the book. I completed most of the writing while on sabbatical in 1998–99, in a quiet office generously provided by Christian Theological Seminary, one of Butler University's near neighbors. In subsequent summers I was able to find solitude for writing in a space in the Butler library, arranged for me by Lewis Miller, the dean of the library.

A number of colleagues have generously read portions of the manuscript and offered feedback and advice. I would like to thank in particular David Andress, John Burney, Alan Forrest, Gary Kates, Michael Sydenham, and of course Lynn Hunt. I would also like to thank the then anonymous (now revealed) readers for Penn State Press, David Troyansky and John Merriman. Both are good friends and valued colleagues, and I have tried to respond to their suggestions and criticisms as fully as possible. Each can at least take some satisfaction in helping to correct my errant sense of geography.

I could not have written this history of the federalist revolt without relying on the work of other historians. I have read, and reread, the books of Alan Forrest, William Scott, and Bill Edmonds and have profited greatly from their careful research and insightful analysis. Alan and I have talked about federalism many times over the years, though not often enough. I corresponded with Bill Edmonds early in my career and regret that I never had the opportunity to meet the man whose work I greatly admire. I have also learned a great deal from the work of Antonio De Francesco and Jacques Guilhaumou, and each has been generous enough to discuss my own work with me. I must also acknowledge the work of Malcolm Crook, even if in the end I reached the conclusion that Toulon was more royalist than federalist.

Finally, a special note of thanks to my wife, Betsy Lambie, for her loving support over the years and her discerning eye as I struggled through the final editing process. We have been married for twenty-five years, and federalism has been there in one way or another for all of them. Having conquered federalism, we can now look forward to another twenty-five years of unity and indivisibility.

INTRODUCTION

More than twenty years have passed since my first trip to France to do research on the French Revolution, but I still remember vividly a conversation in the Calvados archives, where I had gone to learn more about the federalist revolt in Caen. As a young, inexperienced historian I frequently had questions about archival citations or eighteenth-century handwriting, and more often than not I turned to Monsieur Le Petit, a gentle and amiable archivist whose family had lived in Normandy for generations. He answered my questions patiently, sometimes more than once, and eventually asked me just what I was working on. When I told him that I hoped to write a history of the federalist revolt in Caen he offered a simple but deeply felt observation: "It is too bad that the Girondins did not win."

Now Monsieur Le Petit could be expected to believe that history matters—he was after all an archivist. But he cared about the defeat of the Girondins not because he was an archivist (his specialty, in fact, was in early modern civil records), but rather because he was a Frenchman. Moreover, his comment suggested not only that the political struggles of the French Revolution still mattered, but also that the victory of the Montagnards over their Girondin opponents was not a foregone conclusion. Indeed, in Monsieur Le Petit's view, had the Girondins prevailed in their struggle with the Montagnards in 1793, the first French republic might have endured much longer.

Some fourteen years later, having written that first book, I had another conversation that reminded me of the enduring relevance of the French Revolution. In 1992 I traveled in Russia with a group of Butler University faculty, on a study tour related to a comparative world cultures course that we all taught together. Just one year before Boris Yeltsin had succeeded Mikhail Gorbachev in power, and the Soviet Union was in the process of falling apart. Our final stop was St. Petersburg, where one morning we met with members of the city council. I was not looking forward to what I expected to be a rather boring session involving the ritual exchange of formulaic greetings and souvenir pins. I could not have been more wrong. We did get pins (I still treasure mine!), but our conversation with four members of the St. Petersburg municipal council was fascinating, and as we sat with them in a room of the Maryinski Palace, redolent with its own rich history, I felt as if I could as easily have been back in the 1790s in Paris or Marseille.

The four deputies, like their forebears in the French National Convention, were all young and all men, but they represented diverse groups and interests. One was a liberal socialist, one a computer specialist, another an environmental activist, and the fourth ardently devoted to the revival of the Russian Orthodox Church. There were 500 deputies on the St. Petersburg municipal council, and as with the members of the National Convention, 750 in number, these men often felt overwhelmed by the difficulty of accomplishing anything in so large an assembly, even as they felt exhilarated by the opportunity to enact real change in their city. They were faced by enormous, concrete problems, but they also confronted more abstract issues of political theory: "Are we," one asked us, "the representatives of our constituents, or have we been elected to vote our conscience as free agents?" Another observed, "In the midst of so many crises, it is a good thing that the people are at present apathetic, or we would all be out on our ears." The Girondins should have been so lucky, I thought. Parisians were scarcely apathetic in 1793, and most of the Girondin leaders met their fate on the guillotine.

As with my earlier exchange with Monsieur Le Petit, this conversation reminded me that revolutionary politics still matter in the world today. Revolutions are moments when people claim their most fundamental rights and proclaim the principle of popular sovereignty. This was true of the French and American revolutions of the eighteenth century, and it was true of the revolutions that swept across central and eastern Europe in 1989. But despite the assertion of the American founding fathers, those rights and that principle are neither self-evident nor universal. In particular, the nature, the extent, and the practice of sovereignty have always been hotly contested, as they were in 1792–93.

In this book I argue that the contestation of sovereignty was the essential issue that divided French revolutionaries in 1792 and 1793 and that very nearly plunged the country into civil war during the months of the federalist revolt. This was scarcely the only pressing concern before the young republic: the foreign war, the fate of the king, the Civil Constitution of the Clergy, the policy toward *émigré* nobles—these were all divisive issues within the National Assembly and throughout France. But underlying the bitter debates and divisions over these issues lay the most fundamental of political questions: Who are the sovereign people and how are they to exercise that sovereignty?

Why had these questions not been resolved in the years between 1789 and 1793? Or, put differently, why did they become so central, so inescapable, in the spring and summer of 1793? There are short answers to each of these questions. To the first, the answer is that the delegates to the Estates-General did everything they could to avoid the issue of popular sovereignty in 1789. They did not even think of themselves as "deputies" or "representatives" at first—

they were delegates sent by traditional corporate bodies, and even when they broke decisively with that tradition they spoke of the "nation," not the "people," as sovereign. The short answer to the second question is that the king was deposed, tried, and executed between August 1792 and January 1793, and this chain of events forced the revolutionaries to confront more directly the vexing issue of just who within the nation might legitimately exercise sovereignty.

This book, which is in some sense a long answer to the second question, focuses on the struggle between Girondin and Montagnard deputies within the National Convention in the months following the fall of the monarchy, and on the tumult in the provinces that accompanied that struggle and then escalated into open revolt after the leading Girondin deputies were expelled from the National Convention in early June 1793. I will argue, however, that the federalist revolt was not simply a response to the expulsion of the Girondin deputies in Paris but was rather the culmination of a political conflict that raged in a number of provincial cities, most notably Lyon and Marseille, throughout this same period. Local and national politics came together at this time in a particularly dynamic fashion, more so than at any other moment in the Revolution. Local politics, by which I chiefly mean municipal politics, asserted a profound influence on national politics, ranging from the leading role that the Marseille volunteers played in the assault on the Tuileries palace in August 1792, to the well-chronicled impact of Parisian radicalism on debate within the National Convention, to the lesser-known fact that a violent upheaval in Lyon preceded by two days the insurrection in Paris on May 31, 1793, that led to the proscription of the Girondins. It was at the level of local politics that the legitimacy of popular sovereignty could be most forcefully proclaimed, and also where it was most hotly contested. The Girondin deputies, as is generally well known, were for the most part products of provincial politics, but it should be noted that this was true for many of the leading Montagnards as well. When these men debated just who the "sovereign people" were or should be, they thought not only of the militants of the Paris crowd, the *sans-culottes*, but of their constituents back home. It was a debate rooted not only in abstract political theorizing, but in the very concrete political experience of the first four years of the Revolution.

Specialists and serious students of the French Revolution will already be familiar with the course of events in those early years, but the general reader will likely appreciate a brief overview so that the conflict of 1793 can be placed in its proper context. No one could anticipate in spring 1789 what lay ahead for France in the next four years, although nearly everyone realized that the country was in crisis: a crisis characterized by a slumping economy, two poor harvests in succession, a nearly bankrupt royal treasury, and a political impasse that rendered traditional monarchical solutions to such problems impractical. King Louis XVI thus resorted to the extraordinary measure of convening the Estates-

General for the first time in 175 years. All male subjects of the realm were called upon to participate in the election of delegates to the Estates-General and to contribute to the drafting of grievance lists, to share with the king and his ministers their thoughts about the problems confronting France. This unprecedented call set in motion the political mobilization of the entire nation.

The delegates who went to Versailles represented one of the three traditional orders, or estates, of the French kingdom: the First Estate, composed of the clergy; the Second Estate, composed of the nobility; and the Third Estate, composed of everyone else. The Third Estate, being more numerous, sent twice as many delegates as the first two, but there was disagreement over how the estates should deliberate at Versailles—together or separately—and over how they should vote—one vote per order or one vote per delegate. These disagreements produced a stalemate, and little was accomplished for some six weeks.

Then, quite dramatically, on June 17 the bulk of the Third Estate, joined by a number of liberal nobles and clergymen, pledged to meet as a body and declared themselves the National Assembly. Three days later, finding themselves locked out of the Third Estate's meeting hall, they swore the famous Tennis Court Oath, declaring that wherever they might gather, there the nation would be represented. This was a revolutionary moment, and some of the conservative noblemen and bishops, recognizing its implications, soon departed, asserting that they had not been elected as deputies of the nation, but rather as delegates to the Estates-General, and therefore had no further business at Versailles. The king, for his part, publicly accepted the fait accompli in a royal session on June 23, but at the same time he took measures to thwart the initiative of the Third Estate. Royal troops were called to the vicinity of Paris, and on July 11 Louis dismissed his finance minister, Jacques Necker, a favorite of the people.

These measures alarmed the citizens of Paris, who mobilized both in defense of their city and in defense of what was already being referred to by some as "the Revolution." On July 14, a crowd of some eighty thousand marched across Paris from the Invalides hospital to the Bastille, ultimately storming the old royal prison and fortress and killing its unfortunate governor, Bernard-René-Jordan Delauney. The king responded by restoring Necker to office and accepting the transformation of the Estates-General into the National Assembly.

July 14 was the first occasion in the Revolution when crowd violence played a decisive role in major political developments, but it would not be the last. On October 4–5, after Louis XVI balked at signing the Declaration of the Rights of Man and Citizen and refused to sign legislation ordering the confiscation of church property and the abolition of privilege, a large crowd of market women marched to Versailles. Angered by the recent increase in bread prices, they met with the king, accosted the queen and her guards, and eventually escorted the royal family back to Paris, where they took up residence in the Tuileries palace.

From this point forward there were those, even among the revolutionaries themselves, who grew gravely concerned about the influence of popular violence, or at least the threat of violence, on political debate. Many of the deputies to the National Assembly recognized, however, that without the violence of the crowd the king would have been able to stymie the reforms that they so ardently desired. At what point, though, they worried, would continued violent protest come to jeopardize the gains of the Revolution and threaten to cast French society into a permanent state of social disorder? As we shall see, this was a concern that dominated public debate in 1792–93.

A great deal was accomplished during the first two years of the Revolution. The deputies of the National Assembly, also known as the Constituent Assembly, worked tirelessly to create a more rational administrative structure for the realm, to resolve the financial crisis of the royal treasury, and to draft a written constitution for the kingdom. The administrative map of France was redrawn, and a hierarchical network of departmental, district, and municipal councils was created, although it was left unclear whether or not these new councils were to play a political as well as an administrative role. All of these local councils were to be elected, not appointed. But whereas the elections to the Estates-General had effectively been by universal manhood suffrage, the Constituent Assembly divided the citizenry into two groups: active citizens, essentially male property owners, who voted; and passive citizens, women and the propertyless, who did not. Sovereignty was to be limited under the constitutional monarchy.

The most pressing problem before the Constituent Assembly was the royal debt, and as already noted, this was to be eliminated by the confiscation of church property, the sale of which at public auction would generate the revenue to repay royal creditors. This proposed solution created new problems, however. Because of the loss of the church's revenue-producing properties, the clergy were to be paid by the state, making them, in the eyes of the deputies, the equivalent of civil servants. The Constituent Assembly therefore drafted the Civil Constitution of the Clergy, which among other things required all clergy to swear an oath of loyalty to the nation, the king, and the law. This proved to be an enormously divisive measure, not only among the clergy (about half of whom refused to swear the oath) but for the nation at large. Louis XVI, a very devout man, approved the legislation with great reluctance.

Louis was also deeply troubled by the legislation abolishing privilege, including the status of nobility. All men were to be seen as equal asserted the Declaration of the Rights of Man. Many aristocrats were understandably offended by this, and some chose to leave France, as did some of the refractory priests who had refused to swear the civil oath. Revolutionaries regarded these *émigrés* as traitors and called for the confiscation of their property. But Louis refused to take resolute action against them, raising suspicions in the minds of some that the king was conspiring with those *émigrés* and with other monarchs of Europe in a counterrevolutionary plot. The king's flight to Varennes, in June 1791, seemed to confirm those suspicions.

Louis XVI and his family were apprehended near the French border and returned to Paris under the escort of the National Guard and several deputies from the Constituent Assembly. Their reception in Paris was, to say the least, a chilly one. Several points merit emphasis here in regard to this perplexing episode. First, before leaving Paris, Louis XVI had left a note denouncing the recently drafted constitution (which, in his view, imposed unwarranted limitations on the powers of the king), as well as the subversive influence of the Jacobin clubs. The most powerful of the Jacobin clubs, which met in Paris, included a number of deputies in its ranks and functioned, some argued, as a kind of shadow parliament. By 1791 a network of affiliated clubs had already begun to spread across France, and there was much debate, both in Paris and the provinces, about whether or not the Jacobin clubs (or any such clubs for that matter) had a legitimate role to play in the new political order.

The second point worth emphasizing is that after his return to Paris, Louis XVI accepted the constitution that he had so recently denounced and pledged to uphold it. Barely one year later he was deposed for allegedly reneging on that pledge. Louis was particularly concerned that under the new constitution he enjoyed only a "suspensive" rather than an "absolute" veto over legislation, which seemed to leave him in a secondary position to the National Assembly. This was an awkward position indeed for a man who had once ruled as an absolute monarch. It raised in a fundamental way the question of where sovereignty lay.

A third important point here is that in the weeks following the king's return to Paris, a schism developed within the Jacobin club. Moderate deputies broke away from the Jacobins to form a rival club, known as the Feuillants. Their position, simply put, was that the Revolution should come to an end and the nation should rally behind a constitutional monarch and a political order dominated by property owners. That position was challenged by a growing popular movement in Paris that favored the declaration of a republic and the dethronement of Louis XVI. The Cordeliers club, to the left of the Jacobins, circulated a petition to that end, but on July 17, 1791, a rally on the Champ de Mars ended in violence, and this, along with the king's acceptance of the new constitution, brought a temporary end to the radical movement and strengthened the hand of moderates. The fear of popular violence and calls for political moderation will be consistent themes throughout this study.

A Legislative Assembly, to be elected under the new system that distinguished between active and passive citizens, convened in fall 1792. Under a proviso put forward by the young deputy Maximilien Robespierre, the members of the Constituent Assembly were not eligible to stand for reelection, so the Legislative Assembly was composed of men new to national politics. Robespierre, who had not been a leading figure in the Constituent Assembly, gained prominence out of office as a journalist, a leader in the Jacobin club, and an activist in Paris municipal politics. Among the deputies of the new Legislative Assembly, the moderate Feuillants dominated at first, but their leadership was soon challenged by a group known initially as Brissotins, after their leading voice, Jacques Brissot. He was joined by a group of eloquent orators from the department of the Gironde, most notably Pierre Vergniaud. With this influx of new talent, the group eventually came to be known as Girondins. These deputies were committed to some form of representative democracy, to the implementation of the Civil Constitution of the Clergy, and to active opposition to France's enemies abroad, especially the Austrian monarchy, suspected by many of supporting the plots of *émigré* aristocrats.

The Brissotins pushed for a declaration of war against Austria, which they achieved in April 1792, convinced that this would rally the nation to the revolutionary government and force the king to reveal his true loyalty. The war, however, went badly, as Robespierre had warned it would, and the setbacks on the battlefield seemed to polarize the nation. In particular, the flagging war effort rendered more problematical Louis XVI's continued refusal to deal harshly with the *émigré* nobles and refractory priests, both groups now seen as actively supporting the forces of counterrevolution. When Louis dismissed his Brissotin ministers in June 1792 for publicly questioning his loyalty to the nation, an active movement to depose the king was rekindled in Paris.

The first eruption of that movement, on June 20, was unsuccessful, and that failed insurrection brought a host of letters from departmental administrations, and even some provincial Jacobin clubs, declaring their support for the king and their opposition to violent protest. Unfazed by those letters, the militants of Paris redoubled their efforts and increased their organization so that on August 10 a disciplined assault on the Tuileries palace, led by the Marseille volunteers, forced the king's abdication. The collapse of the monarchy once again placed the debate over sovereignty squarely before the French people and their representatives.

We will follow that debate closely in the chapters that follow, as it played itself out both in Paris and the provinces, but let us sketch out its main contours here. The most prominent voices were those of Vergniaud and Robespierre. Robespierre, from his position in the Jacobin club, had openly advocated insurrection against the monarchy and later described August 10 as a triumph of "the people." Vergniaud, who presided over the Legislative Assembly on the eve of

August 10, turned away a petition from the section assemblies of Paris calling for the king's ouster, claiming that the sections of Paris represented only a portion of the people of France.

Both Vergniaud and Robespierre were elected as deputies to the new national assembly, known as the National Convention, made necessary by the de facto collapse of the constitutional monarchy created by the constitution of 1791. Pointing to the glorious triumph of the people on August 10, Robespierre and others insisted that those elections be by universal manhood suffrage, and this was in fact adopted, both nationally and locally. Even as those elections were being conducted, however, violence erupted once again in Paris. Responding to ominous reports from the battlefront, militants invaded the prisons and executed some thirteen hundred prisoners, supposed fifth-column sympathizers of the advancing Prussian and Austrian forces.

The September massacres, as they came to be known, shocked the nation and revived fears among the propertied classes of mob violence and anarchy. Vergniaud and his supporters denounced the perpetrators of the violence, including Robespierre, and demanded that they be brought to justice. The Montagnards, so-called because they occupied the highest seats in the National Assembly, described the violence as regrettable but necessary, linked the September violence to the August 10 insurrection, and characterized the prison executions as a kind of people's justice. Over the coming months, every major issue before the National Convention—the trial of the king, the debate over a new constitution, the conduct of the foreign war—would be touched by this ideological dispute. The Girondins, appealing to the rule of law, saw in the prison massacres a weapon to be directed against their Montagnard/Jacobin opponents. The Montagnards countered that attack by defending the "good people of Paris" and appealing to the ideal of popular sovereignty. The Girondins' response to this was to insist that provincial Frenchmen were a part of the people, too, and that in any case it had not been the "good" people of Paris who had invaded the prisons in September.

On one level, the opposition between Montagnards and Girondins can be seen as a struggle between the champions of the Paris *sans-culottes* on one hand and the champions of provincial France on the other. It was easier for the Montagnards to mobilize their Parisian supporters, however, than for the Girondins to mobilize provincial France, and on June 2, 1793, yet another Parisian insurrection ousted the Girondin leaders from the National Convention. Many departmental administrations protested this proscription of the Girondins, and four provincial cities—Caen, Bordeaux, Lyon, and Marseille—rebelled against Paris and the Montagnard-dominated Convention. This "federalist revolt" very nearly plunged France into civil war, but the federalist leaders (mostly departmental administrators) could not generate popular support for a march on Paris, and the movement never constituted a serious threat to the central government. This is more apparent today than it was at the time. The federalist rebels did everything they could to exaggerate their numbers in order to gain new allies, and the government used those exaggerated claims as justification for an increase in the power and authority of the central government. In July 1793 Robespierre joined the Committee of Public Safety, the group of twelve men who would serve as the executive branch of government for the next year. Its first task was to quell the provincial rebellions. The repression of the federalist revolt, particularly in the city of Lyon, would mark the first manifestations of the Terror in France. Roughly 10 percent of the Terror's victims were charged with the crime of federalism.

The Committee of Public Safety, citing the internal rebellion and the foreign war, never implemented the democratic constitution that the deputies of the National Convention passed in late June 1793 and the voters of France endorsed later that summer. The Montagnards, ruling in the name of the people, never allowed the people to rule themselves. In July 1794 the Terror claimed Robespierre as one of its final victims, and in the Thermidorian reaction that followed, many of the Girondin deputies who had survived the Terror returned to office, as did their supporters in the provinces. The September massacres, and the threat of crowd violence, became once again a focal point in political debate, and a number of prominent "terrorists" were tried and executed or deported. The rule of law, a vengeful law, was now established. The window of opportunity for popular democracy had seemingly passed.

I would agree with Monsieur Le Petit, my archivist friend, that 1792–93 represented a missed opportunity for the young French republic, although I am not sure that I agree with him that France would have been better off under Girondin rule. It is my view that the federalist revolt and the events leading up to it present us with an unusual opportunity to see revolutionary politics not just through the filter of national rhetoric, but through provincial rhetoric and actions as well. It is the one point in the Revolution where national and local politics came together in a most striking fashion. The struggle between Montagnards and Girondins may in some sense have pitted Paris against the provinces, but it was not only the Parisian *sans-culottes* who called for popular sovereignty. Nor was the federalist revolt simply a reaction to the proscription of the Girondins. It grew out of a longstanding struggle over sovereignty that was waged both in word and in practice in cities throughout France, a struggle that came to a head precisely at the moment that the battle between Girondins and Montagnards reached its crisis point in the capital. What was at stake was no less than the future of the French republic, a future that was determined not just by ideology, but by social and political antagonisms as well.

There have been many accounts or studies of the struggle between Girondins and Montagnards, and in recent years each of the federalist cities has been the focus of a monograph. It has been more than one hundred years, however, since Henri Wallon wrote the only history of the federalist revolt, and no one has attempted an overarching study of both the conflict within the National Convention and the revolt in the four principal federalist cities. That is the task that I undertake in this volume. It is a work of interpretation and synthesis, drawing on the research of a great many historians as well as on my own archival investigations. It presents a narrative account of these complicated events as well as, I hope, some persuasive analysis.

The book begins with the words of the most prominent Girondin leader, Pierre Vergniaud. Many years ago Michael Sydenham argued that our understanding of the Girondin deputies was largely a product of Jacobin propaganda, generated after the Girondins had been ousted from the National Convention. Mindful of that admonition, I wanted to let the Girondins speak for themselves, in dramatic fashion, by presenting their own defense at their trial in 1793. But their Jacobin prosecutors, fearful of the eloquence of the Girondin orators, silenced them at their trial. So I have turned instead to a letter that Vergniaud wrote to two of his accusers, and later to the notes that Vergniaud jotted while awaiting trial in prison. We hear as well, in Chapter 1, from the Girondins' accusers, and I will sketch briefly the outlines of the federalist revolt in the provinces.

Having begun at the end of the story, I then turn to the beginning and in Chapter 2 examine the roots of the Girondin-Montagnard conflict within the National Convention. That conflict endured some eight to nine months, paralyzing the work for which the deputies had been sent to Paris. Standing like bookends at either end of that struggle were two insurrectionary upheavals—the August 10, 1792, assault on the Tuileries palace, and the May 31, 1793, *journée* by which the Parisian *sans-culottes* forced the proscription of the leading Girondins. In the interim, three other dramatic events shaped the political debate within the Convention: the September massacres, the trial of Louis XVI, and the impeachment of Jean-Paul Marat. In Chapter 2 I will examine each of those events and their impact on the evolving debate over sovereignty.

That debate ended in violence, at least the threat of violence, in Paris, but Chapter 3 begins instead with a violent upheaval in Lyon that occurred on May 29, two days before the march on the National Convention. The Lyon insurrection reminds us that the provinces did not always wait to follow the Parisian lead while it also makes clear that the Montagnards and their allies did not have a monopoly on violent protest. The May 29 revolution in Lyon was a victory for supporters of the Girondins, and their proscription from the Convention just days later placed the political triumph of the Lyonnais rebels in immediate jeopardy. This chapter examines both of these late May insurrections and then turns to the revolt against the proscription of the Girondin deputies in each of the four federalist cities. The emphasis here will be to establish clearly the chain of events in early June 1793.

General histories of the Revolution have customarily given the federalist revolts short shrift, leaving readers to think of them as disjointed and ineffectual at best, or openly counterrevolutionary at worst. My aim in Chapter 4 is to challenge that view by analyzing the federalist program. The failure of the federalist cities to unify was a key factor in their defeat, but there were serious efforts to join the federalist departments together, and the manifestos and declarations of the various federalist centers make it possible to speak of a federalist program. Theirs was not a truly "federalist" vision—they did not advocate a federated republic as their opponents charged. But they did hold Paris in suspicion and they advocated a political system that would value order over mobilization of the populace. They were not counterrevolutionaries, at least not for the most part, but the federalist rebels did put forward a vision of a republic quite different from that advocated by the Parisian *sans-culottes* or presented by the Jacobin constitution of 1793.

Federalist republicanism was not simply a reaction to Parisian radicalism, nor a loyal following of Girondin leadership. The politics of the federalist rebels grew as well, perhaps most importantly, out of the crucible of local politics, and Chapter 5 focuses on local contexts. Just as Chapter 2 explored the roots of the Girondin-Montagnard conflict, in Chapter 5, I seek to trace the evolution of local politics in the four federalist cities from the early years of the Revolution up to 1793. The emphasis is on 1792–93 when the definition of sovereignty was changed due to the events of August 10. The introduction of universal manhood suffrage in the fall elections of 1792 altered the composition of municipal councils across France, nowhere more dramatically than in Lyon and Marseille. Moderates felt threatened by the newly elected Jacobin councils, and they mobilized their allies and supporters to unseat those councils in spring 1793, claiming at the time the mantle of popular sovereignty. When, in the name of the people, the Parisian *sans-culottes* ousted the Girondin deputies from the National Convention on June 2, the moderates in Lyon and Marseille saw their own recent victories placed in immediate jeopardy. Thus, the local and national conflicts were very much intertwined. We will see that the same was true in both Caen and Bordeaux, though in somewhat less dramatic fashion.

The pronouncements of the Jacobins in Paris and the federalists in the provinces both tended to exaggerate the threat represented by their opponents to the safety of the republic. In Chapter 6, I attempt to look beyond that rhetoric to assess, through letters and private reports, the range of contemporary perspectives on the federalist revolt. How threatened did Parisians feel by the federalist calls for a march on Paris? How persuaded were the people of the provinces that the federalist rebels spoke on their behalf? This chapter seeks to present some of the voices of those rarely listened to and seldom heard.

The federalist revolt collapsed fairly quickly in most quarters, and its gravity was exaggerated by the Jacobins in Paris. Yet it cannot be denied that the repression of the federalist revolts marked the first manifestations of the Terror in France. No city suffered more during the Terror than Lyon, and in Bordeaux and Marseille as well the guillotine claimed hundreds of victims in the wake of the federalist upheaval. In Chapter 7, I will examine the dynamics of that repression, focusing in particular on the role of the representatives on mission but also considering the more positive measures taken by the National Convention to quell the rebellion, most notably the drafting of a new constitution. The constitution of 1793, the most democratic of the Revolution, held considerable promise for the young republic, tragically never realized. It was never enacted, replaced in 1795 by a far more conservative document. But from Gracchus Babeuf in 1796 to Louis Blanc in the mid-nineteenth century, the constitution of 1793 remained an inspiration for French republicans.

Having begun the book with the words of Pierre Vergniaud, I conclude with words from Robert Lindet, one of the accusers to whom Vergniaud addressed his public letter in summer 1793. No one did more than Lindet to try to avert the tragedy of the federalist revolt. Sent by the Committee of Public Safety to Lyon in June 1793, he reported back in his letters that there were many good republicans in that city, and that the differences between Lyon and Paris could be peacefully resolved. Later that summer Lindet led an "army of pacification" to Caen, and the repression of the revolt in that city was almost bloodless. In Lyon, by contrast, nearly two thousand of those "good republicans" were eventually executed. Robert Lindet, certainly one of the most remarkable of the French revolutionaries, later defended the Terror against its Thermidorian detractors. Although he did not deny its excesses, neither did he see it as the simple product of ideology. Unlike most of the revolutionaries, whether Girondin or Montagnard, Lindet seemed capable of overcoming deeply felt political divisions. But in spite of his defense in 1794 of the regime of the Committee of Public Safety, one suspects that Lindet would not have denied that in the name of popular sovereignty the Montagnards had overseen the stifling of participatory democracy. In this lay the real tragedy of the federalist revolt and the Terror that followed.

One

GIRONDINS ON TRIAL

My heart is prepared; it braves the blade of assassins as well as that of the executioner.
My death will be the last crime of our modern Decemvirs.
Far from fearing death, I hope for it: for soon the people, enlightened by it, will free themselves at
last from their horrible tyranny.

—*Pierre Victurnien Vergniaud*

In the final days of June 1793 the city of Paris was uneasy. At the beginning of the month twenty-nine deputies, the leaders of the Girondin faction, had been purged from the National Convention. Some of those deputies had fled to the provinces, seemingly bent on leading a revolt against the capital. But Pierre Vergniaud, the most celebrated orator among the Girondins, remained in Paris under house arrest, and as the month drew to a close he wrote an open letter to Bertrand Barère and Robert Lindet (both of whom were members of the Committee of Public Safety), accusing them of being impostors and assassins.

Published in pamphlet form, Vergniaud's letter accused its addressees of being impostors and assassins. They were impostors, he argued, because they refused to publish formal charges against the proscribed Girondin deputies; they refused to let them speak in their own defense before the National Convention; and they accused the Girondins of fomenting rebellion in the departments, for which they themselves should be held responsible. They were assassins, wrote Vergniaud, because they refused to confront the proscribed deputies in a court of law, preferring to strike them down from behind.[1]

Pierre Vergniaud was the leading spokesperson for the Girondin faction within the National Convention. So eloquent and powerful was his rhetoric that his opponents denied him the opportunity to speak at the October 1793 trial of Girondin leaders. What some have described as the first revolutionary show trial thus presented only one side of the conflict: the Montagnard indictment of the Girondins as counterrevolutionaries. To hear the Girondins, we must turn

---

1. "Vergniaud, Député du Département de la Gironde, à Barère et à Robert Lindet, membres du Comité de Salut Public de la Convention Nationale" (Paris, June 28, 1793).

to letters and to the notes Vergniaud prepared while he awaited trial. These letters and notes will give us some sense of what was at stake for the Girondins in summer 1793.

The fate of the Girondins was not decided only in Paris, however. Four provincial cities rose up in protest of their proscription, supported by a majority of the departments in France. The federalist rebels in these cities were concerned for the safety of the proscribed deputies, but their actions were much more broadly focused and motivated. Issues of sovereignty were very much on the minds of provincial Frenchmen, just as they were on the minds of Vergniaud and the others in Paris. At that moment, indeed, provincial politics and national politics were inextricably intertwined.

There is much that is interesting in Vergniaud's open letter as well as much that is curious and ironic. For example, why did Vergniaud choose to address this letter to Bertrand Barère and Robert Lindet? The two were to be the only members of the first Committee of Public Safety who remained as members of the "Great Committee," reconstituted on July 10, 1793. This significant detail might be sufficient answer to our question, but Vergniaud could not have known this when he penned his letter at the end of June.

Perhaps Vergniaud addressed these two for the role they had played in the ongoing struggle between Girondins and Montagnards. Far from being radical Montagnards, however, both Barère and Lindet could be described as moderates. It is true that Barère had issued the first report to the National Convention on the proscribed deputies, characterizing the insurrection of June 2 as a triumph for liberty; and even as Vergniaud wrote, Lindet was at the head of an "army of pacification" intent on subduing the rebellion in Caen, where a number of the proscribed deputies had sought refuge. But earlier in May, Barère had sponsored the creation of the Commission of Twelve, a committee widely perceived as the very spearhead of the Girondin campaign against the Commune of Paris. Lindet, for his part, had returned from an early June mission to Lyon, another of the federalist centers, optimistic about the chances of rallying the many good republicans in that city to the cause of national unity. He was not, in other words, an advocate of harsh repression or vindictive justice.[2]

Is it possible that Vergniaud hoped to shame the two deputies toward clemency by this public appeal? The opening words of the letter render null this possibility: "Men who cowardly sell your consciences and the good of the Republic in order to preserve a fleeting popularity, and acquire an elusive celebrity!" These are hardly words likely to gain the sympathy of Barère or Lindet.

2. See Michael J. Sydenham, *The Girondins* (London, 1961), 2, for a discussion of Barère's report. For Lindet's missions to Lyon and Caen, see Paul R. Hanson, *Provincial Politics in the French Revolution: Caen and Limoges, 1789–1794* (Baton Rouge, 1989), chap. 5.

Indeed, it is difficult to know what Vergniaud hoped to accomplish by publishing this inflammatory letter. A nineteenth-century biographer of Vergniaud, C. Vatel, expressed astonishment that any printer in Paris dared to publish the piece and speculated that Vergniaud may have principally hoped to arouse support in the provinces for opposition to the Montagnards. The pamphlet was in fact reprinted in both Caen and Lyon, and it almost certainly reached Bordeaux and Marseille as well.[3]

The tone of Vergniaud's pamphlet, however, is more justificatory than incendiary. Rather than defending himself and his Girondin colleagues who were accused of inciting rebellion in the provinces, he attacked their Montagnard opponents. Vergniaud leveled three specific charges against Barère, Lindet, and their colleagues. First, he accused them of deceiving the departments about what had happened in Paris at the end of May and of deceiving Paris about what was going on in the departments. Secondly, he accused them of disquieting both Paris and the departments by their flagrant violation of the confidentiality of the mails. Finally, he berated them for failing to bring specific charges against the proscribed deputies within three days of their arrest as required by law. A prompt report, Vergniaud asserted, would have averted the revolt, either by showing the deputies' guilt or by proving their innocence.[4]

This is scarcely a call to arms, although presumably those who arranged for the reprinting of the pamphlet in Caen and Lyon hoped that it would rally the faltering spirits of their supporters. Vergniaud seems to have been more concerned with justifying the past actions of the proscribed deputies and the current actions of those who had risen in their support. Yet he is careful to direct attention away from the deputies themselves. The insurgent departments had rebelled, he argued, not for the sake of the deputies, but rather for the sake of the National Assembly whose integrity had been violated.

Vergniaud, who has often been described as the master rhetorician of the National Convention, seems oddly unsure of his rhetorical strategy in this piece. It is inflammatory but stops short of being an exhortation to rebellion; and while justifying the actions of the insurgent departments, it also observes that the rebellion might easily have been avoided. As a preliminary effort to defend the actions and motivations of the proscribed deputies, this pamphlet, at a scant six pages, seems wholly inadequate. Nor, given its brevity, is it any more persuasive as an indictment of the Montagnards. It is not as if he could not have said more. For example, in mid-April, on the heels of the celebrated exchange in the National Convention between Vergniaud and Robespierre, Marguerite Elie

3. C. Vatel, *Vergniaud: Manuscrits, Lettres et Papiers, pièces pour la plupart inédites, classées et annotées* (Paris, 1873), vol. 2, 194–98.

4. "Vergniaud . . . à Barère et Lindet," 3–4.

Guadet had published a forty-eight-page pamphlet defending the words and actions of himself and his Girondin colleagues and castigating Robespierre and the Montagnards.[5] Vergniaud, denied the stage of the National Convention, seemed unable to produce with his pen the sort of brilliant and eloquent argument that had once flowed so easily from his tongue.

Unwilling to enter the arena of rebellion with his colleagues who had fled to Caen in early June, Vergniaud may have been hoping to take center stage once again at the trial he assumed must come eventually. He certainly had the opportunity to flee Paris. While under house arrest, Vergniaud petitioned the National Convention on June 16 to be allowed to leave his apartment, freedom that the deputy Birotteau had been granted the day before. When his petition was approved, Vergniaud chose to remain in the capital, whereas Birotteau immediately took flight to Lyon.[6] In late July he was imprisoned in the Luxembourg palace, then transferred within a week to the Force prison and later to the Conciergerie. During his imprisonment, Vergniaud prepared notes for his defense, a defense that he would not be allowed to deliver in court.

A fellow prisoner in La Force, a man by the name of Champagneux, lamented that Vergniaud and his colleagues gave little effort to their defense, seemingly resigned to the inevitability of their conviction and execution.[7] That criticism is belied by the survival in the archives of detailed notes, in Vergniaud's hand, outlining a strategy of defense and indicating relevant supporting documents.[8] These notes may have been prepared after Vergniaud's transfer from La Force to the Conciergerie in early October, but Champagneux's impression of the deputy's casual approach to this momentous event would also be consistent with Vergniaud's longstanding habit of speaking from sketchy notes rather than from a prepared text. Another of Vergniaud's biographers, Claude Bowers, has observed that his "speeches were the ripe fruit of his meditations" and that while "seemingly bored and languid in repose, the moment he mounted the tribune all contemporaries agree that he was metamorphosed, transported."[9] He had ample time to meditate while in prison, to be sure, and these notes convey vividly his own sense of the divisions that had shattered both the unity of the National Convention and that of the young French republic.

Vergniaud organized his notes under five main headings, corresponding to the principal accusations against him and his colleagues. He stood accused of

5. Marguerite Elie Guadet, "Réponse de Guadet, Député de la Gironde, à Robespierre, Député de Paris. Prononcée dans la Séance du 12 Avril 1793," A.D. Gironde, 8J706.

6. C. Vatel, *Vergniaud*, vol. 2, 193–204. Vergniaud would later be accused of attempting to flee Paris, a charge he vigorously denied.

7. Vatel, *Vergniaud*, vol. 2, 233–34.

8. A.N., W292B, no. 204, plaquette 3. Vergniaud's notes are also reproduced in Vatel, *Vergniaud*, vol. 2, 253–318.

9. Claude G. Bowers, *Pierre Vergniaud: Voice of the French Revolution* (New York, 1950), 4–6.

royalism, of federalism, of having conspired to sow civil war, of having initiated the war between France and the rest of Europe, and of having belonged to a faction within the National Convention. His responses to each of these charges were followed by a section of general observations and an appended section in which he addressed the charge that he and the others had slandered the city of Paris. Throughout most of these notes, Vergniaud was careful to focus on his own words, behavior, and actions, deflecting implicitly the serious allegation that the Girondins had acted as a conspiratorial faction. But he began his general observations with a rhetorical question, expressed in the first person plural: "How can there be so many accusations, if we are innocent?" That ominous question, to which he offered no answer, was followed by two interesting fragments: "Spirit of party, hatreds" and "Division over the people or measures called revolutionary."[10]

In these "general observations" lay the heart of the dilemma for Vergniaud and the other accused Girondins. Responding to the specific charges was not so terribly daunting a task, and Vergniaud pursued it systematically in his many pages of notes. The fugitive deputies had done so as well, with the publication of a pamphlet in mid-July that responded to Louis-Antoine Saint-Just's report to the National Convention.[11] So ludicrous did they find the charges against them that they adopted a satirical tone in their pamphlet, referring mockingly to Saint-Just as "Monsieur le Chevalier" and poking fun at the supposed charges against "Buzot's counterrevolutionary horse." To Vergniaud as well as the deputies in Caen, the dual charges that they were both royalists and federalists were clearly contradictory. How could one advocate a restoration of the monarchy and at the same time favor a decentralization of governmental power? And if the people in arms in Caen and Marseille were truly federalists, why were they marching to Paris? Why did they not simply remain at home? In regard to the charge that they had fomented civil war, which Saint-Just alleged was proven by their flight to Caen, the deputies pointed out the absurdity of now being denounced for something that they had done after their proscription on June 2! The proscribed deputies and their supporters in the provinces sought only to restore the unity and integrity of the National Convention and thereby that of the republic itself.[12]

It was more difficult for Vergniaud and the other proscribed deputies to deny that a "spirit of party" and "hatreds" had existed within the National Convention. Vergniaud, for his part, observed in his notes that a national legislature

10. Vatel, *Vergniaud*, vol. 2, 253–65.
11. "Observations sur le rapport des Trente-deux Proscrits. Par une Société de Girondins" (Caen, July 13, 1793). St. Just read his report before the National Convention on July 8. The response of the deputies in Caen was based on excerpts published in the newspapers.
12. Ibid., 11.

could not exist without freedom of opinion, and the liberty to freely express that opinion, and that a tyranny of the majority (*un parti dominateur de la majorité*) would stifle that liberty.[13] Yet the Girondins themselves had moved to impeach Jean-Paul Marat in spring 1793, and Vergniaud had done nothing to allay the impression of hatreds within the National Convention by his published denunciation of Barère and Lindet as "assassins" and "impostors." The fugitive deputies, for their part, fueled the public impression of irresolvable divisions within the Convention with the pamphlet they published in Caen. Defending the impeachment of Marat and the creation of the Commission of Twelve to investigate an alleged conspiracy between the sections and Commune of Paris, they referred to "that commune that had stolen more than 30 million livres from the nation over the course of eight months"; to the mayor of Paris, Jean-Nicolas Pache, "who could not account for more than 80 millions"; to the Committee of Public Safety, which spent "350 millions per month"; to the "honest montagnards who had marched to assassinate them (the Girondins) on the night of March 10"; and to the "montagnard missionaries, Monsieur le Chevalier St. Just among them, who had everywhere preached anarchy, murder, and pillage."[14]

These harsh words evoke as well the "division over the people or measures called revolutionary" to which Vergniaud had referred in his handwritten notes. This division had plagued the National Convention since its earliest days. The September massacres of 1792, seen by the Montagnards as the regrettable but salutary justice of the people, were condemned by the Girondins as the bloodthirsty excesses of a mob of scoundrels orchestrated by the power-hungry triumvirate of Marat, Robespierre, and Danton. Many, though not all, of the Girondin deputies had opposed the creation of the Revolutionary Tribunal in March 1793. And the "representatives on mission," sent into the provinces at the same time to oversee military recruitment, had been drawn almost entirely from the ranks of the Montagnards.

In his seminal work on the Girondins, published some forty years ago, Michael Sydenham observed that the scope and seriousness of the accusations against the proscribed deputies escalated as the summer of 1793 progressed. In his report to the National Convention on June 6, Barère spoke vaguely of the proscribed deputies as being guilty of errors more than crimes and said nothing of specific charges or a trial. For the time being the deputies were to remain simply under surveillance. One month later, on July 8, Saint-Just alleged the existence of a longstanding conspiracy (linking the charges of royalism and federalism) but called for the indictment of only the nine deputies who had at that

13. Vatel, *Vergniaud*, vol. 2, 263.
14. "Observations sur le rapport des Trente-deux Proscrits," 15.

point fled Paris for Caen. By the end of the month, when Saint-Just's decree was finally adopted, the number of the accused had grown substantially and the charges against them had multiplied. Why? In the intervening weeks, Charlotte Corday had assassinated Marat; an expeditionary force from Normandy had been turned back by a Parisian army; and open rebellion had flared up in Lyon, Marseille, and Bordeaux. By October 3, when Jean-Pierre Amar, a member of the Committee of General Security, delivered the final indictment to the National Convention, the range of charges had expanded to include conspiracy with the *émigré* princes and complicity with Lafayette, and the list of the accused had mushroomed to embrace the seventy-five deputies who had signed a June petition in support of the original thirty-two proscribed deputies and ministers.[15]

If the charges against the Girondin deputies ever had any coherence or firm basis in demonstrable fact, both evaporated in the indictment crafted by Amar. No wonder that Vergniaud had included that ominous question toward the end of the notes for his defense: "How can there be so many accusations, if we are innocent?" As he paced his cell in the Conciergerie and looked over at the faces of the friends who stood accused with him, Vergniaud might well have inverted that question: "How can we be innocent, if there are so many accusations?" Logically, of course, the accused deputies could not be both royalists and federalists at the same time, but in the minds of the jurors they need be only one or the other to be guilty. Vergniaud and the others could defend themselves eloquently by pointing to the lack of concrete evidence linking them to General Charles Dumouriez, or Lafayette, or any of the other traitors with whom they had allegedly conspired. To this the prosecutor Antoine Fouquier-Tinville need only respond that conspirators naturally did everything they could to hide or destroy the evidence of their conspiracy.

What Fouquier-Tinville and the Committee of Public Safety feared most in an open trial was the eloquence of the accused deputies, particularly that of Vergniaud. That fear proved amply justified when Vergniaud rose to respond to the vicious testimony of Jacques-René Hébert. Fouquier-Tinville did what he could to curtail the testimony of the accused, but there was little he could do when jurors chose to put questions directly to the deputies. After some days, with the trial threatening to spin out of control, Fouquier-Tinville went to the Committee of Public Safety with a plea for help. Robespierre responded with the infamous decree, approved by the National Convention, that "if the judgment of a case brought to the Revolutionary Tribunal has been prolonged three

---

15. Sydenham, *Girondins*, 21–28. Robespierre intervened to secure the removal of the seventy-five from the decree of accusation.

days, the president will open the following session by asking the members of the jury if their conscience is sufficiently enlightened, and if the jury answers yes, it will pass immediately to judgment."[16]

We return again to Vergniaud's prescient question: "How can there be so many accusations, if we are innocent?" How could a jury *not* find the proscribed deputies guilty, given the number of charges against them? How could a jury distinguish between the deputies sitting before them and those Girondins who had fled to Caen to rally the federalist rebels? When they poked fun at "Monsieur le Chevalier St. Just" or the "*honest* Montagnards" and denounced the scoundrels and anarchists of the capital, the fugitive deputies may simply have been indulging in subtle sarcasm. But radical revolutionaries and criminal trial juries are not known for their appreciation of subtle sarcasm. How, at the end of October, could a jury of Parisians doubt the guilt of the Girondins, given the revolts in the provinces and the fatal letter that Vergniaud had written to the Bordelais at the beginning of May?

To place that letter in context, we must first consider the last of Vergniaud's great speeches before the National Convention. Through the first six months of the Convention's existence, Vergniaud had for the most part held himself apart from, or above, the fray between the Girondins and Montagnards. Jean-Baptiste Louvet and Charles Barbaroux were the most vocal denunciators of Maximilien Robespierre, Jean-Paul Marat, and Georges Danton, and one senses that Vergniaud might have questioned their political judgment in that regard. But when Robespierre rose in the National Convention on April 10 to accuse the Girondin deputies of conspiring with Philippe Egalité to restore the monarchy, mentioning Marguerite-Elie Guadet, Armand Gensonné, and Vergniaud by name, the latter felt compelled to reply. Vergniaud responded systematically to Robespierre's accusations, "pulverizing the charges," as Claude Bowers put it.[17] It was a brilliant performance, made all the more so by its spontaneity, in contrast to the laborious, stultifying delivery of the text that Robespierre had prepared in advance. Robespierre had pointedly accused the Girondins of corrupting public spirit in the departments of France through their correspondence. Vergniaud replied to that charge by praising the patriotic acts of his own department, the Gironde, but closed his comments, as was his wont, with a rhetorical flourish: "As to my correspondence, here in two words is the secret: I never write letters."[18]

Unfortunately for Vergniaud, that truth would not hold in the weeks that

16. Bowers, *Pierre Vergniaud*, 485.

17. Ibid., 369.

18. For the full text of this speech, see H. Morse Stephens, *The Principal Speeches of the Statesmen and Orators of the French Revolution, 1789–1795* (Oxford, 1892), 361–84. This particular line can be found on page 371. A more thorough discussion of these two speeches will follow in chap. 2.

followed. On May 4 and 5 he wrote two letters to his constituents in Bordeaux, urging them to be more forceful in their addresses to the National Convention. Frustrated by their recent silence in the face of growing turmoil in Paris, Vergniaud exhorted them: "Men of the Gironde, rise up! The Convention has been weak only because she has been abandoned; support her against the furies who menace her.... Then the Convention will truly be worthy of the French People. Men of the Gironde, there is not a moment to lose.... If you remain apathetic, arms folded, then the chains have been prepared and crime will reign."[19] To a Parisian jury, those words sounded like slander against the people of their city and an incitement to rebellion in the provinces. Given the feebleness of the rebellion in Bordeaux, it might have been better had Vergniaud never written.

BORDEAUX

The Bordelais did respond to Vergniaud's entreaties, however. On May 8 and 9 a pair of addresses were drafted in Bordeaux to be sent to the National Convention. The first, by the Bordeaux Jacobin club, was a forceful address, though not exceptional among the many such letters and petitions that flooded the National Convention in May and June from provincial clubs and administrations. The Bordelais defended their representatives and called for respect for the National Convention as a matter of principle. In their words, "We declare to the National Convention, that the deputies of the Gironde *have not ceased to be worthy of our esteem, of our recognition, and that their political principles, which have always seemed to us to be those of the majority of the Convention, have always been ours as well.*" They went on to denounce those leading the nation toward anarchy (in pursuit of their own selfish interests), as opposed to those who would "base liberty on laws." "Yes, we believe with *the majority of the Convention*, that the national representation *is not free.* . . . It is not free, because a municipality [the Paris Commune] contests it and steals from it sovereign power."[20]

Perhaps the most striking words in the address were these: "The deputies of the Gironde have become the representatives of the entire nation; the whole republic sees them as its delegates." These words capture one of the essential elements in both the struggle between Girondins and Montagnards and the federalist revolt that followed the proscription of the Girondin deputies: the struggle over political sovereignty. Seen from the provinces, the aggressive ac-

---

19. Vatel, *Vergniaud*, vol. 2, 153. Alan Forrest describes this letter as "nothing less than a clarion call to revolt and counterrevolution." In his testimony before the Revolutionary Tribunal, Vergniaud offered a considerably more benign interpretation of these letters, but to no avail. See Alan Forrest, *Society and Politics in Revolutionary Bordeaux* (London, 1975), 99.

20. A.D. Gironde, 8J368, "La Société Républicaine de Bordeaux, à la Convention Nationale."

tions of the Paris Commune and the riotous behavior of the Parisian *sans-culottes* represented a usurpation of national sovereignty, which legitimately resided only in the National Convention. Yet just as the Montagnards justified the actions of the Paris crowd by insisting that they represented the will of "the people," here we see the Bordelais claim for their threatened deputies a similar status as representatives of "the entire nation."

The second address came from the sections of Bordeaux and was more violent in tone. They had sent their deputies to Paris in good faith, "to work among men." Instead, they found themselves "surrounded by bloodthirsty tigers." Threatened by the knives of assassins, perhaps they had already perished. The Bordelais, in any case, would not stand idly by: "we are immediately organizing half of our national guards; we will send them to Paris . . . and we pledge to save our representatives or to die on their tombs."[21]

This message, read on the floor of the National Convention, elicited a harsh response. Louis Legendre, a deputy from Paris and a butcher by trade, scornfully observed that those who claimed to be under the knives of assassins had nary a scratch to show their constituents. He also questioned the authenticity of the address, suggesting that it had been signed by only a few clerks and represented the views of their masters, not those of the people of Bordeaux. How had it been drafted, and who in fact had signed it? Stung by these veiled accusations but denied a return visit to the rostrum of the Convention, the leaders of the Bordeaux delegation published their reply. Skirting the issue of who had drafted the address, Satire Leris and Pierre Duvigneau observed that it had been signed by the presidents and secretaries of all of the sections of Bordeaux, and that this had been done in the meeting hall of the municipal council in a public session. Moreover, the address also bore the signatures of the members of the municipal, district, and departmental councils, further evidence that it was the legitimate expression of the citizens of Bordeaux.[22]

This exchange, like the address from the Bordeaux Jacobin club, raised issues of sovereignty. From the perspective of Bordeaux, the decorum of the National Convention had disintegrated into vindictive squabbling, with the moderate faction, led by their own esteemed deputies, intimidated and threatened by the ruffians and scoundrels of the street who followed the likes of Hébert and Marat. To the Bordelais, national sovereignty resided in the National Convention, and it was being usurped by the Paris Commune and the Parisian *sans-culottes*. From

21. Henri Wallon, *La Révolution du 31 mai et le fédéralisme en 1793* (Paris, 1886), vol. 1, 154.

22. A.D. Gironde, 8J368. Satire Leris was a municipal official in Bordeaux; Pierre Duvigneau would later sit on the *Commission Populaire de salut public* of the Gironde, the body created to coordinate resistance to the National Convention in June. Their reply to Legendre was appended to the message from the Bordeaux Jacobin club and published in Paris by the printing shop of Antoine-Joseph Gorsas.

the perspective of Paris, expressed here by Legendre, it was the Bordelais who were staking an unjustified claim to national sovereignty. Why should the Girondin deputies, most of whom seemed so contemptuous of Paris, be regarded as representatives of "the entire nation"? Clearly the Parisian activists did not view them as their representatives.

The contention here was not only over the nature of national sovereignty, but over sovereignty at the local level as well. The Parisian deputies and leaders of the Commune were well schooled in the contentious and volatile popular democracy of the Paris sections and clubs.[23] Legendre's skepticism about the origin of the message read before the National Convention grew out of that experience. Was the message from Bordeaux truly an expression of views widely held in the city, or was it the work of a minority? It was well known in Paris that the Jacobin club had severed its affiliation with the Bordeaux Jacobins in February 1793 because of the latter's moderate views and that radical politics in Bordeaux found their home instead in the hall of the Club National.[24] The Club National, however, had been closed down in March. If the radicals of Paris claimed to represent "the people," then who gave voice to the politics of "the people" in the city of Bordeaux?

The Bordelais did not, as they had promised, immediately send one-half of their national guardsmen toward Paris. But one month later, in the wake of the proscription of the Girondin deputies, local authorities took steps to declare the department in a state of insurrection and began preparations to launch their march toward the capital. Coordinating those efforts was the *Commission Populaire de Salut Public*, composed of representatives from the three administrative bodies meeting in Bordeaux (departmental, district, and municipal councils), plus representatives from other towns and districts of the department. On June 9 the members of the commission issued a declaration announcing their intentions and justifying its actions. That document received wide circulation, both within the department and to the rest of the country, including Paris. It declared the department of the Gironde to be in a state of insurrection, given the violation of the National Convention and the abrogation of the rule of law. The rebels pledged to take no action that would isolate them from other parts of the republic, ordered the formation of a departmental force to join with those from other departments in a march to Paris to restore the liberty of the Convention, appealed to all citizens to join that force and to support it with voluntary contributions, and ordered representatives sent to all other departments to inform them of their actions and solicit their support. The message also included the

23. On this topic, see Raymonde Monnier, *L'Espace Public Démocratique: Essai sur l'opinion à Paris de la Révolution au Directoire* (Paris, 1994).
24. Forrest, *Society and Politics*, 69.

oath of loyalty that all members of the Commission Populaire had been asked to swear: "a solemn oath to make eternal war against tyrants, traitors, and anarchists; to preserve the liberty, equality, and security of people and property, the unity and indivisibility of the Republic; and to exercise only those powers confided in them by the People in order to reestablish the respect due the Sovereignty of the nation."[25]

Two days later the *procureur-général-syndic* (an official who represented judicial authority; the *procureur-général-syndic* was attached to the departmental administration, the *procureur-syndic* to the district administration, and the *procureur* to municipal councils), Jean Roullet, wrote a letter to the minister of the interior, Dominique-Joseph Garat. Roullet sought to temper the more bellicose pronouncements being made by the Commission Populaire. He explained to Garat that "it has so often been said to the People of Paris, or to those who are called the People, that they are sovereign and all powerful; they have been pushed so often to take toward the Representatives of the Empire [the National Convention], the countenance and tone of the Sovereign, and of a Sovereign that menaces, that the Peoples of the Departments have finally come to believe that they can appropriate for themselves a portion of that language, and that they too are their own masters, above all when it is a matter of freeing themselves from oppression and becoming the liberators of their Representatives." Roussel informed Garat that he had helped to curb calls in Bordeaux for a break with the National Convention, assuring him that all those supporting the insurrection in Bordeaux were committed to the unity and indivisibility of the republic and the integrity of the Convention. "Citizen minister," Roussel pleaded, "I am obliged to tell you that the people of this region are truly made for the Republic. They are worthy of it." They wished only to defend the National Convention and to protect the republic from the threat of civil war.[26]

But the threat of civil war loomed more ominously over France than it had at any time since 1789. Peasant rebellion had been raging in the Vendée since March and showed no signs of abating. In Marseille and Lyon insurrectionary committees had also been formed, and they were issuing decrees and making plans quite similar to those emanating from Bordeaux. In Caen, too, where representatives from ten Norman and Breton departments would gather, preparations were being made for a march on Paris.

25. A.D. Gironde, 8J368, "Arrêté de la Commission Populaire de Salut Public du département de la Gironde," June 9, 1793.

26. A.D. Gironde, 8J368. This letter from Roussel, along with the declaration of the *Commission Populaire de salut public* and its letter to the National Convention, were printed together in pamphlet form later in June in Montpellier. It is that pamphlet that is contained in this file.

CAEN

A number of the proscribed Girondin deputies made their way to Caen in the first weeks of June, both to seek refuge and to support provincial resistance to the Montagnard Convention. In Caen, on July 13, they published their response to the decree of accusation introduced in the National Convention by Saint-Just. July 13 was to be a fateful day. One week earlier, on July 7, rebel leaders in Caen had scheduled a public parade and review of the volunteer battalions in the hope of generating more volunteers for the modest force that had thus far been organized for the march to Paris. General Félix Wimpffen was on hand to review the troops and give them their marching orders, but only seventeen additional men stepped forward, a disappointing response that had two signifi-cant consequences.[27]

The rebel leaders in Caen (not only from Calvados, but from the neighboring Norman and Breton departments as well) decided to press on with their plan of action rather than wait for an upswell of popular support that might never materialize. By the second week of July they had at their disposal perhaps as many as two thousand troops—a combination of volunteers, national guards-men, and regular soldiers. They ordered them to bivouac in and around Evreux, from which they would launch their march toward Paris. This they did on July 12, laying over in Pacy-sur-Eure for one night. Late the next morning, at the château of Brécourt near Vernon, they encountered a volunteer force dispatched from Paris, the so-called army of pacification. Shots were fired, a few men on both sides may have been wounded, and both armies ignominiously turned tails and fled. Although not immediately apparent, the fiasco at Brécourt on July 13 marked the beginning of the disintegration of the revolt in Caen. By month's end the Girondin fugitives would flee toward Brittany, and the city would sur-render to Robert Lindet and the army of pacification.[28]

The miserable turnout on July 7 would have another consequence as well, one that made a more vivid impression on the deputies of the National Conven-tion and the radicals of Paris. Two years before, a young woman, an ex-novitiate, had taken up residence in Caen and befriended several of the local revolutionary leaders, in particular Jean Charles Bougon-Longrais, an ambitious and impetu-ous young man who, in 1793, was *procureur-général-syndic* of the department and an active leader of the federalist movement. In June 1793 that young woman, Charlotte Corday, met a number of the fugitive Girondin deputies. An ardent supporter of their cause, she attended the festivities on July 7. Appalled by the

---

27. See chap. 3 for a lengthier overview of the events of the revolt in each of the federalist cities. For a fuller discussion of the revolt in Caen, see Hanson, *Provincial Politics*, esp. chap. 4.

28. Ibid., 150–56.

apparent lack of courage among her compatriots, Charlotte Corday set out for the capital on July 9, determined to strike a blow against the anarchists of Paris by assassinating Jean-Paul Marat. She bought a knife in a shop at the Palais-Royal, gained entrance to Marat's apartment by promising information about the Girondin deputies in Caen, and stabbed him to death in his bath.[29]

This dramatic act by Charlotte Corday can hardly be considered integral to either the federalist revolt or the politics and fate of the Girondin deputies. But neither of those can be fully understood without taking into account the impact of Corday's knife blow. The debacle at Brécourt, on that same day, might have made the revolt in Caen appear laughable to the Parisians. Instead the martyrdom of Marat seemed to show the extremes to which the rebels and their supporters would go. The Girondin deputies would most likely have been convicted and executed without the assassination of Marat. At their trial in October, Vergniaud would scoff at the notion that he and the others, in confinement at the time, could have had anything to do with the attack. Yet in the minds of Parisian radicals there was a clear link. All winter and spring the Girondin leaders had complained publicly of being threatened by the knives of assassins. Yet it was they who had led the impeachment effort against Marat in April, and it was he who had now been cut down by a knife. His death made the federalist threat to the republic seem all the more ominous.

LYON

Moderates and radicals had struggled for control of municipal politics in Lyon throughout 1792–93, with the radicals gaining control of the municipal council in late 1792 and placing their candidate, Antoine-Marie Bertrand, in the mayor's office in February 1793. Emboldened by their electoral victories, Lyon Jacobins urged a tax on the rich to finance revolutionary programs and threatened those who resisted their policies with arrest and trial before a revolutionary tribunal. Moderates sought support from their allies in Paris, which came in the form of a May 15 decree from the National Convention forbidding the creation of a revolutionary tribunal in Lyon. With political opposition temporarily at a stalemate, tensions exploded into violence on May 29 when moderates succeeded in ousting the radicals from municipal government by an armed rebellion organized through sectional assemblies. Thus, on the eve of the proscription of the

---

29. See Robert Patry, *Une Ville de province: Caen pendant la Révolution de 1789* (Caen, 1983), 407–15, for a brief discussion of Corday and her background; and C. Vatel, *Charlotte de Corday et les Girondins* (Paris, 1864–72), for a fuller though somewhat romantic treatment.

Girondin deputies in Paris a violent shift in political fortunes had occurred in Lyon, the second largest city in France.[30]

From the very outset, two avenues of response were open to the government in Paris. Within days of the rebellion in Lyon, Robert Lindet proposed to his colleagues on the Committee of Public Safety that he be sent to Lyon without specific orders or authority but with the limited task of investigating the situation and reporting back to Paris. The Committee assigned Lindet that mission, and on June 3 the National Convention approved the order. Lindet arrived in Lyon on June 8, and although he was ill received by local authorities and the sectional assemblies he was optimistic in his letters to his colleagues in Paris about the prospects for a peaceful resolution of the troubles in Lyon. Lindet described the city as agitated but orderly. "No one wants a tyrant," he wrote in this first, undated letter, "all adhere to the same language: the words republic, unity, and indivisibility are on everyone's lips."[31] It was a difficult situation, though, and in his next letters Lindet urged the Committee to draft for publication an official report on the events of June 2 and to hasten the completion of a new constitution. "I have refrained from praising, or blaming, anyone," he wrote on June 10; "I felt I should not betray any sign of either approval or disapproval, but implored people not to rush judgment of events before knowing the true causes."[32]

The alternative to conciliation was advocated by Edmond-Louis-Alexis Dubois-Crancé, Montagnard representative on mission to the Army of the Alps. Convinced that the events of May 29 represented the victory of counterrevolution in Lyon, Dubois-Crancé favored sending the army against the city. In the first week of June he issued that order, only to see it countermanded by Lindet. The Lyonnais found themselves in a quandary. Uncertain about the implications of the insurrection of June 2 for their city, they did not know whether to pursue the politics of conciliation offered by Lindet or to prepare to resist the assault promised by Dubois-Crancé. As reports began to arrive from other cities of plans for resistance to the National Convention, the Lyonnais had to evaluate whether that movement would ultimately support or jeopardize the achievement of their own recent rebellion.

The Lyonnais were no doubt encouraged to cast their lot with the federalist movement by envoys and messages from Marseille, where moderates had also used the vehicle of sectional assemblies to oust local Jacobins from municipal

---

30. See W. D. Edmonds, *Jacobinism and the Revolt of Lyon, 1789–1793* (Oxford, 1990), esp. chap. 6, for a thorough discussion of these events, which will also be considered in more depth in this work in chaps. 3 and 5.

31. F. A. Aulard, *Recueil des Actes du Comité de Salut Public avec la Correspondance officielle des représentants en mission* (Paris, 1891), vol. 4, 509.

32. Ibid.

office earlier in May. Resistance in Marseille forced the Montagnards to keep the Army of the Alps in Grenoble, and the armed force that was reported to be gathering in Caen also promised to keep the National Convention occupied elsewhere. The rebels in Lyon therefore turned their attention to finishing their own business. On July 1 they created a *Commission Populaire, Républicaine et de Salut Public* to coordinate departmental resistance to the Convention. Within two weeks that body ordered that the Jacobins arrested on May 29 be brought to trial. Principal among those was Joseph Chalier, a firebrand who had unsuccessfully run for mayor in 1792 but who was the acknowledged leader of the Jacobin resurgence in 1793. Two days after the assassination of Marat, Chalier was brought to trial in Lyon, accused of inciting his followers to murder and civil war. The judges found him guilty, condemned him to death, and on July 16 Chalier mounted the scaffold. The Jacobins in Paris now had another martyr to place alongside Marat.[33]

MARSEILLE

At the mouth of the Rhône River, some two hundred miles south of Lyon, the sectional assemblies of Marseille had also declared themselves in a state of insurrection against the National Convention. But whereas Lyon had been viewed as a hotbed of aristocratic intrigue since the early days of the Revolution, Marseille had established its revolutionary pedigree in 1789 with popular upheavals against symbols of royal despotism, had added to that reputation in 1790–91 by the envoy of Jacobin "missionaries" to neighboring towns and districts, and had confirmed it when the Marseille *fédérés* led the assault on the Tuileries palace on August 10, 1792. (The term *fédérés* is a reference to those national guardsmen from throughout France who journeyed to Paris in July 1790 to celebrate the Festival of Federation.) Like Lyon, however, Marseille had been riven by political conflict in 1792–93. Local Jacobins gained control of the Marseille municipal council in January 1793 and used the dual bases of the club and the council to initiate a number of radical measures in the winter and early spring. Moderates responded by mobilizing their supporters in sectional assemblies. After the Jacobins forced the mayor, Jean-Raymond Mouraille, from office in early April, the sections went on the offensive. Early in May they created a General Committee to coordinate their efforts. Avoiding the open bloodshed that would strike in Lyon later that month, the General Committee ordered the quiet arrest of leading Jacobins and by early June had dismissed both the municipal and departmental councils and closed down the Jacobin club as well.[34]

33. See Edmonds, *Jacobinism and the Revolt of Lyon*, 203–28, for a discussion of these events.
34. For a full discussion of these events, see Willam Scott, *Terror and Repression in Revolutionary Marseilles* (London, 1973), esp. chaps. 3 and 4.

As in Lyon, the struggle for political power in Marseille became entwined with and complicated by the struggle between Girondins and Montagnards in Paris. Consolidation of the victory won by moderates in Marseille would depend upon a reversal of the victory won by the Montagnards on June 2. But in contrast to Lyon, the revolutionary credentials of the Marseillais placed them in a better position to achieve that by leading provincial resistance to the National Convention. Thus, on June 12 the General Committee issued a manifesto to all of the departments of France: "To arms, Frenchmen, to arms!" the manifesto began, "the National Representation is violated, your Deputies are in irons." Paying little mind to the fact that they themselves had recently ousted the duly elected authorities of Marseille, the members of the General Committee went on to observe that "an ambitious and criminal municipality [the Paris Commune] has attacked the national sovereignty; a disorganizing faction, having broken all social bonds, having violated all the pacts among Nations, having covered all of France in ashes, blood and tears, dares to prepare chains for her; chains forged by a few scoundrels in the infamous lair of the Jacobins."[35]

Two weeks later, on June 26, the General Committee was joined by representatives from the departments of the Hautes-Alpes, the Gard, and the Gironde. They adopted a resolution calling on all departments to send two delegates to Bourges, thereby creating an alternative national assembly, and designated seven towns—Marseille, Lyon, Toulouse, Bordeaux, Rennes, Strasbourg, and Rouen—as centers for the marshaling of troops to be sent against Paris.[36] Four days earlier, the departmental force of the Bouches-du-Rhône had left Marseille, bound for the capital, hoping to retrace the steps of the *fédérés* of 1792.

For the rebels in Marseille (as for the Parisians, the Bordelais, and the deputies of the National Convention), the issue of sovereignty was a principal concern. To bolster its claim to represent the citizens of Marseille, and indeed those of the department as well, the General Committee convened a departmental electoral assembly on July 13, and that body issued yet another declaration to the country. They adhered to all previous declarations and actions not only of the General Committee but of the Popular Commission of Bordeaux as well. Brushing aside the accusation of federalism that had already been leveled against them by the anarchists in Paris, they avowed their movement to be a holy insurrection, one uniting Marseille with Bordeaux, Nîmes, Caen, Lyon, and many other departmental *chefs-lieux* (the administrative capitals of departments). "Paris boasts of having reclaimed its rights on May 31. Well, we declare that in doing so they have usurped ours." Only the French people could decide who

35. A.D. Bouches-du-Rhône, L1953, "Adresse des Marseillois, à leurs frères des quatre-vingt-cinq Départemens."
36. A.D. Bouches-du-Rhône, L1967.

was right: "There is no government except that which the people wants; there can be no [just] measure except that which the people approves. If one consults the many corners of France, one will see on what side there is error, and on what side there is truth. Our supposed federation is the union of good citizens against license and excess. There exists today a schism; it is the inevitable schism between the good and the wicked." Yes, the people of the Bouches-du-Rhône were marching in arms, but only against the tyranny of the factious in Paris. They implored the good citizens of the capital to join them in that cause.[37]

That appeal, issued on the very day that Jean-Paul Marat was struck down, was unlikely to be heeded by the good Parisians. Nor would the Marseille volunteers ever reach the capital to deliver their message personally. Indeed, they never set foot outside the department of the Bouches-du-Rhône. Troops from the Army of the Alps, under the command of General Jean-François Carteaux, turned them back just past Avignon, and on August 25 Carteaux and his army entered Marseille. The grand plan of the General Committee for a coordinated march on Paris from all compass points of the republic lay shattered. Even the hope of a unified resistance movement in the Midi had proven to be far beyond the capabilities of the federalist rebels.

With the capitulation of Marseille, the Army of the Alps turned its attention to Lyon. Dubois-Crancé could now pursue the policy that he had proposed to initiate in early June. Today we can see that the federalist revolt had begun to unravel within weeks of its inception. The armed engagement at Brécourt was almost farcical, the volunteer forces of Bordeaux and Marseille never left the confines of their respective departments, and the Lyonnais never raised a volunteer force to march to Paris. But by laying siege to the city of Lyon, the army of Dubois-Crancé managed to generate a serious armed resistance to the republic. The Lyonnais fought bravely in defense of their city, for by now it was essentially a battle of self-defense, and the siege was not lifted until October 9. Three days later the National Convention would declare "Lyon n'est plus." The repression in Lyon endured for some months to come, but on the last day of October, just three weeks after the fall of Lyon, the Girondin deputies marched to the guillotine in Paris.

Vergniaud and the others rode to the guillotine on October 31 singing *La Marseillaise*, just as they had done when leaving the courtroom after hearing the verdict pronounced against them. It was a poignant moment, one in which the deputies displayed both courage and dignity. Yet there was irony in that moment as well. The *Marseillaise* had first been sung in July 1792 by the Marseille volunteers en route to the capital where they led the charge against the Tuileries

37. A.D. Bouches-du-Rhône, L1965, "Déclaration de l'Assemblée électorale du Département des Bouches-du-Rhône à tous les François," July 13, 1793.

palace. The fall of the monarchy, for which the Girondin deputies had vociferously clamored, may well have been the hour of their greatest victory. Yet is was also the beginning of their troubles, for they were far more successful in opposition than they would ever be in power.

Charles Barbaroux, the fiery young deputy from Marseille, had called the Marseille volunteers to Paris with a famous letter, in which he called for "six hundred men who know how to die." He would call on the Marseillais again in summer 1793, but this time they did not respond. Nor was Barbaroux with his colleagues in Paris as they sang their song on the way to the guillotine. He had left Paris in June for Caen, where he did what he could to rally the federalist rebels. With the collapse of the revolt in Normandy, Barbaroux fled first to Brittany and then by boat with several of the others to the Gironde, where he remained in hiding for nearly a year. Captured in late June 1794, nearly dead from a self-inflicted wound, Barbaroux was escorted to Bordeaux, Vergniaud's hometown, where like most of his fellow Girondins he died on the guillotine.

Two

GIRONDINS VERSUS MONTAGNARDS

The battle in those days was between the friends and the enemies of liberty; the battle today is between friends of the Republic on both sides.

—Dominique-Joseph Garat

In the summer of 1793, Dominique-Joseph Garat served as minister of the interior, responsible for preserving order within France. Although he resigned that post in August, well before the Terror began, he stood accused before the National Convention in 1795 as an exterrorist. Garat was a man of letters with a talent for writing, and his self-defense before his accusers became a lengthy memoir, one that remains interesting reading today.

In that memoir, Garat recalled a conversation he had with Maximilien Robespierre just before the riotous attacks on Girondin printing presses in Paris on the night of March 9–10, 1793. Garat had gone to speak with Robespierre about the factional quarrels within the National Convention, hoping to find some way to alleviate them. Robespierre would have none of it, asserting with conviction that Brissot, Louvet, Barbaroux, and the other Girondins were conspirators and counterrevolutionaries. "I couldn't keep from laughing," recalled Garat, "and the laugh that escaped my lips brought a bitter response." Robespierre chided Garat that he had always been too tolerant, that during the Constituent Assembly he had even been willing to believe that the aristocrats loved the Revolution. Garat insisted that not all noblemen were aristocrats and reminded Robespierre that he, too, had found it possible to work with some patriotic ex-nobles. In any case, those battles had nothing to do with the present differences and were best forgotten, leading Garat to his final admonition.

Garat, ever the moderate (some would say opportunist), always seeking balance, recalled a similar conversation with Jean-Baptiste Salles, one of the Girondin deputies who would be proscribed on June 2, 1793. Salles, he remembered, was just as convinced as Robespierre that there were conspirators against the Revolution, that Robespierre himself had been in league with Danton, Marat, d'Orléans, Lafayette, Mirabeau, and the Duke of York. This will strike readers today as an unlikely group of conspirators, but such wild accusations flew freely in the tumultuous days of 1793. Garat's response to Salles, and his implicit message to his readers, was that the true conspirators against the republic were the monarchs of Europe and the passions of the republicans.[1]

Following their dramatic victory at Valmy in September 1792, the French armies did reasonably well at holding the monarchs of Europe at bay. The deputies of the National Convention did rather less well at controlling their passions, despite the advice of Garat. Garat went beyond individual conversations in his efforts, frequently bringing deputies from both sides together at dinner parties in his apartment. Others, too, made efforts to convince their colleagues to set aside personal differences in order to work for the common good, all to no avail. The political differences that had their seeds in the disputes over the September massacres germinated during the trial of Louis XVI and flowered into virulent personal enmity in the winter and spring of 1793, with the riots and vandalism of March 9–10, the impeachment of Jean-Paul Marat, and the formation of the Commission of Twelve. Rumors and accusations of planned assassinations flew on all sides, made plausible by the assassination of Lepelletier on the eve of the king's execution. The partisan factionalism would persist, despite entreaties from the departments, until one side could marshal the strength to oust the leaders of the other, bringing France to the brink of the civil war that all had claimed to fear.

That conflict erupted almost immediately after the National Convention convened in September 1792, and over the next eight months a series of events and controversies exacerbated the conflict and gave greater definition to the two competing factions. It is important that we consider that series of events in Paris, not only to understand the nature of the Girondin/Montagnard opposition, but because the federalist revolt was not simply a reaction to the proscription of the Girondin deputies. It grew out of the same set of ideological differences that lay at the heart of the divisions within the National Convention. There were three key issues, I would argue, that divided the Girondins from the Montagnards: the legitimacy of revolutionary violence, the nature and locus of political sovereignty, and the role of Paris (and its unruly crowd) in national politics. Each was a factor in public debate very early in the Revolution, but a series of seven events from just before the election of the National Convention through the first eight months of its existence served to highlight those issues

---

1. Dominique-Joseph Garat, *Mémoires sur la Révolution* (Paris, 1795), 50–62. Garat was denounced by Marat as a royalist and arrested in October 1793 as a Girondin sympathizer but weathered this accusation as he had earlier ones. He went on to preside over the Council of Ancients under the Directory and served the government of Napoleon as well. Although we would be well advised to exercise caution when evaluating the details of Garat's recollections, his *Mémoires* do not have the air of partisanship about them. In the atmosphere of 1795 he would have had every reason to vilify Robespierre, for example, and he chose not to do so.

and heighten the antagonisms between the opposing factions. The first of these, the August 10 assault on the Tuileries palace and the prison massacres of early September, loomed over the deputies as they stood for election and poisoned the atmosphere in Paris as they gathered for the first session of the Convention on September 20. The debate about the September massacres was particularly bitter. The other five events—the trial of the king, the riots of March 9–10, 1793, the treason of Dumouriez, the impeachment trial of Jean-Paul Marat, and the formation of the Commission of Twelve—marked the crystallization and denouement of the irreconcilable opposition within the National Convention between the Girondins and Montagnards.

THE FALL OF THE MONARCHY

August 10, 1792—the fall of the monarchy—is a date that assumed iconographic importance in France almost immediately. Celebrated the following year as a national holiday, it is described in most histories as a wholly justified armed uprising against royal despotism and treachery, the last great untarnished insurrection of the Parisian crowd. It was a moment of national unity, as the *fédérés* from Marseille and Brest joined with the *sans-culottes* of the faubourgs Saint-Antoine and Saint-Marcel to topple Louis XVI from his throne and usher in the first French republic. Its importance as such is signified by the Montagnard efforts on August 10, 1793, to heal the wounds opened by the federalist revolt with a national celebration.

Several of the leading Montagnards and Girondins played key roles on August 10. Vergniaud presided over the Legislative Assembly during the uprising; Barbaroux had summoned the Marseille *fédérés* to the capital; Robespierre was a principal spokesman for the insurrectionary Paris Commune; and Georges Danton took charge of the situation at the Hôtel de Ville. But the unity that August 10 seemed to embody began to unravel within weeks of that glorious victory, and by spring 1793 opponents in the National Convention would hurl accusations against each other as to just what role they had, or had not, played on that memorable occasion.

The events of August 10 are of significance to us here not only because of the roles played by leading Girondins and Montagnards (to which we shall turn in a moment), but because of the relation between this successful insurrection and the failed uprising of June 20, which directly preceded it, and the insurrection of May 31–June 2, which led to the proscription of the Girondin deputies. Each of these insurrections made reference, in a sense, to that which had gone before. The intense planning that went into the August 10 assault on the Tuileries was meant to avoid the debacle of June 20, when the Parisian crowd had invaded the grounds of the Tuileries palace in a relatively disorganized fashion, hoping to force Louis XVI to withdraw his veto on three measures of national defense but succeeding only in forcing him to wear a Phrygian cap. Alarmed by this disrespectful treatment of the king and his family, and perhaps out of touch with the current of politics in the capital, departmental administrations across the country sent messages of protest to the Legislative Assembly. Many of these administrators had already been confronted by unruly crowds in their own *chefs-lieux* and considered the preservation of public order to be of paramount importance.

Three important consequences emerged from this failed uprising. Most of the departmental administrators who signed the letters of protest came to regret their action after the August 10 insurrection. Some were voted out of office in the elections that fall, while others were denounced as royalists in the purge of departmental councils following the collapse of the federalist revolt. In Paris, radical revolutionaries—leaders of the sections, members of the Commune, leaders of the Cordelier and Jacobin clubs—learned from the mistakes of June and took pains to plan and organize the insurrection of August 10. But the deputies of the Legislative Assembly, chastened by the letters of support for the king that poured into the capital in late June and early July, proved reluctant to embrace the burgeoning popular movement in the Parisian sections, even when its overwhelming support became obvious. That reluctance alienated the Parisian *sans-culottes* from the Legislative Assembly and raised the issue of sovereignty in a most fundamental way.

There is no need to review here in detail the events of August 9–10.[2] We must emphasize, though, that the August insurrection and the insurrection of May 31 stand like bookends at either end of the tumultuous first eight months of the National Convention. With the fall of the monarchy, the result of an insurrection that they had not made, the Girondin deputies found political power within their grasp. On May 31 they found themselves the targets of a Parisian insurrection, rather than interested bystanders, and by June 2 their hold on power had dissolved with their proscription. Much had transpired in the intervening eight months, but the events of August and September 1792 loomed large throughout.

On July 29 an ultimatum signed by forty-seven of the forty-eight sections of

2. The standard works in French include F. Braesch, *La Commune du 10 août* (Paris, 1911); Albert Mathiez, *Le 10 août 1792* (Paris, 1931); Marcel Reinhard, *10 août 1792: La Chute de la royauté* (Paris, 1969); and Michel Vovelle, *La Chute de la Monarchie, 1787–1792* (Paris, 1972). For brief accounts in English, see George Rudé, *The Crowd in the French Revolution* (London, 1959), 95–112; and David P. Jordan, *The Revolutionary Career of Maximilien Robespierre* (Chicago, 1985), 104–16, who points to Robespierre's description of the uprising in his newspaper, *Le Défenseur de la Constitution*, as the best contemporary account.

Paris was delivered to the Legislative Assembly, demanding the removal of King Louis XVI. Fewer than one hundred of the original seven hundred and fifty deputies of the assembly now sat in regular attendance. They referred the petition to a committee and on August 4 issued a reprimand to the Paris sections along with their reply that the assembly would take no action. As David Jordan put it, the "Legislative thus declared its nullity: it was time to act."[3]

The march of the Parisian national guardsmen and the provincial *fédérés* along the banks of the Seine from the faubourgs Saint-Antoine and Saint-Marcel to the Tuileries palace was largely unimpeded. By the time they reached the Tuileries, Louis XVI had abandoned the Swiss guards to their fate and placed himself and his family at the mercy of the Legislative Assembly. Pierre Vergniaud, presiding over the assembly, issued the decree suspending the king from office and calling for the election of a National Convention. When he came under attack in spring 1793, Vergniaud would proudly recall that he had stayed at his post in the midst of the crisis, calmly fulfilling his duties, while Robespierre had been cowering in his cellar.[4]

The attitude of the leading Girondin deputies toward the insurrection of August 10 was ambiguous at best, however. Brissot, Pétion, and others played a role in instigating the June 20 uprising, but only Barbaroux could be said to have actively participated in the planning for August 10. In theory, the Girondins were ardently opposed to the monarchy and were its most vocal critics in summer 1792, most notably Vergniaud in his speech before the Legislative Assembly on July 3. But in practice, given the presence of Austrian and Prussian troops on French soil and the growing militancy of the Parisian populace, they feared the anarchy that might follow the monarchy's collapse. Ladan Bouramand has argued persuasively that the Girondins' republicanism depended very much on the existence of a king. Before August 10, the Girondins could focus on the king as enemy and pursue an aggressive republican politics. But after August 10, the Girondins were fighting a rearguard action against the radicalism of the Paris crowd as champions of a legal republic, but not a revolutionary republic.[5]

In the eyes of Parisian radicals, Vergniaud had committed two compromising acts in the days leading up to August 10. In late July, Vergniaud, Gensonné, and Guadet had sent a letter to Louis XVI, using the court painter Boze as an

---

3. Jordan, *Revolutionary Career*, 110.

4. Claude G. Bowers, *Pierre Vergniaud: Voice of the the French Revolution* (New York, 1950), 362. Vergniaud made this comment in his April 10, 1793, speech before the National Convention.

5. Ladan Boroumand, "Les Girondins et l'idée de République," in François Furet and Mona Ozouf, eds., *La Gironde et les Girondins* (Paris, 1991), 233–64. In the same volume, Jean-Denis Brédin attributes a similar argument, making specific reference to Vergniaud, to Alphonse Aulard: "Avant le 10-Août Vergniaud vitupère contre les intrigans de la Cour. Après le 10-Août, il combat les excès populaires." See Brédin, "Vergniaud ou le génie de la parole," 367–87.

intermediary, in which they outlined a course of action that might preserve both the nation and the constitutional monarchy. Although the letter became known only much later, it was cited at the trial of the Girondin deputies as evidence of their royalism. Of more immediate consequence to Vergniaud's reputation in Paris was his response to the Mauconseil section's August 4 declaration that it no longer recognized the authority of the king. Vergniaud presided over the Legislative Assembly on that occasion as well and in that capacity observed that the "Assembly, considering that sovereignty belongs to all the people and not to a section of the people, and that there would no longer be government or Constitution and that we should be delivered to all the disorders of anarchy and of civil discord if each citizen or each Section, isolated from the empire, should disregard such oaths at pleasure and refuse obedience to laws or constituted authorities which no longer pleased . . . decrees that it is a matter of urgency that the Assembly . . . annul as unconstitutional the resolution or decision of the Mauconseil Section, and invite all citizens to restrict their zeal within the limits of the law and to guard against the intrigues of those who, by such violations, seek to compromise the public tranquillity."[6]

The citizens of Paris ignored that admonition, of course, and in the face of the assembly's irresolution deposed the king themselves. Vergniaud's critics, or enemies, would charge that even when faced with that fait accompli he proposed a decree to the assembly that called not for the king's abdication, but only his suspension from office.

Vergniaud and his allies would later point out that Maximilien Robespierre was nowhere to be seen on August 9 and 10. But in the days following the insurrection, he emerged as the champion of the Paris Commune, of which Vergniaud and the Girondins were to be so critical. Before August 10, Robespierre represented the section of the Place Vendôme on the general council of the Commune. Although not involved in the preparations for the insurrection, when the Legislative Assembly called into question the legitimacy of the Commune's authority he took responsibility for preparing a justificatory address from the Commune to its constituents, which he presented to the general council on September 1. In that address, Robespierre justified the actions of the Commune in very simple terms: "of all the mandatories of the people, they alone were the people, in every respect."[7]

David Jordan argues that it was only in the weeks before August 10 that Robespierre became convinced of the necessity, and utility, of insurrection, which he finally endorsed in a speech before the Jacobins on July 29. Like Verg-

---

6. Bowers, *Pierre Vergniaud*, 220.

7. Raymonde Monnier, *L'Espace Public Démocratique: Essai sur l'opinion à Paris de la Révolution au Directoire* (Paris, 1994), 136.

niaud, he had initially feared the void that would be left should the Legislative Assembly disintegrate along with the monarchy, but he came to view the movement building in the sections as an expression of the popular will. In the account of August 10 that he published in *Le Défenseur de la Constitution*, Robespierre described that day as a victory of the people and celebrated "the triumph of the 'passive' citizens who have now avenged their exclusion from the politics of the Revolution."[8]

This was a pivotal period in the Revolution with regard to the question of sovereignty. The Constituent Assembly had established a category of "passive" citizen in 1790, denying the vote to those men who did not pay tax equivalent to three days' labor, a measure that Robespierre had ardently opposed in parliamentary debate. The National Guard had similarly been restricted to men of the propertied classes in towns, cities, and villages throughout France. Because of the war crisis, however, the ranks of the National Guard in Paris had been opened to "passive" citizens in the weeks following the June 20 uprising. In the words of David Jordan, "In June and July Paris democratized itself."[9] It was this development that prompted Robespierre to characterize August 10 as a triumph for the "passive" citizens.

Raymonde Monnier also emphasizes the importance of this period for the democratization of Parisian politics, pointing to the intense activism of sectional assemblies and popular societies, acting not in isolation but in constant communication with each other and with the general council of the Commune at the center. Monnier sees this as a revival of the radical activism of 1791, temporarily snuffed out by the massacre on the Champ de Mars. In 1792, that activism would be carried beyond Paris by the *fédérés*, who tended to gravitate toward the most popular quartiers of the capital where they fraternized in the clubs and sectional assemblies. Not only did the sectional assemblies urge the *fédérés* to maintain communication after they had returned to their homes, many also sent their own representatives out to the departments in the late summer and autumn months of 1792. The democratization of Paris would be carried to the nation in another sense in the aftermath of August 10, with the declaration of universal manhood suffrage.[10]

THE SEPTEMBER MASSACRES

If the people were sublime on August 10, their image was soon tarnished by the September massacres in the prisons of Paris. For five bloody days radicals from

8. Jordan, *Revolutionary Career*, 113. The quotation is Jordan's paraphrase of Robespierre's sentence.

9. Ibid., 106.

10. Monnier, *L'Espace public démocratique*, 135–39.

the sections of Paris, joined by national guardsmen and some of the provincial *fédérés*, moved from one Paris prison to another, eventually massacring just under half of the prison population, some 1,100 to 1,400 people. In some cases the killing took on the appearance of summary justice, preceded by trials in the streets or in prison courtyards. But more often popular vengeance was visited indiscriminately. Most of those killed were common criminals, not the treason-ous counterrevolutionaries who, Parisians had been told, were lurking in the prisons, waiting for the opportunity to kill the families of patriots who had de-parted for the army.[11]

The context of the massacres was twofold. Most important, the war against Austria and Prussia was going badly. Defeat at Longwy on August 23 had prompted a call-up of 30,000 additional volunteers, most of them to be recruited in Paris. Marat and others had publicly warned those volunteers not to leave their families behind unprotected against the traitors in the prisons. That dan-ger became more real on September 2 when news arrived in the capital that the fortress at Verdun had fallen to the enemy.

In addition, the ongoing struggle for political legitimacy between the Legis-lative Assembly and the Paris Commune contributed to the atmosphere of fear and panic. The assembly's hesitation on the eve of August 10 had weakened its legitimacy in the eyes of many Parisians, and its August 11 decree calling for the election of a National Convention left it in an ambiguous position. Many of its decrees through the rest of August were simply endorsements of initiatives that had originated with the Commune, which now claimed to represent the will of the people. But on August 30 the Legislative Assembly moved to quash the power of the Commune with a decree that ordered the replacement of the current council by new elections, a move designed both to strengthen the au-thority of the National Assembly and to empower moderate elements within the sectional assemblies of Paris. The move backfired—public outcry forced the Assembly to revoke its decree on September 2, the day that the massacres began.

This jockeying for power between the Legislative Assembly and the Com-mune may explain why neither body took any action to halt the massacres, al-though both certainly were informed shortly after they began. The Girondins later alleged that the Commune was complicit in the massacres, was perhaps even responsible for ordering them, and the boldest among them—Louvet and

---

11. My discussion of the September massacres relies principally on Scott Lytle, "September 1792 Massacres," in Samuel F. Scott and Barry Rothaus, eds., *Historical Dictionary of the French Revolution* (Westport, Conn., 1985), vol. 2, 891–97; Patrice Gueniffey, "Paris Commune," in Fran-çois Furet and Mona Ozouf, eds., *A Critical Dictionary of the French Revolution* (Cambridge, Mass., 1989), 519–28; D. M. G. Sutherland, *France 1789–1815: Revolution and Counterrevolution* (Oxford, 1986), 153–55; and William Doyle, *The Oxford History of the French Revolution* (Oxford, 1989), 188–93. See also Pierre Caron, *Les Massacres de septembre* (Paris, 1935).

Barbaroux—would explicitly name Marat, Robespierre, and Danton as a blood-thirsty triumvirate guilty of unleashing the massacres to further their own quest for dictatorial power. The most damning evidence in this regard was a September 3 circular to the departments, printed on Marat's press, defending the massacres as a salutary act of public safety and exhorting those in the provinces to follow suit in order to defend the *patrie* against traitors.

As Marcel Dorigny has shown, however, the leading Girondins were not quick to condemn the massacres. Antoine-Joseph Gorsas described the first massacres as a "terrible but necessary justice" in the September 3 issue of *Le Courrier des quatre vingt trois départements* and emphasized in a subsequent issue that the justice of the people had spared the innocent. Jean-Baptiste Louvet, linked closely to Jean-Marie Roland, then minister of the interior, did not publish *La Sentinelle* during the days of the killings, but on September 8 he described the massacres as justified and reported that the innocent had been spared. Jacques-Pierre Brissot was more restrained in *Le Patriote français*, choosing neither to defend nor condemn the violence that he reported. Roland did condemn the incendiary rhetoric of Marat and the Commune's usurpation of authority but described the massacres as a regrettable but necessary measure "over which perhaps a veil must be drawn."[12]

Vergniaud may have been the first to draw back the veil. In a speech before the Legislative Assembly on September 16 he denounced the Paris Commune and its Committee of Surveillance (on which Marat sat) for their complicity in the prison massacres, suggesting that those who carried out the killing were little more than "hired assassins." He also pointed an accusatory finger at Robespierre, suggesting that he had targeted deputies of the Legislative Assembly for assassination in a September 2 speech before the Commune where he denounced the faction of the Gironde for conspiring to place the duke of Brunswick on the throne of France. Far from accepting the prison massacres as necessary, Vergniaud concluded by demanding "that the members of the Commune answer with their heads for the safety of all prisoners."[13] Was this a warning for the future, or a call to avenge past crimes? Surely the deputies of the assembly would have heard it in both ways.

Four days after Vergniaud's speech the National Convention held its opening session. The Girondins controlled the ministries, with Roland as minister of the interior, and the leading Girondin deputies all gained election from provincial departments. The leading activists from the Paris clubs and Commune, however, no longer criticized the Girondins from outside the halls of the assembly

12. Marcel Dorigny, "Violence et Révolution: Les Girondins et les massacres de septembre," in Albert Soboul, ed., *Girondins et Montagnards* (Paris, 1980), 103–20.

13. Bowers, *Pierre Vergniaud*, 249–54.

but sat across from them as delegates from the department of Paris. Robespierre, Billaud-Varenne, Legendre, Danton, Fabre d'Eglantine, Desmoulins,
Fréron, Panis, Sergent, Robert, and even Marat all now sat as deputies, and the
conflict between the Commune and the Legislative Assembly carried over into
the first weeks of the National Convention. Would the Convention, too, see its
authority challenged by the city of Paris? Would insurrectionary politics now
drive the Revolution, or would the Girondins succeed in crafting a constitution
that would restore the rule of law?

Developments in the early fall suggested that the Commune would back away
from its militancy of the summer and respect the authority of the Convention.
Chastened perhaps by public outrage at the massacres, it ordered an investigation of its Committee of Surveillance. By the end of September it had withdrawn
support of the commissioners sent out to provincial departments in the aftermath of August 10. As one of its final acts the Legislative Assembly had called
for municipal elections throughout France. Although in many provincial towns
and cities these elections marked a radicalization of municipal councils, in Paris
the opposite occurred. The new general council was more moderate than its
predecessor, with fewer than 20 percent of the incumbents reelected to office.
Astonishingly, Jérome Pétion was reelected as mayor, despite the public abuse
he had endured before and after the August uprising. Pétion declined the office,
choosing to retain his seat in the Convention, and it took several rounds of
voting before Nicolas Chambon, a moderate, emerged victorious, defeating in
the process three candidates supported by the Jacobin club.[14]

Within the National Convention, however, the tension between the leaders
of the Parisian delegation and the Girondin faction continued to build.[15] It
reached the boiling point on October 29 when Roland delivered a report on the
state of the country and Paris, a report that was highly critical of the Commune
and called for the creation of an independent armed force to protect the Convention against the threat of anarchy in the capital. On the same day, Louvet
rose in the Convention to denounce Robespierre.

Louvet was not the first to denounce Robespierre by name—Rebecqui and
Barbaroux claimed that honor, and Roland's report included at least an oblique
accusation. But Louvet focused his lengthy speech explicitly on Robespierre,
brushing aside Danton's entreaty that it was time for the deputies to deal with
issues rather than personalities. He promised his audience facts to support the
allegations that had been floating in the air for some time, but instead he produced only innuendo. Employing a tactic that the Montagnards would them-

---

14. Gueniffey, "Paris Commune."
15. For a detailed account of the acrimony in the Convention from late September through
October, see Michael Sydenham, *The Girondins* (London, 1961), 123–30.

selves master the following summer, Louvet accused Robespierre of participating in a secret conspiracy against the public good. As an indictment of Robespierre, Louvet's speech was a miserable failure—one week later Robespierre defended himself on the floor of the Convention against the accusations and emerged from the fracas more popular among Parisians than before, while Louvet faded into relative obscurity. Camille Desmoulins likened the battle between the two men to Hercules at grips with an enraged basset hound.[16]

But if Louvet's speech was a tactical failure—and it has been suggested that Vergniaud, Gensonné, and Condorcet opposed it—it reveals considerable insight into the dilemma that confronted the Girondins at that moment.[17] How could they attack the perpetrators of the September massacres without seeming to attack the people of Paris, and how could they separate the massacres themselves from the glorious uprising of August 10? Louvet, as a native Parisian and former activist in the Lombards section, certainly had the credentials to attempt this, and he did so with emotion. He spoke of Robespierre's growing ascendancy at the Jacobins, where he was held up as some sort of god by his adoring supporters. Robespierre flattered those supporters, Louvet asserted, as being "the people of Paris, then as simply the people, and then as the sovereign," never missing the opportunity when championing the sovereignty of the people to insist that "he, too, was people." Louvet knew well the people of Paris, among whom he had lived all his life. The people of Paris knew how to fight, they had been at the Tuileries on August 10 (it will be remembered that Robespierre had not). They did not, however, know how to assassinate, and they had not been at the prisons on September 2. To link the prison massacres to August 10 (as Garat had done some days before in a speech to the Convention) was not only to sully that glorious victory, it was to impugn the people of Paris as well. The revolution of August 10 belonged to everyone—to the Parisians, to the deputies of the Legislative Assembly, to the *fédérés* of Finistère and Marseille. The massacres of September belonged only to Robespierre, to Marat (whose name Louvet could not bring himself to pronounce until the very end of his speech), and to their conspiratorial cabal. Louvet did not then deny the sovereignty of the people. What he disputed was Robespierre's claim to embody that sovereignty, charging that he had in fact betrayed it. The argument was rhetorically brilliant, but unfortunately neither Louvet nor the other Girondins had a popular movement to back up their words. However dubious it may have been for Robespierre to claim that his supporters were "the people," he did have a popular movement behind him, one rooted in the clubs and sections of Paris.

16. The text of Louvet's speech and the characterization by Desmoulins can be found in H. Morse Stephens, ed., *The Principal Speeches of Statesmen and Orators of the French Revolution* (Oxford, 1892), vol. 2, 458–74.

17. Bowers, *Pierre Vergniaud*, 273.

Indeed, that popular support for Robespierre in Paris would be in evidence on the occasion of his reply to Louvet. On the night of November 4 a crowd of his supporters lined up outside the Manège, and the following day some seven to eight hundred people, many of them women, crowded into the galleries to cheer on their champion. If the Girondins could not separate Robespierre from his base of popular support in Paris, however, they might hope for greater success in the provinces. In the days following this exchange in the Convention, Roland, who as minister of the interior controlled a sizable budget for "public instruction," ordered 15,000 copies of Louvet's speech printed and distributed in the departments.[18] No copies of Robespierre's reply were ordered.

THE TRIAL OF LOUIS XVI

The issue of sovereignty was also central to the trial of Louis XVI, with the claims of Parisians once again pitted against those of citizens in the departments. The key vote in the trial, among the four roll-call votes, was that on the *appel au peuple* (appeal to the people), the Girondin proposal that the king's sentence be referred to primary assemblies so that the people of France might either ratify the judgment of the Convention or decide Louis' fate themselves. Before the trial began, however, Robespierre reiterated his earlier assertion that the will of the people had been expressed in Paris on August 10. On December 3, 1792, he spoke in opposition to the need for any trial at all: "The great question with which you are occupied is settled by this argument: Louis has been deposed by his crimes. Louis denounced the French people as rebels; to punish them he called upon the arms of his fellow tyrants. Victory and the people have decided that he alone was a rebel. Therefore, Louis cannot be judged; he has already been condemned, else the Republic is not cleared of guilt."[19]

The deputies of the National Convention ignored Robespierre's call for summary execution and over the next three weeks reviewed the evidence against the king and listened to Louis speak in his own defense. On December 27 Jean-Baptiste Salles proposed the *appel au peuple*, which has generally been interpreted as a Girondin attempt to save the life of the king. Not surprisingly, Robespierre and Vergniaud played major roles in the debate over this proposal.

Robespierre spoke first, on December 28, briefly repeating his earlier contention that Louis had been judged and condemned by the people on August 10. Since the Convention had adopted other procedures, however, he would address

18. Jordan, *Revolutionary Career*, 123–26.
19. Michael Walzer, *Regicide and Revolution: Speeches at the Trial of Louis XVI* (New York, 1992), 131.

and oppose this new proposal on different grounds. "Why should the representatives of the nation pronounce on the crime," he asked, "and the nation itself
pronounce on the penalty?" Any delay in the judgment of Louis would unneces-
sarily endanger the safety of the nation and undermine the sovereignty of the
people. How could thousands of primary assemblies be expected to review the
evidence against the king in an expeditious fashion and reach a consensus as to
his sentence? In the midst of war, for the Convention to refer Louis' fate to
primary assemblies would be to acknowledge its weakness, to abdicate the responsibility that the voters had entrusted to their deputies when they elected
them in September. Such a course of action would be an open invitation to
royalists and *feuillants* to come out of hiding in order to manipulate the assemblies. Could the working people of France reasonably be expected to devote
long days, even weeks, to such deliberations? "But citizens," he asked, "will
those who are found in the primary assemblies really be the people?" To appeal
to the sovereignty of the people, Robespierre argued, was in fact a veiled attempt
to destroy the sovereignty of the people by making the country vulnerable to
civil war.[20]

Vergniaud spoke in favor of the *appel au peuple* three days later. Without
naming Robespierre, he acknowledged the emotional force of his "very moving
speech" yet asserted that the application of reason to the question would yield
a very different conclusion. But while appealing to reason, perhaps in an effort
to restore a note of civility to their proceedings, Vergniaud could not restrain
himself from introducing some of the same themes that had characterized the
rancorous debates of the early autumn.

For Vergniaud, as with Robespierre, sovereignty was at the heart of the matter: "What is the sovereignty of the people of which we hear so much, and to
which I should like to think our homage is not mere words, to which I am sure
the National Convention, at least, renders sincere homage?"[21] The deputies had
voted that the decree abolishing the monarchy, and the draft of a new constitution should be presented to the people in primary assemblies for ratification.
Why should not the same be done in regard to the fate of the king? Primary
assemblies need not be asked to determine the sentence themselves, they could
be asked to ratify the decision of the Convention. As to the suggestion that this
would be a disruptive, contentious, time-consuming process, Vergniaud contrasted the law-abiding departments to the intrigue and tumult of the capital:
"Discord! you thought perhaps that agitators exercised the same control in the
departments which a shameful weakness permitted them to usurp in Paris; that

20. Ibid., 178–94.
21. Ibid., 195.

is a very great error. . . . In the departments, the general will is obeyed; it is understood that public and private liberty are founded on that obedience." Deliberation in primary assemblies would be orderly and expeditious.[22]

Warming to his task, Vergniaud followed the logic of his argument, which took him back to the prison massacres, to "the brigands who, in the month of September, sought to found their power on the debris of the monarchy." Who were these brigands? No one in the Manège could have doubted that the reference was to Robespierre and his supporters. Robespierre had warned in his speech that the *appel au peuple* would invite civil war, but Vergniaud asserted that it was they, in fact, who wished for civil war: "Yes, they want civil war, these men who make the assassination of friends of tyranny a precept and who, at the same time, designate as friends of tyranny those whom their hate wishes to sacrifice." How could those supporting the *appel au peuple* reasonably be accused of wanting civil war? "Civil war for having proposed that homage be rendered to the sovereignty of the people! In your opinion then, is sovereignty of peoples a calamity for mankind?"[23]

Vergniaud concluded his speech with a look toward the future, warning that the greatest threat to the republic lay not in foreign enemies, but rather in those who would manipulate the people in their aspiration for dictatorial power, who would not hesitate once again to unleash the assassins of September in pursuit of their ambitions. In that scenario, it would be Paris herself who would suffer the most: "Paris, your posterity will admire your heroic courage against kings, but they will never conceive of your ignominious servitude before a handful of brigands, jetsam of the human race, who moved in your breast and tore you apart by their tumultuous ambitions and their fury. Who could inhabit a city where desolation and death reign?" But was this a reference to the future or to the past? And if to the future, where did hope lie? Vergniaud's answer to this was clear: "liberty would find its realm and its defenders in the departments."[24]

The fate of the *appel au peuple* did not ride on this speech, but two key elements of Vergniaud's argument must have weighed on the deputies' minds as they cast their votes. Vergniaud had spoken first of the "weakness" of the people of Paris in the face of agitators and later of their "ignominious servitude before a handful of brigands." But how did this image square with the "heroic courage" that the people of Paris had shown on August 10? How could one grant them symbolic sovereignty on one occasion and deny it so easily on another? In his effort to pay the people of Paris a compliment, Vergniaud seems rather to have impugned their character. If the people of Paris could slip so easily from hero-

---

22. Ibid., 200.
23. Ibid., 202–3.
24. Ibid., 206–7.

ism to ignominy, from courage to weakness, why should the "obedient" people of the departments not be similarly vulnerable? Indeed, there had been violence in the departments in early September as well, though not of the magnitude of the massacres in Paris. And even as the *appel au peuple* was being debated, royalist agitation in Rouen touched off a violent riot, seemingly confirming Robespierre's warning about the danger of civil war.[25]

The *appel au peuple* came to a vote on January 15, with many of the deputies once again offering lengthy speeches to explain or justify their positions on the issue. The tally suggests that the deputies did listen to the speeches of their colleagues and perhaps to the news from Rouen, for many of them now voted against the position that they had defended in the previous weeks. Several of the deputies associated with the Girondins voted against the *appel au peuple*, most notably Marie-Jean Condorcet but also Charles-Antoine Chasset, who would later join the federalist rebels in Lyon. The proposal was decisively defeated, by a vote of 414 to 281, with ten deputies abstaining. Whether or not the Girondins viewed the *appel au peuple* as a means to save Louis XVI, its rejection by the deputies clearly marked for them a political defeat and a victory for the Montagnards.[26]

The trial of the king marked an ironic strategic shift in the political conflict between Girondins and Montagnards, pointing again to the debate over where sovereignty lay in this period. In one sense, of course, the struggle between Girondins and Montagnards had to transpire within the halls of the national assembly, since that is where they sat as deputies. Back in August and September, however, the Legislative Assembly, dominated by Brissotins/Girondins, had struggled, and failed, to assert its authority vis-à-vis Paris and the Commune, while Robespierre championed the sovereignty of the people, in particular the people of Paris. In attacking the September massacres and their alleged leaders, the Girondins had attempted to reclaim for the Convention its legitimate authority and succeeded in circumscribing the powers of the Paris sections and

25. David P. Jordan, *The King's Trial: Louis XVI vs. the French Revolution* (Berkeley, 1979), 153–54.

26. Michael S. Lewis-Beck, Anne Hildreth, and Alan B. Spitzer have found that this vote, more than any of the others in the king's trial, supports Alison Patrick's contention about the existence of a Girondin faction within the National Convention: Lewis-Beck, Hildreth, and Spitzer, "Was There a Girondin Faction in the National Convention?" *French Historical Studies* 15, no. 3 (spring 1988): 532–33. See also Alison Patrick, *The Men of the First French Republic* (Baltimore, 1972), 92–94; and Jordan, *King's Trial*, 173–77. These three sources can scarcely be said to agree on every point. Jordan asserts that "there was little correlation between political allegiance and the voting on the appeal," but I would defer on this matter to the more sophisticated statistical analysis of Lewis-Beck, Hildreth, and Spitzer. Where Patrick sees the vote as predictable, based on earlier speeches and pamphlets, Jordan emphasizes the shifts between late December and mid-January. Even on the rather straightforward matter of vote counts the three disagree, as follows: Lewis-Beck et al., 414 to 281; Patrick, 418 to 277; Jordan, 424 to 283. All agree that there were ten abstentions.

Commune. When the trial of the king opened, however, it was Robespierre and Saint-Just who most eloquently asserted the authority of the Convention to decide the king's fate, though being careful not to question the sovereignty of the people, whereas the Girondins explicitly championed that sovereignty in their campaign for the *appel au peuple*. They failed in that campaign, in part due to their own inconsistencies, in part due simply to the impracticality of the plan. In the wake of that failure, political strategies would shift once again. The Montagnards would move to redress their weakness in the departments by monopolizing the appointments as representatives on mission in March and April. And the Girondins, conceding the failure of their effort to defeat the Montagnards by appealing to the people of the departments, would renew the battle within the Convention and against the radical sections of Paris.

THE RIOTS OF MARCH 1793

The antipathy between the *sans-culottes* of Paris and the Girondin deputies came to a head in late February and early March 1793. Steadily rising prices, particularly for sugar, incited a wave of riots and attacks by women on grocers, beginning on February 25. Even Robespierre spoke critically of these riots, characterizing them as unworthy of the patriotic *sans-culottes* of Paris.[27] For the Girondins, whose ardent defense of free trade drew the ire of the crowd, the riots seemed the work of the same lawless and anarchistic elements responsible for the prison massacres.

The violence took on a more explicitly political aspect on March 9 and 10, one day after the first public reports of recent military defeats in Belgium. With Danton urging the sections to mobilize for the war effort, the focus of Parisians turned once again, as it had in September, to enemies within the country. The Girondin deputies, widely perceived as the war party within the National Convention, were now blamed not only for the setbacks on the battlefield but also for trying to conceal the bad news from the public. Jérome Pétion and Pierre Beurnonville, the minister of war, came in for particular criticism, and during the night of March 9 an armed band of some two to three hundred, mostly soldiers, sacked the printing presses of Gorsas, Brissot, and Condorcet.

The first calls were now heard in the sections of Paris for the arrest of leading Girondin deputies, and in the days that followed Vergniaud would assert before the Convention that their lives had been spared on March 9 only because they had been warned and had gone into hiding. The evidence for this is slim, but it

---

27. See Jordan, *Revolutionary Career*, 135–38, for a discussion of Robespierre's reaction to the riots.

would become a constant theme in Girondin rhetoric for the remainder of the spring. There is evidence that Jean Varlet, future leader of the *enragés,* tried to galvanize the riots into full-scale insurrection, but the effort was unsuccessful. Although there were calls in the Jacobin club for the dismissal of Armand Gensonné, then president of the Convention, the club held back from the movement in the streets on the evening of March 9. In the following days, the Commune ordered François Hanriot to mobilize the National Guard and order was soon restored.[28]

Two important pieces of legislation emerged from the Convention in the aftermath of the riots. The first authorized the envoy of "representatives on mission" from the National Convention to the provinces, principally to assist in the recruitment effort, though their purview would extend far beyond that task in the months to follow. The second called for the creation of a revolutionary tribunal. Although the Montagnard deputies were the principal advocates of that measure, the first prominent defendant before the Tribunal was Marat, the bête noir of Vergniaud and the Girondins.

Through all of this the National Convention continued to govern without benefit of a constitution, the drafting of which had been the principal reason for which the Convention had been elected in the first place. The deputies had created a nine-member committee to undertake that task on October 11, 1792, a committee dominated by Girondins and led by Condorcet, but its work was delayed by the trial of the king. Condorcet's constitution—it was recognized as such even at the time—was presented on the floor of the Convention on February 15. It was a lengthy and complicated document (Girondin supporters would sarcastically observe that it was too long for its Montagnard critics to read) and did not come up for formal debate until the middle of April. Almost immediately, however, Condorcet's draft was attacked at the Jacobin club for its proposal to increase the authority of government ministers and to strengthen the role of departmental administrations, both viewed as usurpations of popular sovereignty. Never seriously debated in the Convention, it became instead a point of contention in the struggle between Girondins and Montagnards, the resolution of which would doom both it and its author to extinction.[29]

28. A. M. Boursier, "L'Emeute Parisienne du 10 mars 1793," *Annales Historiques de la Révolution française* 44, no. 2 (1972): 204–30. See also Sydenham, *Girondins,* 153–57.

29. See Keith Michael Baker, *Condorcet: From Natural Philosophy to Social Mathematics* (Chicago, 1975), 321–30, for a brief discussion of Condorcet's constitution and its reception. Girondin members of the constitutional committee included Vergniaud, Gensonné, Pétion, and Brissot. When the Montagnard Convention produced its own constitution in late June, Condorcet published an anonymous pamphlet attacking it. The authorship of the pamphlet being transparent, Condorcet was denounced and his arrest decreed. He went into hiding in Paris but fled the capital in March 1794 for fear of compromising the safety of his protectors. Apprehended shortly thereafter, he committed suicide in prison.

THE TREASON OF GENERAL DUMOURIEZ

Relative calm had returned to Paris in the week following March 10, but the military situation in Belgium and Holland continued to deteriorate. On March 18, Charles Dumouriez's army was defeated at Neerwinden and suffered a further setback at Louvain on the 21st. General Dumouriez now began negotiations with the Austrians, pledging to march his army on Paris in order to subdue the rebellious sections and restore the constitution of 1791. When the Convention sent four deputies to the front to investigate and possibly arrest the general, Dumouriez arrested them instead and turned them over to the Austrians. Unable to rally his troops to his cause, however, Dumouriez went over to the Austrians on April 5, taking the son of Philippe Egalité, duc d'Orléans, with him.

The treason of Dumouriez gave new fodder to both the Girondins and the Montagnards in their battle with each other. The Montagnards, led by Robespierre and Marat, were the first to denounce Dumouriez as rumors of his treason reached Paris, though restrained somewhat by allegations from the right that Danton had compromised himself while on mission to the army in Belgium.[30] Allegations of Girondin complicity with Dumouriez soon surfaced, accompanied by charges that this was all part of their plotting to preserve, now restore, the monarchy. For their part, the Girondins tried to turn the table on the Montagnards by accusing them of an alliance with Orléans (who sat with the Montagnards in the Convention) and Dumouriez, seeking to restore a monarchy in which they would exercise dictatorial power from behind the throne. In the long run, the charges of Girondin conspiracy seemed more plausible since they had been in charge of the war ministry when Dumouriez was appointed. But in the short run, the Convention ordered the arrest of the entire Orléans family, to be incarcerated in the Château d'If in Marseille, a decision that would both tarnish somewhat the reputation of the Montagnards and fuel the moderate rumor mill in Marseille.[31]

In Paris the news of Dumouriez's treason served to escalate the crisis that had begun with the riots of March 9–10, with the difference that now the Jacobins were prepared to assume leadership of the sectional movement. Augustin Robespierre, Maximilien's younger brother, speaking before the Jacobin club on April 5, called on the sections to petition the National Convention and "force us to put the unfaithful deputies under arrest."[32] Just four days previously the deputies themselves had sacrificed their parliamentary immunity by passing a decree, proposed by the Girondin Jean Birotteau, which authorized the arrest of depu-

---

30. See Norman Hampson, *Danton* (Oxford, 1978), 104–11, for a discussion of Danton's role in the Dumouriez crisis.

31. William Scott, *Terror and Repression in Revolutionary Marseille* (London, 1973), 85–86.

32. George Rudé, *The Crowd in the French Revolution* (Oxford, 1979), 120.

ties "against whom there should exist strong presumptions of complicity with the enemies of liberty, equality, and the republican government."[33]

The sections responded quickly to Augustin Robespierre's appeal. On April 8 representatives from the Bonconseil section presented a petition before the Convention demanding the arrest of the leading Girondins, including Vergniaud, Guadet, and Buzot. Two days later the section of the Halle au Blé expanded the list to include twenty-two deputies, and this became the standard figure as the petition circulated among the sections in the following weeks.[34] Paris seemed poised once again on the eve of a revolutionary insurrection. Yet in this instance the target was not a despotic king but the National Assembly itself, and unlike their predecessors in the Legislative Assembly, the deputies of the National Convention would not wait passively as the insurrection gathered force. The militants of the Paris sections, however, would remember very well the reluctance of the Legislative Assembly to take decisive action. On April 1, an insurrectionary assembly meeting at the Evêché palace took the title of *Assemblée centrale du salut public et de correspondance avec les départements* (Central Assembly of Public Safety and of Communication with the Departments).[35] Once again the locus of sovereignty would be very much an issue of contention.

On April 10 Maximilien Robespierre rose in the National Convention to denounce a "powerful faction that is conspiring with the tyrants of Europe to give us a king with an aristocratic constitution." He accused that group of having opposed the fall of the monarchy; of having supported Lafayette; of having foolishly led France into war against Austria and later undermined the war effort; of having calumniated both Paris and the Paris Commune; of having sown division within the Convention and corrupted public opinion in the departments of France; of having proposed the *appel au peuple* during Louis' trial; and of having conspired with Dumouriez in his treason against the republic. He concluded his speech by naming Brissot, Vergniaud, Gensonné, and Guadet.[36]

The deputies had been slinging accusations against each other for the past six months, but aside from Louvet's ill-conceived denunciation of Robespierre nothing so specific or extensive had been heard before the Convention. Ambiguous calumny was one thing—it had seemingly become a standard part of rhetorical strategy in the Convention—but the decree of April 1 revoking parliamentary immunity had raised the stakes, and in the face of a brewing insurrection the Girondins could not let these charges go unanswered. Vergniaud rose immediately to respond to Robespierre, not asking for the week's delay that the Incorruptible had needed before answering Louvet's denunciation in

33. Patrick, *Men of the First French Republic*, 109.
34. Rudé, *Crowd in the French Revolution*, 120–21.
35. Morris Slavin, *The Making of an Insurrection* (Cambridge, Mass., 1986), 67–68.
36. *Le Moniteur Universel*, no. 103 (April 13, 1793).

the fall, and in one of his most brilliant speeches he addressed the accusations one by one.[37]

There is no need here to review systematically Vergniaud's speech. It was by all accounts a successful effort. His two-hour speech was interrupted by applause at numerous points, and even the galleries, filled with Robespierre's supporters, grew silent as Vergniaud warmed to his task. Claude Bowers writes that Vergniaud demolished Robespierre, concluding that the "counterattack of Vergniaud, made without preparation or meditation, had been so brilliant and crushing that Robespierre's attack had been forgotten before the session closed."[38] The speech looked both to the past and the future, revisiting issues and controversies from the summer of 1792 and anticipating the defense that Vergniaud would prepare for his trial in the summer of 1793.

Vergniaud parried the specific allegations made by Robespierre quite deftly. Many of them were based on rumor and innuendo, and these Vergniaud turned back on his accusers, asserting that they were the real calumniators of Paris, that they were the true conspirators with Dumouriez. Vergniaud defended his conduct on August 10 and defended the legitimacy of the *appel au peuple* as well. Far from calumniating the Paris Commune, he had simply called for a public accounting of its finances, an opportunity for those officials to demonstrate their zeal in the administration of public funds.[39]

Robespierre had accused them of being moderates. Well, Vergniaud responded, he had scarcely been a moderate on August 10, when Robespierre had been cowering in his cellar, and he was certainly not a moderate in his defense of liberty. But if, under the pretext of revolution, one must defend murder and brigandage to be called a patriot, then yes, he was a moderate.[40]

Vergniaud had heard much talk in recent days of insurrection, and he admitted that it made him groan. To what end would that insurrection be directed, he asked. To transfer the exercise of sovereignty to the republic? But the exercise of sovereignty was confided to the national representation. Therefore, those who spoke of insurrection must wish to destroy the national representation, to place sovereignty in the hands of a few, ultimately in the hands of a dictator. They were, in effect, not defenders of national sovereignty, but conspirators against liberty and the republic.[41]

Vergniaud concluded his speech by reminding his colleagues that less than

37. See Morse Stephens, *Principal Speeches*, vol. 1, 361–84, for the full text of Vergniaud's speech.

38. Bowers, *Pierre Vergniaud*, 373. This quotation comes toward the end of a lengthy discussion and summary of this speech.

39. Stephens, *Principal Speeches*, vol. 1, 369.

40. Ibid., 377.

41. Ibid., 378.

one month before he had stood before them to denounce the March 10 conspiracy against the National Convention. On that occasion, he admonished them, "you ordered, by a decree, that the guilty should be prosecuted before the Revolutionary Tribunal; the crime was confirmed. What heads have fallen? None. What accomplice has at least been arrested? None. You yourselves cooperated in rendering your decree illusory."[42] Every bit as much as Augustin Robespierre's speech before the Jacobin club, this was a call to action. Three days later the deputies of the Convention responded by voting a decree of accusation against Jean-Paul Marat. It was a terrible tactical mistake.

THE IMPEACHMENT OF MARAT

Although Marat's name had been linked to those of Danton and Robespierre back in the days following the September massacres, both deputies had at times publicly repudiated him and the Montagnards tended to maintain a healthy distance between themselves and the "friend of the people."[43] On April 5, however, Marat had assumed the presidency of the Jacobin club, and on that same day he signed a circular that denounced the generals (especially Dumouriez) and the moderates within the Convention and exhorted the departments to march to the defense of Paris.[44] From the perspective of the Girondins, this was essentially an invitation to the radical Jacobins of the departments to march to the capital to join the insurrectional movement that was brewing in the sections. They themselves had appealed to the departments, and would do so again, but to protect them from Paris, not the reverse. In making such an appeal Marat seemed to have made himself vulnerable, and his presidency of the club made the other Jacobin leaders vulnerable as well. The Girondin deputies thus made their move.

Their standard bearer in this instance was Marguerite-Elie Guadet, an experienced deputy from Bordeaux (he had sat in the Legislative Assembly as well) whose antipathy toward the Montagnards and Parisian radicals was well known. Guadet spoke before the Convention on April 12, a speech that was both a follow-up to Vergniaud's response to Robespierre and a denunciation of Marat. He called for Marat's impeachment and trial before the Revolutionary Tribunal.[45] The following day the deputies voted to do precisely that, charging Marat with incitement to pillage, murder, and attacks upon the National Convention.

42. Ibid., 380.
43. Louis R. Gottschalk, *Jean Paul Marat: A Study in Radicalism* (New York, 1927). See pages 181–83 for a discussion of Marat's relations with the Montagnards.
44. Ibid., 156.
45. See Stephens, *Principal Speeches*, vol. 1, 422–47, for the full text of Guadet's speech.

Only 376 deputies voted on the matter, 226 in favor of the charges. Some 374 deputies, many of them Montagnards, were away on mission in the departments.[46]

Marat went into hiding until April 23, the eve of his trial. Presented in evidence against him were his writings and speeches of the past seven months, which his accusers no doubt saw as eloquent and sufficient proof of his guilt. The jury thought otherwise. Just forty-five minutes after listening to Marat deliver his own defense they returned a unanimous verdict of acquittal. Throngs of supporters escorted Marat back to the Convention in triumph and then on to the Jacobin club. Marat's overwhelming popularity in Paris had been clearly demonstrated, as had the vulnerability of the Girondins.[47]

The Girondins had not yet played their last card, however, and within the Convention their numbers and eloquence still gave them the capacity to carry votes. Guadet once again took the podium on May 18 and charged that an insurrection against the Convention was being prepared in Paris. He called for the dissolution of the Commune and the transfer of the National Convention to Bourges. Instead the deputies voted to create a Commission of Twelve, dominated by Girondins, to investigate the situation in Paris and the alleged improprieties of the Commune. On May 24, Louis-François-Sébastien Viger reported to the Convention that the Commission of Twelve had found evidence of a planned insurrection and called for the arrest of Jacques-René Hébert, the *procureur* of Paris, for having published a denunciation of the Girondins in his newspaper, *Le Père Duchesne*. The deputies on the Commission of Twelve now became targets themselves for the wrath of the insurrectionary sections, and their names were added to the list of deputies whose proscription would be demanded on June 2.

The battle between Girondins and Montagnards had thus become a battle between the Girondins and the militants of the Paris sections, "the people," as Robespierre had called them in the days following August 10. Vergniaud had always been careful not to malign the people of Paris, directing his barbs instead against those unscrupulous and ambitious men, like Robespierre and Marat, who misled them. Other Girondin deputies were less prudent. In his speech of April 12, which had led to Marat's indictment, Guadet had responded to Robespierre's charge that he and his colleagues had calumniated Paris:

> We have not calumniated Paris, if we have put forward only those facts that are absolutely true: for to calumniate is to do what you do, to lie in order to defame: but cite for us a single false accusation that we have

46. Gottschalk, *Marat*, 157.
47. Ibid., 158–61.

leveled against Paris. The massacres of September, can you deny them? The pillages of February, can you deny them? The brigandage committed against Gorsas and the printer of the *Chronique*, can you deny them? The orders of the sections, orders in which folly rivals insolence, can you deny them? The insubordination of the council of the commune, its usurpations of power, its habitual revolt against the laws and the National Convention, can you deny them? The anarchy that reigns in Paris, the system of disorganization that is publicly preached, at the same time that murder and pillage are publicly called for, can you deny these? Finally the threats made against the National Convention, the state of oppression under which it is held, the calls for the proscription of its members, can you deny these? What do you then say of calumny, when far from imputing these horrors to the citizens of Paris, we have charged them to the brigands that this city shelters, and to the leaders who direct them?[48]

The conciliatory tone of the last line could scarcely blunt the pointed barbs that came before. They represented a virtual indictment of the actions of the sections and the Paris Commune. Such words might resonate within the halls of the Convention, might draw nods of assent from many of the deputies. But in April and May the Girondins had carried their battle beyond the walls of the Convention, with the indictment of Marat and the formation of the Commission of Twelve. Marat was triumphally escorted by the people of Paris back to the halls of the Convention that had tried to expel him. The people of Paris would return to the National Convention again on June 2, this time bearing arms, to demand the expulsion of the Girondins.

48. A.D. Gironde, 8J706, "Réponse de Guadet, député de la Gironde, à Robespierre, député de Paris, prononcée dans la séance du 12 Avril 1793." Guadet's speech was published in pamphlet form, printed on the press of Antoine-Joseph Gorsas.

Three

REVOLT IN THE PROVINCES

May 29, 1793, was a day of violent insurrection in Lyon, the second largest city in France. The uprising began at seven o'clock in the morning when a National Guard battalion seized control of the arsenal and made it the headquarters for the *Comité des Sections*, an ad hoc steering committee for the sectional movement that had emerged in Lyon that spring with the aim of ousting radical Jacobins from control of municipal politics. Tensions had been high in Lyon for some time, and the Jacobin municipal council had anticipated such a challenge. They had appealed for support to P. C. Nioche and A. F. Gauthier, two Montagnard representatives on mission, and on May 27 word reached town that troops from the Army of the Alps, stationed in Grenoble, were marching toward Lyon to support the Jacobin municipality. That news precipitated the crisis of the twenty-ninth, which the Jacobins proved unable to manage. After a few minor skirmishes in the afternoon, two columns of national guardsmen from the arsenal converged on the Hôtel de Ville, where a pitched battle raged for more than two hours. The Jacobin municipality and its supporters were routed. Evidence suggests that only about twenty-five were killed and thirty wounded, although estimates of casualties were wildly exaggerated at the time. Victorious on the field, or streets, of battle, the moderate sections petitioned the departmental administration, already controlled by moderates, to suspend the municipal council and name a provisional council in its place, which they did. The following day, Nioche and Gauthier, essentially under house arrest at the arsenal, endorsed those actions and issued an order commanding the troops en route to Lyon to return to their garrison in Grenoble. Thus ended Jacobin control of the city of Lyon.[1]

News of the revolt of Lyon and the supposed slaughter of eight hundred patriots was reported on the floor of the National Convention by Joseph Cambon on June 2.[2] At that moment the Convention was itself surrounded by armed battalions of the Paris National Guard and some eighty to one hundred thousand Parisians. The Paris sections had been in a state of declared insurrection since May 31, with the aim of securing the proscription of the leading Girondin

1. W. D. Edmonds, *Jacobinism and the Revolt of Lyon, 1789–1793* (Oxford, 1990), 186–201.
2. Morris Slavin, *The Making of an Insurrection: Parisian Sections and the Gironde* (Cambridge, Mass., 1986), 110.

deputies from the National Convention. By the end of the day that aim had been achieved—under the watchful gaze of the Paris crowd the deputies passed a decree placing twenty-nine of their colleagues and two ministers under provisional arrest. As in Lyon, a political shift had occurred, though in the opposite direction. The Montagnards now controlled the National Convention. The leading Girondins had been expelled from office, their ultimate fate still uncertain, and some seventy-five of their supporters, signatories of a protest against the proscription, would be similarly expelled in early October. But unlike the insurrection that had marked the shift in power in Lyon, the one in Paris was peaceful and bloodless. The threat of violence was certainly there, in the crowd of Parisian militants gathered in the Tuileries gardens and in the ranks of Hanriot's national guardsmen who stood between the crowd and the hall in which the Convention met. But through three days of protest and demonstration not a single deputy was attacked, no heads were paraded on pikes, no blood was shed. So impressive was the order maintained by the crowd on May 31 that even Vergniaud, the leader of those deputies targeted for proscription, was moved to propose a decree observing that the people of Paris had deserved well of the republic.

Such a decree must seem paradoxical to us today, as it did to many at the time.[3] The reader will recall that Vergniaud had been among the first to condemn the September massacres, had called for the heads of those responsible for the riots in March, and in early May had written two letters to Bordeaux imploring his constituents to support the Convention "against the furies who menace her." In the last week of May Vergniaud had again spoken before the Convention: "I also declare, and it is good for all Parisians to hear me, that if through persecution, outrages, and violence we should be forced to retire; if a fatal schism were thus provoked, the Department of the Gironde would no longer have anything in common with a city which would have violated the national representation and broken the unity of the Republic."[4] Why then, on May 31, did Vergniaud make his motion in praise of Paris? The only reasonable answer would seem to be that at that moment it was still not clear what the outcome of the insurrection would be.

Georges Lefebvre has written that the insurrection of May 31–June 2 "was the best organized *journée* of the Revolution."[5] The fact that there was no violence was no doubt a product of that organization. But the events of those three days did not run entirely according to script, nor is it clear that all who were involved in the planning of the insurrection were in agreement as to just what

---

3. Morris Slavin reports that a spokesman for the Commune reported Vergniaud's motion to the General Council with the words, "This . . . will astonish you perhaps." Ibid., 202 n. 65.

4. Claude G. Bowers, *Pierre Vergniaud: Voice of the French Revolution* (New York, 1950), 395.

5. Cited in Slavin, *Making of an Insurrection*, 110.

that script should be. Without recounting in detail the events of those days, it will be worthwhile to examine the key elements of the upheaval for three reasons. First, because issues of sovereignty were at stake, it is important to sort out who exactly was responsible for the proscription of the Girondin deputies: Robespierre and the Jacobins, the Montagnard deputies more generally, the Commune of Paris, the sections of Paris, or some combination of those groups? Second, we must attempt to establish the relation of this insurrection to that of August 10, 1792, and to the failed insurrection or riots of March 9–10, 1793. Finally, because the federalist revolt itself erupted in response to the insurrection of May 31–June 2, it is important to consider what people in the departments knew about the events in Paris and to understand that all of those involved—the Montagnards in the Convention, the authorities of Paris, the Jacobin club, and the proscribed deputies themselves—did everything they could to influence and control the reports that were being relayed to the provinces. It is as true today as it was in 1793 that an understanding of the federalist revolt must rest in part on an understanding of the insurrection in Paris that triggered it.

THE *JOURNÉES* OF MAY 31–JUNE 2, 1793

The first calls for the proscription of Girondin deputies had come in the first week of April, just before the celebrated exchange in the Convention between Robespierre and Vergniaud. On April 15, Jacques Hébert and Jean-Nicolas Pache, the mayor of Paris, presented to the Convention a petition from thirty-five of the forty-eight sections of Paris demanding by name the proscription of twenty-two Girondin deputies. Vergniaud, Louvet, and Gensonné all denounced the petition as a "veritable conspiracy against the sovereignty of the people."[6]

During the final two weeks of April, all eyes in Paris were focused on the trial of Jean-Paul Marat. But earlier in the month, on April 1, delegates from twenty-seven of the Paris sections meeting in the Evêché palace on the Ile de la Cité had adopted the name *Assemblée centrale du salut public et de correspondance avec des départements.* By mid-May that assembly numbered some five hundred delegates, one hundred of them women, and had begun actively to prepare for insurrection. It was this, in large part, that prompted the formation of the Commission of Twelve on May 20, on the motion of Bertrand Barère.

The Evêché assembly was not the only body claiming to represent the people

---

6. Ibid., 14–15. My discussion of the insurrection is drawn principally from Slavin's book, as well as from George Rudé, *The Crowd in the French Revolution* (Oxford, 1979), and Michael J. Sydenham, *The Girondins* (London, 1961).

in Paris at this time. Section assemblies continued to meet regularly, and in many of them there was an ongoing struggle between supporters of the Montagnards and those favoring the Girondins. It would be a mistake to see the sectional movement in Paris as monolithic or unanimous in spring 1793. The Central Council of the Commune also had to be reckoned with, and it had grown more moderate with the elections of late 1792. Finally, there was the General Council of the department of Paris, and this body, too, convened a special assembly on May 29 in the hall of the Jacobin club, which itself might exercise a claim to represent the will of the people.

On May 29 the Evêché assembly created a Central Revolutionary Committee, consisting at first of just nine members but expanded the next day to twenty-five, with the new members coming from the other constituted authorities in Paris mentioned above. That increase reduced the influence of Jean Varlet and the *enragés* (the "angry ones," a pejorative term for Parisian militants) on the Central Revolutionary Committee, thereby restraining somewhat the radical agenda of Parisian militants. When the insurrection began on May 31, then, two assemblies were meeting side by side in the Evêché—the Central Revolutionary Committee and the General Council of the Paris Commune. The goals of the proposed insurrection were essentially twofold: the elimination of the Commission of Twelve (already abolished by the National Convention on May 27 but reinstated the following day), and the proscription of the leading Girondin deputies (the precise number ranging from twenty-two to thirty-four). Even among the Montagnard deputies, however, there was reluctance to go so far as proscription, and on June 1 the Convention referred the matter to the Committee of Public Safety.

One of the extraordinary things about this insurrection is that it endured for three days. It is surprising, on the one hand, that the energy of the crowd could be sustained—and there were sizable crowds in the streets on all three days—and, on the other, that the energy of the crowd did not spill over into violence in the face of the frustrating delays of May 31 and June 1. Playing a central role in sustaining the insurrection while preventing violence were the forces of the National Guard under the command of François Hanriot. His twenty thousand troops, stationed not only at the Tuileries palace, where the Convention now met, but at the Place du Carrousel, the Place de la Revolution, and the courtyard of the Palais-Royal, served both as a source of pressure and a source of protection for the threatened deputies.

In that tense situation, the Committee of Public Safety ultimately proposed a compromise, presented to the Convention by Bertrand Barère on June 2. His report called not for the arrest or proscription of the deputies but rather for their voluntary suspension from office for a limited period of time. At that point, Isnard, Fauchet, Lanthenas, and Dussaulx stepped forward to resign, but this was clearly not enough. The Girondins' harsh denunciations of the Paris Commune and the sections over the previous months, coupled with the arrests ordered by the Commission of Twelve only ten days before, left the Commune and the sections in no mood to compromise. Hanriot's troops forced the issue, and proscription—not resignation—was the result.[7]

That the Montagnards were uncomfortable with the pressure that had been applied on them on June 2 is shown by their actions in the days that followed. Robespierre, who had sanctioned the insurrection on May 29 but not led it, praised the people of Paris for once again saving the Revolution and promised them "the most popular constitution that has ever existed," but he also supported moves to curtail the powers of those bodies that had led the popular insurrection.[8] Almost immediately after the proscription of the deputies the Committee of Public Safety demanded that the Commune remove "dangerous elements" from the Central Revolutionary Committee; on June 6 it presented a decree to the Convention seeking to curtail the independence of all insurrectionary committees; and on June 8 the Central Revolutionary Committee "was transformed into the *Comité de Salut public*" of the department of Paris, effectively making it a part of the revolutionary administrative structure.[9]

This was a victory for the sections of Paris, and it went beyond what the Montagnards and Jacobins might have desired. The record shows that both Danton and Barère denounced the outrage being committed against the integrity of the National Convention in the midst of the confrontation on June 2.[10] And though willing to proscribe the Girondins, the other deputies were not willing to order their arrest. They were placed instead under house arrest, a gentle confinement from which many of them managed to escape. It would be months before formal charges were filed against those deputies who remained in Paris.

The deputies who fled, and those in the Convention who had opposed the insurrection and proscriptions, emphasized to their constituents in the provinces that the Convention had acted under duress, had been coerced by the armed militants of Paris, and had not been able to deliberate freely on June 2. That they were right can scarcely be doubted. Since March, if not since September, the Girondin deputies had been warning their constituents that they were

---

7. See Slavin, *Making of an Insurrection*, 72–75, for a discussion of the shifting constitution of the Central Revolutionary Committee; 96–97, for those sections which did not support the call for insurrection; and 127–41, for a discussion of the *enragés* and the important role played by women in the insurrection. See also Rudé, *Crowd in the French Revolution*, 122–25, for a discussion of the composition of Hanriot's force and the sections from which it was drawn.

8. See David P. Jordan, *The Revolutionary Career of Maximilien Robespierre* (Chicago, 1985), 144–47.

9. Slavin, *Making of an Insurrection*, 148–51.

10. Ibid., 114 and 150.

threatened by "the knives of assassins," yet those knives had remained in their sheaths throughout the insurrection. Both the Jacobin club and the Convention emphasized in their reports that the insurrection had been peaceful, and in that regard it was an even more glorious expression of popular sovereignty than August 10 had been. But did the people of France see June 2 as an expression of their sovereignty as well, or would they view themselves as disenfranchised by the militant sections of Paris? Had the people of Paris "deserved well of the Republic," or had the "majesty of the Convention been outraged?"

The Montagnard deputies themselves must have worried about this during the first weeks of June. The motivation within the National Convention for proscribing the Girondins had been, ostensibly, to remove an obstructionist faction so that the Convention might get on with the business of governing. The war effort had faltered in spring 1793; intensified recruitment efforts had elicited resistance in numerous departments and had provoked serious rebellion in the Vendée; and political uncertainty, the provisioning demands of the war, and spiraling inflation had combined to produce economic difficulties in both town and country throughout France. All of these challenges demanded urgent attention. But having removed the impediment to effective governing within the National Convention, the Montagnards now faced the very real possibility that the country would not respond to its leadership. The threat of civil war was more serious now than it had ever been before.

THE FEDERALIST REVOLT

The Montagnard deputies had every reason to believe that support in the departments for the proscribed Girondins would be widespread, and early indications confirmed those fears. In January the Girondins had attempted to refer the fate of the king to departmental primary assemblies but had been thwarted in that effort. In their debates with the Montagnards, and their denunciations of Paris, Girondin deputies frequently made rhetorical appeals to their constituents in the departments, and as the crisis grew in the spring many, like Vergniaud, had written letters to their constituents soliciting their active support. Many departmental administrations responded to those appeals in April and May, sending letters and delegations to the National Convention decrying the factionalism that impeded its work and denouncing the violent brigands and anarchists who in their view dominated Parisian politics.[11]

The first reports of the events of May 31–June 2 seemed to confirm the

---

11. See Henri Wallon, *La Révolution du 31 mai et le fédéralisme en 1793* (Paris, 1886), esp. vol. 1, 144–77, for examples of these letters.

alarms and warnings that Girondin deputies had issued earlier in the spring, and they brought a flood of letters from departmental administrations and other local authorities protesting the proscription of the Girondin deputies. Although historians have tended to exaggerate the scope of these protests, often claiming that as many as two-thirds of the departments initially joined in the federalist revolt, it would be no exaggeration to state that a majority of the departmental administrations expressed opposition to what they viewed as a violation of the integrity of the National Convention.[12] Some forty-seven departments protested by letter the May 31–June 2 revolution, while thirty-four departments either declared open support for the Montagnard Convention or remained indifferent. Most departmental administrations did nothing beyond their letters of protest, but thirteen departments engaged in prolonged resistance to the National Convention in what has come to be known as the federalist revolt (see table 1).[13]

The departments engaging in prolonged, active revolt were clustered around four urban centers: Caen in Lower Normandy, Bordeaux in Aquitaine, Marseille in Provence, and Lyon in Maconnais (see map 1). Lyon, Marseille, and Bordeaux were the three largest cities in France after Paris, and that alone meant the revolt posed a very serious challenge to the republic. Caen was a commercial port of some significance, but its location made it strategically important for other reasons. Its proximity to Paris made it an early rallying point for those proscribed deputies who fled the capital. It lay in a rich agricultural region and was important in providing both grain and dairy goods for the populace of Paris. Caen's good relations with the city of Rouen, to the east, presented the danger that Rouen, too, would be drawn into the revolt and that the Seine, an important lifeline for Paris, might be blockaded. Finally, Caen's position near the coastline gave it easy access to England, then at war with France. As the revolt in Normandy crumbled in late July, the commander of the rebel forces there, General Félix Wimpffen, would indeed propose collaboration with the British.

It is our task now to deal with the beginning of the revolt, not the end. I

---

12. Examples of general histories that exaggerate the scope of the revolt include Albert Soboul, *The French Revolution, 1787–1799* (London, 1972), 317; J. M. Thompson, *The French Revolution* (Oxford, 1966), 366; J. M. Roberts, *The French Revolution* (Oxford, 1978), 53. More recently, William Doyle, *The Oxford History of the French Revolution* (Oxford, 1989), 241, acknowledges this exaggeration, but another recent history, D. M. G. Sutherland's *France, 1789–1815: Revolution and Counterrevolution* (Oxford, 1985), 187, repeats the exaggeration that some sixty of the eighty-three departments joined in the protests.

13. My breakdown of departmental alignment relies essentially on Henri Wallon, *La Révolution du 31 mai*, but also on my own extensive research in departmental archives. Bill Edmonds arrives at slightly different numbers in " 'Federalism' and Urban Revolt in France in 1793," *Journal of Modern History* 55 (March 1983): 23–24. See my first book, *Provincial Politics in the French Revolution: Caen and Limoges, 1789–1794* (Baton Rouge, 1989), 9–10, for a discussion of the discrepancies between Edmonds' figures and my own.

TABLE 1 Departmental Alignment Following the May 31 Revolution

Jacobin departments (departments supporting the Montagnard Convention)

Aisne	Haute-Loire	Nord
Allier	Haute-Marne	Oise
Ardennes	Haute-Saône	Pas-de-Calais
Ariège	Haute-Vienne	Saône-et-Loire
Aube	Haut-Rhin	Seine
Bas-Rhin	Indre	Seine-et-Marne
Basses-Pyrénées	Indre-et-Loire	Seine-et-Oise
Charente-Inférieure	Loiret	Seine-Inférieure
Cher	Loir-et-Cher	Vosges
Corrèze	Meuse	Yonne
Creuse	Moselle	
Eure-et-Loir	Nièvre	

Federalist departments (departments protesting the Girondin proscriptions)

Ain	Finistère	Maine-et-Loire
Alpes-Maritimes	Gard	Manche
Ardèche	Gers	Marne
Aude	Gironde	Mayenne
Aveyron	Haute-Garonne	Meurthe
Basses-Alpes	Hautes-Alpes	Morbihan
Bouches-du-Rhône	Hautes-Pyrénées	Orne
Calvados	Hérault	Puy-de-Dôme
Cantal	Ille-et-Vilaine	Pyrénées-Orientales
Charente	Isère	Rhône-et-Loire
Côte-d'Or	Jura	Sarthe
Côtes-du-Nord	Landes	Somme
Dordogne	Loire-Inférieure	Tarn
Doubs	Lot	Var
Drôme	Lot-et-Garonne	Vienne
Eure	Lozère	

Departments engaging in prolonged resistance

Ain	Finistère	Mayenne
Bouches-du-Rhône	Gard	Morbihan
Calvados	Gironde	Rhône-et-Loire
Côtes-du-Nord	Ille-et-Vilaine	
Eure	Jura	

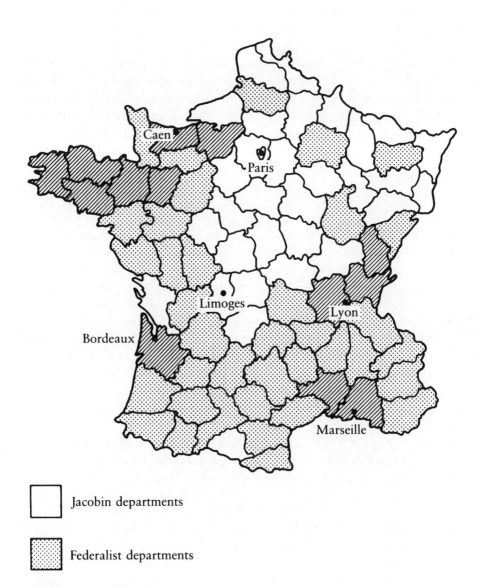

Jacobin departments

Federalist departments

Departments engaging in prolonged resistance

Map 1.   Departmental Alignment in June 1793 (map by Colleen Baker)

propose to do so, in the pages that follow, one city, or region, at a time, in order to establish a narrative line and to present an overall picture of the federalist revolt with as much clarity as possible. It is well to bear in mind, however, that such a sequential treatment can also be deceptive. The revolts did not happen, after all, one after the other. The ultimate failure of the revolt rested in part on the fact that the four centers never did manage to unite, and individually each, with the exception of Lyon, was defeated with relative ease. In early July, however, the specter of revolt in all four cities at the same time, coupled with exaggerated reports of rebellion elsewhere, seemed very threatening indeed to the government and the people of Paris.

CAEN

Elected authorities in Caen—the Caen municipal council, the district council, and the Calvados departmental council—had frequently expressed their concern to the National Convention about dissension within that body during its first eight months of existence and about the apparent anarchy that prevailed in the streets of Paris. Two Calvados deputies to the Convention, Gabriel de Cussy and Claude-Jean-Baptiste Lomont, had maintained a regular correspondence with their constituents and encouraged them to express their views by writing letters to the Convention. Late in October, de Cussy, who had been a municipal officer himself, sent a copy of Louvet's denunciation of Robespierre to his former colleagues, accompanied by the suggestion that a departmental guard might be necessary in order to expel a handful of scoundrels from the Convention so that it might get on with its business.[14]

Early in January, in the midst of the king's trial, the thirteen Calvados deputies sent a letter to Caen warning that a *"parti désorganisateur"* was at work in Paris, sowing the seeds of anarchy, and that even "Pache himself, the Minister of War, is very suspect to the true friends of the Republic."[15] Pache, of course, was mayor of Paris by the time of the May 31 insurrection, and the Caennais would be very suspicious about his role in those events. As the crisis grew in late winter and early spring, correspondence between Paris and Caen increased, with the letters from de Cussy taking a particularly alarmist and vitriolic tone.

Despite an early April letter from de Cussy exultantly reporting the indictment of Marat, administrators in Caen remained deeply concerned about the divisions within the Convention. On April 19, the departmental and district

14. A.C. Caen, I33 (Affaire de la garde départementale de la Convention, lettre de Cussy). For a fuller discussion of the events of the revolt in Caen, see Hanson, *Provincial Politics*, esp. chaps. 3 and 4.

15. B.M. Caen, Rés. Fn. Br. C289.

councils meeting together drafted an address to the National Convention, exhorting the deputies to overcome their bitter disputes and work together for the good of the country. Should that prove impossible to accomplish in Paris, however, they offered the deputies the following advice:

> Elected of the people, you know it, France is not in Paris; she is formed by eighty-four Departments; if in one you are insulted, in another you will be respected, obeyed: there you will find a shelter from the furor and the plots of rascals; there you will enjoy your rights and Liberty; there you will live among the French, Republicans, brothers who will know how to ward off from you daggers and assassins. But before leaving the first cradle of Liberty, make a final effort; brave the storms; spurn the rumors of a few careerists; punish the conspirators; work to give sage Laws to a great People; save your country; obtain happiness for your fellow-citizens; above all, make yourselves respected; and if a few scoundrels again lift their blasphemous voices, think of us, speak, and you will be avenged.[16]

This letter is striking in a number of ways. As in so many of the letters and speeches from this period, the issue of sovereignty looms large—Paris was only one of the eighty-four departments of France, and a disreputable one at that, and the Caennais offered the deputies a safe haven, away from the storms of the capital, for their deliberations. The letter also seems to foresee that the crisis in Paris was nearing its denouement—"make a final effort" to rise above the conflict, it reads. But at the same time the Caennais sound pessimistic about the outcome. In the last line they promise not to protect the deputies from scoundrels but to avenge them.

Claude Lomont also wrote frequently to Caen in April and May, most often addressing letters to his friend Pierre-Jean Lévêque, president of the departmental administration. His letters conveyed deepening pessimism about the situation in Paris and a growing sense of urgency. In a May 15 letter, Lomont admonished the departmental council for the mildness of their most recent address to the Convention and urged them to take a bolder tone, much as Vergniaud had exhorted the Bordelais earlier in May. Indeed, Lomont forwarded to Lévêque a copy of the most recent address from Bordeaux, urging him to compare it to the last letter from Calvados and to do better in the future.[17] The Calvados administrators responded to Lomont's entreaty with a final letter drafted after news of the Convention's tumultuous session of May 27 reached

---

16. A.D. Calvados, L10024 (Procès-verbaux du Conseil Général du département). Also quoted in Hanson, *Provincial Politics*, 93.

17. Hanson, *Provincial Politics*, 94–95.

Caen. They pledged to create a departmental force to protect the Convention's meeting hall and promised "a war to the death against Anarchists, Proscribers, and Factionists."[18]

Officials in Caen made good on their words in the following days and weeks. When news of May 27 reached Caen, Louis Caille, the *procureur-syndic* of the district, issued an order convening sectional assemblies in Caen. Delegates from those assemblies had joined a meeting of the municipal, district, and departmental administrations on the evening of May 30, and it was this body that drafted the final Calvados address to the National Convention. That assembly also approved a resolution calling for the creation of a departmental armed force to march to the aid of the Convention. More urgently, a special delegation was formed to carry their address to Paris, led by Louis Caille and Pierre-Jean-René Lenormand, then president of the departmental administration.

The delegation of nine members arrived in Paris on June 2, in time to witness the final stages of the insurrection and learn of the proscription of the Girondin deputies. They remained in Paris until June 5, conferring with deputies from Calvados as well as with Barbaroux, Lanjuinais, Pétion, and Valazé, all among the proscribed deputies. Finding Paris a threatening and intimidating environment and failing in their mission to deliver the Calvados address on the floor of the Convention, the delegation started back to Caen on June 5, stopping in Evreux and Lisieux to share with officials in those towns their report on the events they had witnessed.

They arrived back in Caen around midday on June 8. The departmental directory immediately convened a special meeting of the three administrative councils, the civil and criminal tribunal, and representatives from the five sections of Caen. The assembly listened to the delegation report on the grim situation in Paris, a report that emphasized the role of scoundrels in the pay of Marat and of the troops commanded by Hanriot. In their version of events, the insurrection of May 31–June 2 was no triumph of the people (whether Parisian or otherwise), but rather a victory for the militant anarchists who had plagued Paris and the National Convention since September. Alarmed by what they heard, those assembled took a personal oath pledging eternal war against those who had violated the Convention and issued an order convening sectional assemblies for that evening, so that the special commissioners could report to the people of Caen as well.

The events of that evening, and the following day, are somewhat confused, but the various accounts that survive agree on a number of crucial developments.[19] Sectional assemblies did indeed meet on the evening of June 8, and on the initiative of section *Liberté* a preliminary declaration of insurrection emerged

---

18. A.C. Caen, I34 (Adresses et députations à la Convention).
19. See Hanson, *Provincial Politics*, 120–51, for a more detailed discussion of what follows.

out of those meetings. Later that night (one account says 2 A.M., another 4 A.M.), a second general assembly convened, although the late hour limited attendance. Notably absent was the mayor of Caen, Jean Le Goupil Duclos, who would later insist that he was not informed of the meeting. Although some of those present claimed later to have dissented, the minutes of the session record a unanimous declaration of insurrection and resistance to oppression until that time at which the National Convention should recover its liberty. Messengers from the neighboring department of the Orne reported similar sentiments there, and the assembly sent envoys to the department of the Manche, just west of Calvados, to request their support for the insurrection. In its most assertive action, the assembly dispatched members of the local Carabot club to Bayeux to arrest the representatives on mission, Gilbert Romme and Claude-Antoine Prieur (of the Côte-d'Or), to be held in the fortified Château of Caen as hostages against the safety of the proscribed Girondins. Finally, the assembly sent word to General Félix Wimpffen, commander of the Fourteenth Military Division, headquartered in Bayeux, inviting him to confer with a newly created provisional committee of insurrection, composed principally of local administrators.

At a second meeting, on the evening of June 9, the first of the fugitive Girondin deputies arrived in Caen—Antoine-Joseph Gorsas and Pierre-François Henry-Larivière, a deputy from Calvados. Gorsas and Henry-Larivière addressed the evening assembly, bolstering the resolve of those present and feeding their sense of outrage. The assembly now voted to break off relations with the National Convention, ordering that no decrees issued after May 27 would be recognized and that henceforth the bulletin of the Convention would not be printed for distribution in Caen. Two other important decisions were taken that evening. The assembly resolved to create a departmental force to march to Paris, and it voted to name sixteen commissioners to travel in pairs to sixteen neighboring departments to invite them to join Calvados in selecting a town from which a central committee could direct the insurrection. As we see, within thirty-six hours of the delegation's return from Paris, a number of key steps were taken to launch an insurrection against the capital and to enlist the support of nearby departments.

These bold and decisive measures attracted to Caen another fifteen fugitive deputies and delegates from eight neighboring departments. It is difficult to appraise the influence of these deputies on the insurrectionary assembly in Caen. Two local memoirists differ in their recollections. Frédéric Vaultier insisted that the deputies kept mostly to themselves, whereas J. B. Renée claimed that the arrival of the Girondins stirred the ardor of the rebels and that the eloquence of Buzot and Barbaroux was particularly persuasive.[20] Pétion's recol-

20. Frédéric Vaultier, *Souvenirs de l'insurrection Normande, dite du Fédéralisme, en 1793* (Caen, 1858), 17; and René Norbert Sauvage, "Les Souvenirs de J.-B. Renée sur la Révolution à Caen, 1789–93," *Normannia* 7 (1934): 21. Other deputies arriving in Caen were François Buzot, Jean-Baptiste Salles, and Denis-Toussaint Lesage (June 12); Charles Barbaroux, François Bergoeing, J. P.

lections, written while he was in hiding near Bordeaux and published years later, are similarly equivocal about the role the deputies played in Caen. He wrote that the deputies agreed not to attempt to influence local authorities and to offer their views only as individuals and only when asked, yet the deputies held organized sessions in Caen, presided over by Pétion and with Barbaroux and Lesage serving as secretaries. What was the purpose of these meetings, if not to deliberate on the current situation and consider ways in which they might affect it? Pétion does concede that he visited meetings of the local Carabot society (the most active club in Caen), though he found the proceedings singularly unimpressive.[21] And once the insurrectionary assembly granted funds to the fugitive deputies (and voted to pay each deputy his usual monthly stipend), they published a number of pamphlets and reports—Barbaroux produced an address to his constituents, Bergoeing published a number of documents from the files of the Commission of Twelve, and collectively they wrote the response to Saint-Just's July 8 report to the Convention. In short, the deputies were not idle. The mayor, Le Goupil Duclos, insisted in his interrogation after the revolt that he had hated to see the deputies in town and blamed them for misleading good citizens with their speeches and pamphlets.[22]

The sixteen commissioners who went to neighboring departments enjoyed considerable success in attracting support for the rebellion against Paris. Two of them, Antoine DeVic and Maurice Renouf la Coudraye, traveled west toward Morbihan and the Loire-Inférieure. In Rennes they found that local officials had already formed a Central Committee of Resistance to Oppression, which they now voted to transfer to Caen. Delegates to the Central Committee began to arrive in Caen on June 23, and its first session convened on June 28. Present were representatives from the Mayenne, the Maine-et-Loire, the Côtes-du-Nord, Finistère, Morbihan, Loire-Inférieure, Ille-et-Vilaine, the Orne, and the Eure. Although the Orne shortly withdrew its support, and the departments of the Maine-et-Loire and Loire-Inférieure were preoccupied by the Vendéan rebellion and thus sent no armed volunteers, this gathering of delegates from ten Norman and Breton departments represented the largest regional conglomeration of the federalist revolt. No other federalist center would succeed in generating as substantial a movement as this. Notably absent in the Central Committee, however, were delegates from Rouen and the Seine-Inférieure, which refused to join in the insurrection.

Duval, J. C. G. Lahaye, and Gabriel de Cussy (June 15); Guadet and Louvet (June 26); Pétion (June 28); Lanjuinais (June 30); A. B. F. Kervélégan (July 2); and E. Mollevaut and Gaspard Duchâtel the next week.

21. C. A. Dauban, ed., *Mémoires Inédits de Pétion, et Mémoires de Buzot et de Barbaroux* (Paris, 1866), 143–47.

22. A.D. Calvados, L10125 (Interrogation of Le Goupil Duclos).

From June 28 to late July, two insurrectionary bodies existed side by side in Caen. The Calvados insurrectionary assembly continued to hold regular meetings, overseeing the recruitment of a departmental armed force and the publication in July of nine issues of the *Bulletin des Autorités Constituées*, which printed minutes of the general assembly, recorded news from Paris, and reproduced addresses from other towns and departments. Its first issue reported that sixty-nine departments supported the protest movement.[23] The Central Committee of Resistance to Oppression took responsibility for coordinating the volunteer forces that were gathering in Evreux for a march on the capital (at the instigation of Buzot, whose home was in Evreux), carried on correspondence with other departments, and oversaw the publication of a number of addresses and proclamations. Most important among these was a twenty-seven-point program outlining the grievances of the federalist rebels and their proposals for the reorganization of political life in Paris.

Key to the success of the federalist program was restoration of the National Convention's integrity and freedom, and for this a march on the capital was essential. Enlisting volunteers for that expedition proved not to be an easy matter, however. Although several Caen and Calvados administrators eagerly stepped forward at the evening meeting on June 9 as the first volunteers for a Calvados battalion, the ranks did not fill behind them. The general assembly issued an appeal to the department on June 10, calling for volunteers for what sounded more like a reprise of the 1790 Festival of Federation than a military exercise—they promised that not a drop of blood would be shed because the majority of oppressed Parisians would welcome their liberators with open arms.[24]

Three times in the following week the general assembly announced, and then postponed, a date for the departure of the Calvados volunteer force for Evreux. Initially projected at four hundred or more, a contingent of two hundred left Caen on June 22 and then only after five men had been conscripted from each company of the Caen National Guard. Joining those troops was the Sixth Battalion of Calvados, originally assigned to combat the Vendée rebellion. Several key administrators accompanied the Calvados force on its march to Evreux, and in their absence public enthusiasm for the revolt seemed to wane and efforts to raise more volunteers faltered. On July 2 the general assembly issued an order that all able-bodied men under the age of fifty who did not have young children were required to enlist, threatening those who refused with fines and imprison-

23. A.C. Caen, I37 (*Bulletin des autorités constituées*, vols. 2–9, June–July 1793). The missing copy can be found in B.M. Caen, Rés. Fn. B402. All nine issues are also printed in Pétion's memoirs, Ibid., 204–26.

24. A.D. Calvados, L189 (Registre des arrêtés du Conseil Général du département du Calvados, 11 août 1792–26 juillet 1793).

ment. A public parade and festival on July 7 produced only seventeen new volunteers, however, and the following day General Wimpffen rescinded the draconian order.[25]

Despite these difficulties in Caen, a modest force did assemble in Evreux. On July 3, a battalion from the Ille-et-Vilaine reached Caen and proceeded on to Evreux. A contingent from Morbihan arrived on July 8, followed the next day by a company of two hundred from the Mayenne. General Wimpffen ordered two regiments of cavalry from the army of the Fourteenth Division to Evreux as well—the dragoons of the Manche and the chasseurs of La Bréteche—with General Joseph Puisaye in command. By July 10 nearly two thousand troops were assembled in Evreux, poised for the next stage of their march toward Paris, where they hoped to meet volunteers from other federalist cities.

LYON

On the face of it, one might have expected the Lyonnais to respond much more quickly and forcefully than the Caennais to the insurrection of May 31–June 2 because the expulsion of the Girondins and the ascendancy of the Montagnards in the Convention so obviously threatened their own insurrectionary turnabout of May 29. But the situation in Lyon was more complicated than that in Caen in a number of ways. In the first place, despite the resounding victory of the moderates on May 29, the political situation in the city and the department remained tenuous and volatile. The first priority for the new municipal council was to present an account of the insurrection to the Convention and the rest of the country that would convincingly demonstrate that May 29 had been a victory for committed republicans and not a counterrevolutionary upheaval. This understandably made authorities in Lyon somewhat cautious in the first weeks of June. A second constraining factor was the presence of Dubois-Crancé and the Army of the Alps in Grenoble. To send an armed force marching off toward Paris would leave Lyon vulnerable to attack from the southeast, and it had been precisely such a fear that had triggered the events of May 29.

News of the May 29 insurrection had prompted the Committee of Public Safety in Paris to send Robert Lindet to Lyon to investigate the situation. Lindet arrived on June 8, on the same coach as one of Joseph Chalier's closest allies, a judge on the district tribunal by the name of Joseph Gaillard, who had been sent to Paris two weeks earlier to lobby for the creation of a revolutionary tribunal in Lyon. His presence on the coach with Lindet compromised the represen-

25. A.C. Caen, I42 (L'Armée Libératrice, mai–juillet 1793) and A.D. Calvados, L16oter (Assemblée Générale des autorités constituées réunies au chef-lieu du département, 1 juillet 1793–26 juillet 1793).

tative's mission in the eyes of the Lyonnais, as did their recent experience with the deputies Nioche and Gauthier. Gaillard was arrested immediately, and the provisional municipal council referred to sectional assemblies the question of whether or not to recognize Lindet's mission. The sections were unanimous in their refusal to accept Lindet's credentials though divided in regard to what to do with the deputy. Section La Guillotière voted on June 9 not to recognize Lindet's mission on the grounds that he had been sent by a Convention that was no longer "one, whole, inviolable and free," observing that they had sworn before, and swore again now, to defend the indivisibility and unity of the republic and the national assembly.[26] Many sections proposed that Lindet be arrested as a hostage against the safety of the proscribed Girondin deputies (word reached Lyon at about this time that such action had been taken in both Caen and Bordeaux), but section Port St. Paul opposed that idea, arguing that to do so would give the impression that the city was in rebellion against the National Convention.[27] Section La Croisette went so far as to insist that Lindet's status as "representative of the people" be recognized even if his mission to Lyon were not.[28]

Bill Edmonds concludes that Lindet accomplished very little by his mission to Lyon, but one might argue that at the very least his presence helped to delay the outbreak of revolt by suggesting to cooler heads (both in Lyon and in Paris) that the difficulties confronting the city might be resolved through negotiation rather than by armed conflict. Although he never met with the departmental administration, and the municipality never shared with him the report already prepared on the events of May 29, Lindet's letters to the Committee of Public Safety conveyed a guarded optimism about the situation in Lyon. Lindet insisted that the majority of Lyonnais remained good republicans, though currently misinformed, misled, and frightened. The resolution to the difficulties in Lyon would come through communication, not repression. In his final letter to Paris, written on June 15, Lindet was as emphatic as possible: "Publish a constitution. Publish the reasons for the indictment [of the proscribed deputies]." With resolve and energy, Lindet admonished his colleagues, all obstacles could be overcome.[29]

26. A.D. Rhône, 1L375. The nomenclature of the Lyon sections is confusing for this period because many of them changed their names during the revolt, and these were changed again during the repression that followed. I have not yet been able to determine what La Guillotière was called before or after summer 1793.

27. A.D. Rhône, 31L21. The minutes of the sectional assembly record the news from Bordeaux that hostages had been taken in that city. Port St. Paul took the name of La Concorde during this period.

28. Edmonds, *Jacobinism and the Revolt of Lyon*, 207.

29. F. A. Aulard, *Recueil des Actes du Comité de Salut Public avec la Correspondance officielle des représentants en mission* (Paris, 1891), vol. 4, 575.

The Lyonnais, too, recognized the need for communication and reliable information—the need to communicate to the nation and to the National Convention the truth about recent events in Lyon, and to secure reliable information about the situation in Paris and the reaction of other departments. To that end, a delegation was sent to Paris on June 8 bearing a report about the insurrection of May 29. The delegation was no more successful in its mission than Lindet was in his. They never presented their report (though it was printed and left with the minister of the interior) and concluded that it was pointless to negotiate with a Convention dominated by anarchists and maratists.[30] Two of the delegates, however, Fain and Durand, sent several letters back to Lyon in the second week of June and these must have influenced opinions in the city. In two letters dated June 11 they reported the arrest of Romme and Prieur in Caen, the news that Calvados and the Eure had refused to recognize the National Convention until the return of the proscribed deputies to their seats, and the receipt in the capital of a letter from Marseille announcing that the departments of the Midi were each naming two representatives to coordinate the march of departmental troops to Paris. They were convinced, they wrote, that "the departmental troops would find only brothers in Paris, that an agreement would be reached at their first meeting." All eyes were fixed on Lyon, they reported. The departments of the Midi must take the first step.[31]

Two days later they wrote that the departments of Normandy had already taken that first step. Troops were en route to Paris from Calvados (a falsehood, as we have seen), with Evreux designated as a point of coordination. On June 14 Fain wrote that members of their delegation had met with a number of the arrested deputies, who were in agreement that "the only means to save the public good is a general insurrection of the departments." Departmental troops would be warmly welcomed in Paris, Fain claimed, and it would be necessary to replace entirely the National Convention, whose unity had been riven by personal squabbles.[32]

The departmental administration and provisional municipal council also sent envoys out to other parts of France, first to circulate a report on the events of May 29 and then to gather information about the reaction to the proscription of the Girondins. Two of these envoys, Alexandre Jacquet and Alexandre-Michel Pelzin, traveled to Marseille in the first days of June. Just two weeks before, Marseille had witnessed a sectional rebellion of its own in which moderates had ousted local Jacobins from power, and a newly constituted municipal council

30. Edmonds, *Jacobinism and the Revolt of Lyon*, 209 and 225. Edmonds notes that one of the leaders of the delegation, the journalist J. L. Fain, returned briefly to Lyon to suggest that the mission be abandoned, but he was sent back to Paris.

31. A.D. Rhône, 1L375.

32. Ibid.

received Jacquet and Pelzin. They wrote back to Lyon on June 8 of the warm welcome they had received and of the enthusiastic support of the Marseillais for developments in Lyon. Marseille, too, had tangled with representatives on mission and had defied the National Convention by the creation of a popular tribunal to judge local anarchists. They exhorted the Lyonnais to do likewise, Jacquet and Pelzin reported, to form a special tribunal to judge the former municipal officials. Encouraged by the news from Lyon, the Marseille General Committee issued orders to shut down the Jacobin club. Authorities in the two cities maintained regular contact in the weeks that followed.[33]

The Lyon municipal council also sent two envoys to Bordeaux, Benoît Girard and Subrin. They arrived in that city on June 7 and addressed a general assembly convened by the departmental administration to consider the national crisis. The minutes of that meeting record that Girard and Subrin reported that liberty had recently vanquished anarchy in Lyon, that the city had been on the verge of falling victim to the criminal maneuvers of anarchists and the Jacobin municipality, but that the rule of law and justice had been restored despite the opposition of Gauthier and Nioche, the representatives on mission. Frequent applause interrupted their report, which the assembly ordered printed and distributed throughout Bordeaux and other towns of the department.[34]

Subrin naturally wrote back to Lyon about the success of their mission, enthusiastically reporting that entire companies of the Bordeaux National Guard were enrolling for a march on Paris and that the volunteer force was likely to be over-enrolled and on the road by early July. He expressed their hope that the Lyonnais had taken similar measures, observing that departmental forces were sure to be well received in Paris and that the Montagnards' most fervent desire was that those troops might remain in their home towns so that the Montagnards could more easily dominate the provinces.[35]

On June 10 the departmental council of the Rhône-et-Loire sent a secret emissary to Bordeaux, accompanied by a delegate from the Jura. The two envoys, Jean-Jacques Tardy and Gauthier (a local man, not the representative on mission Gauthier), made a number of stops en route to Bordeaux, including one in Limoges on June 17. They carried with them a joint address from their two

33. A.D. Rhône, 1L375, for the June 8 letter from Jacquet and Pelzin. See William Scott, *Terror and Repression in Revolutionary Marseilles* (London, 1973), 71–107, for a discussion of the events of May in that city and the June 3 order closing the Jacobin club. Alexandre Michel Pelzin, it is interesting to note, was a native of Marseille, son of the merchant Alexandre Honoré Pelzin. An ardent anti-Jacobin, he fled Lyon during the siege, apparently finding refuge in both Paris and Marseille. He returned to Lyon after Thermidor, edited a moderate newspaper, and was arrested in Year IV for his association with known royalists. See Bruno Benoît and Roland Saussac, eds., *Guide Historique de la Révolution à Lyon, 1789–1799* (Lyon, 1988), 151–52.

34. A.D. Gironde, 3L7.

35. A.D. Rhône, 1L375.

departments calling for an assembly of *suppléants* to the Convention in Bourges and for the designation of regional centers for the coordination of departmental forces. They also presented a list of some thirty-eight departments that they claimed would support such a plan.[36]

So numerous were the reports and addresses coming into Lyon from other towns and departments that the provisional municipal council created a separate committee in mid-June to sort them. Some of these addresses applauded the Lyonnais for the strong stand they had taken on May 29, while others were declarations of protest against the proscription of the Girondins and calls for action against the anarchists in Paris. They all affirmed the Lyon moderates in the rightness of their actions to date and gave them confidence that the rest of the country would support resistance to the Montagnard Convention. The promise of such support was often vague and abstract and would ultimately prove illusory. But on June 20 exhilarating news circulated among the sections that the volunteer force from Marseille would arrive in Lyon in a matter of days.[37]

In this highly charged atmosphere, full of both fear and anticipation, the various assemblies and administrative councils in Lyon moved tentatively toward a declaration of open rebellion. On June 18 the departmental administration issued an order convening primary assemblies throughout the department on the twenty-fourth to elect delegates to a special assembly that would meet in Lyon on June 30. This order seemed to stimulate activity in the sectional assemblies of Lyon, which had been meeting *en permanence* (in continuous session) since mid-May. On June 19, section de la rue Buisson unanimously declared itself to be in a state of resistance to oppression and called for the creation of an armed force that would join with the Marseillais in a march toward Paris. They called on the departmental administration to recruit volunteers from throughout the department and to communicate these measures to all other departments of the republic so that they might follow this example.[38] The department took no immediate action, but the provisional municipal council endorsed the plan for an armed force on that same day and initiated recruitment within the city. Roughly half of the thirty-two sections sent delegates to a June 21 meeting, but recruitment proceeded slowly, with people waiting, perhaps, to see what would come from the primary assemblies and the projected departmental assembly.[39]

The insurrectionary mood in Lyon gained a boost on June 23, a Sunday, with

36. On the Tardy and Gauthier mission, see Edmonds, *Jacobinism and the Revolt of Lyon*, 210–11; for their stop in Limoges, see Hanson, *Provincial Politics*, 110–12.

37. A.D. Rhône, 31L21 (minutes from section La Concorde, formerly Port St. Paul).

38. A.D. Rhône, 31L8.

39. Edmonds, *Jacobinism and the Revolt of Lyon*, 212–13.

the return of the commissioners sent to Paris at the beginning of the month. As in Caen, members of the delegation split up to address sectional assemblies. Citizen Cuzin (or Cusin) reported to section Concorde that the mission had essentially been a failure. Their nominal leader, Jean-Emmanuel Gilibert, who had presided over the June 6 assembly that dispatched them, had been delayed leaving Lyon and never joined the commissioners in Paris. At any rate, the group never appeared before the Convention, which Cuzin reported to be badly attended and dominated by Montagnards. Bread was short in the capital, though one could see it floating in the Seine (a commentary on Parisian wastefulness?!). The mood in Paris was much like that in Lyon on the eve of May 29.[40]

Voters gathered in primary assemblies on June 24 to elect delegates to the departmental assembly, which would meet on June 30 and take the title of *Commission Populaire, Républicaine et de Salut Public de Rhône-et-Loire*. Turnout was relatively high in Lyon sectional assemblies for which records survive, but elsewhere in the department support for the Popular Commission was lukewarm at best. Of the 207 delegates in attendance at Popular Commission meetings during the first days of July, more than half were from Lyon and its immediate environs.[41]

One day before the first meeting of the Popular Commission, authorities in Lyon sponsored a civic festival at which a delegation from Marseille appeared to present a crown of oak leaves to the Lyon National Guard for its valiant defense of law and liberty on May 29. Reinforced in their conviction of having done right in their revolution of the sections and reassured that their brothers to the south would support their resistance against Paris, the Lyonnais delegates to the Popular Commission pushed for an explicit declaration of insurrection. The delegates were not of a single mind, however. Deputies from some of the rural districts were openly skeptical of the proposed rebellion against the National Convention.

The decisive role in steering the Popular Commission to an open declaration of insurrection may have been played by the fugitive Girondin deputy Jean-Baptiste Birotteau. Minutes from the July 3 meeting report the delegates debating whether or not to recognize the decrees issued by the National Convention since May 31, a clear indication that at that late date not all were prepared to break with the government in Paris.[42] Birotteau, a deputy from the Pyrénées-Orientales who had been proscribed on June 2, arrived in Lyon on July 4 and delivered a stirring address to the Popular Commission that evening. For weeks now the Lyonnais had been inundated by letters and reports recounting the

40. A.D. Rhône, 31L21.
41. Edmonds, *Jacobinism and the Revolt of Lyon*, 212–24.
42. A.D. Rhône, 1L378.

outrages committed on June 2 and the deplorable situation in Paris, but for at least some of the more skeptical delegates from the rural districts of the Rhône-et-Loire, Birotteau's firsthand account provided persuasive confirmation.

The National Convention, Birotteau reported, no longer existed. The majority of deputies was either in chains or had scattered in fear. The rump of the Convention consisted of twenty-two former nobles, eighteen priests or monks, and a dozen "judges of 2 September." The people of Paris, he said, had been misled and had taken to the streets without knowing to what end. He and the other proscribed deputies, targeted by the knives of brigands in the pay of anarchists, had been saved only through the efforts of good Parisians, thirty thousand of whom had themselves been included on the lists for proscription! Today eleven-twelfths of the inhabitants of Paris awaited the people of the provinces, anxious to restore liberty and happiness to France. It was not to civil war that Birotteau called the Lyonnais, he assured them, but rather to the fraternal embraces with which Parisians would greet them when they arrived in the capital.[43]

By the end of the evening the Popular Commission had voted to break with the nonexistent National Convention, and in the following days active measures were taken to make real their rhetorical rebellion against Paris. Noel Pointe, a Montagnard deputy en route to supervise the arms factory in Saint-Etienne was arrested, and on July 8 the Popular Commission sent a National Guard battalion to secure that source of weapons. The Popular Commission published an address to the citizens of the department reporting on the decisions taken on July 4 and listing by name the forty-one departments that had already declared themselves in resistance against oppression. But the address also warned its readers against the propaganda of the Montagnards, which accused the leaders of the rebellion of royalism and counterrevolution, of seeking to restore the Old Regime through civil war. It was the anarchists who had pushed France to the brink of civil war, not the members of the Popular Commission. Although not as sanguine as Birotteau about the fraternal embraces that awaited them, they were confident that the courage of their constituents would suffice to defeat the new tyrants and restore liberty to France. As to the charge that they favored royalism, the address pointed out that on the evening of July 4 all present had sworn an oath that "neither *dîmes*, nor seigneurial dues, nor feudal dues would ever be reestablished; and that all would die rather than see the return of any privilege under whatever form."[44]

This is a curious oath to be sworn in summer 1793 by an assembly dedicated to upholding the unity and indivisibility of the republic, an oath unlike those

43. A.D. Rhône, 1L375; and Edmonds, *Jacobinism and the Revolt of Lyon*, 224–26. Birotteau's speech was summarized in a four-page "address to the French" published that week in Lyon.

44. A.D. Rhône, 1L378.

sworn in the other federalist cities. Why did the delegates to the Popular Commission feel compelled to swear it on the evening of July 4 and then to publish it in their address to the department? Even given the Montagnard propaganda, why would the Popular Commission dignify it by explicitly responding to these rumors of royalist intentions? Perhaps because some of the delegates from the countryside had raised such concerns themselves during the course of the evening's debates. Unlike the other federalist cities, Lyon had a reputation, largely deserved, as a haven for *émigrés* and royalists early in the Revolution, and the Lyonnais were sensitive to the possibility that others would misinterpret the events of May 29. The Lyonnais could not afford to be isolated if they were to succeed in their resistance to the National Convention, and Lyon's relations with its hinterland were not always friendly.

Suspicions that the brewing insurrection might have a royalist tinge would have been fed by the July 8 appointment of Louis-François Perrin, a former count and lieutenant-colonel in the constitutional guard of Louis XVI, as commander of the departmental force. Edmonds observes that the Popular Commission did all it could to keep Perrin "out of the public eye" and that "elaborate arrangements were made to dispense him from taking the republican oath."[45] General Perrin could not keep an entirely low profile, however, for on the date of his appointment he had no departmental army to command. Only on July 13 did the Popular Commission issue a decree ordering the formation of a departmental force. And although the provisional municipal council of Lyon had ordered the creation of a volunteer force nearly a month before, on July 19 Perrin felt obliged to send a written appeal to the sections of Lyon, exhorting them to shake off their lethargy and step forward to enlist—sectional deliberations were all well and good, but the time had come to act. While Perrin wrote stirringly of their mission to save the republic, his address also made it clear that measures were being taken to fortify the defenses of Lyon itself.[46]

Perrin's appeal to the sections of Lyon came three days after the execution of Joseph Chalier, the leading Jacobin activist in Lyon, who had been under arrest since May 29. The National Convention had issued a decree on June 21 suspending all legal proceedings against the Lyon Jacobins, but this was not the first time that the Lyonnais defied Paris, and the Popular Commission had also voted not to recognize any action taken by the Convention after May 31. There had been considerable public agitation in Lyon throughout June for the trial of the Jacobin radicals, and the Popular Commission may have ordered the trial to proceed in order to avert popular violence in the city. But it may also be that the Popular Commission took this step in order to increase the likelihood that

45. Edmonds, *Jacobinism and the Revolt of Lyon*, 227.
46. A.D. Rhône, 31L5.

General Perrin's appeal for volunteers would be favorably received in Lyon. If so, that attempt to mollify Lyon moderates came at a high price, for the execution of Chalier, coming just three days after the death of Marat, permanently alienated the Paris Jacobins, including Maximilien Robespierre, who now sat on the Committee of Public Safety.[47]

Robert Lindet's optimism of early June about the prospects for reconciliation with the good republicans of Lyon now seemed sadly misplaced. Although Lyon and the department of the Rhône-et-Loire had been cautious and tentative through the third week of June, the creation of the Popular Commission and its declaration of resistance to oppression; the decree calling for a departmental army and the appointment of Perrin as its commander; and the trial and execution of Chalier all placed Lyon firmly in the federalist camp and rendered nil the possibility of negotiation with Paris. Lindet was now at the head of an army marching toward Calvados, and the task of subduing Lyon would henceforth be turned over to Dubois-Crancé and the Army of the Alps.

Before we turn to consider the situation in Marseille, whose support for Lyon was crucial if the rebellion in the southeast were to succeed, a final comment about the dynamic between the Lyon sections and the Popular Commission is in order. In the first week of June, departmental administrators were at pains to establish that the insurrectionary movement was the work of sectional assemblies in Lyon, and the calling of primary assemblies in late June to elect delegates to the Popular Commission was meant to confirm this. Sectional politics had been vital and active in Lyon since 1790, and the uprising of May 29 was in one sense a reaction against the usurpation of the sections' role by the Jacobin club.[48] During the federalist revolt most of the sections in Lyon were careful to assert that they were only deliberative bodies with no authority to issue orders themselves. They similarly resisted the idea of creating a central committee for the sections, since the earlier creation of a central committee of the clubs of Lyon had led to the abuses of the Jacobins. The role of the sectional assemblies was to debate public issues and to share their views with each other and with their elected officials, to whom they had delegated political power and administrative authority.[49] While acknowledging the limit to their own powers, though, the sections felt that their elected officials should be accountable to them. But on

47. Edmonds, *Jacobinism and the Revolt of Lyon*, 227–29.

48. Edmonds makes this point throughout chaps. 3–6 of *Jacobinism and the Revolt of Lyon*, but also see Edmonds, "The Rise and Fall of Popular Democracy in Lyon, 1789–1795," *Bulletin of the John Rylands Library* 67, no. 1 (1984): 408–49; Edmonds, "A Jacobin Debacle: The Losing of Lyon in Spring 1793," *History* 69, no. 225 (1984): 1–14; and Antonio de Francesco, "Le Quartier lyonnais de la Croisette pendant les premières années de la Révolution (1790–1793)," *Bulletin du Centre d'histoire économique et sociale de la région lyonnaise* 4 (1979): 22–45.

49. See A.D. Rhône, 31L21 (minutes of the sectional assembly of La Concorde, July 12, 1793) for an example of such a discussion.

July 20, when the sections petitioned the Popular Commission to admit four representatives from each section to its meetings, the proposal was tabled, and the preliminary discussion makes it clear that Popular Commission meetings had not been open to the public to that date.[50] While the initiative for the revolt in Lyon lay with the sections, then, it passed to the Popular Commission in July, and there is some evidence that the concerns and goals of the Popular Commission were at odds with those of the sectional assemblies of Lyon.

MARSEILLE

A sectional insurrection in May had changed the balance of power in Marseille as well, although the dynamics of sectional politics in Marseille were rather different from those in Lyon.[51] As in Lyon, Marseille Jacobins had gained control of the municipal council and the mayor's office in early 1793. The outcome of those elections had been hotly contested, with moderates alleging that the Jacobins had manipulated electoral assemblies by drawing up fixed slates of candidates in advance (these elections will be more thoroughly discussed in Chapter 5). During the winter the Jacobin club and municipality worked in tandem to implement measures against perceived enemies of the Revolution. In February the club created a Central Committee, whose principal function seems to have been the denunciation of suspects. Food shortages, price increases, and depreciation of the *assignats* all played into the hands of the Jacobins, and in March they secured the creation of a revolutionary tribunal. Shortly thereafter the municipal council ordered the disarming of all suspect citizens, and arrests soon followed.

As in Lyon, the Jacobin municipality proved unable to revitalize a local economy that had been crippled by revolutionary upheaval, the flight of *émigrés*, and the ongoing war against most of the European powers. This rendered their popular base of support fragile, and their aggressive policies quickly alienated the propertied elite of Marseille. As William Scott puts it, "What is beyond question is that the clubbists demanded measures which were far too ruthless and wide-ranging to win the wholehearted approval of those who had controlled the destinies of the city, that they provoked these people to a reaction against Jacobinism, with its very real threat of terror, and forced people who had hith-

50. A.D. Rhône, 1L378.

51. In addition to archival sources, the account that follows relies principally on Scott, *Terror and Repression*, esp. chaps. 3–5; on Jacques Guilhaumou, *Marseille républicaine (1791–1793)* (Paris, 1992), esp. chap. 4; and on Michael L. Kennedy, *The Jacobin Club of Marseille, 1790–1794* (Ithaca, 1973).

erto been indifferent to the political struggle to enter political activity, and to enter on the side of the enemies of the Jacobins."[52]

The story of the struggle between club and sections in Marseille is a particularly complicated one, and a good example of the way in which local and national politics often interacted in 1792–93. Moderates utilized sectional assemblies as a vehicle to mobilize opposition to the Jacobins, and the months of April and May witnessed an ongoing struggle that essentially focused on the question of whether the club or the sections were the more legitimate expression of popular sovereignty in Marseille. The club demanded that only "good citizens" be allowed to attend sectional meetings, while the sections demanded that the club refrain from meeting when sectional assemblies were in session. Sectional assemblies challenged the legitimacy of the revolutionary tribunal, protesting to the National Convention, but the Jacobin club found allies in the Montagnard representatives on mission, Moise Bayle and Joseph Boisset, who ultimately declared the sectional assemblies to be counterrevolutionary.

Moise Bayle, a member of the Bouches-du-Rhône delegation to the National Convention, was an ardent Montagnard who had been a vocal advocate of the death penalty for Louis XVI. Early in the Revolution he had served as a municipal councilor in Marseille and as *procureur-général-syndic* of the departmental administration. Also prominent in the Bouches-du-Rhône delegation to the Convention was Charles Barbaroux. A revolutionary firebrand in 1789, Barbaroux was among the founders of the Marseille Jacobin club, served as secretary on the municipal council in 1790–91, and in early 1792 was sent to Paris as a lobbyist to the Legislative Assembly for the city. It was his letter that brought the Marseille *fédérés* marching to Paris to lead the charge against the Tuileries palace on August 10, 1792, and Barbaroux was the first deputy elected to the National Convention from the Bouches-du-Rhône.

During his time in Paris as a lobbyist, Barbaroux had grown close to the Rolands and their circle, and his effective advocacy of Marseille's interests during this period and in the Convention earned him many friends back home. But he was also an early critic of Robespierre, and his support for the *appel au peuple* during the trial of Louis XVI alienated not only Bayle and the other Montagnards in the Bouches-du-Rhône delegation, but also many of the *fédérés* and the Jacobin club in Marseille. In response to the campaign for the *appel au peuple*, which became quite a divisive issue in Marseille, the Jacobin club adopted a motto in January that marked one of the first instances in which "federalism" was used as a pejorative epithet: "Mort du tyran: point de fédéralisme" (Death to the tyrant, no federalism).[53]

52. Scott, *Terror and Repression*, 48.
53. For the Jacobin motto, see Scott, *Terror and Repression*, 64; for a good biographical sketch of Barbaroux, see Michael Kennedy's entry in Samuel F. Scott and Barry Rothaus, eds., *Historical Dictionary of the French Revolution, 1789–1799* (Westport, Conn., 1985), vol. 1, 56–57.

Each of the contending factions in Marseille thus had its own allies in Paris, and when Moise Bayle arrived in March he came not only as a representative on mission from the National Convention to assist with military recruitment, but also as a likely supporter of the Jacobin cause in Marseille. Bayle and Boisset arrived in Marseille late in March, followed closely by the Second Battalion of Marseille *fédérés*, which had been sent to Paris in October 1792 to steel the resolve of the Convention in bringing the king to justice. Barbaroux had tried to enlist the Second Battalion as a counter to the militant sections of Paris in the ongoing struggle between Montagnards and Girondins, and their presence served as a model of sorts for those deputies who favored calling a departmental guard to Paris to protect the National Convention. Although they were of little help to Barbaroux or the Girondins in Paris, the *fédérés* of the Second Battalion (most notably their commander, Dominique Girard) would play a substantial role in the sectional movement of April and May in Marseille and in the federalist revolt that followed.[54]

Among the first actions taken by the representatives on mission in Marseille was the levying of a new battalion of six thousand men, to respond to reports of counterrevolutionary violence in the neighboring department of the Gard and to prevent those disturbances from spreading throughout the region. Although justified on the face of it—the southeast had been plagued by counterrevolutionary violence throughout the early years of the Revolution—moderates suspected that this force would become a political weapon for the Jacobin municipality, which just the month before had ordered the disarming of suspects and had called for the creation of a revolutionary tribunal.

Presiding over the municipal council was Jean-Raymond Mourraille, a man in his early seventies who had been mayor since November 1791. Although an early member of the Jacobin club, Mourraille was not a part of that cohort of radical Jacobins newly elected to office in January 1793, some of whom suspected the mayor for his friendship and correspondence with Charles Barbaroux. Emboldened by the arrival of Bayle and Boisset and angered by Mourraille's perceived interference with the departure of the new battalion, on April 10 the radical clubbists denounced Mourraille and the *procureur* of the city, Etienne Seytres, and called on Bayle and Boisset to dismiss them from office. Section assemblies, too, joined in the denunciation of Mourraille and Seytres, accusing them of extortion and embezzlement and linking them to the strong-arm tactics of the Savon brothers, two porters who were radical clubbists active in the March campaign to disarm suspects.

Bayle and Boisset took these charges seriously, dismissed the two officials from office, and ordered all four before the Marseille Popular Tribunal, a special

54. Scott, *Terror and Repression*, 39, 61–63, 282–83.

court that had been formed in fall 1792 at the initiative of sectional assemblies, though never officially recognized by the National Convention. As they would later put it in their report to the Convention, how could they fail to act on a denunciation that was so broadly supported? But the dismissal of Mourraille from office rather than healing the divisions within the city seemed to exacerbate them. Mourraille, denounced by both club and sections, had at least been able to mediate between the two, a task that the representatives on mission proved incapable of managing.

Despite their action in the Mourraille and Seytres case, which ultimately worked to the benefit of the sections, Bayle and Boisset never gained the confidence of the sectional assemblies. Two events external to Marseille would doom their mission to failure. On April 8, the National Convention ordered that Philippe Egalité and the Orléans family be sent to Marseille and imprisoned in the Fort St. Jean. Bayle and Boisset assured the Marseillais that this order showed the confidence of the National Convention in their city, but the approach of the second royal family of France proved a source of consternation rather than honor. Moderates, mindful of Girondin propaganda, feared that Orléans would launch a coup from Marseille, supported by Bayle and Boisset's battalion of six thousand, and march back to Paris to take his place at the head of a government dominated by Marat and the other bloodthirsty Montagnards. Marseille Jacobins, for their part, associated Orléans with the treason of Dumouriez and the maneuverings of the Girondins. No one in the city welcomed the arrival of this royal prisoner.

News from Aix-en-Provence, located just to the north of Marseille, would further complicate the deputies' mission. Earlier in the year, Jacobins in Aix had murdered several prisoners. Now, meeting *en permanence*, the sections of Aix ordered the arrest of a number of leading Jacobins implicated in those murders. Bayle and Boisset sent a trio of departmental administrators to investigate and after hearing their report ordered the closing of the sections of Aix on April 21. Not surprisingly, the Marseille *sectionnaires* feared that a similar fate awaited them, and they protested against this action and also took steps to disband the battalion of six thousand that was still in the process of formation. Fearing for their own safety, Bayle and Boisset fled Marseille at the end of April and took refuge in the nearby town of Montélimar.

From that more secure position, Bayle and Boisset issued an order on May 2 declaring the sections of Marseille counterrevolutionary and suppressing the Central Committee of the sections as well as the Popular Tribunal. The deputies included in their order the observation that, "calling themselves Sovereign, the sections act as if national Sovereignty belonged to them . . . the words THE SOVEREIGN SECTIONS OF MARSEILLE openly manifest a tendency toward federalism."[55] As if to confirm that last observation, the sections willfully ignored the deputies' order. On May 9 they formed a new General Committee, composed of three delegates from each section, and this body effectively controlled Marseille for the rest of the month. Although the judges of the Popular Tribunal resigned on May 27 (pursuant to a decree from the National Convention), before doing so they conducted the trial of Mourraille, Seytres, and the Savons, acquitting the first two and sentencing the Savon brothers to death. The trial itself provided an opportunity for activists from the sections to introduce evidence chronicling the abuses of the Jacobin club. On the basis of that evidence, the General Committee ordered the arrest of a number of leading Jacobins on the night of May 18–19. By early June, pushed along by reports from both Paris and Lyon, the General Committee had dismissed both the municipal and departmental councils and had closed the Jacobin club. As in Lyon, political fortunes had shifted dramatically in Marseille in the space of a few short weeks. Unlike the situation in Lyon, the revolution of the sections of Marseille had been virtually bloodless.

Marseille was more distant from Paris than any of the other federalist cities—it took at least four or five days for news to travel to and from the capital—and that distance played a role in the way that the revolt unfolded in Marseille in June. The Marseille *sectionnaires*, as with those in Lyon, felt obliged to explain their revolution to the National Convention and the rest of France, knowing full well that Bayle and Boisset would be submitting their own report, and to that end a deputation from the sections set off for Paris, arriving in the capital on May 23. Although the delegation did appear before the Convention on May 25, they were jeered and hooted by the galleries. In a letter dated May 29, one of the delegates, Marcel, shared with his compatriots back in Section 3 his conviction that their mission would be futile. Marcel was right, of course. Sometime before the proscription of the Girondins, he abandoned his colleagues, fled the capital, and returned quickly to Marseille, where he arrived on June 6. The rest of the delegation spent another week or so in Paris, shuffling back and forth between various ministries and committees, and returned more slowly to Marseille, by way of Lyon, arriving a full month after Marcel.[56]

There was no question in Marseille, as there had been in Caen, of waiting

---

55. Cited in Scott, *Terror and Repression*, 88–89. See also the *Compte Rendu à la Convention Nationale*, submitted by Bayle and Boisset and published in Paris in June 1793.

56. A.D. Bouches-du-Rhône, L1973 (May 29, 1793, letter of Marcel); L1968 (early June letter of Marcel, date illegible; and a copy of the report of the delegation to Paris, delivered to the General Committee on July 7). It is impossible to know when Marcel's letter of May 29 reached Marseille—probably not much before he did. Nor is it easy to reconstruct the itinerary of the full delegation because they mentioned very few dates in their report.

for the return of the sectional delegation before deciding what course of action to pursue in the face of the national crisis. Nor does one get the sense that the Marseillais themselves felt threatened by what might be happening in Paris. That events in the capital could affect Marseille was clearly recognized—hence the mission of Barbaroux to the capital as municipal lobbyist in 1791–92. But the Marseillais also firmly believed that they could affect events in the capital, as they had done in August 1792 and hoped to do again in 1793. Just days after the sectional delegation had left, on May 27, the municipal council sent an address to the Convention demanding that Marat be tried again, this time outside of Paris. Four days later the sections followed this up with their own address denouncing Marat and calling for his retrial: "Marat is the assassin of liberty. Liberty, as you well know, is entirely linked to property; to attack the latter, is to violate all the Laws, is to annihilate all of the sacred Rights of Man and the Citizen."[57] This address is reflective of the fact that men of property now dominated the sectional assemblies, but also of the degree to which the Marseillais reacted to events in Paris based on speculation about what had happened and what might happen. This would be true of the federalist revolt generally, in all of the provincial centers, but nowhere more so than in Marseille. By the time that these addresses could have arrived in Paris, they must have seemed laughable to those who read them and indicative of the degree to which the Marseillais were out of step with the current of national politics. From the perspective of the Marseillais, however, it was they as much as the Parisians who had saved the nation on August 10, 1792, and they were prepared to do so again.

That the Marseillais remained uncertain about what had happened in Paris even after the return of Marcel on June 6 is made clear by the speculative tone of the document circulated among the sections that evening. "Perhaps intrigue has triumphed at this moment in Paris," it began, "perhaps the national representation has been cut by the swords of assassins, perhaps our deputies, our brothers, have fallen victim to the fury of scoundrels, perhaps the unity of the Republic that we have sworn to maintain to the death has already been broken asunder." If so, then they must take active measures for the safety of Marseille and the republic, and must by all means maintain regular communication among the sectional assemblies.[58]

Also on June 6, delegates from Lyon arrived to elaborate on the reports of the insurrection in that city that had first reached Marseille on June 2. The initial reports—of six hundred brave patriots dead, the victims of an equivocating administration, weak in the face of anarchists on one hand and meddling representatives on mission on the other—had prompted considerable debate in

57. A.D. Bouches-du-Rhône, L1969.
58. A.D. Bouches-du-Rhône, L1972.

sectional assemblies. The situation in Lyon sounded strikingly similar to their own, and although the Marseille sections would exhort the Lyonnais to follow through on their insurrection and bring the anarchists to justice, they were motivated to finish their own business by the news from Lyon. Thus, in the first days of June the sections proposed that both the municipal council and the departmental administration be dismissed, to be replaced by provisional bodies (as had occurred in Lyon), and they called the Popular Tribunal back into existence, to sit in judgment over the Jacobins now forced from office. The two urban insurrections fed on each other—each gathered force and confidence from reports of the other, and they fed into the federalist revolt in each city as well.[59]

June 12 marked both a culmination of sorts to the insurrection of the sections in Marseille and a beginning to the federalist revolt in that city. The General Committee of the sections, formed in early May, had convened electoral assemblies in the city, and on June 12 they elected a provisional municipal council. Twenty-one of the twenty-four urban sections participated (there were eight rural sections as well), and each sent two representatives to the new municipal council. Of the forty-two delegates initially named, twenty-two listed their occupation as either *négociants* (wholesale merchants) or bourgeois, and another half-dozen were identified as manufacturers of one sort or another or ships' captains. Ten were artisans or shopkeepers, with just two professionals (an architect and a lawyer) and one *portefaix* (porter) rounding out the group. The world of commerce was overwhelmingly dominant on this council.[60]

It was not the provisional municipal council that would guide the city through the federalist revolt, however, but rather the General Committee of the sections. On June 12 it drafted an address to all of the departments of France, effectively declaring Marseille in a state of insurrection against the National Convention and calling upon the rest of the country to join them. Unlike such addresses from the other federalist cities, this one offered no euphemistic language about going to fraternize with the Parisians: "To Arms, Frenchmen, To Arms!" it began, "the National Representation is violated, your Deputies are in irons." A portion of this address is worth quoting at length because it makes clear both the intentions of the Marseillais and their sense of the relation between what had just happened in Paris and the recent events in their own city:

> An ambitious and criminal municipality has attacked the national sovereignty; a disorganizing faction, after having broken all social ties, vio-

59. A.D. Bouches-du-Rhône, L1964 (minutes from the deliberations of section 2, meeting on June 2 to discuss the reports from Lyon and consider appropriate responses).

60. A.D. Bouches-du-Rhône, L1951bis. This dossier contains a list of the names and occupations of the members of the provisional municipal council. The other three sections eventually sent delegates as well, but their occupations are not noted.

lated all the pacts that Nations have made between themselves, after having covered France with ashes, with blood and with tears, dares to prepare irons for her; irons forged by a few scoundrels in the infamous den of the Jacobins! Frenchmen! Will your generous hands be chained? Will crime triumph over virtue; audacity and intrigue over justice and liberty? Will twenty million men receive their laws from the factious few?! No, Marseille will defeat them; Marseille is in motion; the same thunderbolts that toppled the throne, will thunder again in that city that is today guilty. Rally around their first trophies, the victors of August 10 will combat and overturn anarchy on those same fields that witnessed their first triumph: Parisians will see the Marseillais a second time; they are en route. Frenchmen, rise up with them, arm yourselves, and march.[61]

The General Committee went on to observe that the Marseillais were taking their siege guns to Paris with them (no fraternal embraces anticipated here) and announced the banner under which they would march: Unity of the Republic, Respect for Persons and for Property. The address was signed by Pierre Peloux, a *négociant*, and Antoine Castalanet, a former royal notary, the two men who would preside over the General Committee from May through August.

For the Marseillais, having marched to Paris twice already, the task of marshaling a departmental force to march to the capital seemed less daunting than it did to other federalist towns and departments. The men of the Second Battalion, recruited by Bayle and Boisset, were likely looking around for something to do, and many would join the expeditionary force. To claim that the Marseillais were already en route was a bit of an exaggeration, but by the time some departments would receive this address, toward the end of the month, an armed force would in fact be on the march.

Why were they marching? This address is interesting in that regard as well. The General Committee explicitly blamed the Paris Commune for the proscription of the Girondin deputies and charged that "ambitious municipality" with criminal and anarchistic impulses. They had violated not only the laws, but also the legitimate social order. Lurking behind the officials of the Commune, of course, were the factious scoundrels of the Jacobin club. These words could just as easily have described the situation in Marseille three months earlier, when a Jacobin municipality had ordered the disarming of decent folk and threatened to send "suspects" (men of property, in all likelihood) before a revolutionary tribunal. Just as the sections of Marseille, and those of Lyon as well,

---

61. A.D. Bouches-du-Rhône, L1953 (Adresse des Marseillois, à leurs frères des quatre-vingt-cinq Départemens).

had triumphed over a Jacobin-dominated municipality, so would they triumph over the Paris Commune, in defense of the unity of the nation and in defense of what they had so recently accomplished in their own cities.

In the days following June 12, letters and messengers from around the country strengthened the resolve of the federalist rebels in Marseille for the path they had chosen. The delegation sent by the sections to Paris wrote back to the General Committee on a regular basis, sending a half dozen letters after May 31, several of them from Lyon, where they lingered for more than a week.[62] At least two deputations from Lyon visited Marseille in June, as did delegates from Nîmes and Bordeaux. On June 17, section 16 ordered the printing of Gensonné's June 2 letter to his constituents in the Gironde, in which he reported the assault on the integrity of the National Convention and implored his compatriots to defend his memory.[63]

Barbaroux sent several letters during this period as well, most notable among them one dated June 6, addressed to the municipal council, which reached Marseille on June 18. "All that I predicted in my earlier letters has come to pass," wrote Barbaroux. He described the proscription of the Girondin deputies, the assault on the Convention led by Hanriot's troops, and he observed that most deputies had now abandoned the assembly. All that remained was "a minority directed by a sovereign Commune." But unlike the tone of resignation in Gensonné's letter, Barbaroux offered hope as well: the provinces could not fail to rise up in the face of this attack. Already the tocsin had rung in Calvados, and armed forces were marching from Finistère, the Gironde, the Jura, and the Ain. Delegates to an alternative national assembly were preparing to gather in Bourges. Although Barbaroux's letter confirmed the fears of the Marseillais, it also confirmed that there was much to be done.[64]

To that end, the General Committee produced a remarkable document in its meeting of June 26, outlining a detailed plan of action. The General Committee was joined on that occasion by delegates from the departments of the Hautes-Alpes, the Gard, and the Gironde. The session began with the adoption of the project approved on June 19 by the Popular Commission of the Gironde (to which we shall turn shortly). Those present saw the need for a more detailed structure to facilitate the measures proposed in Bordeaux. Thus they proposed the designation of seven "secondary directorates," to be located in Marseille, Bordeaux, Lyon, Toulouse, Rennes, Strasbourg, and Rouen, and identified those departments that would send delegates to each directorate. They further designated Lyon, Tours, Evreux, Beauvais, and Châlons-sur-Marne as the towns

62. A.D. Bouches-du-Rhône, L1968.
63. A.D. Bouches-du-Rhône, L1971.
64. A.D. Bouches-du-Rhône, L1968. See also Scott, *Terror and Repression*, 108–16, for a discussion of the situation in Marseille during early to mid-June.

where departmental forces would gather for their march to Paris. Though never realized, this was an ambitious plan, one that the Montagnards could easily point to as evidence that a federalist plot had been hatched in the provinces and that the web of conspiracy stretched across many departments.[65]

The General Committee circulated this document to the sections of Marseille, but only eighteen of the thirty-two sections of the city adhered to it, striking evidence that the revolt did not enjoy wholehearted support. William Scott has observed that signs of opposition to the revolt had appeared in the sections as early as the first weeks of June. He notes that the section leaders responded with *"visites domiciliaires* to the homes of people who had behaved in a surly manner in sectionary assemblies, nocturnal patrols to break up meetings which the Jacobins were said to be holding fairly frequently in and around Marseilles, the summoning to their assemblies of trust-worthy but lazy 'egoists,' as well as the disarmament and arrest of real, tangible Jacobins and the weeding out of Maratists from the companies of the National Guard."[66] As in Lyon, sectional assemblies continued to meet throughout June and much of July, regularly sending messengers to consult with other sections and share their views. Section 10, strategically located in the center of town, appears to have played a pivotal role in molding the initiatives that emerged from these deliberations. But unlike the sections of Lyon, which insisted on the limitations to their own authority and refused to create a central body that might coordinate their actions (as the Jacobins had done), the sections of Marseille had named their own General Committee early in May and willingly ceded their authority to that body. They formalized that tacit cession on July 9 by granting the General Committee unlimited powers, powers that were increasingly used to stifle dissent within the city as the revolt wore on.[67]

By early July the departmental force, which left Marseille on June 22, had occupied Avignon, a strategic point on the east bank of the Rhône River. It would march no farther than that, but in the second week of July it appeared that the Marseillais were making good on their promise to return to Paris. The Lyonnais anticipated their imminent arrival, and in Bordeaux the Popular Commission entertained the illusion that the project they had launched on June 19 was being realized across the nation.

BORDEAUX

It is scarcely surprising that Bordeaux took a leading role in the provincial resistance to the insurrection of May 31–June 2 since five of the proscribed deputies

65. A.D. Bouches-du-Rhône, L1967.
66. Scott, *Terror and Repression*, 118.
67. A.D. Bouches-du-Rhône, L1933.

(Vergniaud, Gensonné, Guadet, Grangeneuve, and Bergoeing) represented the Gironde in the National Convention. The Bordelais petitioned the Convention on several occasions during the spring, exhorting the deputies to set aside their factional disputes and to deal sternly with the anarchistic elements of Paris that threatened the integrity of the national legislature. In May they promised to send their national guards to Paris to protect their deputies, and in June they mobilized to make good on that promise.

Bordeaux, like Marseille, was distant from Paris—roughly a four-day journey—and confirmed reports of the proscription of their deputies first arrived on June 6 or 7. The Bordelais were not isolated from national news, however. Several of their deputies wrote regularly from Paris, including Armand Gensonné, Jean-Baptiste Boyer-Fonfrède, and Jean-Antoine Grangeneuve. Grangeneuve was a particularly important source of news about the capital as his brother, Jean Grangeneuve, was both a departmental administrator and a leader of the Bordeaux Jacobin club.[68] In May especially the various local administrations and the Jacobin club received numerous letters from the capital (as we have seen, even Vergniaud wrote two letters that month), so the Bordelais were able to follow quite closely the developing crisis, though at a few days' delay and from a certain perspective.

News reached Bordeaux from other parts of the nation as well. On two different occasions in May the Bordelais were moved by addresses received from Nantes, whose citizens shared their concerns about the freedom of the Convention and the excesses of Parisian militants. The Bordeaux Jacobin club, which had broken its affiliation with the Paris club in December 1792, maintained an active correspondence with a number of clubs throughout the south and southwest. Members of the club were particularly heartened on May 24 to receive word from Marseille that the reign of law had replaced that of anarchy in that city and that their Jacobin club would soon be regenerated.[69]

The minutes of the departmental administration suggest that news of the proscription of the Girondin deputies first arrived in Bordeaux on June 6, in the form of a copy of the June 3 issue of the *Feuille du Soir*. The minutes record that the reading of that newspaper produced strong feelings of indignation among those assembled, who immediately voted to convene a special meeting of the departmental, district, and municipal councils for the following day. The administrators also voted to reprint and distribute that issue of the *Feuille du Soir*, to send an extraordinary courier to Paris to inform the National Convention

---

68. Many of the letters from the Bordeaux deputies can be found in A.D. Gironde, 12L19. In addition to archival sources, the discussion that follows relies principally on two books by Alan Forrest: *Society and Politics in Revolutionary Bordeaux* (Oxford, 1975), and *The Revolution in Provincial France: Aquitaine, 1789–1799* (Oxford, 1996).

69. A.D. Gironde, 12L14.

of the actions being taken in Bordeaux, and to send couriers to neighboring departments as well. During these deliberations a messenger arrived from section Brutus to propose sending an armed force to Paris.

The message drafted by the departmental administration emphasized the "cries of fury and vengeance" ringing forth in all of the public places of Bordeaux upon hearing the news from the capital. The members of the departmental administration warned the deputies of the Convention that the people of Bordeaux were already proposing extreme measures in response to the outrage that had been committed, and they expressed honest doubts about their ability to control the popular effervescence. Citizens were flocking to section assemblies in a mood of indignation and despair.[70]

It is a striking feature of the federalist revolt at its outbreak that in each of the main centers authorities took pains to present the revolt as a popular movement. Either they credited section assemblies with the responsibility (or later, blame) for instigating the movement (as in Bordeaux, Caen, and Marseille), or they convened primary assemblies in order to allow popular opinion to express itself (as in Lyon). It is difficult to know how to interpret this. To be sure, local authorities in virtually every city and town of France had confronted at some point in the early years of the Revolution their inability to control the collective fury of the crowd, most often in situations of grain shortage or excessive prices, but sometimes in connection with incidents having to do with provocative actions taken by reactionary aristocrats or by non-juring clergy. Perhaps local officials were genuinely concerned in June 1793 about their ability to control the actions of their constituents. But they were also gravely aware of the potential consequences of a declaration of resistance to the National Convention, particularly if its integrity did not prove to have been irreparably violated. Departmental administrators would certainly recall the official and popular denunciations that had befallen their unfortunate colleagues who had chosen to send expressions of support to Louis XVI after the aborted insurrection of June 20, 1792. It is hard not to suspect that the tendency of local officials to credit the revolt to the sections, to primary assemblies, to "the people" in some sense was in large part due to their desire to shift responsibility from their own shoulders onto those of their constituents in the event that the expressions of protest, and perhaps insurrection, should fail to achieve their goal. This interpretation seems all the more compelling given the almost total lack of popular support for a march on Paris in each of the federalist cities only weeks after these initial declarations of revolt.[71]

---

70. A.D. Gironde, 3L7 (Bordeaux Jacobin club, minutes of June 6, 1793).

71. See Antonio de Francesco, "Popular Sovereignty and Executive Power in the Federalist Revolt of 1793," *French History* 5, no. 1 (March 1991): 74–101; and Paul R. Hanson, "The Federalist Revolt: An Affirmation or Denial of Popular Sovereignty?" *French History* 6, no. 3 (September 1992): 335–55, for the beginnings of a debate on this issue.

In regard to Bordeaux, Alan Forrest has commented on the "astonishing una-
nimity among the sections in support of insurrection," although he also characterizes the Bordeaux sections as "among the most confirmed bastions of social
conservatism" and notes that the "vast majority of the sectional assemblies
[were] dominated and controlled by tightly knit groups of middle-class citizens." Still, they met frequently during late May and on into June, and Forrest
concludes by characterizing them as "one of the staunchest sources of support
to the federalist cause."[72]

In the first days of June, in any case, there was widespread concern in Bordeaux about the attacks on their deputies in Paris and a desire to respond forcefully, whether in word or in action. The June 7 meeting convened by the
departmental administration was attended by representatives from all of the
local administrative bodies, the courts, and the sections as well. Also appearing
were the two delegates from Lyon—Subrin and Girard—eager to report on the
May 29 insurrection in their city. Thus, as the Bordelais prepared to deliberate
on the recent events in Paris, they were very much aware of the recent developments in Lyon and Marseille. In their report to the assembly, frequently interrupted by applause, Subrin and Girard made special note of the representatives
on mission Nioche and Gauthier, who had opposed the sectional movement in
Lyon. This prompted some discussion as to whether or not to arrest the deputies P.-L. Ichon and P.-A. d'Artigoyte then on mission in Bordeaux. Although
not technically placed under arrest, they were heavily guarded during their brief
stay in the city. Later in June two other representatives on mission, Jean-Baptiste Treilhard and Jean-Baptiste-Charles Mathieu, sent explicitly by the Committee of Public Safety to investigate the situation in Bordeaux, received a
similarly hostile reception.[73]

The most important decision to emerge out of the June 7 meeting was the
creation of the *Commission Populaire de Salut Public*, hereafter referred to as the
Popular Commission. This was a body of some fifty members drawn from the
already existing administrative and judicial bodies in Bordeaux, and it would be
this group of men that would lead the revolt over the next two months.[74] With
the creation of the Popular Commission the Bordelais had effectively declared
themselves in revolt against the National Convention, though an official declaration would not come for two more days.[75] It was an act of revolt because it
created an administrative entity at the departmental level that had not been
authorized by the Convention, and it represented a formal step that would later

72. Forrest, *Society and Politics*, 108, 159–60.
73. A.D. Gironde, 3L7; Forrest, *Society and Politics*, 112–13.
74. Forrest, *Society and Politics*, 125–30. I will discuss the composition of the Popular Commission, and the administrative bodies formed to lead the revolt in the other cities as well, in chap. 4.
75. Ibid., 109.

be cited as evidence for the charge of federalism leveled against the rebel departments.

This may strike us as a legal nicety today, for the Gironde and other departments went on to make clear their state of rebellion in much more dramatic ways. But at the time this seems to have been a substantive issue for a number of departmental administrations, who went no further in their protests than the writing of letters precisely because to do so would have been to exceed their administrative authority.[76] It was this concern, in part, that prompted local leaders in Caen, Lyon, and Bordeaux to convene sectional assemblies or primary assemblies to endorse their declarations of revolt. From their perspective, it must be admitted, Parisian militants had been defying the authority of the national government for years, both under the Legislative Assembly and the Convention. Many departmental administrations, of course, had demanded that the Paris Commune be censured for precisely that reason, as had some deputies in the Convention. For those deputies in the Convention, and for local authorities, two major issues of revolutionary politics were at stake here. First, did citizens endow their elected assemblies (whether municipal councils, departmental administrations, or the National Assembly) with sovereignty once they had voted for their delegates? That is to say, did they cede sovereignty to their elected assemblies? And second, if this was in fact the case, what circumstances would justify the defiance of constituted authorities in the name of the sovereignty of the people? These were not small questions, and in spring and summer 1793 both the insurrectionary Commune in Paris and the federalist rebels in the provinces were claiming the mantle of popular sovereignty.

In Bordeaux, the Popular Commission quickly took steps to mobilize the department for a march to Paris and to enlist the support of other departments. The resolve of the federalist leaders was strengthened by the arrival, on June 8, of a letter from Armand Gensonné describing the events of June 2. It was a remarkable letter, written in the midst of the tumult and before the vote to proscribe the deputies had actually been taken. Gensonné foresaw his fate clearly, however, and his letter has the tone of a last testament. Although he blamed the faction within the National Convention that was orchestrating the insurrection, he also wrote in defense of the people of Paris, who had been either seduced or misled by the conspirators. Gensonné did not urge his constituents to take up arms, but he did exhort them to examine carefully the charges against him (should there be any) and never to doubt his devotion to the republic, for which he was now prepared to die. The minutes of the meeting where

---

76. Such was the case for the departmental council of the Seine-Inférieure, which declined to join the revolt despite repeated entreaties from the rebel leaders in Caen. See Hanson, *Provincial Politics*, 135.

this letter was read aloud record that those assembled, moved by sadness, sat in silence for some moments. They then ordered that copies of the letter be printed for distribution in Bordeaux and to the other departments of France.[77]

On June 9 the Popular Commission issued statements addressed to the National Convention and to the towns and villages of the Gironde announcing the insurrectional movement that it had launched. Both statements included the solemn oath to resist tyranny that all members of the Popular Commission had sworn; announced their order calling for the creation of a departmental force, to collaborate with such forces from other departments in restoring liberty to the National Convention; and announced that delegates would be sent to the other departments to enlist their support.[78]

Two days later the Popular Commission named eighteen commissioners to travel in pairs to nine different regions of the country. Those assigned to visit distant towns and cities, such as Rouen, Lyon, and Marseille, were charged with making stops along the way as well. Only the border departments of the north and northeast were neglected in the assignments. The commissioners were to relay the principles of the Bordelais to those with whom they met and to report back to Bordeaux on the state of public opinion throughout the nation. Not all of those appointed accepted their mission, but those who did played an influential role in furthering the federalist revolt in other cities, most notably Lyon and Marseille. Their letters back to Bordeaux were also important because they tended to ignore expressions of opposition to their principles and to exaggerate declarations of support, allowing the Popular Commission to operate in what Forrest has characterized as a world "of blissful self-deception."[79]

Although the Popular Commission announced the formation of a departmental force in its published addresses of June 9, it was not until June 14 that it issued a formal decree outlining in detail the formation of a force of twelve hundred men, just over half of whom were to be recruited in Bordeaux. As in the other federalist cities, the departmental force proved difficult to fill, and the decree seems to have generated open opposition to the revolt in a few of the Bordeaux sections. The first such expression of opposition came on June 9 when section Liberty refused to recognize the authority of the Popular Commission, but those sections expressing reluctance tended to be peripheral and their recalcitrance did little to dampen the enthusiasm of the Popular Commission.[80]

77. A.D. Gironde, 3L7.

78. A.D. Gironde, 8J368.

79. For the decree assigning commissioners to visit particular regions, see A.D. Gironde, 12L37; for Forrest's discussion of the commissioners, see *Society and Politics*, 136–43 (passage quoted, p. 140).

80. A.D. Gironde, 12L37 (minutes of section Liberty, June 9, 1793). I will explore the issue of sectional opposition to the revolt in Bordeaux as well as in the other cities more thoroughly in Chapter 5.

As we have already seen, Subrin and Girard, the messengers from Lyon, had reported to their compatriots that support for the resistance movement was strong in Bordeaux and that they expected the departmental force to be over-enrolled and on its way to Paris very shortly. Such was not to be the case. In his most recent work Alan Forrest writes that the "force that was finally assembled and which marched out of the gates of Bordeaux was a caricature of the ambitions of the Commission."[81] Efforts to recruit volunteers for the force were hampered by the fact that weapons and supplies were in very short supply. But it must be noted that in recent months Bordeaux had sent battalions both to the Vendée and to the Pyrenees front. The subprocureur of Bordeaux, J. Amand Tustet, later recalled that after failing to fill the departmental force by volunteers or by drawing lots within National Guard companies, the Popular Commission finally ordered a general assembly of the Guard on the Champ de Mars in Bordeaux. But several companies boycotted the assembly and as at the comparable assembly in Caen, very few new recruits stepped forward.[82]

Originally projected at twelve hundred men, viewed as a modest goal in early June, the departmental force that left Bordeaux in early July numbered only four hundred, and that number was achieved only after the Popular Commission offered to pay recruits a daily stipend. Forrest characterizes the force as "for the most part simple working-men, lured by bribes or by terrorization into exchanging the dull, soul-destroying monotony of life in the *faubourgs* for a brief, fleeting moment of action, of colour and excitement."[83] As it turned out, their expedition was more brief than exciting. At the end of July the departmental force turned back to Bordeaux and disbanded, discouraged by the news from Normandy and having never left the boundaries of the Gironde. On August 2, the Popular Commission itself dissolved. It would be mid-October, however, before the departmental administration of the Gironde would once again acknowledge the authority of the National Convention.

The rapid collapse of the federalist revolt tells us something about the level of popular support for the movement. Even in the principal cities it was difficult to raise troops for a march on Paris and with the exception of Caen, none of the federalist centers succeeded in mobilizing support from the surrounding region. In the case of Caen that support came mostly from neighboring departments and not from the other towns and districts of Calvados. Still, it would be a mistake to underestimate the seriousness of the federalist challenge to the republic, particularly if we consider the situation as it was in mid-July rather than

---

81. Forrest, *Revolution in Provincial France*, 195.

82. B.M. Bordeaux, MS 1865, Tableau des Evénements qui ont eu lieu à Bordeaux depuis la Révolution de Quatre-Vingt Neuf, jusqu'à ce jour (Prairial, an II), rédigé par J. Amand Tustet (subprocureur de la commune).

83. Forrest, *Society and Politics*, 154.

two to three weeks later. Forrest's claim that the federalist leaders in Bordeaux operated in a world of illusion could be said to be true of the rebel administrators in Caen, Lyon, and Marseille as well. But if they had limited success in generating active resistance to the Convention in their own cities and departments, they did manage to convince each other that the movement was thriving everywhere else. And in each city the federalist leaders harbored the hope that good news from elsewhere would galvanize the lethargic populace into action.

Just as they put on a bold and encouraging front in their communications to each other and to the other departments of France, so did the federalist rebels exaggerate their strength in the addresses and manifestoes that they sent to Paris. Félix Wimpffen promised to march to Paris at the head of sixty thousand brave Normans. The Marseillais pledged to rally all of the departments of the Midi to their cause, and Parisians had already witnessed the battalions of Marseille marching into their city on two previous occasions. The Popular Commission in Lyon circulated an address claiming that fully half of the departments of France had declared their resistance to the Convention. The assassination of Marat on July 13 and the execution of Chalier three days later would have convinced many Parisians that the threat from the federalist cities was to be taken seriously. Moreover, it was in the interest of the Committee of Public Safety, as it contemplated the charges to be filed against the proscribed deputies, to exaggerate slightly the seriousness of the provincial revolt, though to be sure the experience in the Vendée had already made clear that such revolts could be bothersome and costly.

Our survey of the revolt as it developed in each of these four cities suggests a number of common elements among them. The proscription of twenty-nine deputies from the National Convention on June 2 served as a catalyst for revolt, but broader political concerns and deep-seated local conflicts also played a crucial role. Departmental administrations and municipal councils in all four cities had expressed their concern about factionalism within the Convention and the threat of anarchy in Paris well before the insurrection of May 31–June 2. They were particularly concerned about the undue influence of the Paris Commune and Jacobin club on national politics, as well as the militancy of the Paris sections. Their perception of the conflicts in Paris grew out of their experience of local politics. Departmental administrations in the Rhône-et-Loire and the Bouches-du-Rhône had seen their authority challenged by radical municipal councils, and moderates in both Lyon and Marseille had used the vehicle of sectional assemblies to topple Jacobin-dominated municipal councils on the very eve of the proscription of the Girondin deputies. Although no comparable sectional rebellion had occurred in Caen or Bordeaux, authorities in the latter city had closed down the radical Club National early in 1793, and the federalist leaders in Bordeaux warmly applauded the news of the sectional upheavals in both Lyon and Marseille. Not only did the struggle over sovereignty in Paris parallel that in these three cities, but in Lyon and Marseille the resolution of that struggle in the nation's capital promised to overturn the recent victory of moderates in those two cities.

In each of the four cities local authorities embarked on the path to rebellion with some caution. As they protested the violation of national sovereignty, they attempted to marshal popular sovereignty in support of their own actions, either through sectional assemblies or through the convocation of primary assemblies. In each city the rebel leaders created a special administrative body to guide the revolt and organize the march on Paris. None of those marches could be termed successful, nor could it be said that the few men who volunteered for the enterprise knew exactly why they were marching to Paris or to what end. Each of the federalist cities sent emissaries around the country seeking to spread the revolt through the publication of their manifestoes or declarations of resistance to oppression, but also to gauge the state of public opinion in other departments. Federalist rebels in each city either arrested representatives on mission from the Convention or entertained such an act, responding in part to their contentious interactions with those deputies in April and May. Local officials often denounced the representatives on mission as "pro-consuls" and complained bitterly that their unlimited powers violated their own authority and sovereignty. To arrest them, however, was an obvious contradiction of their professed devotion to the integrity and inviolability of the National Convention.

That there were contradictions and inconsistencies within the federalist movement is hardly surprising. At moments of crisis men are prone to rash, sometimes ill-considered actions. Was the federalist revolt anything more than that? Who exactly were the men who took the lead in this revolt against Paris and the Montagnard Convention? Was there in fact a national movement as the rebels themselves proclaimed? Can we speak of a federalist program? These are the questions to which we shall now turn.

$\mathcal{F}our$

THE FEDERALIST PROGRAM

On June 8, 1793, Moyse Bayle and Joseph Boisset published an account of their mission to the departments of the Drôme and the Bouches-du-Rhône, submitted as an official report to the National Convention. In that lengthy report, they referred to the movement of the sections of Marseille and Aix as a "system of counterrevolution or federalism." Less than two weeks later Bayle published a separate letter addressed to his constituents in Marseille and the Bouches-du-Rhône, who had by then declared themselves in a state of open rebellion against the Convention. Bayle defended his actions while on mission to the southeast, presented evidence against those deputies proscribed on June 2, and dated his letter: Paris, June 20, 1793, Year II of the French republic without federalism.[1]

As the summer wore on, the revolts in the provinces increasingly came to be referred to as "federalist revolts," and the proscribed deputies would be accused of advocating "federalism" or a "federalist" constitution. One sees these terms in discussion on the floor of the Convention, in the reports of Saint-Just and Jullien, and in the indictment of Amar. In early June some of the leaders of the provincial revolts were at pains to defend themselves against the accusation of "federalism." To be seen as a "federalist" came to be virtually synonymous with being seen as a counterrevolutionary, though, to be sure, there were other varieties of counterrevolutionary as well. When the Law of Suspects was passed in September 1793, to be "a partisan of federalism" was singled out for particular opprobrium.

But what exactly did the term mean? It meant many things, which was a part of its utility. It became a convenient epithet, and just as there has been controversy about the legitimacy of applying the label "Girondin" to the proscribed deputies and their allies, so has there been debate about the appropriateness of the label "federalism" or "federalist revolt." Some would argue that the "federalists" were federalists only in the eyes of their enemies. Michael Sydenham suggested some years ago that the provincial movement might more accurately be termed the "republican revolt of 1793" since none of the rebel departments enunciated a truly federalist vision of government. Nor were the revolts, as some

---

1. Moyse Bayle and Joseph Boisset, "Compte rendu à la Convention nationale" (Paris, 1793). The deputies' original report and Bayle's letter have been bound together, along with several supporting documents, in a single pamphlet of seventy-five pages. A copy is held in the Newberry Library, Chicago (FRC 2154).

historians had previously argued, royalist in character (one is reminded of Saint-Just's charge that the proscribed deputies were both royalist and federalist at once).[2]

I would agree, certainly, that neither the proscribed deputies nor the provincial rebels were truly "federalists" or advocates of "federalism." Nor were they royalists, though in Lyon and Marseille in particular, and the other two cities to a lesser degree, royalists did step in at the latter stages of the revolt to try to salvage resistance to the Montagnards. But if the term "republican revolt" is to be useful, it must imply that the opponents of the rebels were not republicans themselves, which was simply not the case. One might argue that the Jacobins did irreparable damage to the republic by the dictatorial regime they put in place during the Year II, but surely the Thermidorians (those deputies who led the 9 Thermidor coup that removed Robespierre from power) and the political elite of the Directory (the regime in power from 1795 to 1799, which included many of those "federalists" who had been purged in 1793 and survived) deserve some of the blame for the eventual demise of the First Republic.

Further complicating this debate over terminology is the fact that in recent years certain historians have suggested that a "Jacobin federalism," or "radical federalism," can be discerned in the early years of the Revolution as well. Raymonde Monnier uses the term "radical federalism" to characterize the sectional movement in Paris on the eve of the Champ de Mars massacre in July 1791 and suggests that the sectional club movement in Lyon in 1790–91 could be thought of in the same terms.[3] Jacques Guilhaumou writes of "Jacobin federalism" in reference to the efforts on the part of the Marseille Jacobin club to revolutionize the region in late 1792 and early 1793 by sending missions to neighboring towns, and also in reference to a congress of Jacobin clubs of the southeast that convened in Marseille in September 1793, after the collapse of the federalist revolt. Guilhaumou thus speaks of two "moments" of Jacobin federalism in Marseille straddling the moderate federalist moment led, at least in Marseille, by sectional assemblies.[4]

Yet if we accept the argument that such a thing as "Jacobin federalism" existed in 1792–93, then we are left in the same quandary that confronts us in

2. Michael J. Sydenham, "The Republican Revolt of 1793: A Plea for Less Localized Studies," *French Historical Studies* 11, no. 3 (spring 1981): 120–38.

3. Raymonde Monnier, *L'Espace Public Démocratique: Essai sur l'opinion à Paris de la Révolution au Directoire* (Paris, 1994), 34, 60; see also R. Monnier, "Mouvement républicain et fédéralisme radical à Paris au printemps 1791," in Bernard Cousin, ed., *Les Fédéralismes: Réalités et Représentations, 1789–1874* (Marseille, 1995), 51–60. Although Monnier suggests the applicability of this notion to Lyon, it is not a terminology that Bill Edmonds employs.

4. Jacques Guilhaumou, *Marseille républicaine (1791–1793)* (Paris, 1992), esp. chaps. 3 and 5; J. Guilhaumou, "Les Fédéralismes marseillais en 1793," in *Marseille en Révolution* (Marseille, 1989), 105–13. See also *Existe-t-il un fédéralisme jacobin? Etudes sur la Révolution* (Paris, 1986), esp. 21–119.

considering the term "republican revolt": how useful is the term "federalist" in explicating or describing the conflict of 1793 if we see federalists on both sides of the divide? Is the term reduced simply to a more or less meaningless epithet? Part of Guilhaumou's intention in positing a Jacobin federalism, I think, is to challenge the notion that the Jacobins were inveterate centralizers, and there is merit in this. It is supported, for example, by the recent work of Jean-Pierre Gros, focusing on the efforts of five Jacobin representatives on mission during the Year II.[5] Guilhaumou's argument suggests that we think about Jacobin centralism, and Girondin federalism, more in tactical than ideological terms, and such an approach can be useful in sorting out the vagaries of the terms "federalist" and "federalism" over the course of 1793.

There are two ways, I would argue, that the term "federalist" had substantive meaning for those Jacobins who sought to label their opponents as such during the early months of the National Convention. The first has to do with the proposal put forward in the fall by Roland and Buzot and repeated the following spring by Guadet and Barbaroux, among others, that a departmental guard be summoned to Paris for the protection of the National Convention. There was no inherent ideological meaning to such a proposal. The *fédérés* who had come to Paris in 1792 were a radical force. They allied themselves with the militants of the Paris clubs and sections and played a crucial role in leading the assault on the Tuileries palace. But those who wished to summon *fédérés* to Paris in the winter and spring of 1793 saw them not as a means to push the Revolution forward, so to speak, but rather as a means to stabilize the Revolution, to bolster the authority of the National Convention. Those advocating such a proposal sought to bring *fédérés* to the capital not to fraternize with the Parisian *sans-culottes* but to protect the Convention against them. What had been seen as a revolutionary measure in 1792 now came to be seen as potentially counterrevolutionary.

The issue of the *fédérés*, or departmental guards, was closely linked to that of the *appel au peuple* during the king's trial, one of the principal points of contention between the Girondins and Montagnards, and the second way in which the term "federalist" took on a certain substantive meaning in this period. To call for the *appel au peuple* was to deny the assertion (made by Robespierre) that the will of the people had been expressed in the Parisian uprising of August 10 and to assert that an alternative will of the people might lie in the provinces. As we saw in the last chapter, Charles Barbaroux tried to use the Second Battalion from Marseille as a counter to Parisian militants during the debate over the *appel au peuple*, and the Jacobin club in Marseille responded by denouncing the proposed referendum as tending toward federalism. Given their shared root,

5. Jean Pierre Gros, *Jacobin Egalitarianism in Practice* (Cambridge, 1996).

and Barbaroux's attempt to use the *fédérés* to pursue an allegedly federalist agenda, one saw in this period an increasing conflation of the two terms in a pejorative sense.

To be a federalist was to be opposed to "the unity and indivisibility of the Republic," an ideal fervently embraced by virtually every deputy within the National Convention. The "sovereignty of the nation" was both the source and the embodiment of that ideal. But where did that sovereignty lie? Had the people invested it in the National Convention in the act of electing deputies? Or did the people retain their sovereignty and the right to exercise it? If so, by what mechanism could popular sovereignty be exercised, apart from general elections? Through the clubs? Through sectional assemblies? Through insurrection? These were vexing questions, not only for deputies in Paris, but also for officials sitting on departmental and municipal councils, and as the stalemate in the National Convention dragged on, commitment to the twin ideals of "the unity and indivisibility of the Republic" and the Convention as the "embodiment of national sovereignty" became more and more wavering, and ideological consistency became a rare commodity.

Thus, when moderates called for the *appel au peuple* during the king's trial, the Jacobins attacked them for seeking to sow division in the country and undermine national sovereignty as embodied in the Convention. The Jacobin club of Marseille joined in that attack in a celebrated address of March 17, in which they denounced all those deputies who had voted for the *appel au peuple* and declared that "we recognize as the National Convention only that tutelary Mountain that is destined, along with us, to save the fatherland." They went on to call upon all republicans and *sans-culottes* to "recognize as their true representatives only the deputies of the Mountain." Naturally this address drew howls of protest on the floor of the Convention, and Bertrand Barère was heartily applauded when he denounced it as an attack on national sovereignty, as a provocation of federalism and civil war.[6] The Jacobins of Marseille, who had denounced the *appelants* as federalists back in January, now stood accused as federalists themselves.

In the aftermath of the king's trial, citizens throughout France grew increasingly concerned about the partisan divisions within the National Convention. How could a Convention so apparently riven by factionalism be seen to embody the "unity and indivisibility of the Republic"? In their efforts to resolve that factionalism, deputies on both sides looked outside the Convention for sources of support—the Montagnards to the people of Paris, and the Girondins to their constituents in the departments. Each side accused the other of advocating federalism, though in different senses. For the Girondins, the Montagnard appeal

6. Guilhaumou, *Marseille républicaine*, 162–66.

to popular democracy would bring on anarchy and thereby undermine the unity of the republic. For the Montagnards, the Girondin appeal to the departments (Paris is only one of eighty-four departments) would undermine that unity by its implicitly federalist agenda. "Federalism" and "anarchy" became equivalent terms, each seen as a threat to the unity of the republic.[7]

Eventually both sides within the Convention came to accept the necessity of eliminating at least a portion of their opposition, an obvious assault on the notion that the Convention embodied the "unity of the nation." For the Girondins, the key to their impeachment of Marat was to convince a jury (a Parisian jury) that his "anarchism" was counterrevolutionary. In this they failed. The Montagnards were more successful at convincing Parisians, at least a large number of them, that the "federalism" of the Girondins was enough of a threat to warrant their proscription. But not only did that proscription violate the unity of the Convention, it also threatened to shatter the unity of the republic.

Once the revolt began, the term "federalist" took on meaning in another sense. Nearly all of those departments that protested the proscription of the twenty-nine deputies went on to dispute the authority of the now diminished National Convention, although the Lyonnais were somewhat reticent about taking that step. Each of the federalist cities eventually refused to register or publicize decrees of the National Convention taken after May 31. They did so, to be sure, in the name of national unity, but the logical inconsistency of rebelling against the national legislature in the name of national unity is as apparent today as it was to most Frenchmen in 1793. From the perspective of the Montagnards and most Parisians, the rebel cities (or departments) had substituted their own authority for that of the Convention, and this was a federalist act.

The term "federalist," then, was in currency before summer 1793, possessed of a range of meanings and leveled as a charge by and against both sides of the political divide. But was there more to the provincial rebellion than the rejection of the authority of the Convention to justify calling it the "federalist revolt"? A number of historians have addressed this question in recent years from a variety of different perspectives. Bill Edmonds argued some years ago that although the "Montagnards had every reason to want their opponents called 'federalists,'. . . there is little justification for calling them that now except the convenience of maintaining an established usage." Still, after examining the provincial protests

---

7. See Monnier, *L'Espace public démocratique*, 60, for a provocative discussion along these lines. Monnier suggests that "le couple fédéralisme/anarchie est la réplique du couple démocratie/anarchie du discours girondin." The June 8 speech of the deputy S. P. Lejeune before the Convention offers an example of this linkage of anarchy and federalism: "chose étrange, ce sont ceux qui n'ont cessé de crier à l'anarchie et au brigandage qui prêchent aujourd'hui l'anarchie dans les départements et provoquent la dissolution de la République." Cited by Antonio de Francesco, "Popular Sovereignty and Executive Power in the Federalist Revolt of 1793," *French History* 5, no. 1 (March 1991): 75.

and revolts at some length, he concluded that "the revolts were not a war of the provincial bourgeoisie against Paris and the Revolution, but a defensive reaction against Montagnard centralism, a reaction whose intensity was directly related to the intensity of preexisting local conflict." In this view, what gave the provincial revolts some coherence was a shared opposition to Montagnard centralism. We are left, then, with a "negative" definition—the "federalists," if they are to be called that, are defined not by what they stood for, but by what they opposed.[8]

Alan Forrest has emphasized more than Edmonds the anti-Parisian element of provincial federalism. He observes that the federalist rebels "rushed to express their outrage at the harm being done by 'malveillants'; they dreamed somewhat nostalgically of a return to constitutionalism; they spoke of a world where the Convention would be freed from illegitimate pressures and where all eighty-three departments could enjoy a measure of real equality without fear of domination from the capital." Like Edmonds, Forrest offers a definition of the revolt in essentially negative terms: "federalism was an intensely confrontational movement, concerned less with the definition of political principle than with the eradication of abuse." It was a "local movement born out of local circumstance." But Forrest would not reduce the federalist revolt to local particularism, suggesting that it represented a kind of "republicanism of the provinces," more traditional and conservative than that of the capital, but one that would come to prevail even in Paris in the years after Thermidor.[9]

Antonio de Francesco, drawing on the work of Edmonds as well as on his own archival research in Lyon, has challenged the traditional view of the federalist revolt as a moderate movement. De Francesco argues that "the Federalist revolt represented a rejection—and not a defence—of the traditional governmental structure in the country." In his view, "the political action of the Jacobins transformed what had been resistance to a homogeneous government authority in the provinces into an attack on executive power which was seen as the main obstacle to the revolutionary impulse of the nation." Provincial voters, and departmental administrations, had followed the lead of Parisian radicals after August 10 by politicizing local administrative councils and asserting the autonomy of local authorities. Thus, de Francesco argues, the federalist revolt was a manifestation of popular democracy in the provinces and not a conservative reaction against the victory of the Parisian *sans-culottes* and the ascendancy

8. Bill Edmonds, "'Federalism' and Urban Revolt in France in 1793," *Journal of Modern History* 55, no. 1 (March 1983): 22–53. The passages cited will be found on pages 28 and 53.
9. Alan Forrest, "Federalism," in Colin Lucas, ed., *The French Revolution and the Creation of Modern Political Culture*, vol. 2 (Oxford, 1988), 309–25; and Forest, "Le Fédéralisme de 1793: Républicanisme de province," in Cousin, ed., *Les Fédéralismes*, 303–11.

of the Montagnards in the Convention. Far from being a counterrevolutionary rebellion, de Francesco sees federalism as a revolutionary movement.[10]

Mona Ozouf, too, has recently challenged traditional interpretations of the federalist revolt, though from a different perspective than that of de Francesco. Like de Francesco and others, Ozouf downplays the importance of the proscription of the Girondin deputies and writes, "what sustained the rebellion was not so much the insult to the representatives of the nation as the fear of another revolution, sparked by rumors of an agrarian law and taxation of the rich." She also questions the "federalism" of the rebellion, rejecting Albert Soboul's emphasis on "provincial and regional differences" in asserting that the origin of the crisis essentially "involved rejection of Jacobin measures and of the *représentants en mission* who embodied those measures." For Ozouf, then, the revolt was more a response to Jacobin radicalism than to Jacobin centralism, and the "federalist" movement itself was more a Jacobin invention than a reality.[11]

Recent historiography, then, leaves open the question of whether the revolt was truly "federalist," although most historians, including myself, would insist upon qualifying the label in some fashion. There is no consensus, though, regarding either what the revolt stood for or against what the federalist cities were rebelling. Nor is there agreement as to just who the federalist rebels were. De Francesco sees the movement as an expression of popular democracy, a revolutionary movement directed against executive power. Forrest sees some popular support for the revolt, though he does not stress this as strongly as de Francesco. But although he, too, sees in the revolt a reaction against Jacobin centralism, Forrest characterizes the movement as conservative, a defense of the interests of the traditional propertied elite in support of what he refers to as a "republicanism of the provinces." Edmonds rejects the notion that the revolt was a movement of the provincial bourgeoisie, emphasizes the importance of "localism" more than the others, and joins Forrest in seeing the revolt as a rejection of Jacobin centralism. Ozouf is closest to Forrest in her social characterization of the rebels, also asserts a hatred of Paris common to the federalist cities (which Edmonds disputes), but is stronger than all but Edmonds in denying the existence of any common "federalist" agenda among the rebelling cities.

Although the image of a federalist revolt that was counterrevolutionary, perhaps dominated by royalists, has long been left behind, we still lack a clear pic-

---

10. Antonio de Francesco, "Popular Sovereignty and Executive Power in the Federalist Revolt of 1793," esp. 74–80; and *Il Governo senza testa* (Naples, 1992). See also my critique of de Francesco's article: "The Federalist Revolt: An Affirmation or Denial of Popular Sovereignty?" *French History* 6, no. 3 (September 1992): 335–55.

11. Mona Ozouf, "Federalism," in François Furet and Mona Ozouf, eds., Arthur Goldhammer, trans., *A Critical Dictionary of the French Revolution* (Cambridge, Mass., 1989), 54–63.

ture of just what the federalist rebels wanted and who they were. These are the two main issues that I will address in the remainder of this chapter, beginning with an examination of the men who stepped forward to lead the rebellion against Paris in Caen, Bordeaux, Lyon, and Marseille.

Generally speaking, it was departmental administrators who led the revolt, though this was not universally the case. Federalist propaganda tended to reflect this, referring almost always to the number of departments (usually exaggerated) that had joined the protest movement. While the revolt was essentially an urban revolt, which Bill Edmonds has emphasized, it was not exclusively so, and while the four principal cities figured prominently in federalist addresses and propaganda, the rebels in each city made concerted efforts to enlist the support of other towns and districts in their departments, as well as in neighboring departments.

In Calvados a half dozen individuals took the lead in securing the initial declaration of revolt and in guiding the movement as it developed through June and into July.[12] René Lenormand, president of the departmental administration in May, led the delegation that traveled to Paris in late May. The report brought back by Lenormand and his delegation triggered the declaration of rebellion on June 8–9. Lenormand had served on the Vire district council in 1791–92 and was a close friend of Gustave Doulcet de Pontécoulant, a moderate deputy in the National Convention who would be proscribed during the summer for protesting the June 2 proscriptions, and who had himself been a departmental administrator in 1791–92.

Pierre Lévêque assumed the position of president of the departmental council during Lenormand's absence in Paris, and he presided over the special assembly that convened on June 9 and officially declared the department to be in a state of insurrection. Lévêque, like Lenormand, had previous experience in local politics as a member of the municipal council of Caen. Lévêque, too, was a close friend of one of the Calvados deputies to the Convention, Claude-Jean-Baptiste Lomont, with whom he corresponded regularly in winter and spring 1793. Lomont had been a departmental administrator in 1790–91 and was president of the Caen Jacobin club in April 1791, before his election to the Legislative Assembly later that year.

Jean-Louis Chatry *le jeune*, who had served two terms on the departmental council, played an active role in the revolt, as did his older brother, Samuel Chatry. The Chatrys were a merchant family, and Samuel had been a member of every Caen municipal council since 1789. Both brothers had been elected

---

12. The following discussion is drawn entirely from my earlier book, *Provincial Politics in the French Revolution: Caen and Limoges, 1789–1794* (Baton Rouge, 1989).

mayor of Caen early in the Revolution, though both declined, fearful that their Protestantism would be a source of conflict. Samuel was reported to have played a crucial role in fueling the insurrectionary mood among the sections of Caen on the evening of June 8 as the anonymous author of an incendiary speech delivered to sectional assemblies. He would go on to serve as a Calvados representative on the Central Committee of Resistance to Oppression once that body relocated to Caen, and in July he presided over the Calvados insurrectionary assembly, after the departmental force had left for Evreux.

Another departmental administrator, Pierre Mesnil, was, like the Chatry brothers, a *négociant* and a Protestant. He had served on the Caen district council before being elected to the departmental administration in 1791. Jean Bougon-Longrais, the departmental *procureur-général-syndic*, had been active in Caen politics since 1789, though too young to hold elected office until 1792. Lenormand, Lévêque, Mesnil, and Bougon-Longrais led the departmental force to Evreux in July, and Bougon-Longrais in particular played an important role in maintaining the flagging spirits of the rebels in the department of the Eure. Adrien Thiboult, also a departmental administrator, was among the first volunteers for the departmental force.

In addition to these men, several individuals who had been linked to the deputy Claude Fauchet during his tenure as bishop of Calvados in 1791 were active in the federalist movement. All of them assumed official positions in the Calvados general insurrectionary assembly on July 1, replacing departmental administrators who had either returned to their regular posts or would soon leave for Evreux. They included Chaix-d'Estanges, former vicar to the bishop and now curé of the parish Saint-Etienne in Caen, who became president of the general assembly; Charles Debaudre, a priest from Bayeux (the seat of the bishopric), who became vice-president; Mariette, also a priest from Bayeux, named assistant secretary; and Dom Mauger, a cleric who had been one of the nine commissioners sent to Paris in early June, named *procureur-syndic* of the assembly. Fauchet, their patron, would be denounced in late July as a Girondin conspirator and subsequently tried and executed in October 1793.

In Calvados, then, departmental administrators were most prominent in the leadership of the movement in its early days. They did not abandon the revolt in July when men close to Fauchet took their places, but rather assumed new roles. Both groups of men had been active in local politics for some time, and several among them had personal ties to deputies in the National Convention who were sympathetic to those proscribed on June 2. Notably absent from the federalist leadership were officers from the Caen municipal council. Samuel Chatry was a notable, it is true, but his influence did not carry the majority of the municipal council. The mayor, Le Goupil Duclos, remained aloof from the movement throughout, and in July he actively encouraged an end to the revolt.

Although sectional assemblies did meet in Caen on June 8–9 and declared their support for insurrection, they cannot be said to have played an active role in the weeks that followed. As we have seen, popular support for the march to Paris was lukewarm in Caen at best.

It is difficult to say very much about the Central Committee of Resistance to Oppression, which moved to Caen in late June after first establishing itself in Rennes, because the committee destroyed all its records before fleeing Caen in late July. Once established in Caen, the Central Committee took responsibility for propaganda efforts, communication with other departments, and the coordination of the various departmental forces. It included representatives from ten Norman and Breton departments (two apiece), and I should think it safe to assume that the majority of these were departmental administrators. The majority of letters and decrees issued by the Central Committee during July bore the signatures of L. J. Roujoux, a departmental administrator from the Finistère, as president, and Louis Caille, the *procureur-syndic* of the district of Caen and another political ally of Claude Fauchet, signing as secretary.

In Bordeaux, too, departmental administrators played a prominent role in the leadership of the federalist revolt. On June 7, the departmental council initiated the creation of the *Commission Populaire de Salut Public*, the body that would guide the departmental revolt into August. The Popular Commission was composed of fifty members, most of them co-opted from already existing administrative and judicial bodies in Bordeaux and the Gironde. Sixteen of the fifty were drawn from the departmental administration, including Pierre Sers, who presided over the Popular Commission just as he had the departmental council. Sers, a deputy to the Legislative Assembly in 1791–92, was a wealthy merchant and shipper from Bordeaux, as were eight of the nine municipal council members from Bordeaux who sat on the Popular Commission. Joining them was the mayor of Bordeaux, François-Armand Saige. Saige was the son of a *secrétaire du roi* and therefore noble. He had served as an *avocat-général* on the parlement of Bordeaux until 1778, when he sold his office and became fabulously wealthy through colonial trade. He was elected mayor of Bordeaux three times, reflecting the degree to which the mercantile elite dominated Bordeaux political life during the early years of the Revolution. The legal elite of the department was also well represented, with twelve members of various courts sitting as members of the Popular Commission.[13]

As in Calvados, the Popular Commission in Bordeaux had difficulty attracting significant support from the other towns and communes of the Gironde. Only 130 of some 559 communes expressed support for the declaration of insurrection, and few went so far as to lend men or material to the cause. Alan Forrest

13. Alan Forrest, *Society and Politics in Revolutionary Bordeaux* (Oxford, 1975), 124–27.

has noted that many "communes, though deluged with pamphlets and other propaganda, would seem to have made no response whatever to the seductive approaches of the Commission populaire," and that "geographically, support was strongly concentrated in those parts of the Department most remote from Bordeaux."[14] There seems to have been some resentment of Bordeaux's political and economic domination within the department, as was also the case for Lyon in the Rhône-et-Loire, and this would greatly limit the ability of the federalist rebels to rally support for their cause.

Nor was the Popular Commission able to enlist the support of neighboring departments for a march on the capital. The Landes, the Charente, the Dordogne, and the Lot-et-Garonne all initially protested the proscriptions of June 2, but none carried their resistance to the Montagnard Convention further than that. When the department of the Haute-Vienne, northeast of the Gironde, learned that the volunteer force had begun its march, it made preparations to turn the Bordelais back.[15]

Aside from this, the principal difference between Caen and Bordeaux was the firm support of the Bordeaux municipal council for the revolt against Paris. This is indicative of the degree to which the social elite of Bordeaux had continued to dominate revolutionary politics in the Gironde. As Forrest has written, "It must already be perfectly clear that the Revolution in Bordeaux and the southwest cannot in the strict sense of the term be called a 'popular' revolution. Rather it was a revolution by a fairly narrow, privileged group within the community, a group that encompassed both the haute-bourgeoisie who dominated the departmental and municipal administrations and the less wealthy members of the middle classes who took part in the affairs of their sections."[16] In his most recent work, Forrest points to the accusation often leveled against the Bordeaux federalists, that they were "a social elite, a small group of wealthy bourgeois intent on using their position to defend their own economic interests." But while acknowledging that they came from "a fairly narrowly defined social stratum," he stresses that "there is no indication that they used their position with their own narrow social and economic interests in view." The "language of the revolt," Forrest observes, "was more political than social."[17] This is not to say, however, that social factors did not influence local politics. As we shall see more fully in the next chapter, one of the most striking features of the early Revolution in both Bordeaux and Caen is the degree to which the social elite dominated local politics. From the perspective of that elite, there was consonance

14. Ibid., 118.
15. Hanson, *Provincial Politics*, 114.
16. Forrest, *Society and Politics*, 181.
17. Alan Forrest, *The Revolution in Provincial France* (Oxford, 1996), 189–90.

rather than discord between their own self-interest and political ideals and those of their city, their region, and indeed those of the nation.

The departmental administration of the Rhône-et-Loire played a less prominent role in the leadership of the revolt than did those of Calvados and the Gironde, which is scarcely surprising given that the movement grew out of the rebellion of the sections of Lyon in late May. The paucity of archival documentation regarding the composition of the provisional municipality of Lyon, created in early June, or the Popular Commission, which first met on June 30, makes it difficult to identify the specific individuals who assumed leadership at the beginning of the revolt, but Bill Edmonds is unequivocal in his characterization of the general social background of the revolt's leadership: "The propertied classes did a good job of dressing up their rebellion in democratic clothes. But the fact that it was primarily their rebellion remains unmistakable in the social composition of its institutions and in the belief that by ejecting the sans-culotte Municipalité the natural order in Lyon's affairs had been restored, or at least an unnatural one removed."[18]

The departmental administration did take two significant actions in June that can be said to have placed it in the federalist camp. On June 10 it dispatched Tardy and Gauthier to Bordeaux, accompanied by a delegate from the Jura, carrying a joint declaration of the two departments calling for an assembly of *suppléants* to the Convention in Bourges. Then on June 19 the departmental council issued a decree ordering the convocation of primary assemblies to elect delegates to the Popular Commission. Thus, the departmental administration can be said to have initiated the creation of the body that would lead the Rhône-et-Loire during the rebellion. Several departmental administrators sat on the Popular Commission, but as a whole the administration confined itself to tending to routine matters of business during July.[19]

The departmental administration's deference to the Popular Commission throughout July became significant as the revolt in other cities began to collapse. Although individual administrators backed away from the revolt in late July, the fact that they had ceded authority to the Popular Commission impeded them from formally declaring the departmental insurrection at an end. The Popular Commission, claiming to have acted in accordance with the will of the people as expressed in primary assemblies, refused to abandon its resistance to the Convention, even as the movement to join in a federalist march on Paris gave way to a defense of a city increasingly dominated by royalist sympathizers. Had the departmental administration maintained control of the situation in late June and early July, it might have been possible to avert the siege and its disastrous consequences.

18. W. D. Edmonds, *Jacobinism and the Revolt of Lyon, 1789–1793* (Oxford, 1990), 220.
19. Ibid., 237.

The man at the head of the Popular Commission was a Lyonnais by the name of Jean-Emmanuel Gilibert. Born in 1741, son of a Lyon merchant, Gilibert took a degree at the Montpellier faculty of medicine in 1763. He returned to Lyon to teach medicine and botany but was called to Poland in 1775 by King Stanislas, whom he served as royal doctor. Gilibert returned to Lyon in 1783 to resume his scholarly and teaching career, and at some point in his young adult life he became a Quaker. He joined the Jacobin club early in the Revolution and played a role in the reform of education in Lyon in 1791–92 while continuing to publish scholarly works. Only in 1793, when he stood as a candidate for mayor, did he become active in municipal politics.

The Jacobins of Lyon, it will be recalled, had gained control of the municipal council early that winter and were attempting to consolidate their position through the creation of a Central Club to coordinate the activities of the various sectional clubs in the city. On the eve of the mayoral election, the Central Club was sacked in a riot. Gilibert won a narrow victory in the voting the next day, but the *procureur* of Lyon, a Jacobin ally of Chalier by the name of François Laussel, ordered his arrest and kept him in jail until he agreed to resign. In May a jury in Macon acquitted him on charges of defying constituted authorities and inciting the riot that had led to the sacking of the Central Club.

Although he played no role in leading the insurrection of May 29, Gilibert was named to the delegation that traveled to Paris in early June and was elected president of the Popular Commission when it first convened. Gilibert signed all of the official decrees and correspondence of the Commission during the first half of July, and on July 12 he was named delegate to the alternative National Convention that the rebels hoped would convene in Bourges. When his term as president of the Popular Commission expired on July 15, he was replaced by Pierre-Thomas Rambaud, a former *avocat du roi* at the Lyon *présidial* court, under whose leadership the rebellion took on a decidedly royalist character. Gilibert remained active on the Popular Commission, however, and completed another term as president from mid-August to early September, in the midst of the siege.

Gilibert's prominence as a leader of the federalist revolt in Lyon raises two important issues. His central role in the events of both February and June underscores the manner in which the conflicts in Lyon municipal politics and the federalist revolt were inextricably linked. One local historian suggests that for Gilibert the insurrection of May 29 and the subsequent revolt marked the ultimate success of the failed coup of February 18.[20] It is puzzling, however, that a

---

20. Jean Rousset, "J. E. Gilibert, Docteur de Montpellier, homme politique à Lyon pendant la Révolution," *Monspeliensis Hippocrates*, no. 17 (fall 1962): 11–27. See also Bruno Benoît and Roland Saussac, eds., *Guide Historique de la Révolution à Lyon* (Lyon, 1988), 134–35, for biographical details.

professed Quaker should have embraced a municipal revolution rooted in violence and equally puzzling that a man of Gilibert's firm republican convictions
should have been willing to compromise in late July with royalists like Rambaud,
whose obduracy would bring bloodshed to the streets of Lyon. If he had been
willing to fight for his principles in February and May, perhaps against his
Quaker conscience, why did he seemingly so easily abandon them later that
summer? In the person of Gilibert, much of the complexity and paradox of the
federalist revolt is readily apparent.

The situation in Marseille resembled that in Lyon to a considerable degree.
Here, too, a sectional upheaval had thrown out a Jacobin municipality, and that
insurrection significantly colored the federalist revolt that followed. Even more
than in Lyon, however, the leaders of the sectional assemblies dominated the
federalist movement, and the General Committee of the sections guided the
department throughout June and July. Sectional assemblies named a provisional
municipal council, dominated by men of commerce, and a provisional departmental administration, which included men drawn from the Marseille sections
as well as some from other towns and communes of the Bouches-du-Rhône.
Presiding over the General Committee were Pierre Peloux, a Marseille *négociant*, and Antoine Castelanet, a former royal notary. Their dual leadership is
suggestive of the importance of the Marseille commercial elite in the movement
and also of the turn toward royalism that the revolt would take in its final days.[21]

Despite that eventual turn toward royalism, at the beginning of the revolt
the expressed goals and ideals of the federalist leaders can scarcely be said to
have been either royalist or counterrevolutionary. What were those goals and
ideals, and did they reflect a common program among the four federalist cities?
If so, how was that program expressed and what measures did the federalist
rebels take to achieve a unified movement?

The most fully developed declaration of a federalist program was that of the
Central Committee of Resistance to Oppression, issued shortly after the committee reconvened in Caen in late June. This document is notable not only
because it represents the most extensive statement of federalist goals on record,
but also because it grew out of the collaboration of delegates from seven Breton
and Norman departments and thus represents the most broad-based statement
of federalist goals available to us. In the discussion that follows I will focus

---

21. See William Scott, *Terror and Repression in Revolutionary Marseille* (London, 1973), esp.
chaps. 5 and 7, for an extensive discussion of the federalist leadership in Marseille. I will include a
more detailed discussion of some of the leading rebels in each city in chap. 7, focusing on the
repression of the revolt.

principally on this document but will refer as well to declarations issued in the other federalist cities.[22]

The Central Committee published what was essentially a manifesto of twenty-seven demands, grouped into four sections. (See Appendix 1 for the full text of the manifesto.) Some of the demands overlapped with each other, and some of the more minor points need not draw our attention, but eight of the demands, or sets of demands, merit discussion. The first of these was a demand for "a solemn Decree abolishing the administrative corps of Paris and the anarchical authorities known under the name of Revolutionary Committees." There are two things worthy of note here—the suggestion that the influence of the Paris Commune was excessive, and the characterization of that body, and of the revolutionary committees, as anarchical. One finds this language—the condemnation of the influence of Paris and of anarchy, and the combination of those two in the same phrase—among all the federalist departments. For example, the "Address of the Marseillais to their brothers in the other 85 departments," issued by the thirty-two sections of Marseille on June 12, reads, "Marat has finally triumphed" and "an ambitious and criminal municipality has attacked national sovereignty."[23] One month later, a "Declaration of the Electoral Assembly of the Bouches-du-Rhône" proclaimed that its members were "in insurrection, not only against that oppression which chokes liberty, but against anarchy, which tears to shreds and devours the many victims whose liberty it has stolen. Paris boasts of having, on May 31, reclaimed its rights. We declare, ourselves, that Paris has usurped our rights."[24] In Lyon, section Concorde circulated a declaration of insurrection in early June, "considering that the Municipality of Paris dares to arrogate to itself frightening powers, by raising itself even above the Convention," and "considering that the city of Paris sees itself as constituting the entirety of the French people . . . , and that consequently she alone should be the master of public opinion and the arbiter of the popular will."[25] An address of the Popular Commission of the Rhône-et-Loire, issued in the first week of July, simply noted, "we are coordinating our actions with those of other departments, in order to overthrow anarchy and despotism."[26]

Linked to these concerns was a second major demand of the Central Committee of Resistance to Oppression: "that the sections of Paris should no longer

22. An earlier version of the discussion that follows was presented to the September 1793 colloquium on federalism in Marseille and published as "Les Centres fédéralistes, avaient-ils un projet commun?" in Cousin, ed. *Les Fédéralismes*, 313–19.

23. A.D. Bouches-du-Rhône, L1967.

24. A.D. Bouches-du-Rhône, L1965.

25. A.D. Rhône, 31L21.

26. A.D. Rhône, 1L378.

meet in permanent session (*en permanence*)." It is not at all surprising to hear this sentiment expressed by the rebels in Caen, where sectional assemblies played a relatively unimportant role in the revolt. In Bordeaux, too, where the sections confided the direction of the rebellion to the Popular Commission, one finds that commission denouncing "that element of the People of Paris who, lacking resource, industriousness and principles, has become the blind instrument of the scoundrels who pay them."[27] It was necessary to neutralize, or direct, that segment of the population little capable of exercising sovereignty. The Marseillais were more blunt: "There exists a schism; it is the inevitable schism between the good and the bad."[28] But in Marseille, as in Lyon, it was the sectionaries who were good, who had overturned the influence of the clubs and the Jacobin municipalities in their two cities in April and May. One would not expect the federalist rebels in Lyon and Marseille to denounce the permanence of sectional assemblies, but it is important to note that the politics of the sections were quite different in the two cities. In Marseille sectional assemblies remained very active during the revolt, though they did grant "unlimited power" to a Central Committee at the beginning of July. In Lyon, by contrast, even though the sections continued to deliberate throughout June and July, they explicitly recognized the limits to their authority, as was expressed very well in a declaration issued by section Concorde: "It is absolutely necessary that the sections act only as sections, lest the government, which in a large state such as France is representative, both in legislative and in administrative matters, be undermined; if the people, after having delegated power to their representatives, continue to assert the authority of the sections, this is an abuse; and it is this abuse that has produced the evils we have suffered."[29] In this last remark, the citizens of section Concorde alluded not only to recent developments in Lyon but also to those in Paris.

A third major demand issued by the Central Committee in Caen read, "that the Revolutionary Tribunal be suppressed; that the conduct of its Judges be rigorously examined." One finds an echo of this complaint in the June 13 address of the Popular Commission in Bordeaux, which referred to the powerlessness of the national High Court and the usurpation of its powers by the Revolutionary Tribunal.[30] And in Lyon and Marseille, where similar concerns were expressed, one sees clearly the intermingling of local and national politics. In May 1793 the Jacobins of Marseille had created a revolutionary tribunal and

27. A.D. Gironde, 8J368.
28. A.D. Bouches-du-Rhône, L1965 (Déclaration de l'Assemblée Electorale du Département des Bouches-du-Rhône, à tous les François, 13 juillet 1793).
29. A.D. Rhône, 31L21.
30. A.D. Gironde, 8J368.

also began to disarm suspects. The creation of this tribunal triggered the revolt of the Marseille sections against the Jacobin municipality. In Lyon, Chalier and the Jacobins failed in their efforts to create a revolutionary tribunal, but they had proposed such a tribunal in February and March. In both cities, then, moderate sectionaries, the federalist rebels of June and July, saw revolutionary tribunals as a weapon of radical Jacobins.

A fourth major point in the manifesto of the Central Committee addressed an issue that had been festering since the previous autumn, demanding "that a Decree order the resumption of the abandoned investigation against the assassins of 2 September, and the prosecution of those men of blood, who for six months had never ceased to provoke murder, either by their writings or by their speeches in public places and in the Popular Societies." As noted above, the sections of Marseille made mention of Marat in the declaration of June 12, and the Bordelais, too, implicated "the men of 2 September" as responsible for the insurrection of May 31 and the proscription of the Girondin deputies.[31] In the struggle for power in the National Convention, the April acquittal of Marat was a serious reverse for the Girondin deputies. For them, the massacres of September and the incendiary rhetoric of Marat were the very incarnation of anarchy and revolutionary violence. There may not have been Marats lurking in every federalist city, but there was a Chalier in Lyon and the Savon brothers in Marseille, and each of the federalist cities had witnessed violent incidents or riots in 1792–93. The federalist rebels, like the Girondin deputies in Paris, wished to restore the rule of law in order to control revolutionary violence and obliterate anarchy.

The Central Committee's fifth major demand was "that a Decree abolish the degenerate Societies of the Cordeliers and Jacobins in Paris, as ridiculous as they were dangerous, and hold guilty members responsible for their actions." Here, too, we see an issue that brought local and national politics together. For example, in October 1791 the local newspaper in Caen reprinted a pamphlet that had first appeared in Paris, bearing the title "No more clubs, it is the general cry." The anonymous author wrote: "all clubs are useless and dangerous; do we have need of men assembling on a regular basis in towns all across the country to debate affairs of state? Do we not have a National Assembly? Do we need several?"[32] At that time there was an active Jacobin club in Caen, but in the months that followed the departmental administration took decisive measures to break its influence and create a new club, the Carabots, which would remain subservient to local authorities throughout 1792–93. Playing a key role in that

31. Ibid.
32. *Affiches, Annonces et Avis Divers de la Basse-Normandie* (October 9, 13, and 16, 1791).

effort was Gustave Doulcet, who in 1793 sat as a moderate in the National Convention and suffered proscription for his protest against the earlier proscription of the Girondin deputies.[33]

In Bordeaux there were two rival clubs, the Friends of Liberty (affiliated with the Jacobin club of Paris but dominated by moderates) and the Club National (more radical than its rival but lacking affiliation with the Paris club and effectively marginalized in Bordeaux politics). Local authorities in Bordeaux, and the Friends of Liberty, came to view the radical rhetoric and actions of the Club National with alarm, and in March 1793 the Club National was closed down, just after the Friends of Liberty had voted to break their affiliation with the Paris Jacobins.[34] In Marseille, of course, the sectional movement was explicitly directed against the influence of the local Jacobin club, which the provisional municipal council shut down in early June. Moderates in Lyon were also suspicious of the influence of clubs. Early in the Revolution each section, or neighborhood, in Lyon had its own club, to be sure, but there was no dominant Jacobin club in the city until Chalier tried to transplant the model of the Paris Jacobins to Lyon in 1793 by the creation of the Club Central. As in Marseille, that club would be closed in the aftermath of the May 29 insurrection. We will examine more closely the role of clubs in the dynamics of local politics in these four cities in Chapter 5. The point to be made here is that in each federalist city moderates had vanquished a radical club in 1792 or 1793, and they saw that victory threatened by the ascendancy of the Paris Jacobins in the aftermath of June 2.

The sixth important demand of the Central Committee in Caen was quite straightforward: "That the Committee of Public Safety be stripped of its dictatorial powers." It is tempting to see in this an expression of federalist opposition to Jacobin centralism, but to do so would be, I think, premature. When the Central Committee's manifesto was published, the Committee of Public Safety was still in the process of defining its own powers and responsibilities. Not until July did the "Great Committee" of the Year II take shape; the scope of its authority would widen as the summer months wore on. In June, the dominance that it would exert over the National Convention was still a thing of the future.

This was clearly not a grievance directly related to the insurrection of May 31–June 2, however. What would have prompted departmental administrators and municipal leaders in the federalist cities to have formulated it? They would have realized, on one hand, that this was not a committee controlled by the Girondins in April and May, though again its domination by the Montagnards

---

33. Paul R. Hanson, "Les Clubs politiques de Caen pendant la Révolution française," *Annales de Normandie* 36, no. 2 (May 1986): 123–41.

34. Forrest, *Society and Politics,* 68–78.

would be more striking after July. More important, the representatives on mission reported to and drew their credentials from the Committee of Public Safety, and the next demand of the Central Committee addressed this issue explicitly: "That the Deputies sent to the armies and into the Departments should return to the post that the Nation assigned to them; that they should account for the sums spent on their extraordinary missions; that a review be carried out of the arrests that they had ordered, as well as the manner in which those arrests had been made; and that they be held responsible for their actions."

By their words and by their actions the provincial rebels made clear their opposition to the representatives on mission. In Calvados, one of the first actions taken by the General Assembly was to order the arrest of Romme and Prieur, and they remained under guard in the Château of Caen until the end of July. Jean-Baptiste Treilhard and Jean-Baptiste-Charles Mathieu felt threatened in Bordeaux in June and abandoned their mission to the city, and Marc-Antoine Baudot and Claude-Alexandre Ysabeau felt lucky to escape Bordeaux with their lives in August, even as the revolt in the department collapsed. Bayle and Boisset feared for their safety in Marseille even before the revolt, and Lindet was threatened by sectional rebels in Lyon in early June. In its address to the citizens of the Gironde, the Popular Commission in Bordeaux had this to say on the subject of representatives on mission: "You were led to believe that the vast powers granted to the representatives sent on mission to the Departments would be used only to expedite recruitment and to foil the plots of the enemies of Liberty; you learned too late that they were veritable Proconsuls, sent out to harness you to the yoke of arbitrary power that the faction they serve would place upon you."[35]

The Popular Society of Bordeaux was preoccupied by the issue of the representatives on mission in spring 1793. There are two reports in the minutes of the Popular Society on the alarming activities of François Chabot in Toulouse. On May 25 the members of the club voted to send an address to the National Convention denouncing Chabot and the other "*commissaires prévaricateurs.*"[36] In the minutes of the sections of Marseille from the end of May there is a motion "to demand the revocation of the decree that had declared the representatives on mission to be inviolable."[37] In all the federalist cities, the representatives on mission were seen as petty despots, as proconsuls, as usurpers of the authority of local constituted authorities and of the sovereignty of citizens of the departments. This may seem a fine point, but what we see here is not so much a

35. A.D. Gironde, 8J368.
36. A.D. Gironde, 12L14.
37. A.D. Bouches-du-Rhône, L1933.

concern over the growing power of the central government, but rather a resentment of the extension of that power, in an arbitrary fashion, back into the departments in the persons of the representatives on mission.

The final demand of the Central Committee was "that no more assignats be created; and that measures be taken to reduce the number of those already in circulation." The creation of assignats had been harmful to the commerce of Bordeaux, Lyon, and Marseille, and one finds echoes of this complaint in each of those cities during the revolt. Each of the federalist cities except Caen also either abolished the grain maximum or suspended its enforcement during the course of the summer.

Beyond this list of demands issued by the Central Committee of Resistance to Oppression, one finds in the federalist rhetoric a consistent preoccupation with the rule of law, the importance of public order, respect for constituted authorities, and respect for property. We might examine once again the oath taken by all of the members of the Popular Commission in Bordeaux: "to make eternal war against tyrants, traitors and anarchists, to preserve the liberty, equality and security of people and property, the unity and indivisibility of the Republic, and to exercise only those powers confided in them by the People, in order to reestablish the respect due the Sovereignty of the nation."[38] The sections of Marseille were even more emphatic in their June 1 address (on the subject of Jean-Paul Marat): "Liberty, as you well know, is entirely linked to property; to attack the latter, is to violate all the Laws, is to annihilate all of the sacred Rights of Man and the Citizen."[39] One finds these same sentiments expressed in the declaration of the electoral assembly of the Bouches-du-Rhône published on July 13: "Sovereignty of the people is our first doctrine; but the necessity and observance of Laws is the second. Respect for persons and property is the foundation of our political creed: for there can be no sovereignty without obedience; there can be no social pact without safeguard."[40] In this same vein, the Popular Commission of the Rhône-et-Loire began its address to the citizens of the department as follows: "The sovereignty of the French People has been violated in the persons of its Representatives; you have been oppressed; in the place of Laws which assure your happiness, some wish to substitute anarchy, to arm the poor against the rich, crime against virtue, the useless hornet against the worker bee."[41]

There were, then, common themes, expressions, and concerns that emerge from the various proclamations and addresses of the federalist rebels. Do they

38. A.D. Gironde, 8J368.
39. A.D. Bouches-du-Rhône, L1969.
40. A.D. Bouches-du-Rhône, L1965.
41. A.D. Rhône, 1L378.

represent what might be termed a truly federalist project? No, and that issue was expressly addressed by the electoral assembly of the Bouches-du-Rhône in its July 13 address: "What would federalism be? The union of several departments, each with a separate government, gathering together in a defensive or offensive alliance to pursue their common interests. Marseille, Bordeaux, Nîmes, Caen, Lyon, and so many other *chefs-lieux*, are they proposing anything of this kind? They are in insurrection: as this is the most sacred of duties, it is the first of rights; it is the last resource against the abuse of power. They are in insurrection, not only against the oppression that stifles liberty, but against anarchy."[42]

The Popular Commission in Lyon also explicitly addressed this issue on July 18, when reproached by messengers from the departments of the Aude and Hérault for participating in a federalist movement. The minutes record that the assembled delegates reaffirmed their determination to preserve "*la République une et indivisible*" and went on to observe that the Popular Commission was "united in interests and sentiments with all of the departments of the Republic; that a federative Republic is in its eyes an impossible government, anarchical and monstrous, especially for the French nation, of which no part can do without the others; that after having so often expressed this view, it is strange that anyone still dares to slander it [the Popular Commission] by accusing it of federalism."[43]

The fact that rebel authorities in Lyon and Marseille were concerned enough to defend themselves against charges of federalism is itself evidence of the degree to which Jacobin propaganda accusing the provincial rebels of federalist intentions had been successful. And to acknowledge the accusations ran the risk, as it always does, of according legitimacy to those accusations, no matter how logical and persuasive the refutations might be. The rebels might assert their devotion to the indivisibility of the republic and might insist upon their respect for the National Convention by calling for an assembly of *suppléants* in Bourges, but they could not hide the fact that authorities in all four rebel cities had decided in June to no longer recognize or register decrees issued by the National Convention after May 31. They would assert, with great conviction, that the integrity of the Convention had been violated, that that bastion of national unity no longer existed. But the majority of departmental administrations in France could not bring themselves to take that step. Some resisted entreaties from the federalist departments because they supported the insurrection of May 31–June 2. Many others, like the administrators of the Seine-Inférieure, refused to follow the path being marked out by Calvados because, in their view, they lacked the

42. A.D. Bouches-du-Rhône, L1965.
43. A.D. Rhône, 1L378.

legal authority either to arrest representatives of the nation or to reject the authority of the National Convention.[44]

The legal qualms expressed by the departmental administration of the Seine-Inférieure remind us that we must consider not only what the federalist rebels said in their many proclamations and decrees, but also what they did in their efforts to resist the Montagnard Convention. Each of the rebel cities either arrested or threatened representatives on mission in June and July. Although we are most struck today by provincial denunciations of these representatives' meddling in local affairs, it should be noted that municipal and departmental officials in each of the federalist cities had complained to Paris during the spring about the inadequacy of measures taken by the central government for the defense of their coasts or frontiers. It was the meddling of the representatives on mission in local politics that most aggrieved the federalist rebels.

Although the rebel leaders denied any intention to create a federated system of government, their actions could be interpreted in a different light. All the federalist centers published their decrees and proclamations and circulated them widely. One still finds them today scattered throughout the departmental archives of France. The rebel assemblies in Caen and Bordeaux sent out numerous messengers to publicize their declarations and to seek support for a departmental march on the capital. As these messengers and reports circulated, the four principal centers of resistance made efforts to link up and coordinate their actions. The Lyonnais and Marseillais were constantly sending delegations back and forth, both cities mindful of the fact that neither could long resist Paris, or Dubois-Crancé and the Army of the Alps, without the support of the other. Delegates from Lyon also visited Bordeaux, and representatives from Calvados reached both Bordeaux and Lyon. The arrival of delegates from Bordeaux in Marseille prompted the drafting of a document that designated provincial centers for the marshaling of troops for the march on Paris and also identified seven "secondary directorates" in the provinces, a proposal that could easily be construed as the basis of a plan for a federated republic. Most important, however, these envoys and missions make clear that the federalist rebels saw themselves as engaged in something much more than a defense of local interests. They may have failed in their efforts to create a unified national movement of resistance to Paris and the Montagnard Convention, but there is ample evidence that this is exactly what they hoped to achieve.[45]

44. See Hanson, *Provincial Politics*, 135–36, for discussion of a June 18 letter from the administration of the Seine-Inférieure to the administration of Calvados rebuking the latter for the insurrectionary actions it had taken.

45. Most of these missions from the federalist cities to each other and to other departments were discussed and documented in chap. 3. The arrival of two delegates from Calvados is noted in the minutes of the Bordeaux Popular Society for June 22, though they are not named. One of them may have been Charles François Duhamel-Levailly, a departmental administrator, who informed

Delegates from the departments never did gather in Bourges, thus no alternative national assembly convened to ratify a common manifesto or declaration of principles. But I would argue that the departmental rebels did share a common vision, as expressed in the various decrees and declarations they issued; they were united by a common project. It was not, to be sure, a federated republic that they envisioned, though one can see why their enemies leveled this charge against them. The federalist rebels were united, however, in their protest of the violation of the National Convention; in their fulminations against the anarchists in Paris and the excesses of the Paris Commune; in their denunciations of the unlimited powers of representatives on mission; in their attacks on the Jacobin and Cordelier clubs; in their call for a republic of laws, founded on respect for property and for duly constituted authority. They justified their rebellion by an appeal to popular sovereignty, but as the Marseillais put it, a sovereignty that acknowledged the necessity of obedience. For the federalist rebels, the politics of the street, of the clubs, was unacceptable.

It is important to emphasize again that the revolts of June and July were not simply reactions to the proscription of the Girondin deputies. The grievances expressed by the federalist rebels extended far beyond the fate of the proscribed deputies, or even the fate of the National Convention, and their demands and complaints echoed those made in countless letters and addresses sent from the departments to Paris in April and May. Among the most eloquent of these were two letters sent by the citizens of Nantes in early May, one addressed to the National Convention and the other to the departments of France. Both circulated widely, and Alan Forrest has commented on the strong impression that they made on the Bordelais in mid-May.[46]

The Nantais began their address to the departments by observing: "Four years of revolution have agitated France, and now we are told that there must be yet a third revolution. Where are we going? What do we want?" Thousands of Frenchmen, they observed, had watered the tree of liberty with their blood. The Bastille had been toppled, the king had been dethroned and executed, liberty and equality had been won, the republic had been declared. "Frenchmen,"

---

his colleagues on June 12 that urgent business required his presence in Bordeaux. He was therefore commissioned to carry official declarations of the rebel authorities with him on his trip. See Hanson, *Provincial Politics*, 136, for this mission. Alan Forrest makes no mention of delegates from Calvados, but see A.D. Gironde, 12L14 for the Popular Society minutes. The minutes of the Popular Commission in Lyon similarly record the appearance of an unidentified delegate from Calvados at a meeting on July 16. See Georges Guigue, ed., *Procès-verbaux des séances de la Commission Populaire de Rhône-et-Loire* (Lyon, 1899), 102.

46. Forrest, *Society and Politics*, 100. Both addresses were ordered printed in Bordeaux, and can be found in Bordeaux archives. See A.M. Bordeaux, Fonds Vivie, MS227, "Les Nantois à tous les Départements de la République;" and A.D. Gironde, 12L32, "Les Républicains formant le conseil général de la commune et les Sociétés populaires de Nantes, à la Convention Nationale."

they asked, "what more do you want?" In the past two years, no further progress had been made. The factious had taken control of public opinion, were threatening the Convention, dared indeed to dictate laws to the Convention—"all social and political ties are collapsing into anarchy."[47] In sum, it was time for the Revolution to come to an end if respect for the law and for property were to be preserved.

The federalist revolt was not, then, simply a "reactive" movement, responding to the June 2 proscriptions. It gave expression to a different vision of what republican politics might be, one closer to the views of the Girondin deputies than to those of the now victorious Montagnards. That vision addressed not only how government should operate, but how sovereignty should be exercised. These were not purely national issues. The federalist rebels were concerned about more than the usurpations of Parisian radicals. When the citizens of the section Porte-Froc in Lyon gathered on June 14 to draft their own address to the French people, an address that would be adopted by all of the sections of Lyon, they, too, made reference to the September massacres. They, too, lamented the recent usurpation of sovereignty and asserted quite bluntly, "sovereignty is not in the clubs."[48] They were not thinking of the Jacobins or Cordeliers of Paris, however, but rather of the various neighborhood clubs of Lyon, which Chalier had tried to unite in the Jacobin Club Central. They were thinking of their own recent triumph over the Lyon Jacobins, an expression of popular sovereignty in their view, a triumph that was now threatened by the events of June 2 in Paris. Their address serves as a reminder that the federalist revolt was not simply a response to a national political crisis but grew out of the experience of local politics in each of the four federalist cities.

47. A.M. Bordeaux, Fonds Vivie, MS227, "Les Nantois à tous les Départements de la République."
48. B.M. Lyon, Fonds Coste, 350579, "Adresse du Peuple de Lyon à la République française," drafted by section Porte-Froc, 14 June 1793.

Five

THE LOCAL CONTEXT OF FEDERALISM

They [the Bordelais] do not want a king; they want a republic, but a rich and tranquil republic.

—General Biron to Minister LeBrun, June 5, 1793

The second cause [of our recent troubles] is the complete ignorance of these people of the true meaning of the words *Liberty, Equality, Sovereignty,* and the false application that they make of them, egged on by evil-doers. They know no other *people* than the class of unfortunates in which they find themselves, and they truly believe themselves to be the *sovereign.* From that springs their self-claimed right to fix prices, to carry out justice, and soon to divide up property.

—Laugier and Girard to Minister Roland, November 6, 1792

Laugier and Girard, silk merchants from Lyon, would no doubt have been happier in the "rich and tranquil republic" envisioned by General Biron's Bordelais than they were in the violent and strife-torn city of Lyon in the early days of the first French republic.[1] Times had been hard for Lyon's silk industry and its workers, and public calm was shattered in mid-September 1792 by more than a week of violence and market disruptions. Laugier and Girard were concerned about that violence, to be sure, but they were also apprehensive about the upcoming municipal elections, with good reason. Those elections would bring to office a municipal council led by Joseph Chalier and dominated by his Jacobin allies, the "evil-doers" (*malveillants*) referred to in their letter. More strife and violence lay ahead for the Lyonnais, far more than they had endured thus far.

The letter by Laugier and Girard, and others like it, suggests the manner in which Lyonnais politics and national, or Parisian, politics were intertwined during this period. Jean-Marie Roland, who sat as minister of the interior when Laugier and Girard wrote to him, had served on the municipal council of Lyon from late 1790 until February 1792 and played an influential role in Lyon politics from the very beginning of the Revolution. He naturally continued to take an interest in Lyon affairs, and he and his wife maintained an active correspon-

---

1. Foreign Affairs Minister LeBrun shared Biron's letter in a report to Pierre Joseph Cambon, then presiding over the Committee of Public Safety. LeBrun's report can be found in A.N., AF II 44, dossier 345. It is also cited in Alan Forrest, *Society and Politics in Revolutionary Bordeaux* (Oxford, 1975), 110–111. See A.N., F⁷ 3686⁶ for the letter from Laugier and Girard to Roland. The letter is also cited in W. D. Edmonds, *Jacobinism and the Revolt of Lyon, 1789–1793* (Oxford, 1990), 135.

dence with a number of Lyonnais after their move to Paris. Joseph Chalier, whose radical policies led to the May 29 insurrection, was in Paris at the time of the September massacres, and in the minds of Lyon moderates was expected to bring the anarchistic politics of the capital back with him to their fair city. They could not think about their own contentious politics without reference to what had transpired in Paris in recent months, nor could Chalier have hoped to radicalize Lyon without the support and advice, indeed the example, of his Jacobin brothers in Paris.

Revolutionary politics in Bordeaux had been much more tranquil than in Lyon, as General Biron's letter would suggest. There had been violent incidents, to be sure, but these were isolated and did not lead to anything that could be characterized as popular upheaval. Continuity, rather than rupture, marked municipal and departmental elections, and the commercial and legal elite of Bordeaux maintained firm control over local politics. The Parisian revolution of May 31–June 2 represented a threat to the republic they had known more than a challenge to one they envisaged.

Like the Lyonnais, however, the Bordelais saw very clearly the implications of the May 31 revolution and appreciated the fact that their own future would be influenced by events elsewhere. They applauded the May 29 insurrection in Lyon as well as the victory of the sections in Marseille. Their understanding of those events was colored by their own political experience, but they joined with those cities, and with Caen, to defend what they took to be a shared vision of the French republic, a vision that embraced national politics every bit as much as local politics. Central to that vision was a conception of sovereignty and how it should be exercised. This is the issue that lay at the very heart of the federalist revolt.

To understand the formation of that vision, we must examine more closely the character of local politics in these cities and the factors that influenced their development, not in isolation but in comparison with each other and with an eye to the ways in which local politics and national politics intersected throughout this period. It should already be apparent that these four cities were not alike in their experience of revolutionary politics between 1789 and 1793, but we can expect to find interesting parallels and commonalities as well as telling differences among the four. One might pair Bordeaux with Caen—cities where a commercial elite dominated the largely passive popular classes in a relatively uncontentious political arena—and contrast them with Marseille and Lyon—cities where local Jacobins mobilized the popular classes to challenge the hegemony of the urban elite in a highly contentious political arena. Why were the politics of Marseille and Lyon so much more contentious than those of Bordeaux and Caen, and what impact did this have on the nature of the federalist revolt in those cities? Why was the sectional movement more vital in Marseille and Lyon, and why were the clubs seemingly more quiescent in Caen and Bordeaux?

To answer these questions we must consider, at least briefly, the nature of the local economies, the social structure of the four cities, and certain aspects of their urban geography. In this chapter I will also discuss the debate over sovereignty in 1792–93, particularly as it found expression in Lyon and Marseille, where it was more explicitly at issue in the federalist revolt than was the case in Caen and Bordeaux. A thorough examination of these issues for each of the four federalist cities would merit a book apiece, and books have indeed been written about each of them. Many of these books have already been cited in the present work, and I shall continue to draw upon them in this chapter while making no effort to duplicate the more exhaustive treatment of local politics that they offer. The focus here is a comparative one, paying special attention to significant differences and similarities in the local politics of these cities and in their relation to Paris. The discussion will be substantial enough, I hope, to make compelling the interpretation offered though not so extensive as to overwhelm the reader with detail.

Let us begin with Caen and Bordeaux, where politics were relatively more consensual in the first years of the Revolution than in Lyon and Marseille. This is not to say that the political control of the social elite was never challenged in Caen and Bordeaux, but rather that the popular classes were never successful in wresting any share of political power from their hands, at least not until after the federalist revolt. Whereas in Lyon and Marseille the local Jacobin clubs managed to achieve a degree of political power on the municipal councils elected in late 1792 or early 1793, in Caen and Bordeaux the social elite succeeded in either neutralizing or co-opting the local clubs, principally through their control of the local administrative bodies.

BORDEAUX

In Bordeaux, indeed, the most powerful political club was a vehicle for the mercantile and legal elite of the city. The *Amis de la Liberté et de l'Egalité* was founded in 1790 by men who would dominate the local administrative bodies and eventually go on to represent the Gironde in the National Convention. Vergniaud, Guadet, Gensonné, Grangeneuve, Ducos, and Boyer-Fonfrède, all proscribed from the National Convention in June 1793, were among its founding members. Pierre Sers, who presided over the federalist Popular Commission, was also among the founders. By 1792, Alan Forrest has observed, "nearly everyone concerned in the running of the city could be numbered among" its two thousand members.[2] Although the membership was large, it did not extend beyond the propertied classes of Bordeaux. At its founding, the entry fee for members was twelve livres, with monthly dues of three livres, and even when those figures were halved in 1791 they remained prohibitive to the artisan and working population of the city. From 1790 through 1793 the *Amis* was a dominant political force in Bordeaux by virtue of its members' positions in elected office but also as a powerful lobbying force committed, as Forrest puts it, "to the maintenance of the established order."[3]

The *Amis de la Liberté et de l'Egalité* was not the only political club in Bordeaux. Several others formed in 1790 and 1791, including an active women's club, though most of these were short-lived. The *Amis'* most vigorous rival was the *Club du Café National*, which by 1792–93 was championing the Montagnard cause in Bordeaux. But in its early days the Club National enjoyed amicable relations with the *Amis*—indeed, one could be a member of both clubs, and the two societies regularly exchanged addresses and shared petitions. Although the Club National concerned itself with the plight of the poor more than its rival, it did not welcome them to membership, which came predominantly from the middling merchant class and liberal professions. Not until after the federalist revolt would the Club National open its doors to artisans and working men.

Still, despite its respectable membership, the more activist agenda of the Club National was a source of alarm to local authorities even at its foundation. While the *Amis* stressed obedience to the laws and respect for property in their early declarations and constitution, the Club National pledged to be the "defender of the sovereignty of the people" and a watchdog over elected officials. As early as December 1790, such expressed ideals prompted Armand Gensonné, then *procureur* of the municipal council, to warn the members of the Club National that "it is against all the principles of the Constitution, contrary to the essence of the government that we have adopted, that a society of any sort should set itself up as a tribunal, should receive complaints, should exercise a sort of public censure."[4] Gensonné conveniently ignored that no constitution had yet been adopted by the National Assembly, and the national debate over the legality of clubs and the limits to the legitimate role that they might play in the political life of the nation still lay in the future, but his speech conveyed very well the consensus among the Bordeaux elite that the clubs should play a secondary role to the duly constituted elected authorities.[5]

---

2. Forrest, *Society and Politics*, 66.
3. Ibid., 67–68.
4. Ibid., 64.
5. On the debate over the legality of political clubs, see Michael L. Kennedy, "The Best and the Worst of Times: The Jacobin Club Network from October 1791 to June 2, 1793," *Journal of Modern History* 56, no. 4 (December 1984): 635–66; and Paul R. Hanson, "Monarchist Clubs and

Despite its more conservative character, it was the *Amis de la Liberté* and not the Club National that was affiliated with the Jacobin club in Paris, which by its own constitution restricted its affiliations to one club per provincial town. The Bordeaux *Amis* retained that affiliation after the Feuillant schism of summer 1791, but in late 1792 relations between the *Amis* and the mother society, and between the *Amis* and the Club National, grew increasingly strained. The September massacres in Paris were a focal point in that growing estrangement. The *Amis* followed the lead of their most prominent founding members, now deputies in the National Convention, and condemned the massacres as well as those leading Jacobins, such as Robespierre and Marat, who tacitly condoned or perhaps instigated the killing. The Club National refused to make such a condemnation, and in the eyes of the Bordeaux elite, most of whom were members of the *Amis de la Liberté*, this rendered the rival clubbists virtual allies of the anarchists in Paris. In February 1793 the *Amis* lost their affiliation with the Paris Jacobins, who now chose to grant that coveted status to the Club National. Scarcely had its members learned of their good fortune then they received the March 8 decree of the Bordeaux municipal council closing the doors of their club.

As Alan Forrest has observed, however, more important than the controversy over the September massacres in determining the fate of the Club National was "its attitude to the whole question of authority and its growing commitment to the ideals of popular sovereignty."[6] As we saw in Chapter 2, Robespierre had credited "the people" with the toppling of the monarchy in August 1792, and that "people" had found its clearest expression and organization in the militant sectional assemblies of Paris. Inspired by that example and having been stymied by its own lack of affiliation with the Paris Jacobins and by its nonpresence on the elected councils of Bordeaux and the department, the Club National mounted an effort in the fall months first to create a Central Committee of the Bordeaux sections and then to pass a referendum that would allow the sections to meet *en permanence*.

Ironically enough, the Club National succeeded on both counts, but with little positive effect for its own future political influence. A Central Committee of the sectional assemblies began meeting in September 1792, but there was so little unity among the sections or enthusiasm for this project that a municipal council order in late November dissolving the Central Committee met with little resistance. The campaign for the permanence of sectional assemblies, again modeled on Paris, further antagonized both the municipal council and the *Amis*

the Pamphlet Debate over Political Legitimacy in the Early Years of the French Revolution," *French Historical Studies* 21, no. 2 (spring 1998): 299–324.

6. Forrest, *Society and Politics*, 75.

de la Liberté. The Club National was clearly searching for a way to mobilize the urban populace and broaden its base of support in Bordeaux. But by the time club supporters had gained a narrow victory in the referendum to grant the permanence of sectional assemblies, in April, the club itself had been closed down by municipal decree. The first significant action taken by the Bordeaux sections, meeting *en permanence,* was to declare their support for the federalist revolt in June.

Why was it so easy for the Bordeaux municipal council and the *Amis de la Liberté* to turn back this challenge from the Club National, first by dissolving the Central Committee of the sections and then by closing the Club National? The answer lies partly in the urban geography of Bordeaux, in the makeup of the sections themselves, and partly in the paternalistic attitude taken by the Bordeaux elite toward the working poor of the city. There were twenty-eight sections in Bordeaux, ranging in population from just under 1,000 (section 28) to nearly 5,000 (section 5) (see map 2). Early in the Revolution, only active citizens were allowed to attend sectional assemblies and only at the invitation of the municipal council. Their role was seen as consultative—they were not meant to initiate proposals for public policy but rather should defer to elected officials.

The most populous sections were located in the Chartrons district and in the old center of the city (sections 2–10). Although some clerks and workers associated with the port lived in these sectins, they were predominantly the neighborhoods of the mercantile and legal elite of Bordeaux, and the domination of that elite in sectional assemblies gave them a profoundly conservative character. Only two of these sections (4 and 10) voted in favor of permanence in spring 1793. The sections that favored permanence tended to be located in the faubourgs of Bordeaux, particularly those of the south and southwest (sections 1, 11, 12, 13, 14, 16, 17, 18, 20, 21, 22, and 26 voted in favor of permanence). These were the poorest neighborhoods of the city, inhabited by workers and artisans. Not only were these sections located on the periphery of the city, but the most militant among them, section Francklin (section 14), the stronghold of the Club National, was located some distance from most of the others. Their peripheral location, their dispersion, and their relatively low population density all worked against the emergence of popular militancy in these sections of Bordeaux.[7]

But the failure of the Club National to galvanize support for its populist agenda was also due to the paternalistic attitude toward the poor taken by the Bordeaux elite, and to the fact that no burning issue or controversy emerged in the early years of the Revolution to jolt the popular classes out of their passivity. In Paris, as George Rudé has shown, the political mobilization of the crowd

---

7. Ibid., 75–87, see note 67 for the breakdown of the vote on sectional permanence.

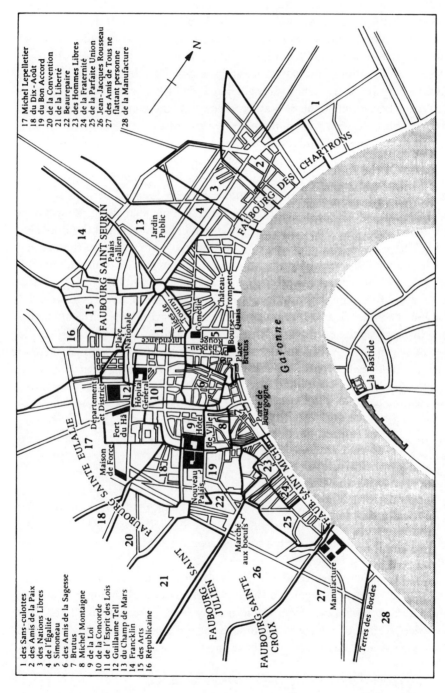

Map 2. The City of Bordeaux with Its Twenty-eight Sections (Source: Alan Forrest, *Society and Politics in Revolutionary Bordeaux* [Oxford, 1975], 79)

tended to coincide with periods of bread scarcity and rising prices.[8] Local authorities in Bordeaux never warmed to the idea of price controls, not even in 1793 when the *maximum* was introduced as national policy. But the municipal council did vote generous subsidies to bakers so that the poor could afford to buy bread even during periods of inflation, a policy made possible by the extraordinary growth of the Bordeaux economy over the course of the eighteenth century. The one moment of market violence in these years came in March 1793, a politically sensitive moment to be sure, just as the municipal council was about to close the Club National and on the eve of the vote on sectional permanence. What instigated the market riots is described by Forrest as essentially a misunderstanding. The municipal council had voted to shift the bread indemnity from the bakers to the sections, a move designed perhaps to allow verification of the true need of those benefiting, but one that also made sectional assemblies beholden to the largesse of the municipal council and the Bordeaux elite. This paternalism of the local authorities served to reinforce the patron-client relations that had long characterized the commercial economy of Bordeaux and to preserve the loyalty of most sectional assemblies to the political leadership of the city. Only in the waning days of the federalist revolt did a handful of sections, led by Francklin, mount a serious challenge to the municipal elite that had led their city down such a perilous path.[9]

The nature of municipal politics in Bordeaux stood in stark contrast, then, to Parisian municipal politics, and the city fathers of Bordeaux must have been perplexed, if not appalled, at the inability of the National Convention to control the unruliness of the Parisian populace. There was a consonance of view between the deputies of the Gironde in Paris—Vergniaud, Gensonné, Guadet, and the others—and their former colleagues on the municipal and departmental councils back in Bordeaux. The sovereignty of the people was vested in their elected officials, in that view, and the people owed respect and obedience to those officials and above all to the law. The apparent gross disregard of the Parisian crowd (egged on by Jacobin radicals) for both the law and elected officials (especially those officials whom they, the Bordelais, had elected!) represented a threat not only to the unity of the republic but to the placid stability of political life in Bordeaux.

The experience of that relatively mild political contention in Bordeaux in late 1792 and early 1793 also colored the response, and understanding, of the Bordeaux elite to the reports from Lyon in early June. Bordeaux, like Lyon, had seen the creation of a Central Committee of the sections; and Bordeaux, like Lyon, had seen a radical club challenge the traditional elite of the city, but in

8. George Rudé, *The Crowd in the French Revolution* (Oxford, 1959).
9. Forrest, *Society and Politics*, 198–200.

Lyon both the Central Committee and the Jacobin club were more powerful than their counterparts in Bordeaux. In Caen, by comparison, the social elite was at least as successful as that of Bordeaux in maintaining control of the political arena.

CAEN

Caen was the smallest of the four federalist cities, with a population in 1793 of roughly 35,000 (Bordeaux and Marseille numbered just under 110,000 inhabitants, and Lyon 150,000 inhabitants in 1790). As with Bordeaux, Caen's economy had flourished during the eighteenth century, particularly between 1725 and 1775, when the population had grown from 27,000 to 40,000. Immigration accounted for approximately 75 percent of that population growth, and most of the immigrants settled in the newer faubourgs of the city. Although Caen, unlike the other three cities, was not a major port, its commercial activity had increased over the course of the century and its leading merchants had dreams of dredging the Orne River in order to make Caen accessible to seagoing vessels. Textile production, once dominant in the urban economy, had declined since 1725 and within that sector production had shifted from woolens to linens and finally to lacemaking, and it also became increasingly rural. Lace was a commercial commodity par excellence—it required little capital investment, it utilized cheap labor (predominantly women and children), and its market extended from Paris and the Breton coast to the North Sea. Thus, on the eve of the Revolution, Caen featured a relatively prosperous commercial economy with a workforce composed of a modest number of wage earners (split between the productive and service sectors), a substantial portion of whom were recent immigrants to the city, working alongside a significant number of artisans and small shopkeepers.[10]

Despite its modest population, Caen was characterized by what Jean-Claude Perrot has described as a level of urbanization that "surpassed Paris, four large ports and several celebrated cities of the interior."[11] After approximately 1770, when the central parishes of the city reached their saturation point, immigrants to Caen tended to settle in the faubourgs of the city, most notably in the faubourg Vaucelles, separated from the central parishes of Caen by the river. Caen's neighborhoods, like those of a modern city, were characterized by a high

10. See Paul R. Hanson, *Provincial Politics in the French Revolution: Caen and Limoges, 1789–1794* (Baton Rouge, 1989), 16–30, for a more extensive discussion of the local economy and social structure of Caen. The most important source on this subject is Jean-Claude Perrot, *Genèse d'une ville moderne: Caen au XVIIIe siècle* (Paris, 1975), 2 vols.
11. Perrot, *Genèse d'une ville moderne*, vol. 2, 951.

degree of social differentiation, with the commercial, legal, and church elite concentrated in the central parishes. The faubourgs resembled small villages, very tightly knit and communal and never well integrated in municipal affairs, either before or during the Revolution.[12]

The Caen political elite took advantage of this urban geography when it drew up sectional boundaries in 1790. Rather than create a large number of relatively small sections, which might have fostered neighborhood politics, the municipal council drew up boundaries for just five sections, averaging some 7,000 inhabitants each (see map 3). The central parishes of the city all lay within three of those sections—Liberté, Civisme, and Fermeté. While the latter two each embraced a sliver of the faubourgs, the bulk of the faubourgs were contained in sections Union and Egalité, and the immigrant population of those two sections was barely represented on the Caen municipal council during the first four years of the Revolution. Of the eighty municipal officers elected to five councils between 1790 and 1793, seventy came from sections Liberté, Civisme, and Fermeté, while only eight came from sections Union and Egalité.[13]

This is not to say that municipal politics in Caen was unchanging during those years. Although the commercial elite played a prominent role on each of the five councils, a substantial contingent of artisans and shopkeepers had replaced the wealthy aristocrats and men of law whose presence had been notable on the first two councils. The shift in the social makeup of the council toward men of more modest means was paralleled by a geographic shift from section Liberté toward section Civisme, the heart of the commercial and artisanal district of Caen.[14]

Politics were generally calm in the city, however, and what political upheaval there was was generally directed toward the noble elite of the Old Regime. In August 1789, an angry crowd killed and dismembered the viscount Henri de Belzunce who had taunted and antagonized members of the newly formed National Guard.[15] Two years later, in the midst of controversy over the Civil Constitution of the Clergy, a crisis erupted on the eve of municipal elections. On the evening of November 5, 1791, eighty-four aristocrats and wealthy bourgeois were arrested after a skirmish outside one of Caen's parish churches. Papers found in their possession made reference to a coalition of aristocrats, allegedly formed to protect "persons and property." The evidence was sketchy and ambiguous, but it was enough in the eyes of municipal authorities to justify locking up the eighty-four in Caen's dungeon and charging them with conspiracy. They stayed in the Château (where Romme and Prieur would be held during the

---

12. Ibid., vol. 1, 54–55, 267, 525; vol. 2, 605, 622, 634–35, 811–16, 926.
13. Hanson, *Provincial Politics*, 217–22.
14. Ibid. See tables on 210 and 220.
15. Ibid., 34–36.

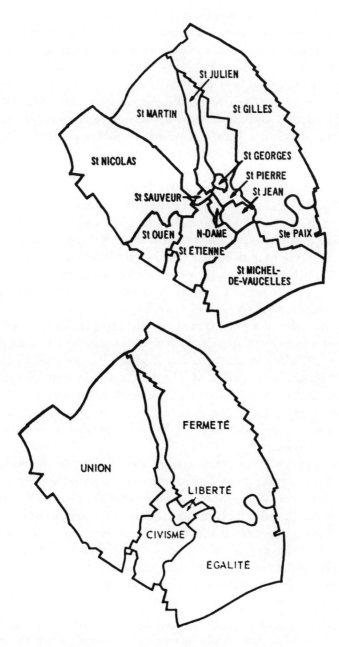

Map 3.   The Parishes and Sections of Caen (Source:
Jean-Claude Perrot, *La Genäse d'une ville moderne*
[Paris, 1975], vol. 1, 43)

federalist revolt) for three months, until the Legislative Assembly ordered the release of all but two of them. The "conspiracy" amounted to little more than a series of meetings in aristocratic households aimed at proposing suitable candidates for the upcoming municipal elections in order to counter the growing influence of the Caen Jacobin club.[16]

The Jacobin club in Caen, founded in August 1790, was neither the bastion of the political elite, as the club in Bordeaux had proved to be, nor as militant and activist as the clubs in Lyon and Marseille would be in 1792–93. The Affair of 84 reveals clearly that the traditional elite of Caen had concerns about the influence of the Jacobins in late 1791. But while the affair and its aftermath marked an end to the dominance of Old Regime nobles and *rentiers* in Caen municipal politics and the rise of the commercial elite, it did not bring the ascendancy of the Jacobin club. Jacobin club members were active in local politics, but no more than three Jacobins sat on the municipal council at any one time. In the months following the Affair of 84, local authorities moved to curb the influence of the Jacobin club, and that history tells us something both about the dynamics of local politics in Caen and about the interaction between local and national politics in the city.[17]

When the Affair of 84 first came to public attention, the Jacobin club had pressured the municipal council to make arrests. In late January 1791, when the Legislative Assembly ordered the release of nearly all those arrested, the Jacobin club and National Guard protested. Their anger was directed more toward the government in Paris than toward local authorities, however, since no elected officials were implicated in the affair and the municipal and district councils went so far as to appeal the decision of the Legislative Assembly before carrying it out on February 3.

At this same time, controversy erupted over the jury list proposed for the departmental criminal tribunal by the *procureur-général-syndic* Georges Bayeux. An unruly crowd of club members and guardsmen had blocked the installation of the tribunal, scheduled for January 23, asserting that aristocrats outnumbered patriots on the jury list. On the following day, a delegation from the Caen Jacobin club, led by Louis Caille and Chaix-d'Estanges, invaded the meeting room of the departmental directory to sustain the protest, denouncing, in particular, the inclusion on the jury list of two university professors who had recently

---

16. Ibid., 39–43.
17. Archival documentation for the Caen Jacobin club is relatively thin. No membership roll has survived in the archives, nor does anything approaching a complete set of minutes exist, though scattered papers, declarations and reports can be found in the municipal and departmental archives, the Caen library, and in the National Archives as well. My discussion here relies principally on the following sources: Hanson, *Provincial Politics*; Hanson, "Les Clubs politiques de Caen pendant la Révolution française," *Annales de Normandie* 36 (1986): 123–41; and Michael L. Kennedy, *The Jacobin Clubs in the French Revolution: The First Years* (Princeton, 1982).

signed a public letter opposing the constitutional oath of the clergy. Although offended by the public disruption and the challenge to their own authority, the departmental directory eventually agreed to a compromise and the tribunal was installed on February 11, the two professors having been dropped from the jury list. Georges Bayeux withdrew from public life, but the campaign of public denunciation against him continued. He was arrested just after the fall of the monarchy and killed by an angry crowd when the Legislative Assembly ordered his release. Bayeux met his fate on September 6, the penultimate day of the prison massacres in Paris.

More significant than the fate of Bayeux or the ultimate makeup of the jury list was the impact this confrontation had on the role of the Jacobin club in Caen political life and its relation to local authorities. The Jacobin club had been active in Caen politics since its founding in late 1790. The issue that most aroused the attention of its members was the debate over the Civil Constitution of the Clergy, and this may explain the zeal of the club in regard to the criminal tribunal. Several men who held prominent departmental positions in 1792–93 played leading roles in founding the club, but in late 1791 and early 1792 the dominant force was Claude Fauchet, who had been elected constitutional bishop of Calvados in May 1791.

There are countless examples of men who began their revolutionary careers at the local level and later played a major role in national politics in Paris— Roland, Barbaroux, Vergniaud, and Lindet are just a few who fit that profile. But in Fauchet we have an individual of national prominence who made his reputation in Paris then went to Calvados to stir things up before being sent back to the capital as a deputy to the National Convention. He is an example of one who moved against the current, so to speak, in establishing a personal link between Paris and the provinces. Fauchet touted himself for having been among *"les vainqueurs de la Bastille,"* but he was most widely known for his leading role in the *Cercle Social,* a club associated in 1791 with the nascent democratic movement of the capital but by 1793 more closely allied with the Rolands and the Girondin deputies.[18]

Fauchet arrived in Calvados, then, with a reputation as something of a radical, and he quickly moved to stimulate more dynamism in the proceedings of the Caen Jacobin club. So successful was he in those efforts that in August 1791 the departmental directory petitioned the minister of the interior, requesting permission to shift their meetings from Caen to the nearby town of Bayeux in order to escape the intimidating presence of the club.[19] As the events of the following February make clear, they were unsuccessful in that petition.

18. Gary Kates, *The "Cercle Social," the Girondins, and the French Revolution* (Princeton, 1985).
19. A.N., F⁷ 3661¹.

The two men who led the protest of the jury list, Louis Caille and Chaix-d'Estanges, were both political acolytes of Bishop Fauchet (Chaix served as his vicar). Faced with the growing militancy of the club and the broadening power base of Fauchet, the departmental administration now tried a different tactic.

Gustave Doulcet de Pontécoulant, a liberal nobleman, was president of the departmental administration at the time, and in that capacity he wrote several letters reporting on the controversy to Cahier de Gerville, then minister of the interior. Doulcet acknowledged that the jury list, the root of the problem, was *"véritablement fort mauvais"* and merited change but noted the directory's reluctance to cede to popular demand by changing it. On February 2, however, Doulcet was able to report a tactical victory to the minister. Assisted by the young secretary of the administration, Bougon-Longrais, Doulcet had managed to drive a wedge between Chaix and Caille at a meeting of the club and had succeeded in neutralizing the popular tumult. As he exultantly concluded to the minister: "At the end of the meeting I was elected President of the Club. I learned of it this morning from a large number of good citizens of this town who had long since ceased going there. They pressed me, they demanded that I accept; myself, I demanded that they attend meetings regularly, and I volunteered. There is the battle decidedly engaged and suffering a necessary fight to the death. Either we restore the authority of the law in Caen, and respect for it in the Club, or we abandon all, business and the country."[20]

In subsequent letters, Doulcet reported presiding over heavily attended, and peaceful, club meetings, and he contemplated making an example of Chaix and Caille. His impulse was restrained, however, by the realization that the two enjoyed the support of Fauchet and by his recognition that they exercised a "prodigious influence over the people of the faubourgs." Doulcet's judgment proved to be sound. Chaix and Caille continued as active members of the Jacobin club (Caille would in fact sit as president two months later), but the club was never again a thorn in the side of elected officials.

In the midst of the crisis over the Affair of 84 and the criminal tribunal, Caille journeyed to Paris, no doubt seeking allies for the Caen Jacobins. But instead he reportedly wrangled with Robespierre and found Charles Barbaroux to be far more sympathetic. As the year wore on, the Caen Jacobins grew increasingly disenchanted with the views and policies laid down by the mother society, and the fall elections were not favorable to the Jacobins and their allies in Caen. Doulcet and Fauchet were elected as deputies to the National Convention, where both eventually allied themselves with the Girondin faction. Indeed, only one of the thirteen Calvados deputies to the Convention—Bonnet de Meau-

20. Ibid.

try—sat with the Montagnards. Bonnet alone dissented from the view of the Calvados delegation, offered by letter when the Caen club sought advice regarding their affiliation with the Paris Jacobins in the wake of the September massacres. Encouraged by their deputies in a course of action toward which they were already inclined, the Caen Jacobins soon severed their ties with the mother society.

Thus, the resolution of a crisis that had threatened to sow political divisions in Caen and mobilize at least a portion of the populace against their elected officials not only managed to keep the peace in early 1792, but also created new political ties that would prove to be important in 1793. Louis Caille, the firebrand of January, was elected *procureur-syndic* of the district administration in the fall, responsible now for enforcing the law rather than flouting it. Doulcet and Fauchet, once competing for influence on the local scene, now sat as allies in the National Convention. Chaix-d'Estanges remained in Caen as curé of the parish St. Etienne, one of the most important in the city. And Bougon-Longrais, who had been helpful to Doulcet in taming the Jacobin club, was elected *procureur-général-syndic* of the departmental administration. In June 1793, each of these men played a role in leading Caen toward revolt.

Even before the split between the Jacobins in Caen and the Paris club, the Caen political elite had taken steps to counter the influence of the Caen club among the popular classes. Early in the Revolution, though the precise date of its origin is obscure, another club appeared in Caen, known as the Carabots. The club had its roots in the popular militia formed during summer 1789— Carabots was reportedly a derivation of *caporaux* (corporals), the rank held by most of its early members. The Carabots, then, were small shopkeepers, artisans, and clerks, and the club seems to have operated more as an informal fraternity than an organized society for the first years of its existence. That changed in February 1793, when fifty Carabots assembled on the Place de la Liberté, a central square ringed by the homes of wealthy *négociants*, to declare formally their political creed. They swore "to maintain the Republic—one, indivisible, and popular—liberty, and equality; to observe the laws that had these principles as their foundation; to exterminate all those who wanted another government." Their declared motto was, "Execution of the law, or death."[21]

The limited evidence we have about the Carabots suggests that they acted as a client group to the departmental administration and the merchant elite of Caen. Several departmental administrators were reportedly members of the

21. See Frédéric Vaultier, *Souvenirs de l'insurrection Normande, dite du Fédéralisme, en 1793* (Caen, 1858), 9–11 and 126–37; Charles Renard, *Notice sur les Carabots de Caen* (Caen, 1858), located in B.M. Caen, Rés. Fn. Br. C315–368; Georges Mancel, *La Société des Carabots* (Caen, 1857); and Hanson, *Provincial Politics*, 51–53.

club, and in the months following their formal installation the club frequently performed tasks at the behest of the administration—assisting with recruitment in March, requisitioning grain and carrying out domiciliary searches in April, inspecting foreign mail in May. The most prominent leader of the Carabots, Jean-Michel Barbot, was chief clerk at the Tribunal of Commerce, presided over by Samuel Chatry, a prominent Caen *négociant*, active in municipal politics and among the most energetic of the federalist leaders in Caen. In June 1793, a number of Carabots accompanied administrators on their journey to Bayeux to arrest the representatives on mission, Romme and Prieur; and late in the month it would be Carabot members, led by Barbot, who formed the core of the Caen volunteer force, paltry though it was, as it marched to Evreux.

As in Bordeaux, the Caen elite effectively controlled the political arena, though the dynamics of local politics in the two cities differed in some respects. In Bordeaux the elite dominated the Jacobin club and with some difficulty turned back a challenge from the more radical Club National in early 1793. In Caen, the Jacobin club itself presented a challenge to local authorities in 1792, one which they met by establishing a more active presence within the club and by patronizing an alternative society, the Carabots. In Bordeaux, sectional activism was effectively harnessed by the municipal and departmental administrations, whereas in Caen there was no sectional movement to speak of. In both cities the immigrant population of the faubourgs was politically marginalized and largely passive throughout the early years of the Revolution, and local politics were controlled by the propertied elite. The republic they desired, so well expressed by the Carabot motto, was one in which respect for the law would be paramount.

In both Lyon and Marseille, by contrast, local politics in the early years of the Revolution were far more contentious, and the political control of the propertied elite was far more tenuous. Indeed, the political elite lost control of the municipal council in both cities in early 1793, regained it through sectional uprisings in the spring, only to lose it once again in the aftermath of the federalist revolt. On the face of it, popular politics look to have been more vital in Lyon and Marseille than in either Bordeaux or Caen, and the sectional movement in the two cities appears to have given the federalist revolt a certain popular base. In both cities, sectional assemblies battled Jacobin clubs, each claiming the mantle of popular sovereignty. But while the outlines of the struggle in Lyon and Marseille seem quite similar, both the club movement and the sectional movement differed in each. An understanding of those differences, and the factors that produced them, will enhance not only our understanding of the local political context out of which the federalist revolt emerged in Lyon and Marseille, but it will also broaden our appreciation of the debate over sovereignty that raged throughout the nation in winter and spring 1793.

LYON

Revolutionary politics in Lyon were enormously complicated, and the following pages can only begin to suggest their complexity and to make clear the folly of easy generalization. With a population of roughly 150,000, the Lyonnais prided themselves at being the second city of France, and a very wealthy city, but one that had experienced an economic downturn in the last decades of the Old Regime.[22] Unlike the other large provincial cities of France, including both Marseille and Bordeaux, Lyon's economy was not buoyed over the course of the century by the expansion of overseas commerce.[23] Lyon's economy relied principally on silkweaving, and unlike the other major textile centers of France, including Caen, the weaving industry of Lyon remained confined to the city itself. Roughly a third of Lyon's population relied for their livelihood either directly or indirectly on the silk industry, which had been in decline for most of the eighteenth century. The value of Lyon silks sold in France dropped by 30 percent between 1769 and 1783, and the 1786 trade treaty with England dealt a severe blow to the industry. Silkworkers engaged in a futile work stoppage in that year, brutally repressed by the city's elite, and by 1789 roughly 22,000 weavers in Lyon were unemployed.[24]

The presence of a large artisanal workforce, concentrated in a single industry racked by economic difficulties, was clearly an important factor in Lyon politics during the early years of the Revolution. It was to this segment of the population that Joseph Chalier and the Jacobins made their strongest appeal in 1792–93. But the *menu peuple* (literally, "little people") of Lyon became active in revolutionary politics as early as 1790, and the character of the Lyon elite is as important as the slumping silk industry in explaining that early activism. Although silk may have dominated the Lyon economy in the eighteenth century, it cannot be said that the silkweaving mercantile elite dominated the social and political life of the city on the eve of the Revolution.

That role was played by a rather narrow group of extremely wealthy aristocratic families who exercised their control of Lyon affairs by virtue of their positions as *échevins* on the Lyon municipal council, known as the Consulat. The Consulat represented a very different sort of municipal politics from that ushered in by the Revolution. There were only four *échevins*, who sat for a two-year term, elected on an annual basis (two each year) by an assembly that was

22. The essential source for the history of Lyon in the eighteenth century is Maurice Garden, *Lyon et les Lyonnais au XVIIIe siècle* (Paris, 1970); for a brief description of Lyon on the eve of the Revolution, see Edmonds, *Jacobinism and the Revolt of Lyon, 1789–1793* (Oxford, 1990), 8–37.

23. Edmonds, *Jacobinism and the Revolt of Lyon*, 17.

24. Ibid., 13–14; and David L. Longfellow, "Silk Weavers and the Social Struggle in Lyon during the French Revolution, 1789–1794," *French Historical Studies* 12, no. 1 (1981): 1–40.

itself dominated by the families of past and present *échevins*. A single term of office conferred nobility. This consular group of noble families, complemented by the magisterial elite of the two most important royal courts in Lyon, the *Cour des Monnaies* and the *Cour de la conservation*, formed a local aristocracy that, though not ancient in its lineage, was far more wealthy than the mercantile elite and was also extremely insular.

Although this predominantly aristocratic elite dominated civic affairs in Lyon, the world of trade and business was controlled by the roughly four hundred *marchands-fabricants* who managed the highly capitalistic silk industry. The economic slump of mid to late century had curtailed their affluence somewhat, but more important, it had widened the gap within the industry between the *marchands-fabricants* and the masters and journeymen who worked the looms. The merchants themselves, while wealthy, were not nearly so wealthy as the aristocratic oligarchy of Lyon, and there was very little intermarriage or social contact between the two groups. Nor was there much interaction between the merchant elite and the other bourgeois professionals of Lyon. The merchants had the reputation, both among the aristocracy and among other bourgeois, of caring only for money. As Bill Edmonds has concluded, "Beyond the sense of distance from the labouring poor, there was little coherence in Lyonnais bourgeois culture on the eve of the Revolution." There was little or no interaction between the mercantile and intellectual elites and little sense of civic involvement among the wealthy merchants. The silk merchants bristled at their social inferiority to the Consular aristocracy, but they were jealously proud of their superiority to the artisans.[25]

Thus, in contrast to Bordeaux and Caen, both prospering cities where the merchant elite stepped eagerly into revolutionary municipal politics in 1789, in Lyon we find a divided elite in a city where economic hardship and social tensions had produced urban unrest as recently as 1786. These divisions within the Lyon elite rendered them incapable of asserting political control in the authority vacuum created by the collapse of Old Regime institutions, and this opened up a political space for the activism of the artisanal population. Two issues in particular drew popular protest. In July 1789 the officers of the Consulat created a new *corps de volontaires* to preserve public order. These seven companies of 120 men each were drawn essentially from the families and employees of the propertied elite, and their creation drew almost immediate opposition, not least because the Consulat seemed intent on thwarting the creation of an independent National Guard. Then in January 1790, "the Consulat established the highest possible tax qualification for active citizenship," and the two issues in combina-

25. Edmonds, *Jacobinism and the Revolt of Lyon*, 20–26; the passage quoted is found on page 26.

tion provoked public agitation both among the middling bourgeoisie and the artisanal population.[26]

That agitation exploded into violence on February 7, in a popular insurrection that had far-reaching consequences. The target of the uprising was the Lyon Arsenal, where the president of the Consulat, Jacques Imbert-Colomès, had recently posted an armed contingent of *volontaires*. After the crowd easily overcame the *volontaires* and seized thousands of weapons, Imbert-Colomès fled Lyon. Under public pressure the remaining *échevins* cut the tax qualification for the right to vote in half and disbanded the *corps de volontaires*. These events did not bring an immediate transformation of municipal politics in Lyon, but the old elite no longer had a monopoly on armed force, and the people of Lyon had proven to themselves that change was indeed possible.[27]

Two men already known to us—they would be on opposite sides of the political divide of 1793—played important roles in the mobilization of popular politics in Lyon in 1790–91, although neither could be said to have been a man of the people. Jean-Marie Roland and Joseph Chalier were both among the notables elected to the Lyon municipal council in February 1790. Chalier resigned his post, though he was returned to the council as an *officier* in November 1791. Roland served on the municipal council through the end of 1791, when he and his wife left Lyon permanently for Paris. The Rolands had spent the previous summer in the capital as lobbyists for the Lyon council, seeking relief of municipal debt from the Constituent Assembly. The political contacts that they made during that period would bring Roland the position of minister of the interior in March 1792.[28]

Roland and Chalier are interesting, and surprisingly similar, political figures in a number of ways. Both were "outsiders" to Lyon. Roland was born in the nearby Beaujolais but spent his early career in Amiens before being appointed royal inspector of manufactures in Lyon in 1784. Chalier was born near Briançon, high in the Dauphiné Alps, and moved to Lyon as a young man in the 1760s to earn his living as a teacher.[29] Both traveled widely in Europe in the 1770s and 1780s, principally in the countries of the Mediterranean. Both were familiar with the world of commerce, though not comfortable in it. Neither was particularly effective as a revolutionary politician, though both were influen-

26. Ibid., 47–49.
27. Ibid., 49–54.
28. The best biography of Roland in English is C. A. Le Guin, *Roland de la Platière: A Public Servant in the Eighteenth Century* (Philadelphia, 1966); the best biography of Chalier remains the short essay by Maurice Wahl, "Joseph Chalier: Etude sur la Révolution française à Lyon," *Revue Historique* 34 (1887): 1–30; see also Edmonds, *Jacobinism and the Revolt of Lyon*, passim.
29. It is interesting to think of Roland and Chalier in the context of the argument that Lynn Hunt has made about the role of outsiders in revolutionary politics. See L. Hunt, *Politics, Culture and Class in the French Revolution* (Berkeley, 1984), chap. 6.

tial—it is impossible to think of Lyonnais politics in the Revolution without placing them at the center of the picture. Both men died in 1793: Roland by his own hand, Chalier on the guillotine.

In 1790 both Roland and Chalier were publicly critical of the merchant elite of Lyon. As early as 1788 Roland had published an essay advocating deregulation of the silk industry, and in the first year of the Revolution he chided the merchant community for its selfishness and lack of civic virtue. While Roland's perspective on the Lyonnais world of commerce was that of inspector, Chalier's was a view from within. He had begun his early teaching career tutoring the children of wealthy *négociants* and moved from that position into the world of commerce itself. He had traveled the Mediterranean as a business agent for two merchant families, the Muguets and then the Bertrands, and had done quite well for himself. When elected to municipal office in 1790, Chalier listed his occupation as *négociant*. His fellow merchants were hardly pleased, however, to read Chalier's February 1790 article in Loustalot's *Révolutions de Paris*, where he described Lyon as "more anchored in aristocracy than ever," a "perfidious city that harbors more sworn enemies of the happiest and most astonishing of revolutions than any other city in France."[30] Chalier found Paris more congenial. He visited the capital in 1789; made contact with Desmoulins, Marat, and Robespierre; acquired a rock from the Bastille during its demolition; was swept up by revolutionary enthusiasm and could scarcely tolerate the revolutionary torpor of the Lyon civic elite. From February 1790 on, that elite viewed Chalier as a kind of traitor not only to his city, but to his class.

In the aftermath of the February 1790 riots, a network of neighborhood clubs began to emerge. By year's end each of the thirty-two sections of Lyon had a club. Each of those neighborhood clubs (and unlike most cities, the electoral sections created by revolutionary legislation were roughly coterminous with the old neighborhoods in Lyon), open to artisans and bourgeois alike, sent three delegates to regular meetings of the Club Central, which were also open to the public. It was at the Club Central that Joseph Chalier wielded his greatest influence, and in the eyes of the propertied elite the Club Central came to symbolize the potential power of an organized popular movement. In Lyon, despite its reputation as a bastion of royalist counterrevolution, there were signs of what we would today call popular democracy, based in the sectional clubs, well in advance of the *sans-culotte* movement that grew out of the sectional assemblies of Paris. Indeed, the salutary example set by the Lyon clubs was trumpeted to the nation in February 1791 by the Parisian journalist Lanthénas in his newspaper *Le Patriote français*.[31]

30. Wahl, "Joseph Chalier," 5.
31. Edmonds, *Jacobinism and the Revolt of Lyon*, 71.

It is important to bear in mind the extremely volatile situation in Lyon, due in part to the continued high unemployment in the silk industry, but also because of the difficulty in securing adequate provisions for the city's population and the fact that Lyon's proximity to the eastern frontier (and its size) made it an attractive haven for fugitive *émigrés* and refractory priests. No municipal council, no matter what its political persuasion or social composition might be, could possibly solve all of these problems. The best they could hope for was to maintain some semblance of public order and civic peace, which the all-too-frequent food shortages or rumors of counterrevolutionary conspiracies constantly threatened to undermine.

It is significant that Lyon's club movement was based in the sections, and significant as well that those sections were based on the traditional neighborhoods of the city. Some sense of the social geography of Lyon is important, then, to an understanding of the dynamics of the club movement that transformed municipal politics in the city in 1791–92. Revolutionary Lyon was divided into thirty-two electoral sections (four of the twenty-eight traditional *quartiers* were split into two sections; see map 4). Two major rivers, the Saône and the Rhône, run through the city, although in the eighteenth century almost all of the city proper lay to the west of the Rhône River. Over the course of the seventeenth and eighteenth centuries, the commercial and administrative heart of Lyon shifted from the right bank of the Saône River to the areas around the Place Bellecour and the Place des Terreaux, located on the strip of land between the two rivers that is today known as the Presqu'Ile.

The other important geographic feature of Lyon, aside from its rivers, and one that is not readily apparent on a two-dimensional map, is its hills. Two hills loomed over the affluent, central neighborhoods of the Presqu'Ile—Fourvière to the west and La Croix-Rousse to the north, and "most of the hillside *quartiers* were weaving *quartiers*, separated by topography and vocation from the rest of Lyon."[32] That topography marked a political separation as well. In the riots of February 1790, social peace was disrupted by the crowd of *menu peuple* who swept down from the hillside *quartiers*, first to the Place des Terreaux and then south past the Place Bellecour to the arsenal. In 1791–92, the clubs of those hillside *quartiers* would mount a more formal challenge to the political elite of the central *quartiers*.

The sectional clubs played an important role in Lyon politics in 1791–92 in two ways. First, most of them held meetings, open to the public, as often as three times per week, and although these meetings were not heavily attended, at least on a consistent basis, they helped to sustain a core of politically well-informed activists in the neighborhoods. Clearly they went beyond the role of

32. Ibid., 77.

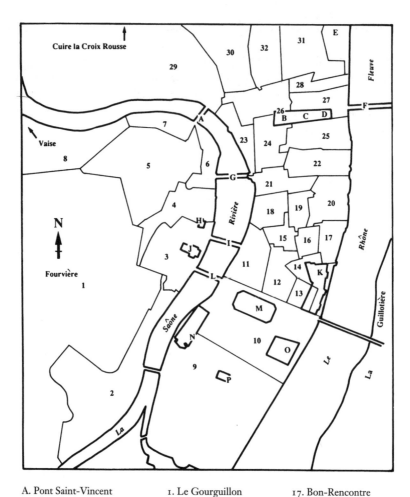

A. Pont Saint-Vincent	1. Le Gourguillon	17. Bon-Rencontre
B. Place des Terreaux	2. Saint-Georges	18. Rue Tupin
C. Hôtel de Ville	3. Porte-Froc	19. La Croisette
D. Comédie	4. Place Neuve	20. Rue Buisson
E. Saint-Clair	5. La Juiverie	21. Saint-Nizier
F. Pont Morand	6. Le Change	22. Rue Neuve
G. Pont de Pierre	7. Port Saint-Paul	23. La Pêcherie
H. Prison de Roanne	8. Pierre-Scize	24. Place Saint-Pierre
I. Pont Volant	9. Bellecour I	25. Le Plâtre
J. Cathedral of Saint Jean	10. Bellecour II	26. Les Terreaux
K. Hôtel-Dieu	11. Port du Temple	27. Le Griffon I
L. Pont de l'Archevêché	12. Place Confort	28. Le Griffon II
M. Place Bellecour	13. Rue Belle-Cordière	29. Saint-Vincent I
N. Arsenal	14. L'Hôtel-Dieu	30. Saint-Vincent II
O. La Charité	15. Rue Thomassin	31. La Grande-Côte I
P. Prison de Saint-Joseph	16. Plat-d'Argent	32. La Grande-Côte II

Map 4.   Lyon and Its Sections, 1789–1793 (Source: W. D. Edmonds, *Jacobinism and the Revolt of Lyon, 1789–1793* [Oxford, 1990], 8)

civic education that political moderates would have preferred for the clubs. This was in part due to the political apathy of the Lyon merchant elite, who tended not to attend the clubs, at least not until 1793, but also because the social elite did not live in those hillside *quartiers*. It was not the poor and the unemployed silkworkers who flocked to the clubs, however, but rather the middling artisans and weavers, those who were eligible to vote in municipal elections.

The results of annual municipal elections reflect the other major impact of these clubs. The earliest clubs may have had some influence on the elections of 1790 (though it is difficult to document), but it is clear that in the elections of autumn 1791 the sectional clubs proposed suitable candidates and the Club Central circulated an endorsed list. Thus, in section Hôtel-Dieu ten "patriot" candidates for ten open seats on the municipal council each received between 164 and 178 votes while no other candidate received more than 11. The result was the election of a council dominated by Roland and his allies, including Joseph Chalier.[33]

Between 1790 and 1793, the occupational character of the council changed from a council dominated by Old Regime officials and wealthy merchants to one dominated by shopkeepers and artisans of much more modest means, and the geographic base of the council shifted as well. The wealthy sections of central Lyon were dominant on the first two councils, whereas the election of 1792–93 brought to office a majority of men from the poorer sections of the hillsides. In the year leading up to that election, both Joseph Chalier and Jean-Marie Roland left for Paris, Roland as an official lobbyist for the city and Chalier to seek redress from the Legislative Assembly for his dismissal from municipal office by the departmental administration of the Rhône-et-Loire. Chalier stood accused of exceeding his authority for having ordered house searches of two men suspected of conspiring with *émigrés*. In Paris, Roland forged close ties with Jacques Brissot and his circle, and Chalier strengthened his links to the Cordeliers and Jacobins. The merchant elite of Lyon viewed Roland as their advocate in Paris. Conversely, when Chalier returned to Lyon in late August, having been exonerated by the Legislative Assembly, they viewed him as an agent of Paris radicals.

On August 24 Chalier delivered one of his typical, highly charged and rambling speeches before the Club Central, calling for the blood of refractory priests and aristocrats. The next day the mayor of Lyon, Louis Vitet, wrote a

33. Edmonds, "Rise and Fall of Popular Democracy in Lyon," 419–21. This article offers a somewhat more extensive discussion than Edmonds' book of the club movement and municipal politics during this period. The voting tallies for section Hôtel-Dieu can be found in A.D. Rhône, 34L1, although similar records for other sections are not contained in this series. Additional evidence that organized slates of candidates were put forward by the clubs can be found in series K of the Lyon municipal archives.

letter to Roland, reporting on the incendiary speech and warning him that in Chalier's politics the sovereignty of the people would be realized only through violence against their enemies. The price of the people's happiness must be the impure blood of their enemies: "he has so inflamed the people (*exalté les têtes*)," wrote Vitet, "that they cannot be controlled and we will soon be seeing horrible rows."[34]

Vitet's words proved to be prophetic. In the days that followed, sectional assemblies and the Club Central issued public calls for stern measures against suspects and alleviation of food shortages and unemployment. The municipal council, now controlled by Roland's allies, was in no position to respond to any of these demands. On September 9, perhaps incited by reports of the massacres in Paris, perhaps responding to the exhortations of Chalier, an angry crowd invaded the prison in the Pierre-Scize neighborhood and killed eight former officers of the royal regiment and three refractory priests. As in Paris, no arrests were made, and some of the sectional clubs celebrated the summary justice of the people, violent though it had been. Vitet blamed "strangers" at the time, a convenient explanation in a large city that saw so many visitors come and go on a regular basis, but in later years he would lay the blame on Chalier and the Club Central. Perhaps he was right to do so, but it is worth noting that acts of popular violence such as this occurred in many provincial towns and cities in early September, prompted not only by the news of the massacres in Paris but by the general mood of panic that prevailed in the country as Prussian and Austrian troops moved closer to the capital.

The violence in Lyon did not end with the prison attack. Market disturbances broke out on September 14, and for a week chaos and disorder reigned in the city. Crowds of men and women roamed through the streets, searching stores and warehouses for grain and other food staples and demanding that prices be lowered. More than a hundred stores and bakeries were pillaged. The municipal council, fearing that the deployment of troops or national guardsmen would only escalate the violence, looked on helplessly in the first days of the riots. Eventually the council sought help from the clubs and conceded the imposition of temporary price controls and the appointment of sectional commissioners. Only then was order gradually restored.

For the *menu peuple* of Lyon, the prison killings and the market riots stood as examples of popular justice directed against the enemies of the people. For the propertied elite of Lyon, those same events represented the realization of their worst nightmare—the collapse of civic order as the uneducated masses ran amok. In early September, before the violence had begun, voters had elected deputies to the National Convention. Among them was Louis Vitet, the man

34. Edmonds, *Jacobinism and the Revolt of Lyon*, 123.

who, as mayor, had managed to sustain calm in the city for most of the previous two years. An election to replace Vitet as mayor was not held until early November. Prominent among the candidates to replace him was Joseph Chalier.

Chalier did not win that election. He lost to Antoine Nivière-Chol, a moderately wealthy merchant who had sat on the previous municipal council as an ally of Roland. The recent riots and the prospect of the rabble-rousing Chalier as mayor seem to have shaken the *haute-bourgeoisie* out of their political lethargy—voter turnout was nearly three times as high as it had been for the mayoral election of 1791, and Nivière-Chol won handily, with 5,129 votes to Chalier's 3,478.[35] Voter turnout for the subsequent municipal council elections was much lower, however, with the result that radical candidates, supported by the Club Central, won nearly every position. Leading the way was one of Chalier's cronies, the former abbé François Laussel, who had also just returned from a sojourn in Paris. Laussel was elected *procureur* of the council, the second most powerful post in the city after that of mayor, and Chalier rebounded from his mayoral defeat by winning election as president of the district tribunal.

The electoral victory of the radical clubbists was even too much for one of the club movement's founders, François Billemaz. "The least of their faults is ineptitude and absolute ignorance," he wrote in a letter to Roland, "all have been made in the same workshop, by Chalier, among the twenty municipal officers one finds fourteen scoundrels, all head-cutters."[36] It had been one thing for the hatters and weavers to gather in sectional clubs and debate the issues of the day, although for some in Lyon even this level of political activity on the part of the *menu peuple* had been suspect. But now not only were the clubbists sponsoring slates of candidates for office, they were themselves winning election to the municipal council.

In the midst of these municipal elections the two silk merchants, Laugier and Girard, wrote to Roland lamenting both the ignorance of the common people and their audacity for claiming sovereignty for themselves. Their letter was dated before the clubbists swept the municipal council elections, and one can easily imagine their alarm at that turn of events. The propertied classes did not sit idly by as Chalier and his allies seized most of the levers of municipal power. They wrote letters to Paris, mostly to Roland, seeking his advice and help. Many of these letters survived and remain in the archives, and they provide an important perspective on Lyonnais politics in this period. They reveal, for example, how fluid political alignments were at this juncture.

In his letter of August 25, for example, in which he reported on Chalier's incendiary speech and warned of the impending troubles, Louis Vitet urged

35. Ibid., 138.
36. Ibid., 133.

Roland to write to Chalier: "A letter from you would influence him a great deal, and this would be a great service on your part to the city, which is so greatly in need of calm at this moment."[37] François Laussel, who would soon be denounced as the "Marat of Lyon," had been sent by Roland to Lyon as an observer in August. Laussel sent at least one report on the market riots of September, emphasizing the nullity of the sitting municipal council (most of whom were Roland's allies!), but in early October Roland revoked his commission because of Laussel's intemperance.[38]

But what could the minister do, beyond writing to Chalier, to help resolve Lyon's troubles? Laugier and Girard had in fact proposed a plan in their letter of November 6:

> The causes of these troubles being well known, the remedies should also be easy to find. To ignorance and idleness one opposes instruction and work. . . .
>
> In vain will the National Convention have ordered the renewal of the municipal council. In vain would the citizens of Lyon apply even the greatest of precautions in their choice of magistrates. Even were those magistrates endowed with a celestial intelligence, they would be unable to contain the ignorant, coarse, indigent, and above all idle mob. . . . But how can we occupy these workers?
>
> The administration [which one is not specified] must commission one or two of the houses of commerce of this city to place orders with different manufacturers (*fabricants*) as if they had been received from Germany, Italy, Spain, etc. Those houses would establish the price of the silks at the moment at which they are given the governmental commission, and the price of the fabrics at the moment at which they are sold, and it is in the difference between those two prices that a sacrifice will be made. But if this plan is accepted, the greatest secrecy will be required to assure its success. If it becomes known that the administration has made work in this manner, the operation will find itself between a rock and a hard place. On the one hand the suppliers will raise the price of silk, and on the other the buyers of the finished fabrics will do everything they can to lower the price they pay. But this plan combines a triple advantage—it will keep the worker employed; it will preserve public calm by eliminating idleness, the source of all disorders; and it will avoid degrading by the giving of alms those souls whom you wish to make a party to a republican constitution.[39]

37. A.N., F⁷ 3686⁶.
38. Ibid. See also Edmonds, *Jacobinism and the Revolt of Lyon*, 130–31.
39. A.N., F⁷ 3686⁶.

In closing, Laugier and Girard assured Roland that one of them would have the honor of discussing this plan with him further the following week, should he so desire. Their letter reminds us that commerce would have taken many merchants back and forth between Paris and Lyon (and Lyon and Marseille) on a regular basis and that, at least in the minds of these two merchants, the salvation of Lyon lay not in politics but in business.

Roland gained a different perspective on the troubles in Lyon from another correspondent, Charles George *l'aîné*. George is an obscure figure—I have not been able to verify his identity in any of the standard sources—but the misspellings and poor grammar in his letters, as well as their content, suggest that he was a middling to poor artisan or silkworker. In a letter dated November 19, he complained of those bakers in Lyon who had refused to comply with the orders of the municipal council. The council, he asserted, had been insufficiently rigorous "toward these men who daily cheat the people," though he admitted that their powers were limited and that "justice is too slow and too mild." George complained bitterly about monopolists and speculators: "It is they who cause all the disorders by buying up silver at a high price and by buying up the harvest while it's still on the stalk, and then crushing the people in the name of liberty, because there are no price controls." George wrote again on November 30 to express his surprise that Roland was opposed to price controls: "You see the disorder that reigns in the republic because of hoarding. We are paying double and even triple, and if grain prices were fixed, as well as drink and other staple goods, that alone would suffice to end hoarding. It would lower prices and restore order to the republic. It would avert insurrection."[40]

For Charles George, then, it was not idle workers who were to blame for the disorders in Lyon, but rather greedy farmers and merchants. These letters show us not only that men of different social backgrounds might have radically different views about the economic and political problems confronting the nation, irreconcilable views in fact, but also that Roland, the erstwhile leader of the "patriot" party in Lyon, was still very much in contact with men on both sides of that social divide. On the question of price controls, however, Roland was firmly on the side of the merchants.

Something of a middle position on these issues was taken by another of Roland's correspondents, Eugène Patrin, a newly elected deputy to the National Convention. On November 23 Patrin wrote as follows to the minister: "I have received a letter from our excellent Vitet who tells me that the new municipality has been entirely named by the party of Marat; that the merchants, all selfish egoists, are obstructing the good measures being proposed by the commissioners sent by the Convention [Vitet among them]; and that Lyon is lost unless

---

40. Ibid.

you come to her aid by guaranteeing work and bread to the workers. It is in you alone, brave minister, virtuous citizen, that the Fatherland places its hope to overturn the ambitious projects of the Dantons and Robespierres, for which Chalier and his ilk are only the instruments."[41]

Neither moderates nor radicals had much hope of resolving the dire economic problems confronting Lyon, but both sides would be more than happy to blame the other for its failure to do just that in the months that followed. What Patrin's letter makes particularly clear is the degree to which the political situation in Lyon had become inextricably intertwined with that of Paris by fall 1792. Patrin and Vitet viewed the electoral victory of the clubbists as the triumph of "Maratists." Chalier and his allies were seen as the tools of Danton and Robespierre (though Laussel, of course, had more recently been in the employ of Roland). The prison killings in Lyon in early September were seen as an extension of the massacres in Paris, brought to Lyon by Chalier and instigated in Paris by his masters, Robespierre, Danton, and Marat.

Chalier and Roland represent two ways that politics moved back and forth between Paris and the provinces, but there were others as well. In the aftermath of the September massacres, the Paris Commune sent emissaries out to the departments to carry its version of those events (as a counter to that being spread by Roland), and at least two of these visited Lyon.[42] But emissaries moved in the other direction, too. In February 1793, Théophile Leclerc, the future *enragé* leader, was assigned to the headquarters of the Army of the Alps in Lyon. Having previously met Chalier in Paris, Leclerc became involved in the meetings of the Club Central, and in May the Lyon Jacobins sent him as their envoy to Paris. On May 29, the very day that moderates regained political control in Lyon, Leclerc was elected to the Central Revolutionary Committee in Paris, the body that would lead the May 31–June 2 insurrection. In June and July, Leclerc was thus unusually well placed to inform Parisian radicals about the political situation in Lyon.[43]

Adding to this multiplicity of contacts between the capital and Lyon was a whole series of representatives on mission who paid visits to Lyon between fall 1792 and the end of May 1793. Vitet, Boissy d'Anglas, and Legendre came in October to help restore calm after the troubles of September. Collot d'Herbois paid an unofficial visit in January, reportedly to solicit signatures on a petition to the Convention opposing the proposed *appel au peuple* regarding the judgment of Louis XVI.[44]

41. Ibid.
42. Edmonds, *Jacobinism and the Revolt of Lyon*, 130.
43. Morris Slavin, *The Making of an Insurrection* (Cambridge, Mass., 1986), 134–35.
44. A.N., F¹ᶜIII Rhône⁸. Collot d'Herbois' presence in Lyon is mentioned in an anonymous letter dated January 15, 1793, addressed to the president of the Convention. The letter writer clearly

Legendre would return to Lyon in March, along with Basire and Rovère, following yet another outbreak of violence in mid-February. The deputies Lacombe-St.-Michel, Saliceti, and Delcher stopped off in Lyon en route to Corsica in late February or early March. Finally, Dubois-Crancé, Albitte, Gauthier, and Nioche visited the city in early May on their way to the Army of the Alps. Gauthier and Nioche returned to the city at the end of the month, of course, and were present for the May 29 insurrection. Most of these representatives on mission were Montagnards, and Lyon moderates resented the intrusions of these national deputies into their local political squabbles, which they preferred to settle among themselves (despite their willingness, only months before, to seek help from Minister Roland, who had since resigned his office). Chalier and the Jacobins, in contrast, recognized that they would need help from Paris if they hoped to consolidate their precarious hold on the reins of municipal power in Lyon.

The ongoing struggle for control of Lyon municipal politics is what brought most of those representatives on mission to the city. Even before the September troubles, moderates had begun a counteroffensive against the radical clubs of the sections. The defeat of Chalier in the mayoral election was one sign of their success, but, as already noted, the more militant clubs of the poorer sections had prevailed in the campaign for municipal council seats. Moderate sections were quick to protest the elections, alleging voter fraud on the part of certain sections (particularly l'Hôtel-Dieu) but essentially calling into question the very principle of presenting an organized slate of candidates and then turning out the vote (or fabricating the vote!) by mobilizing the members of the radical clubs. Particularly galling to moderates was the role played in this by the Club Central. Such criticism was not new—moderates had first mobilized opposition to the Club Central back in the summer of 1791, responding to the Club's efforts to stimulate popular opinion against the monarchy following the flight to Varennes—but it now became more intense and sustained.[45]

During the winter months, Lyon moderates pressed their campaign against the Jacobins by creating rival clubs in the sections or by convening sectional assemblies. The municipal council opposed the permanence of sectional assemblies and attempted to shut them down, but the moderate sections had an ally in the more conservative departmental administration. For their part, Chalier and his supporters hoped to use the organizational network of the Club Central to reinforce their tenuous electoral victory and create a more solid popular base in the community. To do that, they attempted to transform the Club Central

---

felt that he was there to stir up trouble. Collot would return to Lyon one year later to oversee the bloody repression of the federalist revolt.

45. Edmonds, *Jacobinism and the Revolt of Lyon*, 100–101 and 137–43.

from a clearing house for sectional communications into an executive arm of the sectional clubs, modeled on what they took to be the role and function of the Jacobin club of Paris. Such a strategy ran counter to the tradition of sectional autonomy in Lyon, and by February it had backfired.[46]

On the night of February 6, Chalier and Laussel presided over a secret meeting at the Club Central where plans were allegedly laid to create a revolutionary tribunal, prepare a list of suspects, and install a guillotine in Lyon. When the municipal council subsequently ordered household searches, and some three hundred suspects were arrested, panic began to spread. Against the wishes of the council, the mayor, Nivière-Chol, fearing a reprise of the September violence, called out the National Guard. Admitting his overreaction, the mayor resigned, but in a special election on February 18 he was overwhelmingly returned to office. Emboldened by that victory, a mob of his supporters sacked the Club Central that evening, only to see their candidate decline his election. J. P. Lacombe St.-Michel, one of the representatives on mission en route to Corsica, wrote in a letter to Paris that the mob was composed of "shopkeepers' clerks, attorneys' clerks, wigmakers, domestics, the rich and those who sell themselves to the highest bidder."[47]

A third mayoral election, on February 27, returned to office another moderate, J. E. Gilibert (future president of the federalist Popular Commission). But Laussel had taken the precaution of jailing Gilibert on charges of inciting insurrection, and after several days in jail he resigned his post. Thus, at long last, the Jacobins of Lyon were able to return one of their own, Antoine-Marie Bertrand, to the office of mayor. Bertrand was a close friend of Chalier; their friendship dated to the 1780s when Chalier was employed by Bertrand's father in his commercial business. But Bertrand's election, rather than consolidating Jacobin power in Lyon, further compromised the integrity of the electoral system.[48]

The Jacobins now controlled municipal government, and they used that base

46. Much of the discussion that follows first appeared, in somewhat different form, in my article, "The Federalist Revolt: An Affirmation or Denial of Popular Sovereignty?" *French History* 6, no. 3 (September 1992): 342–48; see also, Bill Edmonds, "A Jacobin Debacle: The Losing of Lyon in Spring 1793," *History* 69, no. 225 (1984): 1–14.

47. B.M. Lyon, Fonds Coste, 553 (Lacombe letter of 2/23/93).

48. A number of sources shed light on the events of February and early March. In addition to Edmonds' judicious account, there are reports from the deputy Tallien, from the sectional assemblies to the Convention, a letter from two elected officials sent to deputies in Paris, and various independent statements made to the municipal or departmental authorities. See Edmonds, *Jacobinism and the Revolt of Lyon*, 148–53; J. L. Tallien, *Rapport et projet de décret sur les troubles arrivés à Lyon, présentés à la Convention Nationale, au nom du Comité du Sûreté générale*, B.M. Lyon, Fonds Coste, 350560; A.C. Lyon, I²3, pièce 8 (Rapport et pétition sur les troubles à Lyon, présentés et lues à la Barre de la Convention Nationale); B.M. Lyon, Fonds Coste, 545 (letter from Achard and Gaillard to Javogues, Pressavin, Dupuy, Pointe and Dubouchet); and B.M. Lyon, Fonds Coste, 561 and 565 (letters from private citizens).

along with the Club Central to mount a challenge against sectional assemblies. Each side defended the legitimacy of its own organization while denying that of the other. Both moderates and radicals claimed to represent popular sovereignty—moderates arguing that sectional assemblies were the purest expression of the people's will and radicals insisting that the clubs best fulfilled that function. But it is clear that both sides were at least as concerned with political power as they were with political legitimacy. Laussel had the power to arrest Gilibert, and he did so. The Jacobins had the power to disarm their opponents, and they did so. Both sides sought allies outside the city, in the departmental administration and the National Convention. Because the Jacobins did not yet control the National Convention, Chalier and his allies in Lyon could do little more than threaten a reign of terror against their enemies; they lacked both the power and the authority to impose it. But the incendiary language that they used—Chalier allegedly proposed setting up the guillotine on one of the bridges in the city, so that corpses could be dumped directly into the Saône and washed down river to the sea—served not only to terrify the propertied elite, but to rally many of the sections to the side of the moderates. By May, virtually all of the sections of the Presqu'Ile, with the exception of l'Hôtel-Dieu, had turned against the Club Central. The political polarization of the city was now clearly delineated along geographic and social lines as well.

Leading that opposition movement was the sectional assembly of La Croisette, one of the few *quartiers* in town that remained socially integrated, with wealthy merchants, artisans, and wage laborers living in close proximity. In March and April La Croisette rallied other sections against the proposal to convert the Club Central into a Jacobin club tied to the club in Paris, and when that effort failed, the La Croisette club shifted tactics. In May the moderates in La Croisette (radicals had broken away and formed a new club in February, called Le Pelletier) opened the doors of their meetings to the public, now calling themselves a sectional assembly rather than a club, and initiated a dialogue among the sections (one that would continue on into the federalist revolt) about the limits to sectional power and authority. In doing so they attempted both to challenge the Jacobins' claim to represent the views of the people, and to criticize them for exceeding their constitutional authority.[49]

Ultimately, the moderates of the sections prevailed not by debating the finer

---

49. A.C. Lyon, I²4, pièce 45 (registre des délibérations du club de la Croisette, 29/10/91 à 13/5/93). Unfortunately la Croisette is the only Lyon section for which such a register exists, and as the dates indicate, it does not extend into the federalist period. There are, however, registers for a number of sectional assemblies (not clubs) in the Rhône archives. These tend to be principally devoted to routine matters, but further research into sectional politics in Lyon (and Marseille) would be well worth pursuing. In this regard, see the very fine article by Antonio de Francesco, "Le Quartier lyonnais de la Croisette pendant les premières années de la Révolution (1790–1793)," *Bulletin du Centre d'histoire économique et sociale de la région lyonnaise* 4 (1979): 21–63.

points of sovereignty and representation, but through armed force. The fear that the Montagnard representatives, Nioche and Gauthier, would bring the Army of the Alps to the aid of the Lyon Jacobins prompted that attack. But the ability of the sectional moderates to overthrow the Jacobin municipality also derived from the failure of the Jacobins to address the economic plight of Lyon silkworkers. One of those silkworkers, by the name of Grégoire, wrote to the representatives on mission Legendre, Basire, and Rovère in March: "They [Chalier and his friends] have forced all those who have wealth to flee the city. . . . I have been without work for more than ten days because he who employs me is a perfectly honest gentleman who fears for his life [*sa tête*] and his property and I will be reduced to starvation if this state of affairs continues because the rich people are fleeing the city and it is only they who can support the poor workers by their spending and their business."[50]

The Jacobin municipality proved no more capable than the Rolandin municipality before it of solving the economic crisis of the city (perhaps less so, given their alienation of the merchant elite). But theirs was as much a political failure as an economic one. Far from rallying the people of Lyon to political activism, the radical clubbists and the moderate section leaders both seem to have alienated them. In his report to the Convention on the insurrection of May 29, the representative on mission Nioche commented that the uprising was watched by "an immense crowd, tranquil and indifferent about all that was happening."[51]

MARSEILLE

The political situation in Marseille in 1792–93 bears striking resemblance to that of Lyon in a number of ways, although the revolutionary experience of the two cities in 1789–92, and their respective national reputations, were strikingly different. Marseille was a city of approximately 100,000 people at the end of the Old Regime, about half of whom were recent immigrants. Population had grown by nearly 50 percent over the course of the eighteenth century. Most of that growth had been concentrated in the old neighborhoods of Marseille (the town walls would not be demolished until 1792), although in the last years before the Revolution there had been some movement by wealthier families into the more open and spacious *quartiers* to the east of the long road linking the Porte d'Aix to the Porte de Rome (see map 5). Marseille was an overwhelmingly commercial city, boasting some 750 *négociant* families as opposed to only 80

---

50. B.M. Lyon, Fonds Coste, 569.
51. Cited in Bill Edmonds, "A Study in Popular Anti-Jacobinism: The Career of Denis Monnet," *French Historical Studies* 13, no. 2 (1983): 243. Edmonds also notes that a Swiss eyewitness to the insurrection was similarly struck by the large, passive crowds.

noble families. Most of those merchants lived in the neighborhoods ringing the old port (sections 16, 18, 10, 8, 4, and 6). The farther one moved away from the harbor, generally speaking, the poorer were the *quartiers*, inhabited chiefly by artisans and dockworkers (sections 19, 15, 11, 12, 14, and 13). Although the social segregation of Marseille's urban geography was not as pronounced as that of Lyon, the sections formed from these poorer neighborhoods remained most ardently Jacobin in 1793 while the wealthier sections ringing the port led the federalist movement.[52]

In contrast to Lyon, the commercial economy of Marseille remained relatively vibrant until 1793 when France went to war with England. Still, there were grain shortages in 1789, and these produced serious riots in the spring, which prompted the reorganization of municipal government and the formation of the first citizens' militia in Marseille. One year later, on April 30, Marseille patriots turned their wrath on the two most prominent symbols of royal despotism in the city—the forts St. Jean and St. Nicolas. The two forts, built during the reign of Louis XIV, stood facing each other on opposite sides of the entrance to the old port. Ostensibly built to protect the port, their equally important function was to control the populace of the city—the batteries of St. Nicolas, in particular, pointed in toward the city rather than out to sea. Both forts fell to the crowd without bloodshed, although popular myth at the time would claim otherwise, perhaps to justify the killing of the commander of the fort St. Jean. Despite efforts to preserve them, the forts were largely demolished in the weeks that followed, and the Marseillais could boast of their own "taking of the Bastilles" as evidence of their revolutionary spirit.[53]

Whereas Lyon gained an early reputation as a counterrevolutionary haven, Marseille rivaled Paris as the most revolutionary of France's cities between 1789 and 1792. The Marseillais elected a "patriot" municipal council in January-February 1790, at a time when the Old Regime oligarchy was still clinging to power in Lyon. Unlike Lyon, where the merchant elite remained largely aloof from revolutionary politics, that first municipality in Marseille was dominated by merchants (although not from the wealthiest merchant families). Merchants also were active in the Marseille Jacobin club, which held its first meeting in April 1790.[54]

The Marseille Jacobins and National Guardsmen established the city's repu-

52. Régis Bertrand, "Marseille à la veille de la Révolution," in *Marseille en Révolution* (Marseille, 1989), 17–25. See also William Scott, *Terror and Repression in Revolutionary Marseille* (London, 1973), 10–19.

53. Monique Cubells, "Marseille entre en Révolution (1787–1789)," and Rolf Reichardt, "Prise et démolition des 'Bastilles Marseillaises,'—événement symbole révolutionnaire," both in *Marseille en Révolution* (Marseille, 1989), 35–41 and 53–61.

54. Scott, *Terror and Repression*, 25–26; on the Marseille Jacobins, see Michael L. Kennedy, *The Jacobin Club of Marseille, 1790–1794* (Ithaca, 1973).

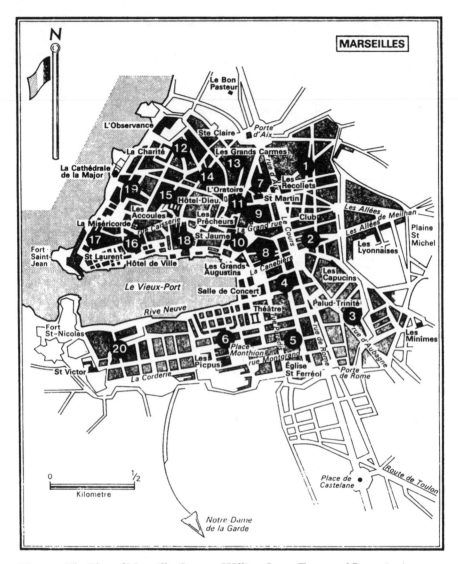

Map 5.   The Plan of Marseille (Source: William Scott, *Terror and Repression in Revolutionary Marseilles* [London, 1973], xv)

tation for radicalism by their repeated forays to neighboring towns and villages in 1791–92 to support their fellow radicals against royalists and counterrevolutionaries. These Jacobin "missionaries" propagated their revolutionary ideals— sometimes through persuasion, sometimes through force—in towns as far-flung as Aix, Arles, Apt, and Avignon. Marseille merchants sometimes grumbled at the frequent absences of the workers who participated on these missions, but they were no doubt relieved that they were exercising their revolutionary fervor elsewhere. Ministers in Paris, too (including Roland), expressed concern that the Marseillais were exceeding their jurisdictional authority and that these forays, rather than consolidating revolutionary constitutionalism, might instead sow disorder throughout Provence. Yet Marseille Jacobins were concerned not only that their nearby neighbors might lack sufficient revolutionary commitment, but that the deputies of the Legislative Assembly and Convention, even the Parisians themselves, might falter as well. Their missionary zeal culminated in the celebrated march of the *fédérés* to Paris in August 1792. In that same month another contingent of Marseille Jacobins marched to Aix and forcibly escorted the members of the departmental council back to Marseille. This relocation of the departmental *chef-lieu* marked the final triumph of Marseille over its Old Regime rival Aix, but it also symbolized the ability of Marseille to flaunt the authority of the national government.[55]

This channeling of revolutionary energies outward did not spare Marseille, however, from the emergence of political and social tensions within the city. As William Scott has put it, a "particularly rapid progress towards extremism on the part of the revolutionary leaders was paralleled by a stubborn current of social conservatism among their richer fellow-citizens."[56] The dispatch of armed contingents of volunteers to Paris and throughout the region cost money, and the special levies to sustain those costs invariably fell upon the rich. Allegations that the Jacobin contingents had committed abuses in the countryside brought calls for inquiries from the law-abiding elite of Marseille, concerned that the reputation of their city was being besmirched, and those calls, in turn, brought accusations from the Jacobins that the wealthy were simply trying to evade the payment of taxes. Poor harvests in 1791 and 1792 not only increased the need for public outlays to procure grain supplies and subsidize prices, but also brought threats from the municipal council against hoarders and speculators. There was no major outbreak of violence in fall 1792, as in Lyon, but there were scattered incidents throughout 1792, including an attack on the Jacobin club.[57]

A sense of civic pride, even euphoria, may have prevailed among certain citizens of Marseille in the weeks following the assault on the Tuileries and the collapse of the monarchy, but there was also a growing sense of social antagonism. In that charged atmosphere, the Marseillais were now called upon to cast their ballots for a new municipal council. The voting began in early January, 1793, and Jean-Raymond Mouraille was reelected mayor by a wide margin. Sev-

55. Ibid., 26–37; and Jacques Guilhaumou, *Marseille Républicaine (1791–1793)* (Paris, 1992), esp. 41–92. Aix had been designated the departmental *chef-lieu* in 1790, a decision much resented by the Marseillais at the time.

56. Scott, *Terror and Repression*, 19.

57. Ibid., 32–35, 48–55.

enty-one when first elected, and by that token alone unusual among revolutionary leaders, Mouraille had been a popular mayor. He had played a role in the
arming of the Marseille *fédérés* and the Jacobin contingents to Aix and Avignon,
but he had also exercised a moderating influence in defense of the merchant
community. He had at one point presided over the Jacobin club and was widely
respected in the city.

The rest of the balloting for municipal offices was far more controversial,
and it was not until March that a full slate of notables could be seated. The first
round of voting for a municipal council also occurred during the first week of
January. On January 11, 1793, 150 citizens signed a petition to the departmental
administration demanding that that balloting be annulled on the grounds that
several sections had sent representatives to a meeting before the election in the
Dominican convent, where they had drawn up a list of twenty candidates (there
were twenty officers on the council), that list then being nominated back in the
section assemblies. This allegation was echoed later in the spring, when section
23 demanded that the entire municipal council be replaced, charging that section 11 had taken the lead in preparing a slate of candidates.[58] The Marseille
Jacobin club almost certainly initiated this organized electoral campaign, which
many Marseillais clearly found objectionable.

The election results themselves tend to confirm these allegations about fixed
slates of candidates. The municipal archives in Marseille contain *procès-verbaux*
(minutes) and handwritten tallies of votes from a number of sectional assemblies
for these elections. The evidence is very striking. Section 13, for example, submitted a *procès-verbal* with twenty candidates, each of whom received 126 or 127
votes. All twenty won election, although one resigned and was replaced. In section 14, too, the same twenty candidates each received between 63 and 68 votes.
Other sections were somewhat less blatant, but a clear pattern emerges. In section 25, eight candidates received 266 votes apiece, and all were elected. The
voters in section 16 cast 129 votes for each of nine candidates, all elected. Although not all sections voted the identical slate of candidates, it is obvious that
an organized slate had been proposed and that the campaign was ultimately
successful.[59]

As in Lyon, a controversial round of municipal elections brought Marseille
Jacobins to power, and they now moved to consolidate their position. In February the Jacobin club created a central committee, which played a role in the
denunciation and disarming of suspects in March and April. This "central committee" seems eerily reminiscent of the effort on the part of the Club Central
in Lyon, also in February, to increase its own autonomous authority. The two

58. A.D. Bouches-du-Rhône, L1964.
59. A.C. Marseille, K38.

situations were quite different, however. In Lyon, the Club Central was attempting to introduce discipline to a loose network of sectional clubs, to modify its own role from that of coordinating committee to one of executive authority, and in the process to create a new Jacobin club in Lyon with links to the Paris club. In Marseille, by contrast, the Jacobin club had always enjoyed affiliation with the mother society, and there was no tradition of neighborhood clubs. The Marseille Jacobins in creating their central committee were building on an already existing base, whereas the Lyon Club Central, by its action, had betrayed its own origins and alienated some of the neighborhood clubs to which it owed its authority.

Yet there are many similarities between the situations in the two cities. In Marseille, too, the deteriorating economic situation made it increasingly difficult for the Jacobin municipality to maintain its base of popular support. Securing an adequate grain supply was an ongoing problem, and the radical measures urged on the municipal council by the club cast fear in the hearts of wealthy merchants and alienated some of the *menu peuple* who depended on them for employment. As in Lyon, an embattled municipal council turned to Montagnard representatives on mission for support, while moderates, denouncing that outside meddling in local affairs, built their base of support in sectional assemblies.

The eventual victory of sectional assemblies over the Jacobin club and the Jacobin municipality in Marseille has generated an ongoing debate over the social composition of the sections over time, and compared to that of the club, beginning with the assertion made by the representatives on mission Bayle and Boisset in April 1793 that "aristocrats" had been flooding into the sectional assemblies during the previous month and a half. William Scott, while lamenting that the "evidence is confused and fragmentary, and in no case is it possible to make a direct comparison between membership before and after the critical weeks of the second half of April," ends by stressing "the continuity of personnel before and after April 1793."[60] John Cameron Jr., citing tax records as evidence, similarly stressed the continuity of sectional personnel and argued that there was no significant social distinction between the membership of the sections and that of the Jacobin club.[61] Michel Vovelle, in a more recent work, presented evidence in support of discontinuity. Focusing on occupational data rather than tax records, he observed that although there was an element of pop-

60. Scott, *Terror and Repression*, 80.
61. John B. Cameron Jr., "The Revolution of the Sections in Marseille: Federalism in the Department of the Bouches-du-Rhône in 1793" (Ph.D. diss., University of North Carolina, 1971). I would challenge Cameron's conclusions on two grounds. First, in comparing *averages* in his analysis of taxes paid, he obscures the importance of those wealthy individuals in some sections who paid very high taxes. Second, he relies principally on the *contribution foncière*, a property tax that none of the working poor would have paid.

ular participation in sectional assemblies throughout the Revolution, its character changed from 1792 to 1793. Vovelle characterized "Jacobin Marseille" of the last half of 1792 as "the small workshop in power" with a heavy participation of artisans and small producers in sectional politics. In spring 1793, their numbers dropped in sectional registers while the participation of merchants, their clerks and employees, and dockworkers increased markedly. He also noted the preponderance of the very old and the very young, with more bachelors and fewer married heads of household, in that same period.[62]

It is unlikely that this debate will be easily resolved. The archival evidence for the Marseille sections is abundant, but it is not consistently so for all sections and it resists statistical manipulation. The further one moves down the social scale, the more difficult it becomes to make positive identifications of individual names or to verify occupational or tax information. Vovelle's conclusions, however, are consistent with contemporary characterizations of the sectional movement and the federalist revolt that followed in Marseille—that it was led and dominated by the merchant community. As in Lyon, where Nioche and Gauthier were struck by the "tranquil and indifferent" crowd that watched the spectacle of the May 29 insurrection, William Scott concludes that in Marseille, the "fall of the Club seems to have left the bulk of the Marseillais indifferent."[63]

In all four federalist cities, then, the year and a half leading up to the revolt witnessed contention for political power and controversy over the nature of popular sovereignty and its appropriate exercise. In Marseille and Lyon, local militants gained control of municipal politics through the vehicle of political clubs and their ability to mobilize voters in support of organized slates of candidates. The electoral success of the Jacobins, which their opponents condemned as illegitimate electioneering, galvanized the moderate elites of the two cities to play the Jacobins' own game—they mobilized their supporters in sectional assemblies and argued that the sections, not the clubs, were the only legitimate expression of popular sovereignty. But they also argued, particularly in Lyon, that there was a limit to that sovereignty, that while sectional assemblies might deliberate, debate, and offer opinions, they had no right to infringe on the authority of official administrative bodies.

Although political contention was less tumultuous and divisive in Caen and Bordeaux, in those cities, too, there was controversy in 1792–93 over issues of sovereignty and the legitimate role to be played by political clubs. In Caen, there was controversy as early as 1791 about offering organized slates of candidates for office, although in that instance an alleged coalition of aristocrats was at the

---

62. Michel Vovelle, "Le Sans-culotte marseillais," *Mesure de l'Histoire* 1 (1986): 75–95.
63. Scott, *Terror and Repression*, 107.

center of the scandal. In both cities elected authorities were challenged by radi-cal clubbists. In Caen, the departmental administration succeeded in taming the Jacobin club by gaining control of its leadership and by sponsoring a rival, the Carabots, that seemingly operated in a clientage relationship to the administra-tive and commercial elite. In Bordeaux, the departmental and municipal author-ities dominated the Jacobin club and successfully stifled a challenge from the more radical Club National in winter and spring 1793. Although the more cohe-sive elites of Bordeaux and Caen had not been forced to "reclaim" their political authority in 1793, they understood well the precariousness of their hold on political power and applauded the May victory of sectional moderates in Lyon and Marseille.

There were really two sets of issues in the debate, or struggle, over sover-eignty in each of these cities. First was the issue of how sovereignty was to be exercised and by whom (we must remember that the electoral franchise was steadily expanded between 1790 and late 1792). In particular, what role could legitimately be played by political clubs in revolutionary politics? The second set of issues (and the role of political clubs figured in this as well) had to do with representation, with the relation between voting citizens and the officials whom they elected. Did citizens cede their sovereignty, as Vergniaud would have it, to their elected representatives once they were voted into office? Or was sover-eignty inherent in the people, as Robespierre argued, and if so, how were they legitimately to exercise it in times of national crisis, or local crisis for that mat-ter? These issues had been debated in abstract terms since the very beginning of the Revolution on the floor of the Constituent and Legislative assemblies and in pamphlets published in Paris. At the level of local politics abstract debates quickly became tangible disagreements, with very real consequences. But practi-cal politics informed principled debate, just as the reverse was true, and we can see this quite clearly in two pamphlets published in Bordeaux and Marseille in late 1791 and early 1792.

Our two pamphleteers were both active in local politics and were both out-siders, in some sense, in their communities. Jacques Monbrion was born in Lourmarin in 1765, moved to Marseille in 1787, joined the National Guard as a grenadier, participated in the 1790 attack on the two forts in Marseille, and became an activist in the Jacobin club, leading several of the Jacobin expeditions from Marseille to neighboring towns and villages. Abraham Furtado was a prominent Jewish merchant in Bordeaux, his family having first settled in Bay-onne after emigrating from Portugal. He joined the Bordeaux Jacobin club early in the Revolution, was elected to the municipal council as a notable in Decem-ber 1791, and served, somewhat reluctantly, as a member of the Popular Com-mission during the federalist revolt. Both men had contacts in Paris. Furtado had visited the capital in 1788 as a petitioner on behalf of the Bordeaux Jewish community; Monbrion journeyed to Paris in 1791 to represent the "conquerors of the Marseille bastilles." During that visit, Monbrion received an enthusiastic welcome at the Cordelier club.[64]

Furtado and Monbrion both wrote their pamphlets in defense of the Jacobin clubs, which had come under considerable attack, both locally and nationally, following the king's aborted flight to Varennes. Louis XVI had left behind a note condemning the activities of the Paris Jacobins, and the Feuillant split in the Paris club was a product of the increasing polarization in Paris between those who now advocated a move toward popular democracy and those (particularly the deputies who broke from the Jacobins to form the Feuillant club) who hoped to salvage the constitutional monarchy and stabilize the revolution. These developments left the Jacobin clubs momentarily vulnerable, but they also opened debate about what the function of political clubs should be. Monbrion and Furtado took very different positions on this issue.

Abraham Furtado argued that the detractors of the Jacobin clubs were in fact partisans of the Old Regime, who asserted, falsely, that the Jacobins wished to subject the laws to the caprices of the popular multitude. On the contrary, he asserted, the Jacobins had played an important role in achieving public confidence in, and respect for, the new laws passed by the Constituent Assembly. To lay the ground for his argument, Furtado posed the question, "What is liberty?"

> Liberty is not the right to do all that one wishes, but rather to not do that which one should not; but to obey with impunity the wise laws that one has made; but to participate in legislation, so as to be more bound to submit to the laws; but to march proudly and without fear under the standard and shield of the law. Liberty constituted by the law, compels a religious respect for it, both from the magistrate who orders and the Citizen who obeys. Woe to the country that possesses a free Constitution, in which this word *Law* does not possess a sort of invisible virtue, which contains and checks, as if by enchantment, all passions, interests, and parties.

Liberty founded in the law, in other words, was quite the opposite from license: "Nothing would excuse the inaction or negligence of magistrates charged with maintaining public order, and suppressing those who would disturb it, if license were to triumph where order should prevail." The role of the Jacobin clubs, one they had performed well to date, was to assist those magistrates by showing the

---

64. Alan Forrest, *Society and Politics*, 56 and 70–71; Jacques Guilhaumou, "Les Jacobins marseillais et la propagation des idées républicaines (1791–92)," in *Marseille en Révolution* (Marseille, 1989), 81–85. Monbrion's mission to Paris is noted in Raymonde Monnier, *L'Espace Public Démocratique* (Paris, 1994), 248 n. 40.

people, not always capable of seeing this for themselves, that the new system of government, and the laws passed by their elected representatives, were actually in their own best interests.[65]

Jacques Monbrion published his "Adresse au Peuple" in February 1792, when he was already a self-avowed republican. Writing in the midst of a constitutional furor over the nature and extent of executive authority, Monbrion devoted most of his pages to a virulent denunciation of the "monstrous veto," asserting that it interfered with the prerogative of the National Assembly and infringed on the domain of national sovereignty. In one emotional outburst he exclaimed that "either the Nation must perish, or this oppressive power (the king) must be struck dead."

What could the people do to protect their rights from the excesses of royal power (an evil that Furtado, too, had acknowledged, though he associated it more with the Old Regime)? Whereas Furtado had stressed the importance of laws and the obedience that the people owed to their magistrates and elected officials, Monbrion lamented that these men were too easily co-opted by the crown. Indeed, "the Departments, the Districts, the Municipalities and the Courts were filled by a crowd of men who, having done nothing for the cause of liberty or to merit the estime of their fellow citizens, were nonetheless rewarded by the people, a people so virtuous as to be easily deceived." One need look no further, Monbrion observed, than the departmental administration of the Bouches-du-Rhône to find a clear example of such perfidy. Even were they to be so lucky as to have trustworthy elected officials, the king had the legal authority to suspend departmental, district, and municipal councils, which explained why so many departmental administrations were devoted to the executive power.

Ultimately, Monbrion argued, "there is only one legitimate authority, the people." Yet even the king appealed to the "opinion of the Nation" for support of his abusive powers. How was the true voice of the people, what historians have come to call "public opinion," to be given expression in the face of these obstacles? For Monbrion the answer lay in the clubs: "It is in their bosom that the citizen is enlightened, and that his patriotism gains its strength; linked by an active correspondence, which redoubles at moments of crisis, these societies form an unbreakable fasces, formidable corps of intrepid defenders of the rights of man." It was in those clubs, Monbrion continued, that public opinion could take form and gain strength: "Public opinion, which at times, in the face of the dangers that menace the executive power, turns away from the goal toward which it

65. Abraham Furtado, "Réflexions sur les Clubs ou Sociétés d'Amis de la Constitution" (Bordeaux, slnd). Although the pamphlet is undated, a reference to the king's flight to Varennes suggests that it was published in summer or fall 1791. A copy of the pamphlet can be found in A.D. Gironde, 8J366.

never entirely ceases to move; public opinion, we say, cannot take shape if the wills are not united en masse in patriotic societies, so that tyranny, which always conserves its unity, cannot fortify itself by the isolated and contradictory wills of individual citizens. In that case, veto after veto will be applied to good laws."[66]

For Abraham Furtado, the principal role of the Jacobin clubs was to assist judicial and administrative authorities in the maintenance of public order by instructing the people about the virtues of the new constitutional regime. This was the role that the Jacobin club of Bordeaux had largely played, and when the Club National of Bordeaux attempted to play a more activist role in 1793, the departmental and municipal authorities shut it down. Jacques Monbrion, by contrast, mistrusted those judicial and administrative authorities. He, too, recognized the need for the people to be enlightened (given their propensity to elect undeserving officials) and saw a role for clubs to play in that regard, but he also envisioned for them a more active role. Clubs would not only mold the will of the people, they would give it strength through unity, give it expression through active correspondence (in order to lobby elected officials), and ultimately, as we have seen in the cases of Lyon and Marseille, provide a vehicle for the people to organize and coordinate their voices in the election of municipal officials. As we have seen in all four federalist cities, nowhere more eloquently expressed than in the letter from Laugier and Girard to Roland, the prospect of the people organized was frightening to the propertied elite. In Bordeaux and Caen a unified elite met that challenge in advance and managed it quite well. In Lyon and Marseille a fragmented elite let power slip from their grasp and were forced to fight a rearguard action, in the end resorting to violence themselves, in order to regain it. But they recognized all too well that the victory of the Montagnards in Paris would almost certainly restore to local office the Jacobins whom they had just defeated.

Abraham Furtado and Jacques Monbrion cannot be said to represent all of the Bordelais or Marseillais, or even all of the Jacobins in their respective cities. But their pamphlets accurately reflect the nature of local politics in their two cities, and theirs are eloquent voices in the national debate over sovereignty and representation that embroiled the French republic in 1792–93. The assault on the Tuileries, the September massacres, municipal elections throughout France in the fall and winter, the trial of Louis XVI, the struggle between Girondins and Montagnards, the insurrection of May 29 in Lyon, the victory of the sections in Marseille, the insurrection of May 31 in Paris, and the federalist revolt that followed—all of these addressed at heart this most fundamental of political issues: who are the sovereign people and how shall they exercise their sovereignty?

66. Jacques Monbrion, "Adresse au Peuple" (Marseille, 1792). A copy of the printed pamphlet can be found in A.N., AD XVI, 26. I am indebted to Jacques Guilhaumou, who first brought this intriguing pamphlet to my attention.

Six

CONTEMPORARY PERSPECTIVES ON THE REVOLT

Oh, Parisians! This is what the factious call a superb *journée*, a beautiful, moral insurrection, and myself I say to you that it is the most horrible attack that one could commit; it is a great, counterrevolutionary movement; it is the dissolution of the Convention; it is the death of the republic and of liberty, it is the complete ruin of Paris; it is not enough to shake your caps at the end of your pikes and bayonets and to cry "Long live the Republic."

—Jean‑Denis Lanjuinais, June 2, 1793

Parisians, without a doubt, have today more than ever done justice to the zeal that the departments have shown for the defense of liberty and of the republic: they ignore none of the sacrifices that the people of the departments have made, and continue to make every day. But republicans, our brothers and friends, the justice that Parisians do to you, they expect in return; what part of the sovereign people has given up more to the Revolution, has done more to build it, has sacrificed more to maintain it? . . .

For ourselves, whatever position you may take, nothing could take from us the sweet consolation, the unique pleasure of having achieved the common good, of having been the authors of a revolution that will be the third in our annals, *without the shedding of blood or tears.*

—Address from Parisians to their brothers of the departments, June 1793

Events seldom speak for themselves, and in the aftermath of the insurrection of June 2, 1793, different versions of the uprising competed for the hearts and minds of literate Frenchmen in both Paris and the provinces. Supporters of the Girondins, men such as Jean-Denis Lanjuinais, who represented the Ille-et-Vilaine in the National Convention, denounced the uprising as a violation of national unity. The Paris Commune, in contrast, defended the insurrection that it had done so much to initiate.[1] What were the people to believe about June 2? Had it been a sweet and glorious blow (remarkably peaceful) in defense of liberty and the republic? Or was it a vile attack on the integrity of the National Convention, a trampling on the liberty of the French people?

Both sides to the conflict—the proscribed deputies and their supporters, on the one hand, the Jacobins and Montagnards, on the other—recognized how

1. B.N., Lb⁴¹ 665, "Second discours de Lanjuinais, député par le département de L'Isle et Vilaine à la Convention nationale, prononcé le dimanche deux de juin 1793, et détails très circonstanciés des faits les plus mémorables de cette journée" (slnd); B.N., Lb⁴¹ 667, "Adresse des Parisiens à leurs frères des Départemens" (Paris, 1793). The second address was prepared by the Commune of Paris.

much was at stake in June 1793. A great deal rested on perceptions, and these two official pronouncements were clearly aimed at molding those perceptions. But how much of this propaganda were people prepared to believe? The fact that the federalist rebels were unable to rally their constituents for a march on the capital suggests that the people of the provinces were not convinced that the National Convention had been illegally violated and that anarchy now reigned in Paris. But other factors might also explain the lack of enthusiasm for a march to Paris—it cost money to mount such an expedition, and a series of patriotic campaigns had already taxed the resources of most people; the war effort and the rebellion in the Vendée had drawn considerable manpower from each of the federalist cities; and economic considerations (the slumping economy in Lyon and Marseille, the impending harvest throughout France) may have left many people disinclined to leave the relative security of home to embark on a campaign whose goals seemed uncertain to them.

What was the public mood, what were people thinking during this critical period? There are a variety of sources, ranging from semipublic reports to private correspondence, that allow us to go beyond the "official record" in gauging public sentiment. The minister of the interior, Joseph Garat, was naturally concerned with maintaining public order, fragile as it was, both in Paris and the provinces. To that end, police spies submitted regular reports on the state of *esprit public* (public spirit or public opionion) in the capital, and Garat sent two separate batches of agents into the provinces in spring and summer 1793. The first of these, proposed by Garat as early as January, were to travel incognito throughout France, gathering information on political and economic conditions in the country. Some thirty-six of these agents set out on mission in May and June, each carrying a copy of Arthur Young's *Voyage en France* and Adam Smith's *Wealth of Nations* (translated into French). A second batch of fifty-two agents was commissioned by Garat in June to distribute copies of the recently completed constitution, particularly in those departments where local authorities could not be expected to publicize the constitution themselves. Both sets of agents sent regular reports to Garat, and their letters are an important source regarding the mood of the country.[2]

A number of representatives on mission, deputies sent by the National Convention, were already in the provinces when the vote was taken in Paris to proscribe twenty-nine of their colleagues. Some of these deputies were present in or near the federalist cities, and others were in neighboring departments. Their letters, too, sent to the Committee of Public Safety, offer telling evidence of the uncertainty that prevailed in the first weeks of June, before an official line was

2. Pierre Caron, *Rapports des Agents du Ministre de l'Intérieur dans les départements (1793-an II)*, 2 vols. (Paris, 1913–15).

established regarding the June 2 insurrection or the brewing provincial revolts. To these letters we might add interrogation transcripts, personal letters, and newspaper reports, from both Paris and the provinces.

This sort of evidence, taken together, will still be suggestive rather than conclusive about attitudes and perceptions in Paris and the departments. Some of Garat's agents were more eloquent, and perceptive, than others. Some interrogators were more interested in settling scores, in sending enemies to the guillotine, than in searching for truth. But these sources offer us a glimpse of the mood of the country as the nation teetered on the brink of civil war.

Over the course of the first five months of 1793, the French nation had grown weary of the factionalism within the National Convention—departmental administrations, municipal councils, and popular societies throughout the country sent letters to Paris calling for an end to the squabbling.[3] It had become clear to many in the provinces that the Convention was no longer the bastion of "unity and indivisibility" that revolutionaries held up as their national ideal. Most people also came to realize that there were competing versions of those divisions. By the same token, in many provincial cities comparable divisions had emerged in late 1792 and early 1793—within the social and political elites, between municipal and departmental councils, between clubs and elected authorities, between clubs and sectional assemblies.

There is evidence of such divisions, to varying degrees, in each of the federalist cities. Representatives on mission, sent out in April and May to assist with recruitment and also to address local political conflicts, not only failed to resolve those divisions in most cases but often managed to exacerbate them. Thus, people in the departments were skeptical about "official" news of the events of May 31–June 2, and deputies and political activists in Paris knew better than to accept at face value the official reports coming from the departments, either about popular reaction to news of the proscriptions or, for example, the official versions of the sectional insurrections in Lyon and Marseille. Everyone, or nearly everyone, understood that pervasive skepticism. This is why the Paris Commune drafted its letter to the departments and why the Marseillais and Lyonnais both sent delegations of citizens to Paris to defend their recent actions before the Convention. The Caennais also sent a delegation to Paris in early June both to deliver their department's protest and to gather reliable information about the events in the nation's capital.

In the midst of what was clearly a national crisis, then, people were desperate to gather information about what was going on and unsure of whom to trust as a source of such information. Partisans of one side or the other, by contrast,

---

3. See Henri Wallon, *La Révolution du 31 mai et le fédéralisme en 1793* (Paris, 1886), 2 vols., for a representative sample of such letters and addresses.

whether in Paris or the provinces, knew exactly what version of events they wished to disseminate. The question for them was how best to get that version out, and how to counter, or control, the circulation of contrary reports.

As an example of the former we might consider a letter, dated June 8, sent by the directory of the district of Morlaix, in Finistère, to the representatives on mission Joseph-Marie-François Sévestre and Jean-Baptiste Cavaignac, in Brest. The district had just been ordered by the departmental administration to raise a contingent of 104 men and to name a delegate to accompany them on their march to Paris in order to restore the proscribed deputies to their seats. The Morlaix administrators asked the representatives on mission what course of action they would advise, so that they might "reconcile the obedience that we owe to the higher authority with the safety of the Republic."[4]

Cavaignac and Sévestre replied immediately, observing that "we feel, as do you, that the two measures ordered by the departmental administration could have very dangerous consequences for liberty, and lead to a civil war that would shatter the Republic and return us to slavery." They went on to say, however, that if it were true that the Convention had been violated, it was indeed the duty of all citizens to rally to its defense. "You see then, citizens, that everything depends on facts and circumstances. We would need more knowledge ourselves to form a clear opinion and to advise a course of action." They therefore counseled prudence, cautioning that private letters might well exaggerate, or even be mistaken about, events in Paris but also observing that the district council was in fact subordinate to the department and should follow its lead unless there was clear evidence that it was abusing its authority.[5]

This exchange suggests several interesting points. Although virtually all of the federalist departments uniformly condemned the representatives on mission in their region as "proconsuls," not all deputies in the field at this time acted capriciously or had alienated local authorities. Nor did all of those deputies (most of whom, like Sévestre and Cavaignac, sat with the Mountain) rush to defend the proscription of the Girondin deputies or condemn out of hand those who were poised to protest that action. To be sure, to counsel prudence and restraint would serve the cause of the Montagnards—each passing day would bring the cooling of emotions and reduce the likelihood of upheaval. For the federalist rebels, in contrast, prompt action was essential if they were to have any chance of undoing what had occurred in Paris.

Paris, too, relied on the representatives on mission for information. On the same day that Sévestre and Cavaignac wrote their letter to Morlaix, the deputies Creuze and Thibaudeau, on mission to the army near La Rochelle, wrote to the

4. A.N., AF II 46, dossier 360.
5. Ibid.

Committee of Public Safety from Poitiers: "The people of Paris are accused of tyranny, and the National Convention of weakness. It is difficult for us to judge the truth of reports that have been dictated, perhaps, by a spirit of party, and all that we can do is to subdue public effervescence and try to rally all good citizens to the national representation." They warned that the current state of crisis must not long endure—the people would not tolerate it, and it would render their recruitment efforts impossible. The people were clamoring for a republican constitution. Creuze and Thibaudeau reported that a coalition of departments was contemplating an address to the Convention and expressed their concern that such an extraordinary action might well undermine the unity of the republic. The potential leadership of Bordeaux in such an effort was particularly worrisome.

Even the representatives on mission Romme and Prieur, who had been arrested by the rebels in Caen, were reluctant to condemn those who protested the recent proscriptions. They wrote to the Committee of Public Safety that their arrest "might serve the cause of liberty, preserve the unity of the Republic and restore public confidence" if the Convention would issue a decree declaring them hostages against the safety of the arrested deputies. The people of Caen, they reported, were full of "love for liberty, for justice and for docility."[6]

Most towns and cities in France had established regular communication links with Paris over the course of the Revolution. Departmental administrations received reports and decrees from both the minister of the interior and the National Convention, and these were circulated to district and municipal councils. Jacobin clubs received circulars from the mother society as well as from other provincial clubs, and most subscribed to one or more Paris newspapers. Deputies to the National Convention corresponded regularly with departmental and municipal councils and with Jacobin clubs back home, sometimes collectively (as a departmental delegation) and sometimes as individuals. Personal letters, between friends or business colleagues, could also be an important source of news from Paris.

Most of the Gironde deputies wrote regularly to their constituents. In late May and early June letters reached Bordeaux from Vergniaud, Gensonné, Grangeneuve, Guadet, Ducos, and Boyer-Fonfrède. All were well known and respected in Bordeaux, active in local politics early in the Revolution, and founders of the Bordeaux Jacobin club. Grangeneuve's younger brother presided over the club in mid-June. The letters from these deputies must have had a profound impact on the Bordelais. As Alan Forrest puts it, they "played a major part in forging their mood of determination."[7]

---

6. Ibid. Creuze and Thibaudeau wrote their letter on June 9, Romme and Prieur on June 10.
7. Alan Forrest, *The Revolution in Provincial France: Aquitaine, 1789–1799* (Oxford, 1996), 185.

One still senses in Bordeaux, however, an element of uncertainty about exactly what had occurred in Paris and what might be done to respond. One finds evidence of this in the minutes of the Bordeaux Jacobin club.[8] As early as May 26, members of the club began to talk seriously of raising a departmental force to be sent to Paris to protect the National Convention. The next day, a letter from Pierre-Joseph Lamarque, a member of the municipal council then in Paris, reported on the arrival of a delegation from Marseille and urged the Bordelais to send one themselves. On May 28, a letter from the deputy Boyer-Fonfrède warned of new plots to assassinate thirty-three deputies and dissolve the National Convention. This alarming news, consistent with the letters sent by Vergniaud early in May, was confirmed by letters from both Vergniaud and Gensonné that arrived in the first week of June.

Pierre Drignac, another municipal councilor, frequently shared personal letters with his fellow Jacobins. On June 1, he sent his friend Bruno Marandon, editor of the *Courrier de la Gironde*, a letter from Boyer-Fonfrède, along with the admonition that the letter was not to be copied under any circumstances. One wonders at the reason for such a precaution. There was nothing exceptional about the letter, which was read aloud to those present. Boyer-Fonfrède described the tumult in Paris, the precarious situation of the deputies from the Gironde, and the growing dominance of Parisian anarchists. When the club appealed to Drignac to allow the printing of the letter for circulation to the sections, he readily consented. Perhaps his willingness was prompted by another letter received on June 1, this one from Grangeneuve, which reported on the events of May 28 and warned club members that one could not expect Parisian newspapers to report these developments accurately.

Over the next two weeks the club was deluged with letters and personal reports, so much so that entries to the minutes became quite sketchy. On June 4 Lamarque returned from Paris, ending a four-month journey around the country. He apparently left Paris before June 2 and so brought no eye-witness account of those events, but he did encourage the Bordelais to send a delegation to Marseille. Drignac shared another letter from Boyer-Fonfrède on June 8, sent via "an unknown citizen," reporting that the Convention no longer existed and that all Paris papers were being edited by Maratists.

Clearly the Paris newspapers were not to be trusted, which rendered personal letters all the more important.[9] These were soon embellished by personal testi-

---

8. A.D. Gironde, 12L14, (minutes of the Bordeaux Jacobin club). Unless otherwise noted, the following discussion relies exclusively on these minutes.

9. Despite what appears to have been a general skepticism toward Paris newspapers, when the departmental administration received a copy of the June 3 issue of the *Feuille du Soir*, including an account of the events of June 2, it immediately ordered that copies were to be printed and sent to neighboring departments. A.D. Gironde, 3L7 (minutes of the departmental council for June 6, 1793).

mony. A citizen from Paris visited the club on June 10 and told the members that although the people and sections of Paris were good, they lived in fear of a repeat of the September massacres and hence remained quiet in the face of Maratist agitation. Another visitor from Paris, present at the same meeting, denounced both Robespierre and Danton. Yet there is something both vague and predictable about these accounts. It is not clear from the minutes when these two Parisians had last been in the capital, and the information they offered had been a staple of anti-Jacobin propaganda for months. One cannot help but wonder if their testimony, as well as the letters from "unknown citizens" being forwarded by Drignac, were not orchestrated in some fashion.

As the summer progressed, propaganda was generated on all sides. We have already encountered, in Chapter 3, a number of the declarations issued by the rebel authorities in the four federalist cities, almost always exaggerating the number of departments engaged in active protest. The letter from the Paris Commune "to their brothers of the departments" attempted to portray the events of May 31–June 2 in the best possible light, and the Commune sent commissioners out to the provinces to carry that message. Garat's agents, too, did everything they could to reassure those they met that the Convention continued to deliberate in freedom and that all was well in Paris.

None of Garat's agents traveled to the Gironde, but in late June or perhaps early July a sixteen-page pamphlet appeared in Bordeaux purporting to be a letter from a citizen of Bordeaux to a friend back home, written after a trip to Paris. The anonymous letter writer had left Bordeaux toward the end of June, full of fear and trepidation, having been led to believe the worst about Parisians. But in the first Parisian cafe he entered people befriended him, even after learning that he was from Bordeaux. He met good *sans-culottes* from the faubourg Saint-Antoine who told him that because Parisians had just voted to accept the new constitution there was to be singing and dancing all day long! All of Paris, the letter reported, seemed to be one big happy family. Even the Jacobins he had encountered "were the best fellows in the world."[10]

The transparency of such a piece is readily apparent to us today, as it likely was to the more worldly and politically active citizens of Bordeaux. But among those Bordelais who had never set foot in Paris, had perhaps never left the boundaries of the department, a letter such as this (given some credibility by the mere fact of its being printed) must have sown a few doubts about the more alarming reports emanating from the capital. Such doubts may have discouraged people from signing up for the departmental force. But others might have been drawn to enroll by the promise of singing and dancing and the camaraderie of Parisian cafes.

10. A.D. Gironde, 8J711, "Lettre d'un Citoyen de Bordeaux, à un de ses amis, dans le département de la Gironde" (slnd).

The arrival in Bordeaux of messengers from other cities and departments presented another source of information, one that tended to confirm the gravity of the situation and convey the impression of a nationwide movement of protest. Subrin and Girard arrived from Lyon on June 7. On June 22 commissioners from the Jura, the Lot-et-Garonne, the Hérault, and another from the Rhône-et-Loire spoke before the Jacobin club, followed by two messengers from Calvados bringing news of the Central Committee of Resistance to Oppression. Reports from Marseille also tended to feed the enthusiasm for revolt in Bordeaux.

But there were voices of caution as well. On June 19, a letter from the deputy Guadet, dated June 14, was read before a meeting of the Jacobin club. Guadet characterized the arrest of representatives on mission (Romme and Prieur had already been arrested in Caen), the sequestering of public funds (authorities in each of the federalist cities would resort to this), and the refusal of protesting departments to recognize the authority of the National Convention as dangerous and impolitic actions. He advised other measures, though the Jacobin club did not choose to record those suggestions in its minutes before forwarding the letter to the Popular Commission.[11]

Whatever the members of the Popular Commission might have thought of Guadet's advice, they forged ahead with the implementation of nearly all the actions he counseled against as well as the formation of an armed force to march to Paris. There was a shortage of volunteers for that force, and some of those who were reluctant to serve wrote letters to the military committee of the Popular Commission to explain their reticence. One such letter came from Jean-Baptiste Duluc, a young man who had moved to Bordeaux from Paris in October 1792, sent by his father so that he might learn about trade. He had joined the National Guard in Bordeaux, and on June 25 the Popular Commission ordered that all National Guard companies draw lots to fill the ranks of the departmental force. Jean-Baptiste had drawn the short straw, but he protested that he ought to be exempt from such service on several counts. First, he was an only son. Second, he had some sort of nose ailment that frequently afflicted him. But most important, his father, mother, sisters, and grandfather all lived in Paris. All this he had shared with his company, but they ignored him. As he eloquently concluded his appeal, "but you, Citizens, you must surely shudder at the thought of a son forced to march against his father." Others petitioned for exemption from service on more mundane grounds (one recruit begged off because he had no teeth), but surely Duluc was not the only one who saw the idea of sending an armed force to Paris as a contradiction of the revolutionary ideal of fraternity.[12]

11. A.D. Gironde, 12L14.
12. A.D. Gironde, 12L37.

Duluc's plea, and implicit warning that the Popular Commission was teetering on the brink of civil war, could have been rooted in self-interest, of course. But another letter survives in the archives, equally impassioned, sent to the Jacobin club of Bordeaux by a former club member who had moved to Rouen to take up a post as teacher in a mathematics school. We know little about L. Prudhomme, as he signed his name, beyond what the letter tells us. The letter is undated, though the text suggests that it was written shortly after the July 13 battle at Vernon. The tone of the letter hints that Prudhomme was a young man ("do not disdain the advice of your student," he wrote at one point) and that he had left Bordeaux for Rouen after the flight to Varennes ("It was amongst you that my passion for liberty and equality was born; I was still amongst you when I first longed for a republican regime"). It is a long letter, more than ten handwritten pages, and it is fascinating both for the depth of feeling it reveals and for the insight it offers into the divide that now separated men who had once been united in their opposition to the monarchy. There is urgency in Prudhomme's letter but not stridency. He is profoundly troubled by the published proclamations of the Bordeaux rebels, fearful of what might lie ahead. But he is writing to friends, not enemies. Even as late as mid-July, after the battle at Vernon and the death of Marat, he remains confident that their differences can be resolved, that the dangerous course being charted by the Bordelais is rooted in error, not malice. Prudhomme's letter was intended to convince, not condemn, and it merits a lengthy consideration.[13]

"My brothers and very good friends," began Prudhomme, a phrase that he repeated many times in his long letter. He apologized for taking so long to reply to the June 24 letter he had received from the Bordeaux club, citing the responsibilities of his school and his public involvement in Rouen: "However, I can no longer put off the expression of my sadness at seeing the purest, the most generous, the most republican of all the popular societies of the republic forgetting its virtues, in order to follow the heat of the delirious passions of a few individuals, desperate because their heinous projects, worthy of the vengeance of republicans, have been exposed. Read my letter to the end, I pray of you, and you will see if I have ceased to merit your friendship." Prudhomme knew, then, that his words were not likely to be welcomed in Bordeaux, but nonetheless he spoke bluntly to his fellow Jacobins. His next paragraph makes clear, however, that he was more than a former club member and hoped that

---

13. A.D. Gironde, 12L32. These letters of Prudhomme and Duluc are also interesting because they illustrate something obvious yet easy to forget in studying this period: life went on for most people even in the midst of revolutionary upheaval. Duluc had come to Bordeaux to pursue a career in commerce. Prudhomme had moved to Rouen to teach mathematics. Yet both remained actively engaged in the Revolution—Duluc in the National Guard, Prudhomme in the Rouen Jacobin club—and committed to the ideals of 1789.

his friendship would earn him their forbearance: "I shared your sentiments in everything, I was always worthy of you; I am therefore one of the family, so do not reject, do not disdain the advice of your student, of your brother, and above all of a brother who cherishes you; but one who prefers the truth and the safety of the republic to you."

In his effort to persuade his brothers in Bordeaux that their opposition to the National Convention had placed the republic in peril, Prudhomme pursued a dual strategy in his letter. He, on the one hand, traced the history of the divisions within the Convention, up to the *journées* of May 31 and June 2 and, on the other, analyzed the implications of their present course of action, trying to make clear that their rebellion jeopardized the very thing they claimed to hold most dear:

> You have trembled, you tell me, over the fate of liberty. What patriot has not bemoaned the troubles, the scandal within the Convention? But, brothers and friends, what has been the cause of those ills, who were the members of that liberticide faction of which you have spoken to me, if they are not the leaders of the right wing? . . . You are in insurrection, and your departmental administrators have joined Bordeaux and their efforts are applauded by the People? But by whom are this people enlightened, who leads them, who proves to them that this assemblage that I call a confabulation, is there for their safety, whereas it is leading them by the shortest route to Despotism, and to feudalism by way of federalism.

Prudhomme could understand the position taken by the Bordelais because he had once shared their view:

> I thought as you do, and my correspondence with my very good friend Boyer-Fonfrède attests to it; I thought that the commune of Paris wished to municipalize France and make itself the center of the national will and strength. May 27 seemed to prove it, but the Convention was in fact surrounded on that day by counterrevolutionaries, who were only after the patriotic members; but they thwarted the infernal cabal by their imposing firmness: firmness that you did not see among the members of the right wing on May 31 and June 2, days on which the thunder of the people rumbled all around them, but without striking them, whatever the cowards might say.

Prudhomme would have hoped to enhance his influence among his former fellow clubbists by this reference to Boyer-Fonfrède, whose reputation among the Bordelais was well known. But he did not shy away from harsh criticism of the deputies of the Gironde and others of the right wing, though he seldom referred to them by name. His letter has a rambling quality to it. He would get ahead of himself in his argument at times and be forced to circle back to complete an unfinished thought. More than once he insisted that he must bring his epistle to an end, only to be carried forward by his fervor and enthusiasm for another page or two. Prudhomme apologized for the "republican frankness" with which he spoke to his friends but asked them: "What do you imagine republicans will think, those who once saw you to be well spoken, so generous, so grand in the face of danger, when now they see everywhere nothing but invitations to federalism; they see on the roads emissaries from Bordeaux attempting to corrupt, the word slips out, yes corrupt those wavering departments, and those already disposed toward federalism; when they see you invite faithful generals to join your cause and that of the other departments pulled along in these liberticide steps." Prudhomme's frank and probing question has become a statement by the end. It is striking that he uses the term "federalism" at several points in the letter, showing that it had gained common usage by mid-July. In his criticism of the deputies of the "right wing" he used both the term "Brissotin" and the term "Girondin," further evidence that this label had at least a limited contemporary usage. He characterized the Girondins as "*hommes d'état*," thereby distinguishing them from the Montagnards, who had not held government posts during the months of factional struggle. He, like the Bordelais, had once held the Girondins in high esteem. They had enjoyed his confidence.

What, then, had shattered Prudhomme's confidence in the Girondin leadership? He was now convinced that the Girondin deputies had been secretly working for the restoration of the monarchy, which he hoped to prove to his Bordeaux brothers, or at least to give them enough evidence to impress them (*pour vous ébranler*). And he would draw that evidence from facts (*dans les faits*, which we might also translate as "deeds"). The "proof" that Prudhomme offered in his letter is interesting not because it was compelling, but rather because it was plausible and bears a striking resemblance to the case that would eventually be made against the proscribed deputies. Prudhomme provided no documentary evidence but rather presented a sort of narrative of events (*les faits*) that were more or less publicly known, interpreted in such a way as to condemn the actions (or inactions) of the Girondin deputies and to call their motivations into question.

Before turning to his evidence of the Girondins' royalism, however, Prudhomme felt compelled to defend the deputies of the Mountain, whom the Bordeaux clubbists had attacked in their most recent letters to him and in a published circular. How, he asked, could they not approve the conduct of the

Mountain "when that conduct has given us a republican constitution, whose principal points of perfection are the respect that it guarantees for property, and the love that it inspires and demands for old age and in that sweet humanity, in that touching pity that one owes to misfortune." This is all that Prudhomme had to say about the new constitution, other than to extol it in general terms, but it is striking that in this single phrase he appeals both to its defense of property and to its concern for the less fortunate in society. How could one oppose the deputies who had drafted a constitution of such noble sentiments, much less the constitution itself? But this, of course, was precisely what the Bordelais seemed intent on doing: "Do you therefore not want the republic? Do you therefore not want liberty?"

Prudhomme could scarcely believe this to be true of his erstwhile comrades, yet their declaration of insurrection in support of the proscribed deputies seemed to suggest otherwise. This brought Prudhomme squarely back to the issue of the Girondins' royalism and in the process set up a very neat rhetorical opposition: to oppose the new constitution (the work of the Mountain) was to oppose the republic; the Girondins, who had undeniably stood in opposition to the Montagnards in the National Convention, must therefore have opposed the republic. But Prudhomme offered more than syllogistic reasoning in support of this allegation. From the very beginning of the Convention, he argued, the Girondins had "profited by their talents and their dinners at the table of Roland" to establish a following among the other deputies, a position they sought to support by the creation of a departmental force. When that effort failed, they turned to the army and General Dumouriez, whom they continued to shield even when the evidence of his treason became virtually undeniable. This alleged complicity with Dumouriez, whose royalist sympathies were now well known, was the most damning proof that Prudhomme had to offer of his charge that the Girondins had conspired to restore the monarchy.

As with his defense of the Montagnards, however, Prudhomme bolstered his case against the proscribed deputies by referring to events and actions that took place after June 2. Those same deputies who had conspired with Dumouriez, for whose liberty the Bordelais had declared themselves in insurrection, had incited the troubles in Calvados and the Eure and in Lyon as well.

In Prudhomme's view, then, the good republicans of Bordeaux had been misled by their elected representatives. But the fact that they were simply misguided rather than being willfully counterrevolutionary in no way diminished the gravity of their actions nor the perilous consequences that would follow should they fail to mend their ways:

> You wish to prevent the breaking of the unity and indivisibility of the republic, but the efforts you have made have broken them: all is in

pieces, the Convention has ceased to be the common center for a number of departments, they no longer communicate with her, they threaten the lives of her emissaries, they intercept her correspondence, so vital to the safeguarding of liberty, they act as sovereigns. Brothers and friends, if this disorder endures, the republic is in grave danger! So many sacrifices, so much blood shed, so many privations, so many vows, so many worries—for what? For what? To replace on the throne, which you had reduced to powder, a monster who will soon devour you!

Far from preserving the unity of the republic or respect for the National Convention, the Bordeaux rebels had imperiled both by their actions. Although Prudhomme did not use the term "federalism" in this passage, he makes clear its essential meaning at the time: the rebel departments were guilty of federalism because they had claimed for themselves the sovereign authority of the National Convention. Ultimately that challenge to the Convention would prove to be counterrevolutionary, he argued, because it would lead to a restoration of the monarchy, the hidden agenda of the proscribed deputies themselves. If all they had fought and sacrificed for was not to be lost, the Bordelais must come to their senses: "Make haste, your attitude emboldens the departments that have followed you, or which pulled you along. Why do Lyon, Marseille, Toulon, Brest, Calvados, etc., supposedly in insurrection in order to resist oppression, why do they not employ their energy to defend our new constitution, so firmly republican, so popular?" Instead those departments, and the Bordelais, resisted the Convention, which had drafted that new constitution, in order to inspire hatred toward the Revolution itself. That resistance (and here Prudhomme indulged his profession) represented "mathematical proof of the counterrevolutionary spirit that guided those departments and towns."

This was an impassioned appeal, less coherent, perhaps, in its original form than as presented here, but expressive of the kind of argument that French republicans were having amongst themselves as the nation confronted the crisis of June–July 1793 and uncannily prescient of the main outlines that official policy would eventually take toward the federalist rebels. Those who had erred in declaring their opposition to the National Convention might still mend their ways and join their republican brothers by rallying to the new constitution. The deputies of the Mountain, so maligned in the months before May 31 as apostles of anarchy and disorder, deserved credit for drafting that new constitution, and the Girondins now stood exposed as royalist conspirators. Their supporters in the departments, Prudhomme argued, including the Bordelais, were the unwitting agents of federalism and civil war.

We cannot know what impact Prudhomme's letter had on the Bordeaux Jacobins—perhaps it persuaded a few of them not to enroll in the departmental force. But there were also letters arriving in Bordeaux in mid-July that sought to bolster the insurrectionary sentiments in the city. One such letter, written by an anonymous Lyonnais merchant on July 2, was ordered printed and posted by the *Commission Populaire* of the Gironde. The letter reported the previous day's creation in Lyon of their own Popular Commission, presided over by that "most pure Republican," Gilibert. Delegates from Marseille had recently joined them in a civic festival, but the city was under constant threat from Dubois-Crancé and the Army of the Alps. Preparations for defense of the city were underway, with eighteen hundred national guardsmen on constant duty (rotated each week), digging defensive trenches and manning the one hundred cannon pieces deployed at the city's perimeter. The republic was in danger, to be sure, though the threat came not from the proscribed deputies but from the Montagnard representative on mission, Dubois-Crancé.

Not all news from Lyon was ominous, however. The letter also reported that seven to eight thousand Marseille volunteers were "at the doors" of Lyon, and that an armed force directed by representatives on mission against the departmental administration of the Jura had been turned back near Lons-le-Saunier by a crowd of some twenty thousand peasants. This letter suggested, then, that a national movement had indeed been mobilized in opposition to Paris and the Montagnard Convention.[14]

The Bordelais Popular Commission had of course tried to encourage that national movement by the envoy of commissioners in June throughout much of the country, and the reports of glowing success they sent back helped to sustain the wavering resolve of the Bordelais.[15] Yet, those commissioners were not always warmly received, as was the case with Etienne Hallot, sent on mission to the southeast with Pierre Lavaugayon. The two went directly to Marseille, where section assemblies were indeed delighted to learn of Bordeaux's declaration of revolt. But from there Hallot journeyed north, accompanied by a representative of the Marseille sections, B. F. A. Fonvielle. Hallot and Fonvielle went first to the Drôme, where the departmental administration, despite its early declaration of protest against the June 2 proscriptions, refused to convene an assembly that the two commissioners might address. Stymied in their effort to rally the people to the federalist cause, the two drafted and printed an open letter to "their brothers of the department of the Drôme." This letter, like those above, tells us something about how the federalist rebels made their case to potential allies, but it also provides indirect evidence of the resistance they encountered.

Like Prudhomme in his letter to the Bordelais, Hallot and Fonvielle began

14. A.C. Bordeaux, MS 228 (Fonds Vivie).
15. See Alan Forrest, *Society and Politics in Revolutionary Bordeaux* (Oxford, 1975), 136–44, for a discussion of a number of those missions.

by flattering their audience, referring to their brothers of the Drôme as "the first apostles of liberty." They called upon the citizens of the Drôme to reclaim their sovereignty, denied to them in the first instance by the Mountain, the new Titans of France, who sought power through murder and pillage, and in the second instance by their own departmental administrators, whose courage had faltered in the face of the bayonets commanded by Dubois-Crancé. Leaving aside their cowardly administrators, however, Hallot and Fonvielle urged the men of the Drôme to direct their "hatred and vengeance" against the new tyrants of the Mountain, listing by name Robespierre, Danton, and Marat as well as the two representatives on mission to the Army of the Alps, Dubois-Crancé and Antoine-Louis Albitte. May 31, they asserted, had been a counterrevolutionary movement, a criminal movement led by those who saw the republic only in Paris, an uprising in response to the "tocsin of anarchy." Now the "tocsin of liberty" was ringing out in the departments. Bordeaux and Marseille had taken the initiative and were showing the rest of France the path that they must follow, against the Montagnards in Paris, in order to reclaim their happiness.[16]

This was a stirring appeal, one that evoked many of the themes we have encountered in previous chapters: anarchy rampant in Paris; the triumvirate of Robespierre, Danton, and Marat intent upon dictatorial power; the opposition between Paris and the provinces, and the Parisian usurpation of national sovereignty. There are interesting embellishments here as well, though: the reference to the people of the Drôme as the "apostles of liberty" and the emphasis on the "proconsuls" Dubois-Crancé and Albitte. One sees here both the old opposition between Paris and the provinces that had been a staple of Girondin rhetoric during the winter and spring, but also an effort on the part of Hallot and Fonvielle to make the menace looming in Paris more immediate and real to the people of a department quite distant from the capital. Finally, it is worth noting, the uprising of May 31 is characterized not only as anarchical but as explicitly counterrevolutionary, just as the Montagnards would increasingly characterize their "federalist" opposition.

As stirring as the rhetoric of this pamphlet may have been, it failed to rouse the citizens of the Drôme, who stolidly refused to join in active resistance to the National Convention. Hallot and Fonvielle seemed to anticipate the reasons for that refusal. At any rate, they devoted the final pages of their appeal to a refutation of two of them: more than a page was taken up by a response to the charge that the rebels of Bordeaux and Marseille favored a "federalist" system, evidence that in the southeast, too, the federalist label was current as early as the first week of July (Hallot and Fonvielle met with the Drôme departmental adminis-

16. A.N., AF II 43, dossier 344, "Adresse des citoyens Hallot, député de la Gironde, et Fonvielle ainé, député des Bouches-du-Rhône, à leurs frères du Département de la Drôme" (slnd).

tration on July 3). They also made reference to the new constitution, already circulating in the departments, deriding it as farcical while asserting that "the majority of the nation refuses to receive it."

According to Alan Forrest, none of the Bordeaux commissioners succeeded in recruiting to the movement any town or department not already committed to the revolt. Most met with polite refusal, as did Hallot in the Drôme; some were lectured about the assault on national unity that was inherent in their protest; and some, as with those who visited the Haute-Vienne, were warned that any march toward Paris would be met by armed resistance. Such skepticism was rarely reported back to Bordeaux (or to Marseille or Lyon), though some of the commissioners were discouraged by their cool reception.[17]

Fonvielle, however, was quite committed to the cause (although in his case that cause may have been royalism).[18] Two weeks after his foray into the Drôme, he was at a meeting of the Popular Commission in Lyon, where he encountered delegates from several other departments. These included men from the Jura, the Ain, and the Doubs (all neighboring departments), and also a delegate from Calvados. The delegates from the Jura and Doubs, departmental administrators, had journeyed to Lyon as mediators, hoping to convince the Lyonnais to avert civil war by examining and voting on the new constitution, as their own constituents had done in recent days. Indeed, both departments, as well as the Ain, had voted to accept the new constitution. This was a significant shift, for these two departments had been among the first to protest the proscriptions of June 2 and to call for provincial opposition to Paris.

The six delegates arrived in Lyon on July 20, where they found the departmental administration essentially helpless, having ceded its authority to the Popular Commission. They circulated about town that day, trying to gauge the public mood, and in their letters home reported the Lyonnais to be suspicious of outsiders (themselves included) and deeply hostile toward Paris and the National Convention. The six appeared before the Popular Commission on July 21, urging its members to recognize the authority of the Convention and to endorse the new constitution. They offered as well to act as neutral mediators between Lyon and the Army of the Alps.

There was little discussion on July 21, but the next day Fonvielle, the unnamed delegate from Calvados, and François Bémani, one of the members of the

17. Forrest, *Society and Politics*, 136–44.
18. William Scott, *Terror and Repression in Revolutionary Marseille* (London, 1973), 80–82. Fonvielle, a native of Toulouse, was a marquis under the Old Regime. He arrived in Marseille in early 1792, having spent the first years of the Revolution in Sête and Montpellier. Fonvielle was among the "new men" who flocked to section assemblies in winter and spring 1793, leading to the defeat of the Jacobin municipality and the closing of the Jacobin club. He emigrated after the revolt in Marseille collapsed. See also *Mémoires historiques de M. le chevalier de Fonvielle de Toulouse* (Paris, 1824), 4 vols.

Popular Commission, angrily denounced this conciliatory proposal. Fonvielle accused the three departments of cowardice and denounced the six delegates as agents of Marat. Despite this inflammatory name-calling, a certain amount of reasoned discussion seems to have followed. One of the Doubs delegates, Bouvenot, insisted that a majority of departments now favored reconciliation. When Bémani responded that the visitors were misrepresenting the Lyonnais position, one of the Jura delegates observed that although they had taken the same position initially and were no friends to the Mountain, they lacked the ability to oppose them with force. Only by accepting the new constitution could they hope to challenge the Mountain in the next round of elections. To this Fonvielle replied that the Jura obviously shared the principles of the Lyonnais but did not dare to act on them, and he was joined by the delegate from Calvados, who taunted the others for their fear, urging them to return to the safety of their homes if they lacked the courage of the brave Normans and Bretons. This deterioration into regional boasting and recrimination prompted a call for recess until the afternoon.

When the Popular Commission reconvened, Fonvielle brought news that the Marseillais had taken Avignon and were marching up the Rhône valley toward Lyon. A letter from Bordeaux was produced, reporting that their departmental force was also en route. Finally the deputy Birotteau spoke, rejecting as folly the notion that good republicans might combat the Maratists who now controlled the Convention by adopting a flawed constitution and hoping for new elections. Only by an armed march on Paris could the departments achieve their purpose. These rejoinders brought the debate to a close, the well-intentioned effort at mediation a complete failure. Although primary assemblies in the Rhône-et-Loire would in fact vote to accept the new constitution on July 28, it was a meaningless gesture that did nothing to avert the looming confrontation between Lyon and the Army of the Alps.[19]

This exchange before the Popular Commission suggests some of the factors responsible for the failure of the federalist revolt. The most obvious is the inability of the protesting departments to raise volunteer forces for a march on Paris. The delegate from the Jura seemed to admit that it was only this failure that had prompted his department to abandon its active opposition to the National Convention and to accept the new constitution, in the hope that civil war might be avoided and that the ascendancy of the Montagnard faction might be contested in future elections. Fonvielle and the others deflected this argument

19. My attention was first drawn to this exchange before the Popular Commission by Professor Michael Sydenham, who very graciously shared with me his unpublished manuscript on the federalist revolt in the Jura, a generosity for which I am very grateful. For an account of the exchange itself, see Georges Guigue, ed., *Procès-verbaux de la Commission populaire, Républicaine et de Salut Public de Rhône-et-Loire, 30 juin à 8 octobre 1793* (Trevaux, 1899), 127–33.

by the convincing (though erroneous) assertion that armed resistance was not only possible, but was in fact being successfully mounted at that very moment in Normandy, Provence, and the Gironde. Although that assertion carried the day, it could not be long sustained, nor could it mask the fact that the rebels lacked both a rallying point and a clear objective. If national unity, or the achievement of a constitutional regime, was the goal, then the Montagnard Convention seemed the most promising prospect for reaching it given the newly proposed constitution. Not only was the new constitution a powerful piece of evidence that the factionalism of the Convention had been overcome, it also made plain the inability of the federalist rebels to present a positive alternative. There had been initial calls for the convocation of an alternative national assembly in Bourges, to be sure, but the call for a march to Paris carried a much more powerful emotional appeal, at least initially. The objective of such a march was essentially negative—either to undo what had been done on June 2, by restoring the proscribed deputies to office, or to reverse the outcome of that day by defeating the Montagnards (or Maratists). This must have seemed to many like an invitation to continue the dissension that had wracked the National Convention from January through May, only on a broader scale—to embroil the entire nation in a political dispute that could only end in civil war.

Fonvielle and the others had berated the six commissioners from the Jura, Doubs, and Ain for their cowardice, citing by contrast the bravery of the Caennais and Marseillais who were resolutely marching toward Paris. Troops were marching, but there was also uncertainty and dissension in Marseille, as revealed by an anonymous letter, dated July 19, addressed to an artillery captain by the name of Rocfer who was stationed at Besançon in the Doubs. The letter began with a reference to the sectional insurrection that spring:

> The looting, and the excesses of all sorts committed by the leaders of the club, led to the resistance to oppression that resulted in the Marseille revolution, but one would be mistaken if one believed that upheaval to have been in the name of true Republicanism. A multitude of aristocrats and royalists came out of their lairs and joined the true Republicans; they were numerous and dominated the sections and the General Committee. Once oppressed, they now became the oppressors. They reign by a system of terror; they fetter thought, and compromise patriotism; they have the Republic in their mouths and royalism in their hearts. From time to time, sparks are struck in the sections; but they are soon snuffed out by delegations from all of the others, and everything ends in accusations.
>
> An order of the sections has declared traitors to the fatherland anyone who proposes to read the new constitution; that oppression has

produced an effect quite opposite to that desired. Tempers are flaring, and we may yet see an upheaval that will return us to the excesses of before.

After a brief reference to Toulon (which appeared to be joining Marseille) and the taking of Avignon, the letter writer reported that primary assemblies in the Gard had just voted to accept the new constitution. This development, he feared, would make it nearly impossible for the Marseille volunteers to join up with those of Lyon. Moreover, the new recruitment effort was going badly. "I do not know after all whether I should be happy or distressed; I wish to crush anarchy, but I shudder to think that we are actually working either for Egalité [the duke of Orléans], or the young Capet [Louis XVII], or the duke of York, or federalism."[20]

Whoever the author of this letter may have been, he shows considerable insight into the divisions that had emerged among the sections of Marseille and suggests as well the doubts and uncertainties that plagued the federalist movement by early to mid July. Official pronouncements and propaganda maintained a brave face—always exaggerating the number of departments in revolt, reporting optimistically on the progress of departmental troops toward Paris, and continuing to excoriate in violent terms the anarchists and schemers who now allegedly controlled the National Convention. But while this letter writer was adamantly opposed to anarchism, he was equally opposed to federalism and suspected many of the rebels in Marseille to be veiled royalists. The sectional movement that had initially championed order and liberty had grown intolerant of those who spoke critically, and sectional leaders forbade public discussion and debate of the new constitution. With each department that voted to accept the new constitution, however, the federalists' claim that the Convention no longer existed grew less and less credible. Even a diminished National Convention held more promise as a symbol of national unity than the rebels' invocation of popular sovereignty and their calls for a march on Paris.

If provincial perceptions of the situation in Paris and the status of the National Convention changed over time, so too did Parisian perceptions of the character of the federalist revolt and the danger that it presented to the security of the capital and the unity of the republic. As noted above, Garat as minister of the interior sent two batches of agents out into the departments, one just before the revolt broke out and the second in late June. Their original mission was to gather information about the state of agriculture, commerce, and industry throughout the country, but the political crisis confronting the nation rendered that mission decidedly secondary.

20. A.N., D XLII, 4.

Letters written by the agents in Bordeaux and Lyon in late May are particularly interesting. Pascal-Thomas Fourcade was sent to the departments of the southwest in the second week of May. Although Bordeaux was not included in his mission, he passed through that city and on May 26 wrote a letter from Pau in which he offered a succinct assessment of the political climate in the city:

> The vast majority of the inhabitants want the Republic; but, misled by the hatred for Paris that has been inspired in them, they blindly follow the royalists who take advantage of those biases to lead them toward ideas of federalism. . . .
>
> Nearly all of the departments [through which he had traveled] are usurping legislative authority, they levy taxes, intercept or refuse to execute official decrees, take arbitrary actions, and generally treat the friends of the Revolution despotically.[21]

As with many of the agents who sent reports to Garat during these months, Fourcade emphasized that public spirit (*esprit public*) was generally good, that people supported the Revolution and favored democracy, but that apathy and antipathy toward Paris were real dangers. His linking of royalism and federalism seems to anticipate what would eventually become official policy, as does his insistence that although the people were good, "the city of Bordeaux has been corrupted."

Garat's agent to Lyon, Clément Gonchon, had accompanied Fourcade on two earlier missions, one to the Eure-et-Loir and the other to Belgium. In May he traveled alone to the city of his birth, where his father, a silk merchant, still lived. Gonchon was a silkworker himself, though he had lived in Paris for some time. He was reportedly present at the taking of the Bastille in 1789, played an active role in Parisian politics, and gained a reputation as the "orator of the faubourg Saint-Antoine." Despite his reputation as an ardent *sans-culotte*, he gravitated toward the Girondins in late 1792, and Louvet supported his failed candidacy in the elections to the National Convention.[22]

Gonchon was sent to the Rhône-et-Loire precisely because he was familiar

---

21. Caron, *Rapports des Agents*, vol. 1, 377–78.

22. I have relied principally on Caron, *Rapports des Agents*, vol. 1, 483–508, for this biographical information as well as the text for all of the letters to be discussed in the pages that follow. I have also consulted the original copies of these letters in the national and departmental archives. Bill Edmonds suggests that Gonchon was first sent on mission by Roland, but I believe he is mistaken in that assertion. Although Gonchon was eventually denounced as a Rolandin, he was not Roland's creature. One might note, in this regard, that François Laussel *was* originally sent to Lyon as an agent of Roland and yet came to be known as "the Marat of Lyon." One cannot always tell a man's politics by his associations. See Edmonds, *Jacobinism and the Revolt of Lyon*, 130, 156, and 215 for his discussion of Gonchon.

with the territory, as was the case with many of the "observer agents" commissioned by Garat. His family and friends in Lyon helped him gain access to sectional meetings and the confidence of the Lyonnais, a confidence that might otherwise have been denied a Parisian *sans-culotte* with impeccable revolutionary credentials. Gonchon sent a series of letters to Garat in late May and June, as well as to the Quinze-Vingts section in Paris. They make for fascinating reading today, as they must have at the time, for the May 29 insurrection in Lyon, which was almost universally denounced in Paris as a counterrevolutionary movement against loyal Jacobins, is described by Gonchon as a glorious victory for all true republicans. His sympathy for Lyon moderates earned him the enmity of Dubois-Crancé and eventual denunciation as a Rolandin, for which he spent a number of months in prison. Gonchon can hardly be considered an entirely neutral observer (not that there were many of these in France in 1793), but his letters yield a number of insights and his presence in Lyon probably served to delay the tragic consequences of the military engagement that he foresaw and warned against.

Gonchon wrote his first report to Garat on May 28, the eve of the troubles in Lyon. Four days earlier he had intervened in a dispute between a small merchant—a supplier of butter for the Army of the Alps—and a group of women who wished to have some of the butter for themselves. Gonchon announced his official status to the crowd, eliciting a derisive cry from the women, who suggested that he had probably been sent by the Convention with orders to protect monopolists. Sensing a potentially dangerous confrontation, Gonchon shifted from Parisian French to the local patois, assuring the women that he was a good *sans-culotte*, as concerned as they about fair prices, but that the people must not take justice into their own hands. He persuaded a few of the protesters to accompany him to town hall, where they spoke with the mayor, Bertrand, who then returned with them to the shop. Gonchon and Bertrand reasoned with the women for hours, on into the evening, and although they could not hold the crowd back from seizing a portion of the butter and selling it at what they deemed to be a fair price, they did prevent the sacking of the shop and the escalation of a dicey situation into full-fledged rioting. In the process Gonchon established himself as both a native son and a Parisian *sans-culotte*, an unusual combination in that place and time. We should not neglect in all this the importance of his ability to speak the local patois.

Gonchon closed his letter with a warning to Garat that trouble was brewing in the city, and he urged that two deputies from the Convention be sent. Indeed, he had heard rumors in town that one of them might be Pierre Vergniaud, which he thought would be excellent because he knew Vergniaud quite well and clearly respected him. It seems incongruous today to contemplate the idea of Vergniaud on mission to Lyon in late May 1793, and the fact that Gonchon considered it a possibility probably says something about his political naivete. At the same time, however, that personal characteristic seems to have allowed him to take individuals, and situations, at face value. There is both a disingenuousness and a frankness about his letters. When he next wrote, trouble had indeed erupted in Lyon, but Gonchon appears to have no inkling of the imminent insurrection in Paris.

Gonchon's letter of May 31 included a lengthy account of the May 29 insurrection. He began by noting the arrival earlier that week of the representatives on mission Gauthier and Nioche, observing that the Lyonnais viewed them with suspicion (particularly Gauthier, it seems). Gonchon reported that the poor of Lyon had been telling him of plans underway in the sections to unseat the municipal council, composed of *sans-culottes*, and replace them with aristocrats. He went on to describe the uprising in a very measured tone, including his own efforts to calm inflamed spirits, as well as those of the representatives on mission, and concluded with the simple observation that sectional forces had triumphed and peace had returned to the city. He promised to send more details the next day, which he did.

I have suggested above that Joseph Cambon's exaggerated report of the death toll occasioned by the counterrevolutionary upheaval in Lyon may well have contributed to the victory of the Montagnards on June 2, the day that Cambon reported the news to the Convention. Gonchon's letter of June 1, arriving some days later, painted a very different picture of those same events: "But, citizen Minister, reassure well the Convention, that she has nothing to fear! The citizens of Lyon have covered themselves with glory; they have shown the greatest courage in the battles that took place in the different neighborhoods of the city, and the greatest generosity toward their enemies, who behaved like scoundrels, for, if they had carried the day, Lyon would have been lost; more than 50,000 men would have had their throats slit."[23]

Gonchon had heard rumors that Dubois-Crancé was directing the Army of the Alps toward Lyon, and he shared his concern about the danger of such a course of action with Nioche. Should Dubois-Crancé march on the city, he wrote to Garat, "I will go before him to instruct him on all that has happened, and to describe for him the courage of the citizens of the sections."

Gonchon wrote again on June 3, continuing to sing the praises of the Lyon sections: "Oh citizen Garat, what a spectacle for a republican who sees on all sides his fatherland in danger! Yes, yes, we will be republicans, despite the intriguers and our enemies of all sorts. We will achieve that true republican virtue that consists of humanity, generosity, the love of good morals, and true courage, and it is the citizens of Lyon, who have been so calumniated, who will be the

---

23. Caron, *Rapports des Agents*, vol. 1, 493.

first to have given the example of true republican character. Search in the history of revolutions; find me a comparable example: being victorious, they have not shed a single drop of blood." One cannot question the revolutionary enthusiasm and idealism of Gonchon, but Garat and the members of the Committee of Public Safety who read this letter, and those that followed, must certainly have had doubts about his judgment. Cambon may have exaggerated the death toll on May 29, but to claim that not a single drop of blood had been shed was to err dramatically in the opposite direction. It is true that the victorious sectionaries did not take immediate reprisals against their Jacobin opponents (though they would do so in July), but Gonchon said nothing in his letters about those who had been killed in the fighting itself. Although the Jacobins in Paris would soon characterize the Lyon federalists as the dupes of royalist counterrevolutionaries, Gonchon insisted in this letter that it had been the Jacobin municipality that had been duped by clever *émigrés*. In his next letter, dated June 11, he informed Garat that he had been the guest of a number of sections, that their civic spirit was very good, and that (over drinks in the bars and cafes) he had even managed to convince a few of the diehard supporters of the club to attend sectional meetings.

Gonchon said almost nothing in his letters to Garat about the mission of Robert Lindet to Lyon, a surprising omission given that Gonchon's assessment of the situation was not dramatically different from Lindet's. Lindet did not, to be sure, sing the praises of the new authorities in Lyon who had refused, after all, to recognize his credentials as a representative of the National Convention. But Lindet, like Gonchon, had insisted in his reports to the Committee of Public Safety that the majority of the citizens of Lyon were good republicans and that a reconciliation of some sort between the rebellious city and the National Convention could better be achieved through negotiation than by armed force.

Even at the end of June, long after Lindet had returned to Paris, Gonchon continued to urge Garat to avoid armed confrontation at all costs. In a letter dated June 28, Gonchon reported that violence was once again on the verge of exploding in the city, largely because of the receipt of the National Convention's decree forbidding the trial of those arrested after May 29. The decree had prompted the provisional municipality to release some of those "arrested illegally," much to the consternation of sectional activists hungry for justice or revenge. One of those released, a former official on the Jacobin municipal council by the name of Odo Sautemouche, made the mistake of stopping in a cafe near the prison for a beer, over which he petulantly castigated the "people" who had abandoned them as "ingrates." The people responded by throwing him in the river, where he perished. Gonchon himself remained in the bars and cafes until two in the morning, trying to reassure those "good citizens" who now feared that this act of violence would bring retribution down on their heads.

Gonchon, too, saw the danger of this, but he insisted to Garat that the Convention's decree had been ill advised. Perhaps one hundred people had originally been arrested, he wrote, but only eight or ten were truly guilty. Had they been tried and punished, all would now be calm in Lyon. But now he feared that all hundred, or more, would be massacred by the people. And if the Convention ordered the army to march against Lyon, "rivers of blood would flow."[24]

On July 1 Gonchon wrote again to Garat, reporting that "all is tranquil for the moment." The popular tumult and demonstrations outside the prisons had ended. In recent days Gonchon had been out in the countryside attending to the task he had originally been assigned. He closed his short letter with the simple promise that "tomorrow I will send you my observations on agriculture."

Gonchon did submit his report on agriculture, but he said nothing in either of these last two letters about the July 1 convocation in Lyon of the Popular Commission, whose existence would make it almost impossible for any sort of reconciliation between Lyon and the National Convention. He wrote in his letter of June 28 that many of the leaders of the sections in Lyon saw the necessity of rallying to the Convention. But the Convention's decree ordering the suspension of all judicial proceedings against arrested Jacobins had once again alienated the Lyonnais moderates, and when local authorities went ahead with the trial and execution of Chalier on July 16, all hope for a negotiated settlement effectively dissolved.

The letters written by Gonchon, Fourcade, and the other agents and representatives on mission to the departments presented a perplexing and somewhat inconsistent picture to Minister Garat and the Committee of Public Safety. Bordeaux, where there had been little violence and where the revolt would dissolve of its own accord, was described by Fourcade as entirely corrupt. Lyon, where counterrevolutionary violence was thought to have claimed eight hundred lives on May 29 and where the revolt would collapse only after a lengthy and brutal siege, was described by Gonchon as a paragon of republican virtue. How were such conflicting reports to be reconciled with the official declarations of the rebel authorities themselves in these two cities, which claimed that they were united, along with most of the other departments in France, in a campaign to defend the indivisibility of the republic and to restore the integrity of the National Convention?

Evidence from Paris suggests that there was considerable debate, and disagreement, both on the floor of the Convention and in the streets of the city as to the nature of the departmental revolts and how best to respond to them. On June 5, the deputy Boyer-Fonfrède asserted that if it had been legitimate for armed men to demand the proscription of deputies on June 2, then other French

24. Ibid, 502–3.

citizens had an equal right to march to Paris under arms in order to demand their freedom. His colleague from the Gironde, the deputy Jacques-Paul Duplantier, did not agree and tendered his resignation on June 7 because of rumors that ten thousand armed men were already on the march from Bordeaux. This gesture elicited an outburst from Jean-François Ducos, another of the deputies from Bordeaux, dismissing Duplantier as a "weak man" and offering himself as a hostage against the safety of the proscribed deputies. The Committee of Public Safety had indeed proposed such a policy, offering themselves as hostages to the protesting departments until the nation could be reassured as to the integrity of the National Convention and calm be restored. Danton had offered to go to Bordeaux himself as a hostage.[25]

During the first two weeks of June, letters of protest poured into the National Convention from departmental administrations and other authorities throughout France. The general tone of reaction, not shared by all deputies to be sure, was one of skepticism and then exasperation. On June 9 the address of protest from the Gironde was read into the official record, prompting the deputy Jacques-Alexis Thuriot to observe that when the Bordelais were better informed as to the events of June 2 they would recognize their error and know who the true anarchists were. Later in the same session a similar letter arrived from Montpellier, to which René Levasseur responded that it bore only elegant signatures: "to find it credible that the contents of this address are the expression of the inhabitants of that town I would have liked to see a few signatures that were not those of office clerks or teachers of handwriting."[26] The Convention went on to vote that in future such letters would be referred to the Committee of Public Safety for review, following Levasseur's observation that while some in the departments might have disapproved of some of the "circumstances" of May 31, the results were generally accepted.

One senses among the deputies of the Convention, then, an initial tendency to discount the seriousness of the departmental protests, but also a desire to get back to work on the task for which they had originally been elected, namely the drafting of a new constitution. If factionalism had impeded that work in the spring and led to the necessary proscription of twenty-nine of their colleagues, then it was crucial that they make progress on that task now and not become mired in interminable debate about reaction to the events of June 2. The deputies were sensitive, of course, to opinion in the capital as well, perhaps more so than to that in the provinces, and Garat had his agents circulating in the streets of Paris to report on the public mood.

Two of them in particular, Dutard and Perrière, submitted regular reports in

25. *Le Moniteur Universel*, issues of June 7–10, 1793.
26. Ibid., issue of June 11, 1793.

the first weeks of June, and they suggested that although an uneasy calm had returned to Paris after June 2, it was threatened both by ongoing concern over the price of food and other staple goods and by reports of the departmental revolts and military reverses at the front. Thus, on June 8 Perrière reported that in the former Palais-Royal (now Palais-Egalité) the news that ten thousand armed men were on the march from Bordeaux had produced heated comments among a group of national guardsmen. One ruffian had gone so far as to apologize for the September massacres and to suggest that there might be a need for more. While his comrades clearly did not share this view, they had said nothing to dispute it. Perrière concluded his letter with the editorial comment that liberty was at the mercy of the first scoundrel to fall upon it, and that given their sheeplike proclivities the people were always in danger of losing it.[27] Two days later he commented on Levasseur's dismissal of the Montpellier letter to the Convention, observing that it was neither the number nor the nature of the signatures on an address that determined its merit but rather what it had to say. It was no more reasonable, he suggested, to assume that all rich people would act only for their own self-interest than to assume that all *sans-culottes* were enlightened enough to avoid being misled.[28]

Another of Garat's Paris agents, La Tour-La Montagne, reported on June 10 that the Committee of Public Safety's proposal to send hostages to the departments had aroused a furor in the city. The general opinion was that such a measure would be harmful not only to Paris and the National Convention, but to the departments as well, that to take such a step would be to plunge the country in the direction of civil war. A far better policy would be to send agents into the departments to enlighten the citizenry as to what had really happened in Paris between May 31 and June 2, which is of course what Garat would eventually do.[29]

The mood in Paris in the weeks following June 2 seems neither to have been one of panic nor bravado. The proscription of the Girondin deputies did not end political divisions within the National Convention, but it certainly muted them, and the growing danger of civil war produced a resolve among the deputies to focus on the business of drafting a constitution. The successful completion of that task would be crucial to the neutralization of the federalist movement.

Evidence also suggests that serious doubts plagued the federalist rebels almost from the outset as to the feasibility of their project and even the goals they hoped to achieve. Although the federalist leaders were able to sustain into July

27. Alexandre Tuetey, *Répertoire général des sources manuscrits de l'histoire de Paris pendant la Révolution française* (Paris, 1890–1914), vol. 9, 211.

28. Ibid., 212.

29. Ibid., 213.

the illusion of widespread departmental resistance to the Convention by controlling the circulation of news, convincing at least some people that as many as sixty departments were prepared to march on Paris, they could not in fact generate the popular support to make that march a reality.

The National Convention for its part, by completing and circulating a new constitution, succeeded in convincing the nation that it was once again the center of the "unity and indivisibility" of the republic. The drafting of that constitution, and the official decree of accusation against the Girondins, offered convincing evidence that the proscribed deputies, now legally charged, had been the source of the problem all along. In this way the Convention both knocked the wind from the sails of departmental resistance and prepared the way for the repression that would follow.

Seven

PRELUDE TO THE TERROR

The Eure and Calvados have not forgotten the resentments to which they were exposed. If blood was not spilled in those departments as it was in the Cévennes, at Bordeaux, at Toulon, at Marseille, that circumstance, unique in the history of the revolution, is due only to the devotion that inspired me to take upon my own head all of the vengeances and all the resentments.

—Robert Lindet, June 1795

The town of Lyon will be destroyed. All those buildings occupied by the rich will be demolished. All that will remain will be the houses of the poor, the homes of those patriots who were slaughtered or proscribed, those buildings solely devoted to industry, and those monuments dedicated to humanity and to public education.

—Decree of the National Convention, October 12, 1793

One would be hard pressed to imagine a starker contrast than that between the repression of the federalist revolt in Caen, overseen by Robert Lindet, and the repression of the federalist revolt in Lyon, carried out under the supervision of the representatives on mission Couthon, Dubois-Crancé, Collot d'Herbois, and Fouché. Only two of the Caen federalists were executed for rebelling against the National Convention, and in both cases only after fleeing Caen and being apprehended elsewhere in suspicious circumstances. In Lyon some nineteen hundred people were executed for participating in the revolt. So numerous were the executions that the guillotine proved insufficient to the task—two hundred were killed by grapeshot on the plain of Brotteaux. Apart from the drownings in Nantes, there is no episode of the Terror more appalling than the bloodletting that occurred in Lyon.

Why was the repression of the federalist revolt so ruthless in Lyon and so lenient in Caen? Part of the answer to that question lies in the circumstances of each town's capitulation to the National Convention. Barely three weeks after the skirmish at Vernon, Caen submitted to the Parisian "army of pacification" without further battle. The representatives on mission Lindet and Du Roy entered Caen peacefully on August 3. Five days later the siege of Lyon began. It endured for nine weeks, during which time the resistance in Lyon took on increasingly royalist overtones. Lyon was not "pacified"—it fell to military conquest, and the repression there resembled reprisal more than revolutionary justice.

Yet early in June Robert Lindet had visited Lyon, and although his visit cannot be described as either cordial or successful, he reported to the Committee
of Public Safety that there were many good republicans in Lyon and strongly
opposed Dubois-Crancé's desire to send military force against the city. Later
that month, Garat's agent Gonchon again warned that if troops were sent to
Lyon blood would flow in the streets. Why did it prove impossible, despite
efforts on both sides, to negotiate an end to Lyon's resistance and avert bloodshed? Did anyone really believe that wholesale executions would restore revolutionary unity?

It is tempting and probably justified to give Robert Lindet some of the credit
for the mild repression in Normandy, and there have been those, to be sure,
who have placed most of the blame for the carnage in Lyon on the shoulders of
Collot d'Herbois and Fouché. The most recent historiography on the repression
of the revolt in Lyon, however, has tended either to challenge the "myth" or
the "black legend" that has attached itself to Couthon and Collot d'Herbois in
particular, or, as in the work of Paul Mansfield, to shift responsibility for the
bloodletting from the shoulders of the representatives on mission more squarely
to those of Maximilien Robespierre.[1] Mansfield's argument raises two issues that
are crucial to an understanding not only of the repression of the federalist revolt,
but to an understanding of the Terror more generally. The two issues are intertwined. By insisting that principal responsibility for the repression in Lyon must
fall on Robespierre, Mansfield is asserting the primacy of the center (Paris and
the central government) over the periphery and, following the interpretation of
François Furet, the primacy of ideology, or discourse, over social factors or local
circumstance.[2]

These issues will be central to the analysis that follows, and I will argue,
generally speaking, that local factors outweighed national policy in the application of repression to the federalist cities, and that social and political antagonisms were more important than ideology in guiding that repression and
explaining its variability from one federalist city to another. Robert Lindet is a
central figure in my argument, both because he played an important role in
crafting national policy as a member of the Committee of Public Safety, and
because he went on mission to Lyon and to Caen in summer 1793. Lindet was
also an unusually perceptive observer of revolutionary politics. It is worth noting

1. See Martine Braconnier, "Le Fédéralisme Lyonnais: Originalité et Mythe d'une répression
(septembre–octobre 1793)," and Michel Biard, "Collot d'Herbois et la Répression à Commune-
Affranchie: Mythe et Réalité," both in Bernard Cousin, ed., *Les Fédéralismes: Réalités et Représentations, 1789–1874* (Aix-en-Provence, 1995), 197–216; and Paul Mansfield, "The Repression of Lyon,
1793–94: Origins, Responsibility and Significance," *French History* 2, no. 1 (March 1988): 74–101.

2. François Furet, *Interpreting the French Revolution*, trans. Elborg Forster (Cambridge, 1981),
and "Terror," in François Furet and Mona Ozouf, eds., *A Critical Dictionary of the French Revolution*,
trans. Arthur Goldhammer (Cambridge, Mass., 1989), 137–50.

his words cited at the beginning of this chapter regarding "vengeances" and "resentments," which point to a combination of local and national factors at play.[3] Lindet fought against those vengeances, not against ideology or political dogmatism, and in the more placid political arena of Caen he succeeded in repressing federalism without resorting to terror. Lyon was of greater strategic importance militarily than Caen, and it had a violently contentious revolutionary history. There were thus many more vengeances and resentments to be overcome in that city. Perhaps Lindet's optimism for Lyon, expressed early in June, was misplaced. But he was not alone in his optimism, and this in itself is remarkable. Even in the midst of national crisis, of near civil war, there were many who held firm to their revolutionary idealism and who were hopeful for the future even as the Terror began to unfold.

The repression of the federalist revolt marks the first wave of the Terror. The three largest cities after Paris were punished for their complicity in the revolt, and this had national implications for the future course of the Revolution. But the Convention and the Committee of Public Safety responded to the federalist threat in ways other than revolutionary Terror, and we must consider those as well. The circulation of a new constitution was crucial to the collapse of the provincial revolts and protests, and in fall 1793 the Convention passed legislation that fundamentally reorganized local political bodies. That reorganization addressed issues of sovereignty that had been central to the federalist movement, and it had serious implications for the future of revolutionary politics.

There are a number of factors to bear in mind when considering the collapse and repression of the federalist revolt. From the perspective of Paris, the central objective of the Committee of Public Safety from early June on through the summer was to prevent the linkage of the several federalist centers and to deny those cities the support of their hinterlands. This was not only a tactical objective from a military point of view, but a strategic objective as well: the unity of the republic was at issue here, and the success of the federalist movement depended on the ability of the rebels both to achieve widespread support and to convince the rest of the country that the National Convention no longer merited the allegiance of the nation. To defeat all four federalist centers militarily would have been a formidable task, as the siege of Lyon ultimately made very clear. It would be far easier to defeat the federalist rebels politically.

To achieve that political victory, the Committee of Public Safety and the National Convention had to accomplish several things. First, they needed to

3. "Robert Lindet au Peuple Français, ou Tableau de la Convention Nationale" (Paris, 4e année de l'ère républicaine). This is Lindet's self-defense, written shortly after his arrest on 9 Prairial, Year III.

discredit the federalist movement among the people of the provinces. Crucial to that task were the agents sent out by Garat and the representatives on mission sent out by the Committee of Public Safety. Second, the National Convention had to convince the nation that it continued to merit its confidence. This required, on one hand, an explanation and justification of the events of May 31–June 2, and, on the other, the completion of a new constitution. Robert Lindet had emphasized this in his early letters from Lyon, and the deputies moved quickly to accomplish both tasks. The next challenge was to communicate those documents because the rebel authorities in most departments refused to publish or register official decrees or orders from the Convention. Here, too, the agents of Garat proved to be useful.

The eventual "pacification" of the federalist strongholds required the deployment of military forces. France remained at war with much of the rest of Europe, the rebellion in the Vendée was still a serious problem, and the possibility that Lyon might be lost to the republic raised grave concerns both about military security and the provisioning of Paris. Only after the four federalist cities had been secured militarily could representatives on mission proceed to purge local administrative bodies and ultimately reorganize departmental political structures.

The National Convention promised lenient treatment to those who admitted their "error" in following federalist leaders. Officials who had protested the proscription of the Girondin deputies or who had declared their resistance to the National Convention after June 2 were given three days to retract such declarations. Those who did were generally dismissed from office but rarely incarcerated or prosecuted. Those who had taken up arms against the republic, however, or who had urged that citizens march against Paris were treated more harshly. Many were imprisoned, and several thousand were executed for their participation in the federalist revolt.

Each of these phases, or stages, of the repression of the federalist movement merits attention. My goal will be not only to elucidate the character of that repression in its own right, but to use it as a lens through which to look backward toward the revolt itself and forward to the Terror proper. One might well argue that it was the federalist revolt, more than any other single factor, that prompted the National Convention to declare terror as the order of the day on September 5, 1793.

Let us begin in July, with a date of symbolic importance. On July 13, Charlotte Corday gained entrance to the apartment of Jean-Paul Marat and stabbed the "friend of the people" to death. Corday's rash act, immortalized forever in Jacques-Louis David's masterpiece, stunned the nation and took on an immediate political significance. Corday gained entrance to Marat's quarters by presenting a note that promised information about the federalist rebels and fugitive

Girondin deputies in Caen. In addition, she carried a letter from Charles Bar-baroux, one of those fugitive deputies, introducing her to the deputy Claude De Perret. That letter not only cost De Perret his life (he was executed on October 31 along with the other Girondin deputies), it provided circumstantial evidence of a link between the fugitive deputies and Corday's heinous act. Marat was instantly transformed into a revolutionary martyr, a more potent adversary to the Girondins and the federalists in death than he had ever been in life.[4]

Corday's act also tells us something about the weakness of the federalist movement. She had left Caen just days before in frustration at the lukewarm response of the Caennais to General Wimpffen's call to arms. Her dismay at the impotence of the federalist rebels in Normandy was confirmed on the very day she killed Marat by the rout of Wimpffen's small army on the plain of Brécourt by Lindet's army of pacification. No one was killed in that battle, and the farcical nature of the confrontation might have done much to deflate the federalist movement elsewhere (as it seems to have done in Bordeaux) had not the assassination of Marat convinced the nation that the federalist rebels were indeed committed enemies of the republic.

A third, less dramatic, event on July 13 suggests to us the possibility that the repression of the federalist revolt could have been much less bloody than it turned out to be. The departmental administration of the Doubs met that day (a Saturday, in fact) in Besançon and reversed its earlier condemnation of the "odious and outrageous violation of the national representation." The adminis-trators further resolved that they would no longer read letters from other de-partments urging resistance to the National Convention but would instead draft an address of their own to all the departments of France warning them against the dangers of a federalist policy. What had prompted this turnabout? Four days earlier copies of the new constitution had been delivered to the city, and this had apparently convinced the Doubs administrators and their fellow citizens that the National Convention remained a legitimate expression of national unity.[5]

This had been the hope of Robert Lindet when he wrote to the Committee of Public Safety from Lyon on June 15, "Publish a constitution."[6] The deputies of the National Convention worked diligently on this task throughout most of the month of June, setting aside their political differences for the moment in

4. See Louis R. Gottschalk, *Jean Paul Marat: A Study in Radicalism* (New York, 1927), esp. 167–70.

5. A.D. Doubs, L55 (Délibérations et arrêtés du conseil du département du Doubs, 3 avril 1793–14 août 1793). I am grateful to Professor Michael Sydenham for sharing with me an unpub-lished paper in which he discussed these events.

6. F. A. Aulard, *Recueil des Actes du Comité de Salut Public avec la Correspondance officielle des représentans en mission* (Paris, 1891), vol. 4, 575.

order to devote every afternoon session to discussion of the proposed constitution. Marie-Jean Hérault-Séchelles began his report on the newly drafted articles during the session of June 10, and after two weeks of discussion and revision the deputies approved the constitution on June 24. Two days later, C. Lacroix underlined the importance of this document: "When the constitution is presented to the people, they will abandon those who have misled them and will rally around this Palladium of liberty."[7]

We should not exaggerate the importance of the constitution of 1793, for it was never enacted and the circumstances in which it was reviewed and voted upon by primary assemblies in July suggest that it was seldom subjected to careful scrutiny or reflection. Still, it contrasted quite sharply with the "Girondin" constitution on which Condorcet had taken the lead earlier in the year and played a major role in nineteenth-century republican memory.

The proposed constitution addressed squarely the issue of sovereignty that had proven to be so contentious over the previous eight months. It confirmed the principle of universal manhood suffrage, which had been introduced in practice in fall 1792 with dramatic effect, particularly in municipal elections. The language of the constitution made clear that the people, rather than the nation, were the source of sovereignty, thereby reversing the formula first uttered by Sieyès and other patriots of the Estates General when they asserted that wherever the National Assembly might meet, there the nation would be found. If sovereignty did not reside in the National Convention (or whatever assembly might replace it), however, the new constitution remained somewhat ambiguous as to how popular sovereignty was to be exercised.

The constitution drafted by Condorcet's committee had proposed a bicameral legislature, which the Montagnards rejected. But whereas Condorcet had suggested an executive council elected directly by the voters, the constitution of 1793 called for a 24-member executive committee chosen by the deputies themselves from among a list of 84 candidates nominated by departmental electoral assemblies. This nod in the direction of departmental authority, however, was more than negated by the fact that the new constitution called for one deputy to be elected for every 40,000 inhabitants, with no regard whatsoever for departmental boundaries. Moreover, departmental and district administrations were to be elected indirectly, by departmental electoral assemblies. Thus, the national assembly and municipal councils were to be the purest expression of popular sovereignty. In this way the political authority and power of departmental administrations, to which the Girondins had appealed in winter 1793 and which the federalist rebels tried to mobilize in support of their cause in June, were severely curtailed.

7. *Réimpression de l'Ancien Moniteur* (Paris, 1847–50), vol. 16, 756.

At the same time that the Montagnards asserted the sovereignty of the people, then, their new constitution strengthened the authority of the national assembly. The executive committee was responsible to the assembly, not to the voters. Whereas the Girondin constitution had included a referendum system, based in the departments, by which voters could force the national assembly to consider a petition or piece of legislation, the constitution of 1793 made recourse to a popular referendum possible but very difficult. Instead of institutionalizing referenda, the Montagnards made provision for the exercise of popular sovereignty by strengthening the clause declaring the people's right to insurrection in the Declaration of the Rights of Man and Citizen.[8]

The deputies of the National Convention ratified the new constitution on June 24, and on June 27 they decreed that primary assemblies should convene throughout the nation within one week of receiving copies of the constitution and instructions for balloting. The instructions were quite flexible—some assemblies voted by voice, others by paper ballot. The goal was to complete the national referendum expeditiously, so that delegates from the assemblies could convene in Paris on August 10 to record the votes and participate in a festival celebrating the new constitution and the unity of the republic.

The new constitution was not the only significant piece of legislation that the National Convention put before the nation in summer 1793. Indeed, one of the first acts following the proscription of the Girondin deputies was a decree authorizing the sale of *émigré* property in small parcels, passed on June 3. On June 10 the Convention authorized the partition of common lands among the peasantry, and on July 17 all surviving seigneurial dues were abolished outright, overriding the 1789 decrees that had called for monetary compensation. Although these measures cannot be said to have been aimed explicitly at undermining the federalist movement, they very clearly would have appealed to the rural population, particularly the small and middling peasantry and in that way served to curtail the ability of the federalist rebels to broaden their base of support. These positive achievements of the National Convention may also have inclined many citizens to cast their votes in support of the new constitution.

One other piece of legislation helped smooth the path of the proposed constitution as it was presented to primary assemblies. Just two days after the constitution was approved, Robert Lindet proposed a decree concerning all departmental, district, and municipal officials who had signed protests of the June 2 proscriptions or declared their resistance to the Montagnard Convention. The vast majority of those officials, Lindet argued, had been misled about events

8. For a cogent discussion of the constitution of 1793, see Clay Ramsey, "Constitution of 1793," in Samuel F. Scott and Barry Rothaus, eds., *Historical Dictionary of the French Revolution, 1789–1799* (Westport, Conn., 1985), vol. 1, 238–42. For the text of the constitution, see Jacques Godechot, ed., *Les Institutions de la France depuis 1789* (Paris, 1970), 79–92.

in Paris and the freedom of the National Convention. Now that sufficient time had passed for the facts to become known, all administrators who had given orders to arm the people against each other, who had intercepted official correspondence, or who had spread spurious reports regarding the Convention ought to be called on to publicly retract their statements within three days or be declared traitors. This decree, adopted by the Convention on June 26, offered a double incentive to those affected—those who retracted could be said to have erred rather than rebelled and would be treated leniently by the government. Those who refused to retract would be declared traitors and could expect to be treated harshly. A great many departmental officials eagerly embraced the opportunity to retract their declarations of protest or insurrection.[9]

It was in this context, then, that the proposed constitution was delivered to primary assemblies in late June and early July. As Malcolm Crook has observed, the "generally conciliatory effect of the referendum is reflected in the huge number of votes cast, despite the civil strife and enemy incursions which prevented assemblies from meeting in over 400 cantons (8 per cent of the total)."[10] It is impossible to arrive at a precise vote count because some assemblies simply reported unanimous approval of the constitution, but roughly speaking, nearly two million citizens voted in the affirmative, with some eleven thousand to twelve thousand voting in opposition. This was the largest voter turnout since 1790, bearing in mind that the electorate had been expanded in 1792 by the elimination of the distinction between "active" and "passive" citizens. The overwhelming vote in favor of the constitution would seem to represent an endorsement of the unity of the nation and the legitimacy of the Convention and a repudiation of the federalist agenda. Still, some ten percent of the assemblies proposed amendments or modifications (including calls for immediate elections or a provision that no sitting deputy could be reelected), and Crook rightly points out that opponents of the Montagnards might have supported the constitution in the hope that new elections would cast them out of office.[11]

How was the new constitution received in the federalist cities? Initially, of course, it was not received at all because rebel authorities in all four cities cut off official communication with the National Convention and refused to publish its decrees and addresses. That blockade of information was countered by the efforts of Garat's agents and by special messengers appointed by the Executive Council of the Convention. Two such messengers, Dufour and Prière, sent to the departments of Eure and Calvados, reported to the Executive Council on

---

9. See *Réimpression de l'Ancien Moniteur*, vol. 16, 755–57, for the text of this decree.

10. Malcolm Crook, *Elections in the French Revolution: An Apprenticeship in democracy, 1789–1799* (Cambridge, 1996), 105. The following discussion of the referendum on the constitution draws substantially on Crook's account.

11. Ibid., 113–15.

July 5: "We are distributing and have distributed all along our route the constitutional act, the address from the Convention to the French people, the announcement of primary assemblies, and the address from the Department of Paris. This distribution has produced the most marvelous effect among the good people of the countryside."[12]

In Calvados the distribution of the constitutional act coincided with the collapse of the revolt and may well have contributed to it. Barely a week after Dufour and Prière wrote their letter the federalist troops were routed at Vernon, and by the end of the month virtually all the authorities in Caen had retracted their declarations of revolt and convened primary assemblies to vote on the constitution.[13] But in the other three cities, copies of the constitution arrived months before the revolt was finally suppressed, to a mixed and sometimes surprising reception.

Nowhere was the reception of the new constitution, and its ultimate acceptance, more perplexing than in Lyon. From the day of its first meeting the Popular Commission made clear its intention to refuse recognition of the National Convention and all of its decrees since May 31 and to prevent circulation or consideration of the proposed constitution. On July 1 the Popular Commission instructed the provisional municipality of Lyon to investigate reports that copies of the constitution were circulating in the city. Four days later, a delegate from the sections of Lyon denounced the constitutional act, drafted by a "band of scoundrels," in the following terms: "After having spent six months opposing all constitutional proposals, they have made one in six days, without discussion, nor examination; eh! who can fail to see that they have presented this constitution solely to incite new troubles and foster disorder? It was at the moment that this new constitution appeared that pillaging began in Paris."[14] The president of the Popular Commission, Jean Gilibert, also went on record opposing consideration of the new constitution, arguing that to do so would accord legitimacy to the Montagnard minority now dominating the Convention and that any constitutional document produced by such a body could only be "vicious and inadequate."[15]

The logical contradiction in such a position is obvious—if the new constitution were inherently "vicious and inadequate," why not conclusively establish this by allowing the people to see it? As the month wore on, public pressure mounted in Lyon for the convocation of primary assemblies to vote on the

12. A.N., AF II 45, dossier 353.

13. See Paul R. Hanson, *Provincial Politics in the French Revolution: Caen and Limoges, 1789–1794* (Baton Rouge, 1989), chap. 5, for a fuller discussion of the repression of the revolt in Caen.

14. G. Guigue, ed., *Procès-verbaux des Séances de la Commission Populaire, Républicaine et du Salut Public de Rhône-et-Loire* (Lyon, 1899), 3, 5, 33–34.

15. W. D. Edmonds, *Jacobinism and the Revolt of Lyon, 1789–1793* (Oxford, 1990), 236.

constitution. That pressure grew in part, no doubt, from the clandestine circulation of smuggled copies of the document. An additional factor, however, was the visit to Lyon of delegates from the departments of the Ain, Doubs, and Jura.

Two delegates from the Jura arrived first, on July 12, and the members of the Popular Commission were shocked to learn that this department, among the first to protest the proscription of the Girondin deputies, was now preparing to convoke primary assemblies to review and vote on the new constitution. The minutes of that day's meeting record at length the unanimous response of the Popular Commission, captured most succinctly in the following passage: "The national representation, reduced by violence to a feeble minority, is absolutely nul; she can neither deliberate, nor propose laws, without usurping the national sovereignty; and as a natural consequence of that principle the French people cannot, indeed must not, at the risk of neglecting their duty, examine the acts and the decrees, of whatever sort, that emanate from that minority."[16] Within a week, however, the Popular Commission had reversed itself and voted to convoke primary assemblies in the Rhône-et-Loire to consider the new constitution. What had prompted this remarkable turnabout? And what were its implications?

During the intervening week the delegates from the Jura had apparently gone back home, only to return on July 20 accompanied by commissioners from the departments of the Ain and Doubs. These three departments, all just to the north of the Rhône-et-Loire, had abandoned their opposition to the Montagnard Convention within the past week by voting to accept the new constitution. The leaders of the rebellion in Lyon were deeply distressed at this news, as was made clear by the stormy reception the six delegates received at a session of the Popular Commission on July 22.[17] The hope of the six delegates—that they might convince the Lyonnais to abandon their rebellious stance—proved illusory. But the terms under which the Popular Commission called for consideration of the new constitution by primary assemblies in the Rhône-et-Loire, and the dialogue of those few days both within and outside the Popular Commission, suggest that the issue of sovereignty remained very much at the forefront of political debate in Lyon at this crucial moment. Indeed, this may have been the point at which the rebellion in Lyon shifted from being a part of a federalist movement, however ill defined, to being a desperate defense of purely local prerogatives.

When the Popular Commission issued its convocation of primary assemblies on July 19, it explained that this was not a contradiction of its earlier policy forbidding publication of any laws or decrees of the National Convention be-

---

16. Guigue, ed., *Procès-verbaux . . . de la Commission Populaire*, 375.
17. This confrontation was discussed in Chapter 6.

cause the proposed constitution was not a law "but rather a simple project that the French people have the right to examine." Furthermore, "the examination of any constitution is an act of sovereignty and no one has the right to restrict the exercise of that sovereignty."[18] Under those terms it is not clear what the vote in primary assemblies would mean, and perhaps it was precisely that ambiguity that the members of the Popular Commission hoped to achieve. In any event, when Lyon voters gathered on July 28, 5,152 approved the new constitution without qualification, 2,049 voted yes with one or more amendments, and 45 voted against. Thus, a higher percentage of voters in Lyon had reservations about the constitution than nationwide, but the document was still overwhelmingly approved. Not only was the constitution approved, the city of Lyon composed a delegation to carry the official tally of votes to Paris and join in the celebration being planned for August 10. Astonishingly, the delegation left Lyon as active preparations were being made for the siege that both the voters and the Popular Commission knew was imminent.[19]

There seems to have been considerable uncertainty among the Lyonnais in this period about the issue of sovereignty or a cynical willingness on the part of some to manipulate that uncertainty to particular ends. How could the Popular Commission authorize a vote on a proposed constitution, apparently sanction the positive result of that vote, and yet persist in its refusal to recognize the authority of the body that had drafted the document? As Pierre Bouvenot, one of the delegates from the Doubs who had been treated so rudely before the Popular Commission on July 22, wrote to his colleagues in Besançon, "if this Commission did not exist, matters would not have gone so far."[20]

Even at that late date, however, the delegates from the neighboring departments did not abandon hope for a peaceful resolution to the looming confrontation between Lyon and the Army of the Alps. The delegates from the Ain offered to journey as intermediaries to the Army of the Alps to plead with Dubois-Crancé on behalf of the Lyonnais. On the evening of July 22, Bouvenot and the others shared dinner with the commissioners from Marseille and Bordeaux whose reports of armed forces marching from their cities had effectively stymied the conciliatory efforts of Bouvenot and the others in that afternoon's meeting of the Popular Commission. In his final letter to Besançon, Bouvenot noted simply that their efforts had not yet proven successful, expressing hope that the vote on the constitution might bring a change. His most critical comments were reserved for the Girondin deputy Birotteau, then present in Lyon,

18. Edmonds, *Jacobinism and the Revolt of Lyon*, 235–36.
19. Ibid., 243, for the voting on the constitution.
20. A.D. Doubs, L172 (Correspondance générale recue des départements (Ain-Lozère), 1790–an VI; and L 55 (Délibérations du conseil général du département du Doubs, 3 avril 1793–14 août 1793). I am indebted to Professor Michael Sydenham for these references.

whose behavior "fully justifies the reproach leveled at deputies of this sort, that of touring the departments for the sole purpose of inciting insurrection and civil war."[21]

One cannot lay responsibility for the siege of Lyon on outsiders, however, whether they be Birotteau, Dubois-Crancé, Robespierre, Collot d'Herbois, or the delegates from Marseille and Bordeaux. The Lyonnais had set themselves on a path of resistance to the Montagnard Convention on May 29, and although circumstances had shifted in the interim, it was not so easy to abandon that path. Section assemblies, many of which had supported the May 29 uprising and most of which had sanctioned the creation of the Popular Commission, now seemed peculiarly unwilling to assert themselves. Consider, for example, the minutes from the July 12 assembly of section Concorde. At this time the existence of the proposed constitution was already known, and the first delegates from the Jura had arrived in town to report the imminent convocation of primary assemblies in that department. There had also recently been talk in some of the sections about creating a *bureau de correspondance*, or general secretariat, among the sections, and it was this idea that section Concorde felt compelled to address on July 12. The minutes expressed the sentiment that motions or resolutions emanating from the sections should not be called *arrêtés*, or orders, as some sections had apparently done, because only constituted administrative bodies were authorized to issue orders. They continued: "It is essential that the sections act consistently as sections, for otherwise the government, which in a large state such as France is representative, both in legislative and in administrative matters, would be subverted; after having delegated their powers, for the people to continue to exercise them in section assemblies would be an abuse, the very abuse that has landed us in our current troubles."[22] It is clear from these minutes that the members of section Concorde felt strongly that sectional assemblies should not exceed their authority or mandate. Unlike the sectional assemblies in Marseille, those in Lyon never moved to create a central organ that might express their collective will or presume to act as an administrative body.

One week later, on the very day that the Popular Commission ordered primary assemblies to review and vote upon the constitution, the minutes for section Concorde record that a delegation from section Rousseau brought alarming reports of the growing danger from the Army of the Alps, and that this news inspired everyone in attendance (no number was given) to enroll in the departmental force. Just four days after that, on July 23, the section elected eight of its members to conduct a preliminary examination of the constitution, which the section then voted to accept on July 28—255 voting to accept it without reserva-

21. A.D. Doubs, L173.
22. A.D. Rhône, 31L21.

tion, 65 voting yes with a variety of amendments. None were recorded as opposing the new constitution. On July 30, the section met to approve the address drafted by the provisional municipal council to be carried to Paris, declaring not only Lyon's acceptance of the constitution but also the city's recognition of the National Convention as the legitimate government of France, along with all of the decrees issued since May 31 except those directed against the city of Lyon.[23] Most important among these was that of July 12, by which the Convention decreed that "Lyon was in a state of rebellion, denounced as traitors those administrators who had convoked or cooperated with the Popular Commission of Rhône-et-Loire, confiscated rebel property, and ordered loyal citizens to leave Lyon within three days."[24]

The situation confronting the Lyonnais in late July was thus extraordinarily complicated. For departments such as the Ain and Jura, acceptance of the constitution (even with qualifications) might reasonably be expected to spare them from harsh retribution for their initial embrace of the federalist movement (though that expectation later proved to be illusory, at least for some administrators). Even if Bouvenot was not quite right in asserting that things would never have gone so far were it not for the Popular Commission, its existence made it much more difficult for the Lyonnais to extricate themselves from the revolt. Lindet's decree of June 26, promising leniency to those administrators who retracted their declarations of protest, did not apply to the members of the Popular Commission. Their constituents, even if they no longer supported resistance to Paris and were unwilling to join in a march on the capital, could hardly abandon the men they had put in place as leaders of the revolt. Moreover, although the Lyonnais may have been lukewarm about a march on Paris, many were quite adamant about punishing those whom they considered responsible for the troubles of late May. Once the Popular Commission responded to that pressure by ordering the trial of Joseph Chalier, who was executed on July 17, the die was essentially cast. Out of this came the apparent contradiction of an address to Paris expressing a qualified acceptance of the new constitution accompanied by an explicit refusal to recognize those decrees of the National Convention directed against the city of Lyon.

In Paris, of course, that refusal was seen as proof that the Lyonnais acceptance of the constitution was not genuine or sincere, and it hardened the resolve of those who believed that the rebels in Lyon must be treated harshly. Thus, while the completion of the constitution did substantially undermine support for the federalist movement nationwide, it proved to be no panacea in the case of Lyon.

23. Ibid.
24. Edmonds, *Jacobinism and the Revolt of Lyon*, 231.

Nor can the publication of the constitution be said to have produced a fundamental shift in Marseille, although the response to news of its distribution does
reveal fissures within the federalist movement in that city developing as early as
the first week in July and also suggests some of the differences between the
sectional movement of Marseille as compared to that of Lyon. As in the other
federalist cities, the authorities in Marseille made clear by mid-June their rejection of the authority of the National Convention and forbade the publication of
any decree or order issued after May 31. In addition, all public officials were
required to swear an oath pledging to uphold that prohibition. It is not surprising, then, that copies of the new constitution were not officially registered or
allowed to circulate in Marseille.[25]

Indeed, when the departmental administration forwarded copies of the new
constitution to the General Committee (the Marseille insurrectionary body) on
July 2, the committee rebuked department officials for having done so, reminded them of the oath they had sworn, and then dismissed them from office,
to be replaced by delegates elected from the sectional assemblies of the city.[26]
At the same time, the Marseille district council was issuing a lengthy statement
retracting its earlier declaration of support for the revolt, rebuking the ill-considered oath that its members had felt pressured to swear, and reaffirming its
acknowledgement of the National Convention as the only legitimate center of
the nation, to which all good republicans should rally. The district officials concluded their statement with an expression of their confidence that "the adoption
of the Constitution to be presented by the Convention, after it has been examined and discussed by the sovereign people, is the only way to save the fatherland, to preserve the unity and indivisibility of the Republic, and to prevent for
all time the return of Royalty."[27]

Predictably enough, the General Committee responded to this declaration
by dismissing the members of the district administration and calling on the
sections of Marseille to replace them. This they were perfectly willing to do.
Barely ten days before, section 4 had circulated a proposal urging that anyone
who spoke publicly in favor of a recent decree of the "so-called National Convention" (condemning the Marseille Popular Tribunal) should be viewed as a
"traitor to the fatherland and particularly to the city of Marseille, a disruptor of
public order, to be arrested and prosecuted as such."[28]

Although at least 23 of the 32 sections of Marseille adhered to this proposal,

25. William Scott, *Terror and Repression in Revolutionary Marseilles* (London, 1973), 114–17.

26. A.D. Bouches-du-Rhône, L1972 (minutes of the General Committee, July 2–3, 1793).

27. A.D. Bouches-du-Rhône, L943 (minutes of the Marseille district council, July 3, 1793).
Concern about a possible return to monarchy was greater in Marseille than elsewhere because
Philippe Egalité and his family were imprisoned in the city.

28. A.D. Bouches-du-Rhône, L1971 (minutes of section 4, June 24, 1793).

it did not succeed in quelling dissent. On July 4, for example, reports circulated among the sections of a disruption in the meeting hall of section 9, and several sections dispatched members to help restore order. This prompted the drafting of what might be called a code of sectional etiquette, first proposed by section 3 and then adopted by a vote of all of the sections. The first point of the document stipulated that "all good and true citizens" were invited to attend section meetings. Point two, however, noted that any citizen who had been called to order twice by the president of the section, yet who persisted in making a motion that tended to disrupt the order and tranquility of the section, would be denounced to the police. Point three expressly forbade all citizens to enter the meeting hall bearing arms. Should disorder continue within a section assembly, despite all efforts by the president to restore order, he was to adjourn the meeting and denounce the troublemakers to the police. These rules were to be clearly posted in all section meeting halls.[29]

Within a week, however, trouble erupted in section 3, the very section that had proposed this code of conduct. It seems that on July 10 a citizen Brait arose to ask why, despite several previous requests, the new constitution had not been read to the section. He demanded such a reading now and was supported by two groups gathered near the door. The president pointed out that two previous votes had rejected proposals for such a reading, but Brait and his supporters were insistent and the meeting collapsed into tumult. A delegation from section 4 arrived to help restore order, at which point the section voted to denounce Brait to the municipal police. They also voted to denounce a certain citizen Bastide, a battalion chief in the National Guard, who reportedly had been reading the constitution aloud to various companies of the Guard. We see then, that even though reading the constitution, or simply proposing that it be discussed, was sufficient grounds to be denounced as a traitor, a number of citizens in Marseille were willing to run that risk in the first weeks of July, and the constitution clearly received some public attention despite the best efforts of the federalist leaders to block its publication. It was not until September, however, after the republican troops under General Carteaux had entered the city, that the Marseillais voted their acceptance of the new constitution.[30]

The response to the new constitution in Bordeaux was much like that in Lyon. Despite having adopted a policy of refusing to recognize any decree issued by the National Convention after May 27, the Popular Commission did nothing to impede the circulation of the constitutional proposal when it arrived in July. There is some evidence in the archives to suggest that pressure to accept the constitution may have come from women in Bordeaux. On July 22, the

29. A.D. Bouches-du-Rhône, L1933.
30. A.D. Bouches-du-Rhône, L1976.

Société des Amies de la Liberté et de l'Egalité, claiming a membership of eight hundred women, wrote a letter to the William Tell section, urging its members to review and approve the constitution.[31] The municipal council of Bordeaux also urged section assemblies to vote in favor of the new constitution, and when the voters overwhelmingly did so on July 25–26, they claimed this as proof of their horror of federalism.[32]

This varied reception of the new constitution in the federalist cities reveals a good deal of confusion about the definition and exercise of sovereignty and the nature of republican politics in this period. The leaders of the revolt in all four cities claimed to be acting in accord with the sovereignty of the people, yet in both Lyon and Marseille they were initially reluctant to allow the people to exercise their sovereignty by examining the new constitution. The sovereign people, it seems, needed to be protected from themselves at times. Just as in Paris earlier in the year, in the struggle between Montagnard and Girondin deputies, elected officials on all sides were eager to claim the mandate of the people. But in practice it was often safer to claim the mandate of the people than to actually give them the opportunity to express it. The propertied elite of both Marseille and Lyon had been quite chagrined, after all, at the mandate extended to local Jacobins in the municipal elections of late 1792. Thus their reluctance to convene primary assemblies to vote on the new constitution.

Once the constitution had been adopted, with reservations, the federalist authorities were left to make sense of that acceptance in the face of their continued resistance to the National Convention, leading to some of the tortured reasoning that we have already examined. At issue here was the status of the National Convention, and as with the concept of popular sovereignty, that status was contested both within the halls of the Convention and in provincial assemblies and administrations. To reiterate the debate within the Convention, both Girondins and Montagnards found it convenient at various points to appeal to a sovereign authority beyond the Convention itself, and at other times to insist upon the ultimate authority of the Convention or the Legislative Assembly before it. Vergniaud, for example, had turned away the petitions of the sections of Paris on the eve of August 10, asserting that they spoke for only a portion of the people, whereas the Legislative Assembly embodied the sovereignty of the nation as a whole. In the debate over the trial of Louis XVI, Robespierre and other Jacobins initially disputed the need for a trial, the "people" having already delivered their verdict. The Girondins prevailed, and the king was then tried before the National Convention. But once his guilt was clearly established, it

31. A.D. Gironde, 12L19.
32. See Alan Forrest, *Society and Politics in Revolutionary Bordeaux* (Oxford, 1975), 132–33 and 171, for a discussion of acceptance of the constitution in Bordeaux.

was the Girondins who insisted that the verdict be decided by the people of France, in primary assemblies, while Robespierre and the Montagnards argued that the deputies of the Convention must take responsibility for making that decision themselves, as they ultimately did.

The bitter debates during the trial of the king and thereafter opened the way for disputation about the "inviolability and indivisibility" of the National Convention. These words appeared frequently in the addresses from departmental administrations and provincial clubs in winter and spring 1793 as they exhorted the deputies to put aside their differences and turn their energy to the most important task at hand, namely, drafting a constitution. These addresses often referred to the Convention as the "Palladium of Liberty," as the symbolic embodiment of the "unity and indivisibility" of the nation. That symbolic ideal had of course been shattered by the proscription of the Girondin deputies, but they themselves had been the first to shake its foundations by their indictment of Jean-Paul Marat. Cherished ideals and exalted political principles were very much at stake in 1793, but it was clearly not just the federalist rebels who at times seemed inconsistent or contradictory in their observance of or pronouncements about those ideals. Why could one not accept the constitution drafted by the National Convention while rejecting other decrees and orders of that same body when the deputies of the Convention had already proven capable of reversing themselves and of proscribing a portion of their own number?

Indeed, tactical considerations seem to have superseded principled concerns very quickly in summer 1793, on all sides. None of the revolutionaries wanted to dissolve the republic, despite the fact that both the proscription of the Girondins and the provincial rebellions threatened its stability. Put simply, the challenge for both sides was to gain control of the ship of state without sinking it. In tactical terms, the Montagnards had a clear advantage: they had their hands on the levers of state power, and their popular support was concentrated in the capital. By drafting a constitution they demonstrated to the nation their ability to govern and reestablished the National Convention in the eyes of the people as a center of national unity.

The tactical obstacles were much greater for the federalist rebels. Their power base was essentially local, and they needed to convince potential allies not only of the justice of their cause, but also of their ability to prevail in a struggle with the National Convention and perhaps with the *sans-culottes* of Paris as well. Their utter inability to mobilize widespread support for a march on Paris doomed their uprising to failure (the experience of the winter and spring had made it clear that expressions of protest alone from the provinces would have little influence on the National Convention), but it also made it possible for the Convention to offer generous terms to those who admitted they had erred or been misled in early June.

This, at any rate, was the opening that Lindet's June 26 decree offered to administrators who had supported resistance to the Montagnard Convention in early June. The decree, in essence, acknowledged the confusion and ambiguity inherent in the conflicting reports that circulated about the events in Paris and allowed the possibility that good republicans might have made honest mistakes in reacting to exaggerated reports from the capital. If those erring administrators retracted their insurrectionary statements now, they would be spared serious punishment.[33]

This decree clearly went further than trying to wean the fainthearted from their support for the federalist movement. It explicitly addressed the leaders of resistance, not only those who had erred in word but those who had taken action aimed either at challenging the authority of the National Convention or at mobilizing armed rebellion (here the deputies chose their words carefully, though, making reference to those who had tried "to arm the people against each other" rather than against the government or against Paris). Although the decree did not promise clemency to those who retracted, it implied as much by announcing that those who failed to retract would be declared traitors. There was ambiguity here, probably intended, leaving room for the Committee of Public Safety and its representatives on mission to determine in the future the severity of punishment for those who had rebelled.

In the short term, however, the decree of June 26 appears to have had its desired effect. Scores of retraction statements were registered in late June and early July—issued by municipal councils, district and departmental administrations, even by popular societies—and it would seem fair to say that in Normandy and perhaps in the hinterland of Bordeaux this decree may have played a pivotal role in dissipating what little support had once existed for the protest and march against Paris. The department of the Eure is illustrative of this point. It was strategically important by virtue of its location on the route between Caen and Paris. Its departmental seat, Evreux, was to be the staging ground for the volunteer forces being gathered in Normandy and Brittany. It was also in some sense a "swing" department politically because its delegation to the National Convention included both François Buzot, one of the proscribed Girondin deputies, and Robert Lindet. For all of these reasons, the Convention paid particular attention to the Eure from as early as mid-June, and when Lindet's decree inviting retractions was issued on June 26, it found receptive ears in his native department.

Nowhere was this more true than in the small town of Vernon. The town council of Vernon had written twice to the minister of war, Bouchotte, and the National Convention (on June 23 and 25) expressing their opposition to the

33. *Réimpression de l'Ancien Moniteur*, vol. 16, 755–57 (session of June 26, 1793).

departmental administration's statement of protest and its plan to mount a departmental march on Paris.[34] The demurral of Vernon, and resistance from the district of Bernay as well, may have broken the solidarity of the Eure departmental council, for by the end of June a number of its members found themselves in Paris. Pierre-Jean-Martin LeComte gave a statement before the Committee of General Security in which he laid principal blame for the insurrectionary posture of the Eure on the shoulders of the president of the departmental administration, though he also had harsh words for several Calvados administrators who had come to Evreux and stirred up resistance. On June 29 he was joined by ten other officials from the Eure in a statement of retraction, and on July 2 the National Convention ordered the lot of them back home.[35]

The lenient treatment of these officials may have contributed to the collapse of the revolt in that department and the ease with which Lindet's army of pacification brought Lower Normandy back under the control of the central government. There was no further military engagement in Normandy after the fiasco at Vernon, and as Lindet and the army approached Caen both the new constitution and the retraction decree were given wide distribution. Because the retraction offer extended for three days from the date of publication (not its issuance in Paris), local officials could still claim eligibility, and between July 21 and 24 all the local administrative bodies in Caen issued statements of retraction. Those retractions would not save them their jobs and many who did not go into hiding spent time in prison during the Year II, but their willingness to admit their error may well have saved them their lives.[36]

The invitation to retract declarations of protest was not as resoundingly successful elsewhere—nowhere did the revolt collapse as quickly or as easily as it did in Normandy—but in all the federalist departments it raised doubts in the minds of some local officials about the wisdom of their past actions and the prospects for success of continued resistance to Paris. It was difficult, after all, to read promptly and accurately the shifting political currents in the capital, and past experience no doubt taught local officials that it was better to make amends for errors than to persist in holding to well-intentioned political positions that events had rendered untenable. Just one year earlier, after the failed insurrection of June 20, a number of departmental administrators had drafted messages of support for the besieged monarchy only to find themselves politically vulnerable after the uprising of August 10. Those who could explain their letters as the product of "error" fared much better in the next round of elections than those who were seen as avowed royalists.

34. A.N., AF II 46, dossiers 359 and 360.
35. A.N., F⁷ 4558.
36. For a fuller discussion of the retractions in Calvados, see Hanson, *Provincial Politics*, 152–56.

This would be the tone taken by many local officials and clubs in summer 1793, as we see in the retraction statement drafted by the Popular Society of St. Sever, somewhat to the south of Bordeaux, on July 7: "It is always a glorious thing for a man, when he has fallen into error, to correct that error upon discovering it. To that end, the address that we now present to the administration conveys the avowal of the error into which we had fallen, and the formal retraction of our previous sentiments."[37] The language of this retraction is typical, though it came somewhat earlier than most others in the southwest, given the ability of the Popular Commission in Bordeaux to control the flow of information from Paris. By late July, however, with the collapse of the departmental march toward the capital, clubs, towns, and districts throughout the region were reversing their earlier declarations and disassociating themselves from the federalist movement. Now recognizing their own precarious position, officials in many of these towns (including Libourne, Cadillac, Blaye, and La Réole) went beyond issuing simple retractions and became hostile critics of Bordeaux's rebellious stance. La Réole, an important district seat, rallied to the Montagnards and became the staging ground for the Convention's representatives on mission in August and September.[38] The collapse of any semblance of local support for the revolt finally led the Popular Commission to announce its own dissolution on August 2, although it would be two more months before all differences between Bordeaux and the National Convention would be resolved, and then by force rather than compromise.

The call for retractions had relatively little impact in the Rhône-et-Loire because Lyon had never managed to attract much regional support for its call to arms and the Popular Commission in Lyon had effectively supplanted local administrative bodies, which therefore had nothing to retract. In the Bouches-du-Rhône, however, the retraction by the Marseille district council on July 3 produced a fissure in local support for the revolt and could be said to have forced the insurrectionary General Committee to reveal its true colors. The district's retraction statement itself was particularly dramatic, beginning with a reference to the "profound abyss" into which the enemies of the republic wished to push it, expressing the fear that the district administrators might be accused "of having been asleep on the brink of the precipice," and ending with an unequivocal retraction of their earlier oath of insurrection. It was not only the presentation of the new constitution that had persuaded them to change their position, but the fact that so many other departments had now abandoned the protest. Insisting that they had never been given the opportunity to thoroughly debate the proposals put before them in June, they not only retracted their oath of insur-

---

37. A.N., AF II 45, dossier 353.
38. Alan Forrest, *The Revolution in Provincial France* (Oxford, 1996), 197–202.

rection (even one member who had never sworn the oath in the first place!), but they additionally condemned the Marseille Popular Tribunal, which stood poised and ready to judge local Jacobins.[39]

This retraction by the district officials, along with the fact that the General Committee now dismissed them from office, gained leniency for them when the representatives on mission arrived in September. But at that crucial moment in early July, it also served to change the tenor of the revolt in Marseille. By dismissing both the district and departmental councils and calling on the sections of Marseille to replace them and by further taking measures to stifle dissent within sectional assemblies, the General Committee was quite blatantly asserting its own power and authority. The earlier principled declarations about the integrity of the National Convention, the unity of the republic, the sanctity of popular sovereignty all faded into the background. As all pretense of a national movement evaporated, and as local support began to crumble around them, the members of the General Committee grew more desperate, and like their counterparts in Lyon they began to look for new allies among those whose sympathies were quite openly royalist.

The new constitution, the news (or propaganda) from Paris that was spread by Garat's agents, the call for retractions, and the promise of lenient treatment for those who had erred—all were effective in turning both local officials and ordinary citizens away from the federalist movement. In Lyon and Marseille, and to a much lesser degree Bordeaux and Caen, armed force would ultimately prove necessary, but there was one other weapon that the National Convention used to advantage in its political battle with the rebel departments: food. The supply and the price of grain had of course been politically volatile issues at several times and in many places during the early years of the Revolution, and the mid to late summer months were the period of greatest vulnerability. For the revolutionary government, the need to insure the provisioning of Paris was of paramount importance, just as it had been for the monarchy before, and this created resentment in the provinces.[40] The issue was further politicized by the passage in spring 1793 of the grain maximum, legislation that was supported by the Montagnards and their *sans-culotte* supporters and opposed by many of the Girondin deputies. Aimed at establishing a ceiling on grain prices, this legislation had the unintended consequence of diminishing supply because some farmers refused to sell their harvest at what they deemed to be unfair prices.

Grain supply, then, was a sensitive matter and local officials knew well from

39. A.D. Bouches-du-Rhône, L943.

40. See Richard Cobb, *Paris and Its Provinces, 1792–1802* (Oxford, 1975), and *The People's Armies* (New Haven, 1987) for discussion of this issue during the Revolution; as well as Cynthia Bouton, *The Flour War: Gender, Class and Community in late Ancien Regime French Society* (University Park, Pa., 1993).

experience that inadequate supplies could disrupt public order and jeopardize their own authority. But if this were true for Caen, Marseille, or Bordeaux, it was doubly true for Paris, and the federalist rebels tried to turn this to their advantage in June. On June 10, the General Assembly in Calvados issued an order suspending all transport to Paris of *denrées de première nécessité*, principally staple foodstuffs. This was in response to a grain shortage in the Caen market and the widespread perception that Paris took far more than its fair share. This boycott of grain shipments alarmed the mayor of Paris, Jean-Nicolas Pache, who wrote to the Caen district council on June 21 to implore them to disavow this barbarous project, citing the threat of anarchy that it might pose and the many sacrifices that Parisians had already made for the liberty of the nation. It is noteworthy that Pache chose to write to the district council, for it seemed that the district administrations throughout France were the first to abandon the federalist movement. But in this instance his tactic offended the insurrectionary assembly in Caen, which brusquely rejected Pache's entreaty, taking the opportunity to lecture the mayor about the parasitism of Paris.

Fortunately for Paris, the efforts of Calvados to blockade the capital did not receive universal support. The northwestern departments in Lower Normandy and Brittany joined in the boycott, but grain continued to travel up the Seine from Le Havre and Rouen. Still, by early July, the bakers of Paris were in serious straits, and on July 14 Pache wrote a confidential letter to Robert Lindet and Jean-Michel DuRoy, then on mission in the Eure, begging them to make their first priority the reopening of trade routes so that grain from that region could again reach the capital. Pache stressed the gravity of the situation by reminding the two representatives that famine in Paris might bring the downfall of the republic.[41]

The collapse of the revolt in Normandy would relieve the immediate pressure on Paris, but grain supplies remained tenuous for much of France throughout the summer months. Late in July, Jean-Baptiste Carrier reported to the Committee of Public Safety that grain shortages in Rouen were a source of serious concern, and when Lindet and DuRoy arrived in Caen the first week of August they found the city to be absolutely lacking in grain. In Lindet's view, the key to regaining the loyalty of the Caennais was to feed them.[42]

If grain could be used to rally wavering patriots to the republic, the withholding of grain could be used as a weapon against the federalist cities, much as the rebels in Caen had tried to use it against Paris. Two decrees issued by the Popular Commission in Bordeaux on July 25 and 26 make it clear that the grain supply had grown quite precarious in the city. As Alan Forrest has observed, it

41. This discussion is drawn largely from Hanson, *Provincial Politics*, 132–34.
42. A.N., AF II 168, dossiers 1379 and 1380.

is ironic that the increase in overseas trade in Bordeaux over the course of the eighteenth century impelled local growers toward the wine business and away from the cultivation of grain, with the result that in most years the city had to import food, especially grain. This made the city more dependent on the central government for a secure supply of grain at the same time that its expanding commercial business inclined the municipal elite to resent state restrictions and interference. The paradox inherent in this became fully apparent in late July, for even as the Popular Commission tried to mobilize its constituents to rebel against the National Convention, it appealed to that same body to make good on an earlier pledge of a loan so that Bordeaux might pay for foreign grain.[43]

Only days after issuing that appeal, the Popular Commission dissolved itself and ended the city's active revolt against the National Convention. Hopeful that this might mark an opportunity to return Bordeaux to the republican fold, the Committee of Public Safety dispatched two representatives on mission to the city—Marc-Antoine Baudot and Claude-Alexandre Ysabeau. Their visit to Bordeaux could scarcely have been more disastrous. They journeyed to Bordeaux from Toulouse, and along their route they spoke with many ardent republicans who assured them that the people of Bordeaux did not share the federalist sentiments of their leaders, that the most populous sections would rally to their support. But when the two deputies arrived in the city, on the evening of August 19, a mob of several hundred angry young men accosted them on the street, disputing among themselves, as Baudot would later report, only as to who might have the honor of striking them first. Fearing for their lives, Baudot and Ysabeau were taken to meet with municipal authorities, where they endured more threats and insults. After passing an uneasy night in the city and unable to shed their hostile escort, the two left Bordeaux, their cab once again jostled by young dandies as they approached the town walls. When they later took leave of their driver, he informed them that he had been offered a bribe to drive their coach off a bridge![44]

Baudot and Ysabeau retreated to the safety of La Réole, where they remained until October. In spite of their inhospitable reception in Bordeaux, they were not entirely pessimistic about the prospects for subduing the city without the use of armed force. Writing to the Committee of Public Safety on August 26, they reported in glowing terms that patriotism prevailed throughout the surrounding towns and villages. They had a "faithful agent" in Blaye, down river from Bordeaux, who would assist them in blocking grain shipments. Not wishing to starve the "people" of Bordeaux, they had sent word to the activists of the "pure sections" of the city (which they estimated at eight of the twenty-

43. A.D. Gironde, 12L37; and Forrest, *Society and Politics*, 5–29.
44. Forrest, *Society and Politics*, 212–14.

eight) that grain, or the funds to buy it, would be made available to them but not to the authorities of the city.[45]

Astonishingly, just two days after the deputies had been hooted out of town the municipal council sent them a letter, signed by the mayor, François Saige, and printed for all to see. The letter expressed concern about their ill treatment, relief that they had not been harmed, and it conveyed the assurance that the miscreants would soon be brought to justice. Having taken care of those niceties, the mayor came right to the point—he hoped that the deputies would do all in their power to secure the funds and grain so essential to the provisioning of the city. Alan Forrest has written of the Bordeaux federalists that "theirs was a world of make-believe that would soon be cruelly shattered." There could be little better evidence of that than this letter.[46]

Baudot and Ysabeau replied diplomatically: they would do what they could, but success would rely in part upon the good efforts of Bordeaux patriots to regain control of their city. For until the federalist authorities in Bordeaux had fully capitulated, which they would not do until October, the central government would do little to assist the city in securing grain, and although the two deputies might make sure that Bordeaux did not starve, they would not be generous in releasing precious grain. As the food supply grew more precarious, local authorities and even the Bordeaux Jacobin club turned to their neighbors for help. On August 28 the Popular Society of Bergerac, in the Dordogne, responded to one such appeal with a rebuke to the Bordeaux club, admonishing them for having allowed themselves to be led, or rather misled, by "those men of the old regime." "How is it possible that you could watch without indignation as your duly constituted officials said to the Representatives of the People, 'We will no longer recognize your Decrees, and we will govern ourselves until you have returned to their positions the Deputies in whom we have confidence?' Is it not obvious that the source of your troubles lies in your refusal to recognize the laws, and that so long as you refuse to conform to the decrees of the Convention, all of the granaries of those Departments in which the laws are observed will be closed to you?"[47] In this manner Bordeaux, which had once hoped to rally the southwest in a movement of popular resistance to Paris, found itself increasingly isolated.

In Marseille, too, grain shortages made it difficult for the federalist leaders to sustain their protest. The British naval blockade along the Mediterranean coast cut off most overseas supplies, and in early July the Committee of Public Safety ordered naval authorities in Toulon to intercept ships destined for Marseille (although that city would soon join the Marseillais in their revolt). By early August there were riots in some of the sections of Marseille over food prices, and on the eighth of the month the provisional municipal council issued an appeal to all citizens, exhorting them to prevent the export of bread from the city. Four days later they issued an additional order requiring all inhabitants of Marseille and its *terroir* (hinterland) to present an exact accounting of their grain within two days to the president of their section. Failure to comply would be punished by confiscation of all unreported grain. At this point the rebel leaders were no doubt preparing for a possible siege, but such measures would inevitably have contributed to the growing dissension in the city.[48]

Armed force was eventually applied against all four federalist centers, although in both Caen and Bordeaux the simple threat of military action was enough to bring the rebels to capitulate—quickly in Caen but only after two months of stalemate in Bordeaux. Marseille fell relatively quickly as well, without any actual fighting in the city itself. But the departmental army did engage in combat, just outside of Avignon, where it was soundly defeated on August 11 by a portion of the Army of the Alps under the command of General Carteaux. Two weeks later he entered Marseille at the head of his troops.

Four days before the decisive battle in the Bouches-du-Rhône, the siege of Lyon began. Even at that late date, despite the execution of Chalier and the refusal of the Lyonnais to recognize the full authority of the National Convention, there were those who hoped that military confrontation might be averted. François Melletier, one of the agents sent to the region to distribute copies of the constitution, wrote to Minister Garat three times in late July. He assured Garat that the vast majority of those he encountered were good citizens, dedicated to the unity and indivisibility of the republic but temporarily misled by outsiders like the Girondin Birotteau. In his last letter Melletier wrote that the constitution was about to be adopted unanimously, with only a few "insignificant reservations," and that all in Lyon was "very calm; one awaits with impatience the reward from the Convention for this loyalty and justice; for how could one demand more than submission to the will of the National representation? And, when one has recognized one's error, would it be prudent or politic to march troops against peaceable citizens, and in so doing to risk making France vulnerable to its foreign enemies?"[49]

The qualified acceptance of the constitution by the Lyonnais could not save them, so long as they refused to accept the decrees of the National Convention condemning the Popular Commission for its rebellious acts. Bill Edmonds has

48. A.D. Bouches-du-Rhône, L1933. See also Scott, *Terror and Repression*, 120–22, for a discussion of the growing food shortage.

49. Pierre Caron, *Rapports des Agents du Ministre de l'Intérieur dans les départements (1793-an II)* (Paris, 1913–15), vol. 2, 267–72, letters of July 20, 28 and 30, 1793.

written that in summer and fall 1793, "something like collective paranoia emerged amongst the Lyonnais, a belief that '*le préjugé est contre nous*.'"[50] It had been impossible for the Lyon federalists to marshal popular support for a march on Paris, either within the city walls or from the surrounding countryside, but rallying people for a defense of their city was a different matter. Early historians of the Revolution in Lyon, following the lead of the representatives on mission who oversaw the suppression of the revolt, argued that there was little popular participation in the defense of the city and that those workers and artisans who joined the fighting did so only because they were forced or misled (as, indeed, many of them would claim in their interrogations after the city capitulated). But although the wealthy and the propertied came to play a more prominent role in Lyon politics in July and August—and it is clear that at least some of them had monarchist sympathies—they managed to find support across the social spectrum and in most of the neighborhoods of Lyon (with the notable exception of the Croix Rousse, where most silkworkers lived).

Faced with a Jacobin-dominated National Convention and the likely return of a Jacobin municipality should their revolt fail the Lyon elite rallied to the defense of property and order, and they portrayed outside forces as a threat to the local community. Whereas in June the Popular Commission had tried desperately to join Lyon to a nationwide federalist movement, at least partly in the hope that such a movement might secure the political gains that Lyon moderates had made on May 29, by August the dream of national resistance lay shattered and the call to defend the city appealed not to national concerns (the constitution, after all, had been approved), but to local autonomy and the right of the Lyonnais to manage their own affairs.[51]

Dubois-Crancé, the representative on mission attached to the Army of the Alps, now became the embodiment of the outside threat, portrayed in the propaganda of the Popular Commission in much the same terms as Joseph Chalier had once been. In a printed letter addressed to the soldiers of the besieging army, they accused Dubois-Crancé of wanting "to complete the massacre begun on February 6; to renew the carnage of May 29 in our city; he wants to restore the municipal council, the club and the scoundrels who hoped to profit by that massacre; this is what he means when he speaks of oppressed patriots."[52] Because Dubois-Crancé had called for military action against Lyon in the early days of June, it was easy for the Lyon rebels to paint him as a bloodthirsty proconsul bent on violent reprisals, and even go so far as to call him a royalist, masking his true views in patriotic rhetoric. This demonization of Dubois-Crancé and

---

50. Edmonds, *Jacobinism and the Revolt of Lyon*, 254.
51. Ibid., 251–55.
52. A.D. Rhône, Fonds Coste, pièce 350583.

his Jacobin allies in Paris made it easier for the committed republicans among the Lyon rebels to tolerate the royalists who were now rallying to their cause.

The siege became a war of attrition. The geography of Lyon—the hills to the north and the west and the two rivers cutting through the city—presented logistical and tactical problems to General Kellerman's army, which was never as large as he or Dubois-Crancé might have liked, because of the revolt in Marseille, the betrayal of Toulon, and the danger of invasion by the *émigré* forces in Turin. Kellerman projected that a force of 25,000 to 30,000 men would be necessary to take Lyon quickly, and his troops never approached that number. They may have been as few as 13,000, certainly no more than 20,000. The leaders of the revolt hoped to raise some 9,000 to 10,000 men for the defense of the city. Despite support for resistance, that hope proved unrealistic, and only with difficulty did the Popular Commission manage to put together a force of some 3,000 men. Some sections of the city met their quotas only through requisition or the drawing of lots. Still, that small force was able to hold off Kellerman's army until early October.

Unable to take Lyon by attack, Kellerman pursued a strategy of encirclement and bombardment. Cutting the city off from outside support was not difficult. By late July there were open manifestations of hostility to Lyon in every district of the Rhône-et-Loire, evidence once again of the degree to which Lyon had alienated its hinterland. In early July a force of some 1,500 had left Lyon to secure the armory of nearby St-Etienne. Unable to hold St-Etienne and harried at various points by local Jacobins, the force made its way back to Lyon by mid-September, managing to slip into the city just before Kellerman completed its encirclement.

The sporadic bombardment of the city took its toll, although more perhaps on morale than in physical damage or casualties. As in the other federalist cities, the steady decline in food supply played a critical role. Given the gastronomic reputation of Lyon, we should not be surprised that its citizens expressed concern about more than just grain. On August 18 the minutes from section Droits de l'Homme record a proposal that municipal authorities order an inventory of all the stocks of gruyère in town and if necessary impose price controls so that the poor could continue to purchase this essential item. On September 8, as the situation grew more grave, section Saône noted its shock that at a time when famine threatened one still saw dogs running loose in the streets and squares.[53] By the end of September the shortage of food had grown severe. With starvation a very real possibility, sectional delegates met on October 8 and on the following day surrendered the city to the Army of the Alps and the representatives of the National Convention.

53. A.D. Rhône, 1L379, and 31L21. I have also drawn extensively in this section on Bill Edmonds' thorough discussion of the siege in *Jacobinism and the Revolt of Lyon*, chap. 8.

There can be no denying that the Lyonnais were harshly punished for their rebellion against the Montagnard National Convention, but the history of the Terror in Lyon also illustrates the degree to which a reliance on revolutionary rhetoric as evidence can lead to exaggeration. The rhetoric cannot be ignored, but it must be placed in context and evaluated alongside what actually happened. On October 12 the Convention issued its infamous decree that concluded with the ominous words, "Lyon made war against liberty; Lyon is no more." Article 3 of the decree announced that "the city of Lyon will be destroyed." More specifically, the houses of the wealthy would be razed, leaving only the homes of the poor and of patriots and buildings dedicated to industry or to public education.

One might add to these pronouncements from Paris an array of sanguinary condemnations made by representatives on mission in fall 1793. Georges Couthon, in one of his letters to the Committee of Public Safety, wrote: "I find myself in a country that is in need of complete regeneration. . . . I believe that the people are stupid here by temperament, that the fogs of the Rhône and the Saône leave in the air a vapor that makes them thick-headed. We have requested a colony of Jacobins, whose efforts, joined to ours, will give the people a new education, and will nullify, I hope, the effects of climate." Collot d'Herbois and Fouché later compared republican vengeance to a "thunderbolt," placed in their hands by the people, and wrote to Paris: "Our enemies need a grand example, a terrible lesson that will force them to respect the cause of justice and liberty. . . . . Their bloody cadavers must be thrown into the Rhône so that along the two banks, at the mouth of the river, below the walls of the infamous Toulon they will terrify the ferocious but cowardly English with the omnipotence of the French people."[54]

For all of his fiery rhetoric, Couthon had little stomach for revolutionary terror in practice. When he received a copy of the Convention's decree in late October, he reportedly went to the Place Bellecour, the central square ringed by the opulent homes of the merchant elite of Lyon, where he struck one of the mansions with a small silver hammer, uttering the words "the law strikes you."[55] When Robespierre and his colleagues on the Committee of Public Safety admonished him for failing to implement their draconian orders more promptly, he requested his recall, and by the end of October he had left Lyon, to be replaced by Collot and Fouché.

---

54. These excerpts are drawn from essays delivered at a 1993 colloquium on federalism held in Marseille, the first by Martine Braconnier, "Le Fédéralisme lyonnais: Originalité et mythe d'une répression (septembre–octobre 1793)," in Bernard Cousin, ed., Les Fédéralismes: Réalités et représentations, 1789–1874 (Aix-en-Provence, 1995), 203–4; and the Collot and Fouché quotations in Michel Biard, "Collot d'Herbois et la répression à Commune-Affranchie: Mythe et Réalité," same volume, 208.

55. Cited in Braconnier, "Le Fédéralisme lyonnais," 203.

The standard reading of the Terror in Lyon has long been that it was largely the handiwork of Collot d'Herbois, who exacted his personal vengeance for having been booed off the Lyonnais stage back in the mid-1780s, but the recent research of both Paul Mansfield and Michel Biard has laid that canard to rest. Collot seems to have fared rather well on the Lyon stage, and his theatrical career was certainly respectable. More significantly, Mansfield has argued that the real responsibility for the harshness of the Terror in Lyon lay in Paris, principally with Robespierre, and Biard has argued that that harshness has been at least somewhat exaggerated. Far from the city being destroyed, only between six and twenty-seven houses were leveled, several of those in connection with urban redevelopment projects. And although the death toll was certainly high (between 1,700 and 1,900), it did not total the "several thousands" that François Furet claimed at the time of the bicentennial.[56]

The Terror in Lyon need not be exaggerated to convince us of its grimness nor attributed either to the personal vengeance of Collot d'Herbois or the ideological zealotry of Maximilien Robespierre to make it comprehensible. The roots of its severity lay both in the multiple instances of local violence, extending back to 1790, and in the willfulness of the city's resistance to national authority, as manifested both in the siege itself and earlier in the execution of Joseph Chalier. There was ample local enmity to fuel the fire of revolutionary justice once it was lit in fall 1793. But as Bill Edmonds has emphasized, it was a justice imposed by the nation, or by those claiming to speak for the nation. Couthon may have departed Lyon before the executions began, but it was his "policy of colonization" that was carried out in the months that followed. Unwilling to leave revolutionary justice in the hands of the "thick-headed" Lyonnais (even the local Jacobins were insufficiently trustworthy), the Committee of Public Safety sent dozens of Parisian *sans-culottes* along with Collot and Fouché, to be followed in November by a "revolutionary army" of some two thousand men.

Local Jacobins now had the armed support they had lacked the previous spring, and they both applauded the harsh justice meted out against their former enemies and benefited from the reorganization of local government with appointments to the municipal council and the various revolutionary committees. But when Robespierre fell on 9 Thermidor, the Jacobins who came to local office during the Terror stood as easy marks for the murderous vengeance of the White Terror, and they were killed not only for their own alleged crimes but for having served as pawns of Paris during the Year II. The end result of this sorry period in Lyon's revolutionary history, extending from the takeover

---

56. See Mansfield, "Repression of Lyon, 1793–94," and Biard, "Collot d'Herbois et la Répression à Commune-Affranchie," and François Furet, "Terror," in Furet and Ozouf, eds., *A Critical Dictionary of the French Revolution*, trans. Arthur Goldhammer (Cambridge, Mass., 1989), 144.

by moderates on May 29, 1793, to the days of the White Terror in 1795, was the total annihilation of any popular political movement, leaving political power in the hands of those who had first claimed it in 1790, the propertied elite of Lyon. From whatever perspective one cares to view it, the Jacobin Terror in Lyon can only be seen as tragically misguided and costly.[57]

The repression that followed the collapse of the federalist revolt in Marseille was substantially less severe for a number of reasons. The first was reputation. Both cities had rebelled against the Convention, but the Marseillais had a reputation for revolutionary activism dating back to 1789. Lyon, in contrast, was viewed throughout the Revolution as a haven for former aristocrats and refractory clergy and had been the scene of counterrevolutionary violence before 1793. Whereas Couthon saw the need for a "colony of Jacobins" in Lyon, the representatives on mission sent to the Bouches-du-Rhône "recognised that Marseilles had always contained some patriots," and they turned to those men for assistance in identifying the leaders of the revolt and to staff the local councils and tribunals.[58] As in Lyon, a series of representatives on mission visited Marseille. Although there were those—notably Barras and Fréron—who pressed for harsh reprisals against the rebels, others—including Albitte and Maignet—called for leniency for those who had been misled. The Marseillais also had defenders in Paris, most notably the deputies Omer Granet and Moise Bayle, both staunch Jacobins with numerous local contacts. The contingencies of geography and circumstance also played a role. With Toulon now in the hands of the English, the Convention had a more serious problem on its hands and could ill afford to alienate the population of a city whose resources would be necessary to return Toulon to French control. Finally, there had been no siege in Marseille, thereby reducing the emotional need to take reprisals.

The repression in Marseille, which extended from September 1793 through spring 1794, is more revealing of the complicated political dynamic that prevailed throughout most of France during this period of the Revolution. The situation in Lyon seemed black-and-white at the time—the armed resistance of the city to the representatives and armies of the nation confirmed its image as a haven for counterrevolutionaries and guaranteed that stiff reprisals would follow. One might debate how harsh the judicial retribution should be, but few outside Lyon would have argued that the city should not be punished, and those who might have argued on strategic grounds for leniency (such as Couthon and

---

57. See Edmonds, *Jacobinism and the Revolt of Lyon*, 282–304. Edmonds labeled this final chapter to his book a "Postscript," and as sound as his overall judgment is, his admonition that the history of the Terror in Lyon remains to be written is still true. The documentation is voluminous, but the topic is politically charged and terribly emotional.

58. Scott, *Terror and Repression*, 129. My discussion here draws heavily on Scott's book, which remains the best local study that we have on the terror in the provinces.

certainly Lindet) would have left themselves politically vulnerable (Lindet was in fact later denounced by Dubois-Crancé for his opposition to early military action against the city).

In Marseille the debate over this issue was quite open, both among the representatives on mission and between them and the Marseille Jacobins. Antoine-Louis Albitte, for example, was optimistic about the revival of republicanism in Marseille as early as September and advocated leniency for those who had been followers, accompanied by severe punishment for the leaders. Stanislas Fréron and Paul-François Barras, in contrast, criticized Albitte for being soft-headed and insufficiently diligent, and they grew more and more intransigent in their demands for harsh measures as time wore on.

One of the striking things about the letters and pronouncements from this period is the pervasiveness of the language of disease. Federalism was described as a cancer, the Marseillais were seen as having been infected or contaminated, local patriots wrote of the need for regeneration or recovery. But although the deputies may initially have seen the Marseillais as capable of assisting in their own cure, by November Barras and Fréron had abandoned that hope. On November 4 they secured from the National Convention a decree declaring Marseille in a state of siege, which effectively increased their own authority. Later in the month they used that authority to dismiss the revolutionary tribunal, which had been convened in September and was composed of local patriots, for failing to aggressively prosecute prominent federalists. They replaced that tribunal with a military commission composed of outsiders and sent the two leading figures of the revolutionary tribunal to Paris to be tried. Even that proved an insufficient remedy in the eyes of the two representatives. In January Fréron wrote to Moise Bayle, "I believe that Marseille can never be cured, barring a deportation of all its inhabitants and a transfusion of men from the North." Later that month Barras and Fréron wrote, "Marseille is the original and primordial cause of nearly all the ills that have afflicted the country."[59]

Such categorical and extreme rhetoric calls out for analysis. The Marseillais might well be blamed for exhorting their neighbors, and even the Lyonnais, to join in the federalist movement, but they could scarcely be held accountable for the revolts in Normandy or Bordeaux, much less the uprising in the Vendée. What could Barras and Fréron have been thinking? In part, no doubt, they were preoccupied by the treason of Toulon, which was the principal focus of their

---

59. Scott, 138–39. Fréron's comment about the need to import "men from the north" calls to mind a conversation from my first research trip to Marseille. Alone in the city for three weeks, I dined on several occasions in a small restaurant on a quiet side street just off the Cours Jullien. The proprietors were a charming young couple who had recently moved to Marseille from Lille. Echoing Fréron's antipathy, they cautioned me that I should always be wary of the Marseillais restaurateurs who were all too quick to switch menus, and prices, on unsuspecting tourists!

mission. But they were troubled as well by what they saw as a desire on the part of the Marseillais to resurrect federalism, and by this they meant plainly and simply a reassertion of local initiative and autonomy. In October an assembly of delegates of some seventy Jacobin clubs in the region had convened in Marseille. Their goal was to assist in the effort to subdue Toulon, but the representatives on mission viewed that gathering as a threat to their authority, and it was largely this that had prompted the November decree declaring a state of siege. This "federation" of provençal Jacobin clubs was not a new phenomenon—it had occurred in the winter of 1792–93 as well and has prompted Jacques Guilhaumou to write of a "Jacobin federalism" in the region.[60]

For Barras and Fréron, then, federalism represented not so much an ideological challenge to Jacobinism as an assertion of local autonomy vis-à-vis national authority. Unlike Albitte, and later Maignet, who looked for local radicals as the foundation upon which a revitalized republicanism could be built in Marseille, Barras and Fréron sought to impose a national definition of what it meant to be a genuine republican and harsh punishment on those who had failed to meet that standard. We have seen this sort of tension between the representatives on mission in Lyon, and it occurred in the other federalist cities as well. In Caen, for example, Robert Lindet complained that his colleagues, Bonnet and DuRoy, both of whom had local roots, would not authorize the arrest of the leading federalists; and Xavier Audouin, on mission in Rouen, berated all three for failing to order even a single execution, whereas in Rouen eight people had been guillotined for cutting down liberty trees.[61]

Indeed, the representatives on mission in summer and fall 1793 confronted a difficult balancing act between national and local imperatives. Their mandates from the Committee of Public Safety were typically broad and flexible, but they remained accountable to the Committee and were obligated to carry out the various decrees of the National Convention. To complete their missions successfully it was essential that they identify local Jacobins upon whom they could rely and gain their confidence, not always an easy task in a period when many in the provinces openly referred to deputies on mission as "proconsuls." Nor were their missions without danger—all the deputies would have been well aware that in Caen, Lyon, and Marseille representatives on mission had been imprisoned, and in Bordeaux Ysabeau and Baudot were threatened with bodily harm. Beyond this balancing of the national and the local, however, the representatives on mission must certainly have been conscious of the work of their colleagues elsewhere in the provinces. For Barras and Fréron, the severe repression underway in Lyon, coupled with the outright betrayal of the Toulonnais

---

60. Jacques Guilhaumou, *Marseille républicaine (1789–1793)* (Paris, 1992), 137–73, 202–32.
61. Hanson, *Provincial Politics*, 177–85.

could only have served as a profound incentive for judicial harshness in Marseille as well. The need to justify that harshness may explain the shrillness of their pronouncement blaming Marseille for "all the ills of the country." But despite those pressures and their shrill rhetoric, the Terror in Marseille was much less severe than in either Lyon or Toulon.

Two judicial bodies oversaw the repression in Marseille: the revolutionary tribunal and the military commission. Barras and Fréron dismissed the revolutionary tribunal in November 1793, but the military commission did not begin operation until the following January and remained in session until March, when Maignet dismissed that body and reconstituted the revolutionary tribunal. Although the military commission was in fact harsher in its judgments, as Barras and Fréron had intended (of the 218 people who came before it, 123 were sentenced to death, 1 was imprisoned, 94 were fined, and none were acquitted), the revolutionary tribunal judged more cases (878) and sentenced more people to death (289). It also acquitted 476 individuals.

Nearly all those sentenced to death were accused in some fashion of federalism. Many of the most prominent leaders of the revolt had fled to Toulon, and then on to Italy, or they had gone into hiding in the countryside. But among the guilty one finds a number of those who served on the General Committee, a number of departmental administrators, and a great many presidents and secretaries of sectional assemblies. The procedures of the revolutionary tribunal, for which the surviving records are more abundant than for the military commission, could scarcely be described as summary judgments. The judges were both thoughtful and thorough in their interrogations, and one senses in the transcripts the gravity with which they carried out their responsibilities. All the accused were questioned at length and given the opportunity to speak in their own defense.

The judges were more likely to be harsh with the leaders than the led. To have served in an official post under the regime of the sections (that is, from early June through late August) nearly always drew a death sentence or prison, but those who had merely attended section meetings or fulfilled minor roles could expect at most a prison term. Similarly, those who had served as officers in the departmental army could expect no mercy from the judges, but men in the rank and file who could claim to have been coerced into service were often released. Those who freely admitted their error, the young, the uneducated, and those from lowly social backgrounds were more likely to be treated leniently. The convicted came from all walks of life—the Terror in Marseille could certainly not be characterized as a class war in any sense—but the greater number came from the ranks of the propertied elite. Those identifying themselves as *propriétaires* were the most numerous, followed by lawyers and other professionals, and merchants (hardly surprising given that more than half of those who sat on the municipal council created by the General Committee of the sections identified themselves as *bourgeois* or *négociants*). Although Barras and Fréron had dismissed the revolutionary tribunal in part because of its failure to aggressively prosecute the prominent merchants of Marseille, thirty-three *négociants* were tried before it, only eight of whom were acquitted.[62]

Repression of the federalist revolt in Bordeaux resembled that in Marseille in many ways, although ultimately it proved to be more mild and the pattern of judicial reprisal was rather different. One would not have predicted this given the circumstances surrounding the collapse of the revolt in the two cities. Whereas General Carteaux entered Marseille without incident on August 25, Ysabeau and Baudot had been almost literally chased out of Bordeaux just the week before. Nearly two months of stalemate followed, and although no siege was required to subdue the city, it was not until October 17 that the two deputies could return, accompanied by nearly two thousand armed troops. They were joined in Bordeaux by two other representatives on mission, Guillaume Chaudron-Rousseau and Jean-Lambert Tallien.

Ysabeau and Tallien were the dominant figures in the months that followed. On the eve of his arrival in Bordeaux, Tallien had expressed in a letter to Paris his skepticism about the newfound republican spirit among its citizens, asserting that only fear and hunger had prompted the Bordelais to modify their attitude. One day after entering the city, the representatives announced their intention to execute those who would "make of Bordeaux a new Lyon," and as in Marseille a military commission was appointed. Bordeaux was effectively placed under military government until May 1794, and although the representatives turned to the militants of section Francklin for support of their policies and assistance in carrying them out, the Year II quite clearly marked the end of local autonomy and the imposition of centralized political rule in Bordeaux.

It might be said that geography smiled upon Bordeaux and spared the city the excesses that were visited on Lyon. With the city of Nantes threatened by the Vendée rebellion, the importance of Bordeaux as an Atlantic seaport grew, as did the potential contribution of its merchant community. Even at the height of the federalist revolt, Bordeaux continued to send volunteers to the Vendée, and the persistence of the uprising there rendered it a more serious concern to the government than the lukewarm republicanism of the Bordelais. The Spanish border to the south represented another potential danger, and should war break out on that front the resources of Bordeaux would be valuable to the defense of the republic. Whereas the representatives on mission in Marseille had worried about that city's influence over neighboring towns and villages, Bordeaux, like Lyon, appeared to have thoroughly alienated the towns of its hinterland, so

---

62. Scott, *Terror and Repression*, chaps. 6–10.

that the danger of renewed resistance spreading throughout the region seemed minimal.

Jean-Baptiste Lacombe served as president of the Military Commission throughout its existence and earned a reputation for ruthlessness that cost him his life after Thermidor. But Lacombe answered directly to Ysabeau and Tallien, and the resentment directed against him may have been due more to the stifling of local political independence under their rule than to the executions ordered by the commission, for the Terror was in fact remarkably mild in Bordeaux. Only 227 individuals were charged with the crime of federalism, and many of those escaped with a prison term or a fine. Between October and May 1794, only 104 executions took place in Bordeaux, prompting the Committee of Public Safety to chastise the representatives on mission for their leniency.

As in Marseille, the judges were thorough in their interrogations, and the transcripts of their proceedings shed light not only on the reasons for their leniency but also on the grounds that served to justify convictions. René Margueritte Magol, for example, was a former notable on the municipal council, became a member of the Popular Commission, went on mission to several departments to seek support for the revolt, actively supported the revolt in his section, and later opposed the new constitution. For this he was sentenced to death on 25 Brumaire. Brunaud-Gabriel Marandon, a thirty-five-year-old native of La Rochelle, claimed in his defense that while he had gone on mission to other departments, he had visited only three of the nine he had been assigned. He was still sentenced to death, principally for his pronouncement in Auch that "the people of the department of the Gironde had reclaimed their sovereignty in order to resist the tyranny of the Mountain in the Convention."[63]

Aman Graves had also gone on mission to other departments during the early phase of the revolt, but he was ordered released on 19 Germinal on the grounds that error was his only crime, that he had been misled and abused by others. He had in fact accompanied Magol on mission, so the judges appeared not to find guilt by association. Lélius Boissel, former *procureur* of Bordeaux, was charged with speaking against the representatives on mission to Bordeaux, and although the judges agreed that he had shown weakness in his public office, there was also testimony that he had spoken against the revolt in his section, and the six months that he had already spent in prison were deemed punishment enough. Most curious among the acquittals was that of Antoine Bonus, a forty-nine-year-old *négociant* who had lived in Bordeaux for thirty-three years. He went on mission up the Atlantic coast, as far north as Nantes, and was a member of the Popular Commission, which named him as one of its liaisons to the departmen-

63. See A.D. Gironde, 5L28, for both of these dossiers. Alan Forrest also discusses both men in *Society and Politics*.

tal force when it embarked toward Paris. The statement he made in his defense was rather feeble (he hadn't really wanted to go on mission, he was a poor public speaker and had exerted little influence, etc.), but he did present four pages of signatures from his section attesting to his republicanism. That this persuaded the judges seems curious because the signatures came from section Brutus, one of the most staunchly federalist in the city.[64]

Cases like this may have eventually prompted the Committee of Public Safety to dispatch Marc-Antoine Jullien, the nineteen-year-old son of a deputy from Toulouse, to take charge of the situation in Bordeaux. Jullien, who sent many of his reports directly to Robespierre, was openly scornful of Ysabeau and Tallien, describing the former as being far too solicitous of prominent Bordeaux families and the latter as far too solicitous of his mistress, Thérèse Cabarrus. During the two months of Jullien's mission, 198 people were executed in Bordeaux, including the fugitive Girondin deputies Guadet and Barbaroux. Pétion and Buzot were apprehended at this time as well, but committed suicide in a field near St. Emilion.

In one of his reports to Paris, Jullien claimed not only to have heightened revolutionary justice in Bordeaux, but to have raised republican spirits as well: "Not long ago, here, a mournful silence greeted the pronouncement of a death sentence in the Military Commission, and the same silence accompanied conspirators to the scaffold; the entire town seemed to secretly bemoan their punishment. Today unanimous acclamations and repeated cries of *long live the Republic* sanction both the conviction and the execution of enemies of the fatherland."[65] But even with the escalation of convictions and executions ordered by Jullien, the Terror claimed just over three hundred lives in Bordeaux. Ysabeau, whose recall to Paris had been engineered by Jullien, returned on mission to Bordeaux following 9 Thermidor and as his first official act reconstituted the military commission that would try and execute Lacombe, symbolically bringing an end to the Terror in Bordeaux. In Paris, Tallien subsequently denounced those deputies who had once repudiated him for moderation, while back in Bordeaux many of the federalists who had been imprisoned during Year II quietly returned to office.[66]

Nowhere was the repression of federalism milder than in Caen. Indeed, in the entire department of Calvados only seven executions took place during the Terror, and the two federalist rebels who paid with their lives for their actions were executed in other departments after being apprehended in compromising

64. A.D. Gironde, 5L7, dossiers Boissel and Bonus; and 5 L 20, dossier Graves. Also see Forrest, *Society and Politics*, 138, 143, 152 for information on Bonus.

65. A.N. AF II 46, dossier 359 (letter of 11 messidor II from Jullien fils to the Committee of Public Safety).

66. Forrest, *Revolution in Provincial France*, 314–16.

circumstances. How are we to explain this extraordinary clemency when in each of the other federalist cities the guillotine was claiming hundreds of lives?

First, let us be clear that Lindet and the other representatives on mission could have found ample justification for taking harsh reprisals. Two of their colleagues, Charles Romme and Claude-Antoine Prieur, had been arrested in Bayeux in early June and remained imprisoned in the Château of Caen until the end of July. In addition, the city had provided safe haven for eighteen of the proscribed Girondin deputies and placed resources at their disposal that allowed them to plead their cause through published addresses and pamphlets. In July, Caen had become the meeting place for the Central Committee of Resistance to Oppression, and the city had provided both volunteers and leadership for the armed force that had gathered in Evreux to march on Paris. Finally, more than one million livres were diverted from the public treasury to pay for the costs of resistance.

But the revolt in the northwest collapsed without any serious armed engagement. As soon as Lindet's decree promising clemency was published in Caen, members of the district and municipal councils sent their retractions to the Committee of Public Safety, and most of the departmental administrators followed suit. By the time Lindet and his army of pacification reached Lisieux in late July, it was clear that the authorities in Caen were eager for some kind of accommodation—they were far more contrite, certainly, than officials or rebel leaders in any of the other three cities. Garat's agents also made it clear to Lindet and his two companions that there was considerable apprehension in Caen about the troops accompanying them. Far from issuing an ultimatum to the Caennais, then, Lindet, DuRoy, and Bonnet wrote a public letter to the city assuring its inhabitants that the army of pacification came to fraternize not to slaughter, to restore liberty not to stifle it.

Lindet and the others entered Caen on August 3, a few days after the release of Romme and Prieur. Many of those most active in the revolt had fled or gone into hiding. The deputies immediately dismissed all local officials and began to hold public meetings in order to gather information about loyal patriots but also to set the record straight regarding the events in Paris in May and June. On August 7 Lindet published a pamphlet detailing why he had voted on June 2 for the arrest of the twenty-nine deputies, citing their conduct since that date as ample proof of their guilt. Three days later the representatives on mission and the soldiers of the army of pacification joined the Caennais in a festival celebrating the fall of the monarchy, though there was some embarrassment among the locals when the rain washed the fresh paint off one of the banners to reveal an old slogan: "Vive la Nation, la Loi, et le Roi!"

Despite the good will on both sides, the work of the representatives on mission soon bogged down. Unlike the other three cities, there had been no strong radical club in Caen whose militants might now step forward to denounce the leaders of the revolt (and this must be counted as another factor explaining the mildness of the repression in Caen). Lindet complained in letters to Paris that DuRoy and Bonnet were reluctant even to order the arrest of the leading rebels for fear of alienating their former colleagues and friends in the area. Not until September, when Charles-François Oudot arrived on mission to replace them, was Lindet able to issue arrest orders for the ringleaders. Jacques Laplanche succeeded Lindet and Oudot in November, but even his ardent Jacobinism and fiery rhetoric brought the arrest total barely to fifty. Another handful of officials were arrested the following March—they had been in hiding for months but gave themselves up, reassured by the fact that the representatives on mission Bouret and Frémanger had just released all the municipal officials arrested the previous fall. Throughout all of this, the guillotine stood idle in Caen, and those arrested for federalism would be released in the days following 9 Thermidor.[67]

Robert Lindet certainly deserves much of the credit for minimizing the impact of the Terror in Calvados, and the citizens of Caen would render him his due by rallying to his defense when he himself stood accused before the National Convention in the months following Thermidor. But it is doubtful that his restraint could have succeeded in the other federalist cities. His presence did little to defuse the tense situation in Lyon in the early days of June, despite his optimism about the prospects for reconciliation. Yet the efforts of Ysabeau and Tallien in Bordeaux, of Maignet and Albitte in Marseille, and even of Couthon in Lyon do make it clear that not all of the representatives on mission were bent on wreaking revolutionary vengeance in the provinces in the early days of the Terror.

If we should be wary of exaggerating the horror of the Terror in Lyon, we should also avoid being misled by the mildness of the repression in Caen. All told, some 3,000 lives were claimed by the federalist revolt—several hundred died in the siege of Lyon on both sides, and just over 2,600 were executed following the revolt.[68] The legacy of this would be clear in the days of the White Terror in both Lyon and Marseille, and Bordeaux, too, saw its share of violence in the Year III. The repression also left its mark in the provinces through the reorganization of local administrative structures.

67. For a more detailed discussion of the repression in Caen, see Hanson, *Provincial Politics*, 159–89.

68. If one tallies the numbers that I have offered in the discussion above, taking Edmonds' highest estimate of 1,907 for the death toll in Lyon, the total is 2,623. An exhaustive search would push that number substantially higher. A number of administrators from Toulouse who wavered in the early summer were eventually tried before the Revolutionary Tribunal in Paris, for example. When the revolt collapsed in Caen, many of those who had gathered there, including several of the Girondin deputies, fled to Brest, and a number of Breton administrators were tried and executed there in the fall. A group of departmental administrators from the Jura were also tried and executed for federalism.

Departmental and municipal officials figured prominently among the victims of the Terror in the federalist cities, and this is hardly surprising—they had taken a leadership role in the protests and resistance. Most of them did not pay for their error with their lives, but all were dismissed from office. The federalist revolt was seen in Paris as principally the work of departmental administrations, and the representatives on mission were therefore charged not only with bringing the guilty to justice but with reorganizing local government. The law of 14 Frimaire II (December 4, 1793) suppressed the departmental councils, presidents, and *procureurs-généraux-syndics*. Only the departmental directories remained intact, with their functions now explicitly restricted to administrative matters. The new law also suspended local elections, with vacancies to be filled by appointments made by representatives on mission. This same law increased the responsibilities of district councils, which had shown themselves to be more reliable than departmental administrations. District councils now assumed responsibility for the enactment of all new laws and reported directly to the Committee of Public Safety through appointed *agents nationaux*, not to the departmental directory, as before.[69]

In the name of protecting the nation against further rebellion, the National Convention severely undermined popular sovereignty by this measure. Less than six months before, the Montagnards had touted the insurrection of May 31 as a victory for the people, much as August 10, 1792, had been celebrated as a victory of the people over the monarchy. Indeed, on the anniversary of that victory the Lyonnais and the Bordelais sent delegations to Paris, and the people of Caen celebrated as well. They celebrated not only the defeat of the monarchy but the overwhelming approval of the new constitution, the most democratic constitution that the revolutionaries would produce.

The official rhetoric of early summer had asserted that the people had been misled by their officials in the federalist cities. But the law of 14 Frimaire made it clear that the National Convention no longer trusted the people to elect loyal republicans to office, acting, no doubt, on reports from the representatives on mission in the provinces. Couthon had written, after all, that the Lyonnais were "stupid by temperament," and Barras and Fréron had written of the need for a "transfusion of men from the North" to Marseille. In June, General Biron had reported that what the Bordelais really wanted was a "rich and tranquil republic," and even Lindet, ever the optimist, lamented the lassitude that prevailed among the Caennais. By withdrawing their trust from the people, the people who had elected them to office, the deputies of the National Convention nullified their base of support (an act they repeated two years later when they man-

69. Jacques Godechot, *Les Institutions de la France sous la Révolution et l'Empire* (Paris, 1951), 282–86.

dated that two-thirds of their number must be returned to office in the elections of 1795). By reducing local government to a purely administrative function and denying its political role, the Convention contributed to the stultification of the political vitality that had fueled the Revolution to that point. It began a process that would continue until 18 Brumaire.

CONCLUSION

On or shortly after September 20, 1792, Madame Roland hosted a banquet to celebrate the declaration of the first French republic. In attendance were Brissot, Pétion, Guadet, Louvet, Boyer-Fonfrède, Ducos, Grangeneuve, Gensonné, Barbaroux, Vergniaud, and Condorcet. They would shortly become deputies in the National Convention, and all would be proscribed from that body in June or July 1793. All except Louvet would die in 1793, most of them on the guillotine, having been denounced as traitors to the republic. They were, to borrow Vergniaud's phrase, like the children of Saturn, devoured by the revolution that had given them birth.[1]

Jean Baptiste Louvet reclaimed his seat in the National Convention following 9 Thermidor, as did all of the surviving proscribed deputies who had protested the insurrection of June 2. Louvet had gone to Caen later that month, to seek haven and to support the federalist rebels who were gathering there. When the revolt in Normandy collapsed, he fled with Pétion, Barbaroux, and Buzot, first to Brittany and then on to Bordeaux, where they found that provincial resistance had also collapsed. All they could do now was hide or flee. Only Louvet survived. On 21 Ventôse III, to honor those who had once supported him and his comrades, Louvet rose in the Convention and proposed a decree declaring that all republicans who had taken up arms in protest of June 2 *"ont bien mérité de la patrie"* (had served their country well). The proposal failed. The federalist revolt, it seems, was an episode that the deputies preferred simply to forget.[2]

Some months earlier, on or near the second anniversary of Madame Roland's dinner party, Robert Lindet similarly stood before the National Convention, not to propose a decree but rather to report on the state of the republic on behalf of the two great committees, the Committee of Public Safety and the Committee of General Security. The date was September 20, 1794, not quite three months after the fall of Robespierre. Lindet warned his listeners: "the genius of faction is still reviving and putting the country in danger. Let us recollect events, the memory of which ought never to be effaced: they will be a useful lesson for us and for posterity." What lessons did Lindet see in those events?

1. The banquet is recounted in J. Guadet, *Les Girondins: Leur Vie Privée, leur vie publique* (Paris, 1861), vol. 2, 5. This is a memoir written by the nephew of the deputy.
2. Bronislaw Baczko, "Les Girondins en Thermidor," in François Furet and Mona Ozouf, eds., *La Gironde et les Girondins* (Paris, 1991), 47–71.

We cannot rehearse all of them here—Lindet's report was thorough and lengthy. But not surprisingly, he did not share Louvet's view of June 2. That date marked the destruction of a faction, he argued, a faction that was impeding the work of the Convention and one that would ultimately have betrayed France. In the wake of that insurrection the country had been divided and the people had been misinformed, but the Convention had produced a constitution and preserved the unity of the republic. In the midst of war, both within France and against her foreign enemies, acts of heroism had been committed, but errors and excesses had occurred as well and innocent victims had been imprisoned. Lindet called on his colleagues to free those unjustly confined: "Restore Liberty to every citizen who has been or may be useful." He made particular reference to the productive citizens of Lyon, Marseille, Bordeaux, and Nantes. But as he had done in summer 1793, Lindet cautioned the deputies not to confuse error with crime: "Error is never to be confounded with treachery or guilt. Prove by the application of principles, and by your conduct, that all men are equal."

But just how was that to be done? Lindet implored his colleagues to preserve the positive in what had been accomplished ("The Revolution is accomplished: it is the work of all.") rather than to allow it to be eroded by personal recrimination and continued factionalism. For rhetorical flourish, Lindet sought analogies in both architecture and navigation: "When an edifice is completed, the architect pulls down the scaffolding, but destroys not his fellow-labourers. The navigator, overtaken by the tempest, relies upon his courage and his skill, which danger renders more active, and fruitful of resources, to save the vessel entrusted to him. When arrived unshipwrecked in the port, no man requires of him an account of his manoeuvres—no man asks if he has strictly followed his instructions."

He concluded his report by appealing to the ideals of 1789: liberty, equality, and fraternity. Among brothers there was no room for despair. Those who had erred should be forgiven; those who had committed crimes should be punished. But the courts could be trusted to pursue that task. For others the key was to work together for the benefit of the republic: "Liberty is the greatest encouragement that can be given to useful men; gratitude will induce them to render service to their country."[3]

Gratitude was not the first virtue of the Thermidorians, however. Nor were they persuaded by Lindet's call for unity and forgiveness. In March 1795 he testified on behalf of his former colleagues Billaud-Varenne, Collot d'Herbois, and Barère—indicted for the excesses they had committed while on mission in

3. Robert Lindet, "The Present State of France: Report of the Committees of Public and General Safety and of Legislation, Presented to the National Convention, September 20th, 1794" (London, 1794). I have relied upon this English translation of Lindet's speech, which is held in the collection of the Newberry Library in Chicago.

the provinces—and two months later he stood before the Convention himself, accused as a terrorist. Lindet fared better than the other three, all sentenced to deportation. He was spared by the amnesty the National Convention voted as it dissolved itself in October 1795. But less than two years later, Lindet returned to the docket, charged now as a supporter of the Babeuf conspiracy. He was eventually exonerated of those charges, but during this period he took refuge in the home of Pierre Mesnil, one of the Calvados administrators he had imprisoned following the federalist revolt. Mesnil, along with a number of other Caennais, had testified on behalf of Lindet at his trial in 1796. A friend of the family thereafter, Lindet became part of the family in 1798 when he married Mesnil's daughter.[4]

Reconciliation was possible, then, for revolutionaries who had stood opposing each other, divided, back in 1793, but it was far more the exception than the rule. For most, the divisions that had been sown in the National Convention in its earliest days and that had burst into virtual civil war in the provinces in summer 1793 were impossible to overcome. Those divisions manifested themselves as personal recriminations to be sure, as much in Thermidor as they had in 1793, but they grew out of heartfelt disagreement over the most fundamental of political questions: Who were the sovereign people and how were they to exercise that sovereignty in the first French republic? This is the issue that lay at the heart of the federalist revolt and that joined it to the struggle between Girondins and Montagnards within the National Convention.

Even as Louvet and the others dined at Madame Roland's, the concept of the "sovereign people" was in the process of redefinition. As we saw in Chapter 2, Robespierre claimed the toppling of the monarchy on August 10 as a victory of "the people," in particular the "passive" citizens who had been denied the vote since 1790. Now they were to be given the vote, and the election of deputies to the National Convention, as well as the local elections to follow, would be carried out under a system of universal manhood suffrage. This experiment with popular sovereignty proved to be problematical on several counts.

First of all, the question of who represented the people lay at the very heart of the drama in the early days of August, with Vergniaud's refusal to accept the petition from the Mauconseil section, Robespierre's championing of the Paris Commune, the inactivity of the Legislative Assembly (in which Vergniaud claimed that sovereignty resided), and the eventual uprising itself, which

4. See A. Montier, *Robert Lindet, député à l'Assemblée Législative et à la Convention, membre du Comité de Salut Public, Ministre des Finances: Notice Biographique* (Paris, 1899); and H. Dupré, *Two Brothers in the French Revolution: Robert and Thomas Lindet* (New York, 1967), for these biographical details. Lindet's statement in defense of his colleagues, which amounted in essence to a defense of the Committee of Public Safety, and his statement in his own defense, both published as pamphlets, are also well worth reading.

brought the Marseille volunteers together with the *sans-culottes* mobilized by the insurrectionary assembly of the sections of Paris. The successful insurrection may have settled the matter in the eyes of Robespierre and the Jacobins, but the debate over where legitimate political authority lay in Paris continued throughout August and September and carried over into the National Convention after that.

Secondly, the call for the election of a National Convention (with all adult males now eligible to vote) prompted an electoral campaign on the part of the Paris Jacobin club. In the wake of the Legislative Assembly's own *Exposition des Motifs*, which both called the elections and offered a rather sterile account of the events of August 10, the Jacobins issued a *Tableau comparatif des sept appels nominaux fév.–10 août 1792*, a summary of the voting on the most important issues debated in the Legislative Assembly during the past year. The intent was clearly to discourage voters from supporting deputies who had cast votes in support of the monarchy. Some people resented this electioneering on the part of the Jacobin club, and some departmental assemblies viewed the pamphlet as an effort to manipulate the vote. The effect is difficult to gauge because the pamphlet was produced in late August and probably reached no more than half the departmental electoral assemblies. But it did set a tone for the departmental and municipal elections that followed.[5]

Even as the departmental electoral assemblies deliberated, however, the prison massacres broke out in Paris, and this added another dimension to the debate over sovereignty. Louvet, as we have seen, took the lead in denouncing Robespierre's defense, perhaps instigation, of the September massacres. If "the people," sublime in August, were to be credited with the overthrow of the monarchy and the foundation of the republic, were they now to be held responsible for the horrible violence of September? The Girondins said yes, while the Montagnards, by and large, said no. But the reputation of "the people," the Parisian people at least, had clearly been tarnished, and in the provinces the image of Parisians as vanquishers of monarchy quickly gave way to an image of Parisians as bloodthirsty anarchists.

In the provinces, the issue of popular sovereignty was problematized in yet a third way. Universal manhood suffrage may have been practiced in the elections for the National Convention, but voter turnout was relatively low and the election was indirect. The final choice of deputies was made by an electoral assembly, composed in almost all cases of the propertied elite, and the same assemblies

5. Alison Patrick, *The Men of the First French Republic* (Baltimore, 1972), 145–51; Michael L. Kennedy, *The Jacobin Clubs in the French Revolution: The Middle Years* (Princeton, 1988), 287–91; and Paul R. Hanson, *Provincial Politics in the French Revolution* (Baton Rouge, 1989), 70–75.

selected the departmental administrations. But these elections were followed by municipal elections, in which citizens voted directly for their representatives in sectional assemblies. Aside from popular insurrection, this was the most direct exercise of political power available to most ordinary people, and in many provincial cities the elections of 1792–93 proved to be quite contentious.

Nowhere was this more true than in Lyon and Marseille. In Lyon the elections were preceded by a week of riotous violence, imported from Paris by Joseph Chalier in the view of the propertied elite. In both cities, local Jacobins presented an organized slate of candidates to sectional assemblies and encouraged their supporters, largely drawn from the artisanal classes and workers, the newly enfranchised, to vote en bloc. This they did, and the Jacobins gained control of the municipal council in both cities, setting off a howl of protest from those who had seen political power slip out of their hands and who now claimed voter fraud on the part of the Jacobin clubs. Although the new voters did not successfully mobilize at the polls in Caen and Bordeaux, they did make their presence felt, and the elites in those cities, too, were alarmed in fall 1792 by the clamor of the popular classes for a more regular exercise of their sovereignty through the clubs or sectional assemblies.

Not only did the municipal elections of 1792–93 present a challenge to the propertied elite's hold on political power, that elite was also troubled by the fact that the exercise of sovereignty on the part of the popular classes, led by the Jacobin clubs, was accompanied by violence or the threat of violence. As in Paris, there had been prison killings in Lyon, followed by a week of market riots in September. In February 1793, the meeting hall of the Club Central was sacked, and in early spring the municipal council, supported by the Jacobin club, called for the arrest and disarming of suspects. Similar calls for domiciliary searches and the arrest of suspects alarmed the propertied elite of Marseille, and in both cities the elite fought back by mobilizing their supporters in sectional assemblies, which they claimed to be the legitimate embodiment of popular sovereignty. In the end, though, the propertied elites of both towns resorted to violence to reclaim the power they had lost in the previous elections.

This first experiment with popular sovereignty occurred, of course, in the midst of a national crisis, and this added to the challenge. The fall of the monarchy meant the collapse of the political center, and the debate over sovereignty took place at a time when there was much disagreement over how much authority could, or should, be vested in the central government. The ongoing concern about food supply and prices; the Vendée rebellion in the west; the encroachment of Prussian and Austrian troops onto French territory; the constant rumor of *émigré* plots; the treason of Dumouriez—all of these contributed to the sense of urgency, even fear, that prevailed throughout this period. For the Montagnards, the mobilization of popular support was the key to meeting the crisis. The Girondins, by contrast, saw danger in that mobilization, the danger of mob violence and anarchy.

That danger had been apparent since the first days of the Revolution, and it underlay the reluctance with which most all of the revolutionaries approached the abandonment of the monarchy and its replacement by a republic. Even when Louis XVI made clear, by his flight to Varennes, that he was opposed to the revolutionary project, most of the deputies remained suspicious of the idea of a republic and held on to the hope that a constitutional monarchy might somehow survive.[6] Among the first to call for the creation of a republic was Condorcet and his group of supporters in the *Cercle Social*, including its founder Nicholas Bonneville and Claude Fauchet, by then constitutional bishop of Calvados and future deputy to the National Convention from that department. Condorcet made the case for a republic in a speech before the *Cercle Social* in early July 1791. Even at that time, though, both he and Bonneville were concerned that the people would need to be taught what a republic was, that the vast majority of the populace was not yet ready to exercise the responsibilities that went along with republican government.[7] Condorcet and others now called openly for the creation of a republic in France, but the violence on the Champ de Mars on July 17 soon discredited the idea in the minds of most deputies. Some may have hoped that a constitutional monarchy would allow an evolution in that direction, but instead the republic was born out of the violence of August 10, 1792, almost by accident.

Bill Edmonds once observed, "No community in eighteenth-century France was free from the fear of popular violence."[8] There are two important points contained in this relatively simple observation. The first is that popular violence was virtually endemic in French society throughout the eighteenth century. Compared to the seventeenth century, the eighteenth century appears to us today to have been relatively peaceful, but food and market riots remained a common feature (as in the Flour Wars of the 1770s), and the maintenance of order was the principal function of both local and national government. The second point, related to the first, is that this reality continued into the revolutionary decade. Indeed, it is undeniable that popular violence grew in the 1790s as royal authority was first challenged and then collapsed. But the Revolution

6. See Pierre Nora, "Republic," in François Furet and Mona Ozouf, eds., *A Critical Dictionary of the French Revolution*, trans. Arthur Goldhammer (Cambridge, Mass., 1989), 792–805, for a thoughtful discussion of the idea, or ideal, of a republic as it evolved in the latter half of the eighteenth century.

7. See Gary Kates, *The "Cercle Social," the Girondins, and the French Revolution* (Princeton, 1985), for a discussion of the influence of this Paris club and its relationship to the Girondins.

8. Bill Edmonds, "Popular Democracy in Lyon, 1789–95," *Bulletin of the John Rylands Library* 67, no. 1 (1984): 413.

did not invent popular violence, and to suggest, as Simon Schama did, that violence was the very essence of the Revolution is a gross oversimplification.[9]

We need to remind ourselves, though, that for elected officials at all levels during the revolutionary decade, the danger of popular violence was a constant preoccupation. For the deputies at Versailles and in Paris, the periodic violent insurrections of the crowd had been essential to the advancement of the revolutionary agenda. But for all the deputies, whether Girondin or Montagnard, those violent upheavals remained problematical, as we have seen in our examination of the relation between August 10 and the prison massacres of September. Not only was the violence itself political, but the subsequent debate about that violence became intensely politicized.

As Colin Lucas has aptly observed, "During the arduous transition from the *ancien régime* to the Revolution, the crowd and the elites coexisted uneasily in the public space of power vacated by the monarchical state."[10] The public space available to both new elites and to the crowd came into full existence almost immediately in 1789, whereas it would be three more years, of course, before the monarchy would vacate fully its position of power and authority. During those three years, the crowd (or "the people," as radical deputies came increasingly to call it) occupied an ambiguous position. Although crowds did not always erupt into violence, the danger was always there, and as such they represented a threat to the property and security of the elites. But the deputies in Paris, and even some departmental administrators, also recognized the crowd to be an essential ally vis-à-vis the aristocracy and royal power. The creation of the National Guard, thus, fulfilled a dual role: it incorporated a portion of the crowd (an increasing proportion as the Revolution wore on) into a citizens' militia that could counter the armed force of royal garrisons yet could also be mobilized in the face of a menacing crowd to preserve order and protect property if necessary.

It is crucial to bear in mind, then, that an angry crowd represented more than simply a threat to public order. For the propertied elite it also represented a rival (or set of rivals) in the contestation for public power, and in summer and fall 1792 that contest changed in fundamental ways. The fall of the monarchy on August 10 transformed the crowd from potential ally in a struggle with a common foe into feared adversary, particularly for moderate deputies and the majority of the provincial elite. Moreover, in the month that followed that same menacing crowd, at least the males in its midst, obtained the vote, and in cities

9. Simon Schama, *Citizens: A Chronicle of the French Revolution* (New York, 1989), xv, as cited in Colin Lucas, "Revolutionary Violence, the People and the Terror," in Keith M. Baker, ed., *The Terror* (Oxford, 1994), 57–79.

10. Colin Lucas, "The Crowd and Politics Between Ancien Régime and Revolution in France," *Journal of Modern History* 60, no. 3 (September 1988): 451.

like Lyon and Marseille they used this new weapon to gain apparent control of municipal politics. For moderate republicans, this was a most vexing development.

Ladan Boroumand has suggested that the republicanism of the Girondins depended very much on the existence of a king, that most of them found it very difficult to embrace a republic resting upon popular sovereignty as its foundation.[11] Yet even before the fall of the monarchy one might argue that many of the Girondins, and their supporters in the provinces, embraced a vision of a republic that rested more on the law than on popular sovereignty for its legitimacy. Claude Fauchet, an early advocate of a republic, argued that the sovereignty of the people must manifest itself under the sanction of the law.[12] Gustave Doulcet, while still a departmental administrator in Calvados, wrote to the minister of the interior in February 1792 that "either we restore the authority of the law in Caen, and respect for it in the Club, or we abandon all." And Abraham Furtado, our Bordeaux merchant, wrote in his 1791 defense of clubs that the law must function as "a sort of invisible virtue, which contains and checks, as if by enchantment, all passions, interest, and parties." The legitimate role of clubs, in Furtado's view, was to educate the people to be responsible citizens. (See Chapter 5 for both of these passages.)

In the months after August 10, this appeal to the law as a necessary foundation for social and political order became more pronounced. The attack on the perpetrators of the September massacres, including Robespierre and Marat, was couched in terms of bringing criminals to justice, whereas Robespierre, of course, defended the massacres as an expression of popular justice, of the people's will. While Robespierre and the Jacobins would have sent Louis XVI to the guillotine without a trial (Louis had already been found guilty by the people on August 10, argued Robespierre), the Girondin leadership insisted upon due process of law. In the January 1793 debate over the proposal to bring departmental troops to Paris for the protection of the National Convention, François Buzot had this to say: "Where I come from [the town of Evreux], laws are observed, authorities are obeyed, and taxes are paid. Here [in Paris], laws are openly violated, authorities are defied, and taxes are never paid."[13]

The food riots of February and the attack on printing presses in March gave the Girondins additional reason to denounce the lawlessness of the Parisian *sans-culottes* and to remind their political adversaries that those responsible for the September massacres had still not been brought to justice. The most vulner-

11. Ladan Boroumand, "Les Girondins et l'idée de République," in François Furet and Mona Ozouf, eds., *La Gironde et les Girondins* (Paris, 1991), 233–64.
12. Rita Hermon-Belot, "L'Abbé Fauchet," in ibid., 340.
13. Cited in L. Boivin-Champeaux, *Notices Historiques sur la Révolution dans le département de l'Eure* (Evreux, 1894), vol. 1, 503.

able defender and ardent champion of popular violence was of course Jean-Paul Marat, and in their final political offensive against the Montagnards, the Girondins again pursued a legal strategy. In the very speech that led to his indictment, Marguerite-Elie Guadet addressed not only the crimes of the "friend of the people" but the crimes of the people themselves, at least those of their most radical leaders: "the insubordination of the council of the commune, its usurpations of power, its habitual revolt against the laws and the National Convention, can you deny them?" (see Chapter 2).

But we can see that the "fear of popular violence" was really twofold: popular violence posed a threat to social order and to property, as it had for centuries, but in the 1790s, and especially in 1792–93, it also came to represent a means by which the crowd could have a dramatic and immediate effect on political power, even lay claim to that power itself. Given that twofold threat, how were the "*honnêtes gens*" (honest men) of the Revolution to control the crowd and preserve order in the face of the collapse of the Old Regime society of privilege and hierarchy, in which deference for one's social betters was embodied in the great chain of being conception of the estates? The answer, simply put, was to build a new regime on respect for the law and property. The beauty of this was that the old elite could claim membership in the new elite by virtue of their property and wealth, and the new regime could stake a claim to the mantle of egalitarianism by asserting that the law applied equally to all and that the ranks of the propertied and wealthy were open to any who were willing to work hard enough to join them.

In the midst of economic upheaval, however, it was difficult to satisfy hungry and unemployed artisans and workers with promises of legal equality, particularly when a large portion of the people were denied the vote. It was precisely in large cities, such as Lyon and Marseille (and Paris), hard hit by the economic slump of the 1780s and the dislocation brought on by 1789, that an organized and active popular movement developed. Bordeaux, a city close in population to Lyon and Marseille, did not see its overseas trade plummet until somewhat later in the 1790s, allowing the merchant elite to maintain firm control of the political arena and allowing Abraham Furtado to argue that the principal role of the Jacobin clubs was to educate the people about the responsibilities of citizenship. Jacques Monbrion, had he migrated to Bordeaux instead of to Marseille, would very likely have had more difficulty publishing a pamphlet that called upon clubs to give strength and unity to the will of the people so that they might challenge a political elite that could not be trusted.

Ultimately, both Girondins and Montagnards proved to be skeptical of the viability of popular democracy in practice. The Girondins, convinced of the inability of the uneducated masses to govern themselves, favored government by a propertied and educated elite, and they were joined in this view by their supporters in the provinces, the federalist rebels of 1793. Legal equality would be achieved by that elite through the crafting of a system of law that would apply to all. In this vision they could appeal to Jean-Jacques Rousseau, whose *Social Contract* had proposed the law as an institution that might mediate the dependency that permeated the social order of Old Regime society. But Rousseau had also warned, in his *Second Discourse*, of the past ability of the rich to dupe the poor through the creation of a legal system that protected property more than individual liberty, and it was that lesson from Rousseau that the *sans-culottes* took to heart in 1792–93.

The Montagnards, then, based their political vision not on the rule of law (though they were not unmindful of its importance), but rather on the will of the people.[14] The incompatibility of these two visions is apparent because, as we have seen, the expression of the people's will could often run counter to the rule of law. Witness the frequent denunciations in the departmental protests, beginning in winter 1793 and continuing on through the federalist revolt, of the anarchism of the Parisian *sans-culottes* and their champions in the National Convention. That "anarchism," however, was perceived not simply as a threat to social order. In the eyes of departmental elites it was emblematic of the political campaign that the popular classes had mounted in any number of provincial cities in fall and winter 1792–93. When Bordeaux federalists asserted that they had reclaimed their sovereignty from Paris in summer 1793, they were thinking as well of the challenge they had faced from the Club National in the previous autumn.

Raymonde Monnier has written, "Paris was the only place [in France] capable of symbolizing the democratic community." But she also observes that the flourishing of neighborhood clubs in Paris that she sees as essential to that democratic community (reaching its zenith between May and September 1793) occurred first in Lyon in 1791.[15] In that first incarnation, however, those neighborhood clubs were almost purely a vehicle for the expression of public opinion or for the education of the people. Only in 1792, following the leadership of Joseph Chalier, did the Club Central emerge to give those neighborhood clubs cohesion and unity and a taste of power. This the Lyon elite viewed as extremely threatening. They accused Chalier, and the Club Central, of pervert-

14. One might see this Montagnard vision as flowing out of the "political discourse" and the Girondin vision as flowing out of the "judicial discourse" that Keith Baker has described as two of the three dominant discourses (the third being "administrative") that prevailed in French political thought in the last decades of the Old Regime. See chap. 5, "French Political Thought at the Accession of Louis XVI," in Keith M. Baker, *Inventing the French Revolution* (Cambridge, 1990).

15. Raymonde Monnier, *L'Espace Public Démocratique: Essai sur l'opinion à Paris de la Révolution au Directoire* (Paris, 1994), 27 and 48. In making this argument about Lyon, Monnier relies heavily on the work of Bill Edmonds, although she exaggerates, I think, the degree to which the club movement in Lyon had coalesced behind a central leadership in 1791.

ing the ideal of popular sovereignty, of misrepresenting the will of the people. The Popular Commission claimed for itself the mantle of popular sovereignty during the federalist revolt, but we have seen how important the discourse of sovereignty remained in the sectional assemblies of Lyon throughout the summer of 1793 and how reluctant the Lyonnais were to follow the Popular Commission into active rebellion against Paris until their own city was threatened by military siege.

The proscribed Girondin deputies who left Paris for Caen in June 1793 hoped that the people of the provinces would rally to their defense and march on the capital to restore the integrity of the National Convention. In that hope they were sorely disappointed. In his memoirs, written while in hiding near St. Emilion, Jérome Pétion lamented that it "was easy to see that the public spirit of the mass of citizens was bad. Caen leaned obviously toward royalism." François Buzot was more harsh in his assessment of the people: "Would one not have to continually shut one's eyes to lead that mob of frenzied imbeciles that one today calls the people?" Disillusioned by the failure of the people (those of Paris and the provinces) to follow their leadership, there was nothing left to Pétion and Buzot but to call for vengeance against their enemies, and this they did with vehemence. These were Pétion's parting words in a letter to his twelve-year-old son: "The greatest torment for me would be to think that so many heinous crimes might go unpunished; vengeance is now the most sacred of duties. Forgiveness would be the most criminal of acts."[16]

These are the words of bitter, defeated men, confronting their own death. That their despair may have harshened their judgment of the people should hardly surprise us. But let us consider as well their enemies, against whom they called for vengeance. Just weeks after Pétion and Buzot fled Caen, Robert Lindet entered the city and moved amongst the citizens who had caused the fugitive Girondins such despair. Like Pétion, he remarked upon the complacence of the Caennais, their political passivity, but he also expressed confidence in their republicanism and their patriotism. During the two months he spent in Caen, Lindet worked hard to recruit those good republicans into municipal and departmental office.

Even young Marc Jullien, who was responsible for hunting down Pétion and Buzot, wrote confidently to Paris that republican and revolutionary spirits were reviving among the Bordelais. But not all of the representatives on mission were so optimistic about the republican potential of the people of the provinces. We have seen Couthon's comments about the polluting atmosphere of Lyon and its stultifying effect on its inhabitants, and Barras and Fréron's conviction that Marseille would need to be repopulated with immigrants from the north before

16. *Mémoires Inédits de Pétion, et Mémoires de Buzot et de Barbaroux* (Paris, 1866), li, 17, 147.

it could be considered truly republican. In the end, the Montagnard deputies grew disillusioned about the viability of popular democracy, and rather than reawakening republican ideals in the provinces they introduced reforms that consolidated political power in Paris and stifled the exercise of the popular sovereignty that they had once defended. The reduction of the size and role of departmental administrations, the appointment of "national agents" as liaisons to district and department councils, the suspension of municipal elections—all these measures tended to inculcate a sense of apathy and resignation among the French people.

It is tempting, then, to see the principal impact of the federalist revolt, or its failure, as the triumph of Jacobin centralism over departmental independence or autonomy. Both Alan Forrest and Bill Edmonds have emphasized that aspect of the revolt in their work, and I would not deny that this was an important result of the Montagnard victory in 1793. But there was more to the federalist revolt than a defense of regional or departmental autonomy. It was an integral part of the debate over sovereignty that had been waged over the past three years at both the national and local levels. The federalist revolt, more than any other event of the Revolution, joined that national and local debate together. The Girondins and their supporters in the provinces, having championed the rule of law, could not mobilize the people in support of their vision in summer 1793 and therefore lost the battle. The Montagnards, however, having ridden the popular movement to power in spring 1793, proved no more capable of realizing their ideal of a government based on the will of the people. Worried on one hand by the unruliness of the people and their tendency to adopt extreme positions, and on the other by their tendency to be duped by their social betters, the Montagnards curtailed the exercise of popular sovereignty in Paris as well as in the provinces. They would reap the bitter fruit of that policy in Thermidor and again on the 18 Brumaire. But the people would pay a higher price. For having imposed the Terror in the name of the people, the Montagnards linked the ideal of popular democracy with the policy of revolutionary terror, thereby discrediting (for at least the next seventy-five years) the legitimacy of popular sovereignty broadly defined.

Appendix:
Demands of the Central Committee of Resistance to Oppression

I

1. Qu'un Décret Constitutionnel assure au Corps législatif une Garde départementale dans laquelle Paris fournira son contingent.

2. Que les Tribunes soient supprimées, ou du moins soumises à une police tellement sévère, qu'elles n'osent plus influencer, troubler les Délibérations.

3. Que dans le lieu de ses Séances, le Corps législatif ne laisse plus défiler des Bataillons armés; qu'il ne reçoive plus de Pétitions que par écrit; qu'un bon Réglement maintienne entre tous ses Membres le respect que se doivent mutuellement les Représentants de la Nation.

4. Que les Députés mis en état d'arrestation, sur le Décret arraché par violence, soient rendus à leurs fonctions, sauf à soumettre leur conduite aux Tribunaux, quand ils auront été légalement accusés.

5. Qu'un Décret solennel casse les Corps administratifs de Paris et les Autorités anarchiques connues sous le nom de Comités Révolutionnaires.

6. Que la Commune de Paris soit divisée en autant de Municipalités qu'elle a de Tribunaux; que ces Municipalités soient formées incessamment, et qu'il ne puisse y entrer aucun Membre des Administrations actuelles de cette Ville.

7. Que les sections de Paris ne soient plus désormais en permanence.

8. Que le Tribunal révolutionnaire soit supprimé; que la conduite de ses Juges soit rigoureusement examinée.

9. Que la commission des Douze, établie pour découvrir les complots tramés depuis six mois contre la Représentation nationale, soit réintégrée et continue ses recherches. Que les auteurs de ces complots soient enfin légalement punis, quels qu'ils soient.

10. Qu'un Décret ordonne de reprendre l'instruction commencée contre les assassins du 2 septembre, de poursuivre ces hommes de sang, qui depuis six mois ne

Source: B.M. Caen, Fn. B2634.

cessent de provoquer au meurtre, soit par leurs écrits, soit par leurs discours dans les lieux publics et dans les Sociétés populaires.

11. Qu'ils soient punis, ceux qui depuis le 31 mai violent à Paris le secret des lettres, et portent de continuelles atteintes à la liberté de la presse.

12. Qu'un Décret abolisse, sous des peines afflictives, les dénominations aussi dangereuses qu'elles sont ridicules, de Cordeliers, de Jacobins, que portent les Sociétés dégénérées de Paris.

13. Que les scellés soient mis sur leurs papiers, et sur ceux de la Commune de Paris et de ses Comités révolutionnaires.

14. Qu'on exécute dans cette ville les Loix relatives aux étrangers, aux gens sans aveu.

II

15. Que la Convention divisant enfin les Pouvoirs, se borne à ceux qui appartiennent à une Assemblée législative.

15bis. Que le Comité de salut public soit dépouillé de sa Puissance dictatoriale.

16. Que les Députés envoyés près des armées et dans les Départements, retournent au poste que leur avait assigné la Nation; qu'ils rendent compte des sommes qu'ils ont touchées pour leur mission extraordinaire; que l'on examine la manière dont ils l'ont remplie, et les motifs des arrestations qu'ils ont ordonnées; que leur responsabilité ne soit pas un vain mot.

17. Que l'on donne au Conseil exécutif la vigueur nécessaire pour faire marcher le Gouvernement.

III

18. Qu'une commission formée d'hommes capables et intègres soit chargée d'examiner les comptes des anciens Ministres et de la Commune de Paris; de rechercher les sources des grandes fortunes qu'on a vu subitement éclore depuis le 10 août; et de rétablir enfin l'ordre dans nos finances.

19. Que l'on informe contre les auteurs des vols faits au Garde-meuble, et des pillages de février.

20. Qu'il ne soit plus rien avancé à la Commune de Paris sur le trésor public; qu'elle paye enfin ses impositions arriérées.

21. Qu'il ne soit plus créé d'assignats; que l'on avise aux moyens de diminuer la masse de ceux qui sont dans la circulation.

22. Que le numérotage, les signatures manuscrites de les endossements des assignats soient rétablis tels qu'ils étaient lors de la première émission.

IV

23. Que la Convention, ayant recouvré sa liberté, son intégrité, soit invitée à donner sous deux mois une Constitution digne de la République Française.

24. Qu'elle indique les Loix qu'elle n'a pas rendues librement.

25. Si la Convention ne croit pas que les haînes qui l'ont jusqu'à présent divisée, lui permettent de s'acquitter désormais des fonctions importantes que le peuple lui a déléguées, qu'elle ait du moins la bonne foi de le déclarer; qu'elle convoque les Assemblées primaires, et que de nouveaux Législateurs puissent bientôt réparer les maux qu'elle a faits à la France.

Article ajoûté

Que la Garde nationale de Paris soit promptement réorganisée, et qu'elle n'ait pour Chefs aucuns des Membres des Administrations et des Comités Révolution-naires du 31 mai.

Bibliography

Archival Sources

In addition to the published sources listed below, the research for this book relied heavily on documents held in French archives in Paris and each of the federalist cities. At the National Archives I consulted documents in series AF II (Comité de Salut Public), DXLII (Comité de Salut Public), DXLIII (Comité de Sûreté Générale), F¹ᵇI and F¹ᵇII (Administrative personnel), F¹ᶜIII (Esprit public et elections), F² (Administration Départementale), F³ (Administration Communale), F⁷ (Police Générale), and W (Tribunal Révolutionnaire). The rich collection of revolutionary pamphlets and newspapers in the Bibliothèque Nationale was also enormously valuable.

In the departmental archives of the Bouches-du-Rhône, Calvados, the Gironde, and the Rhône, I worked principally in Series L. The municipal archives of Bordeaux, Caen, Lyon, and Marseille contain valuable documents as well, particularly in Lyon and Marseille, where municipal politics were so contentious in 1792–93. The municipal libraries in each of those cities also contain extensive collections of revolutionary pamphlets, proclamations, and other printed sources. The Lyon municipal library is particularly rich in this regard.

In the United States, I was able to do substantial research in the Newberry Library in Chicago and the Lilly Rare Books Library at Indiana University in Bloomington, both of which have extensive collections of revolutionary pamphlets and newspapers.

Published Primary Sources

Aulard, F. A. *Recueil des Actes du Comité de Salut Public avec la Correspondance officielle des représentants en mission*, 28 vols. Paris, 1891.

Bulletin des autorités constituées, nos. 1–9, June–July 1793. A.D. Calvados.

Caron, Pierre. *Rapports des Agents du Ministre de l'Intérieur dans les départements (1793-an II)*, 2 vols. Paris, 1913–15.

Dauban, C. A., ed. *Mémoires Inédits de Pétion, et Mémoires de Buzot et de Barbaroux*. Paris, 1866.

Delasalle, Paul. *Documents inédits sur le fédéralisme en Normandie*. Le Mans, 1844.

Garat, Dominique Joseph. *Mémoires sur la Révolution*. Paris, an III [1795].

Julien, Jean (de Toulouse). *Rapport fait au nom du Comité de Surveillance et de Sûreté Générale sur les administrations rebelles*. Paris, 1793.

Réimpression de l'Ancien Moniteur, seule histoire authentique inaltérée de la révolution française depuis la réunion des Etats-Généraux jusqu'au consulat, mai 1789-novembre 1799, 32 vols. Paris, 1847–50.

Stephens, H. Morse. *The Principal Speeches of the Statesmen and Orators of the French Revolution, 1789–1795*, 2 vols. Oxford, 1892.

Tuetey, Alexandre. *Répertoire général des sources manuscrites de l'histoire de Paris pendant la Révolution française*, 11 vols. Paris, 1890–1914.

Vatel, C. *Vergniaud: Manuscrits, lettres de papiers, pièces pour la plupart inédites, classées et annotées*, 2 vols. Paris, 1873.

Secondary Sources

GENERAL

Agulhon, Maurice. *Pénitents et francs-maçons de l'ancienne Provence*. Paris, 1968.

Albert, Madeleine. *Le Fédéralisme dans la Haute-Garonne*. Paris, 1932.

Applewhite, Harriet B. *Political Alignment in the French National Assembly, 1789–1791*. Baton Rouge, 1993.

Baczko, Bronislaw. "Les Girondins en Thermidor." Pages 47–71 in François Furet and Mona Ozouf, eds. *La Gironde et les Girondins*. Paris, 1991.

Baker, Keith Michael. *Condorcet: From Natural Philosophy to Social Mathematics*. Chicago, 1975.

———. *Inventing the French Revolution*. Cambridge, 1990.

Benoit, Bruno, ed. *Ville et Révolution française*. Lyon, 1994.

Boroumand, Ladan. "Les Girondins et l'idée de République." Pages 233–64 in François Furet and Mona Ozouf, eds. *La Gironde et les Girondins*. Paris, 1991.

Bossenga, Gail. *The Politics of Privilege: Old Regime and Revolution in Lille*. Cambridge, 1991.

Boursier, A. M. "L'Emeute Parisienne du 10 mars 1793," *Annales Historiques de la Révolution française* 44, no. 2 (1972): 204–30.

Bouton, Cynthia. *The Flour War: Gender, Class and Community in late Ancien Regime French Society*. University Park, Pa., 1993.

Bowers, Claude G. *Pierre Vergniaud: Voice of the French Revolution*. New York, 1950.

Braesch, F. *La Commune du 10 août*. Paris, 1911.

Brédin, Jean-Denis. "Vergniaud ou le génie de la parole." Pages 367–87 in François Furet and Mona Ozouf, eds., *La Gironde et les Girondins*. Paris, 1991.

Calvet, Henri. "Subsistances et fédéralisme," *Annales Historiques de la Révolution française* 8 (1931): 229–38.

Caron, Pierre. *Les Massacres de septembre*. Paris, 1935.

Censer, Jack. *Prelude to Power: The Parisian Radical Press, 1789–1791*. Baltimore, 1976.

Chaumié, Jacqueline. "Les Girondins et les Cent Jours," *Annales Historiques de la Révolution française* 43 (July–September 1971): 329–65.

———. "Les Girondins." In Albert Soboul, ed., *Girondins et Montagnards*. Paris, 1980.

Cobb, Richard. *Paris and Its Provinces, 1792–1802*. Oxford, 1975.

———. *The People's Armies*, trans. Marianne Elliott. New Haven, 1987.

Comninel, George C. *Rethinking the French Revolution: Marxism and the Revisionist Challenge*. London, 1987.

Cousin, Bernard, ed. *Les Fédéralismes: Réalités et Représentations, 1789–1874*. Aix-en-Provence, 1995.

Crook, Malcolm. *Elections in the French Revolution: An Apprenticeship in Democracy, 1789–1799*. Cambridge, 1996.

De Francesco, Antonio. "Popular Sovereignty and Executive Power in the Federalist Revolt of 1793," *French History* 5, no. 1 (March 1991): 74–101.

———. *Il Governo senza Testa: Movimento democratico e federalismo nella Francia rivoluzionaria, 1789–1795.* Naples, 1992.

De Luna, Frederick A. "The 'Girondins' Were Girondins, After All," *French Historical Studies* 15, no. 3 (spring 1988): 507–18.

DiPadova, Theodore A. "The Girondins and the Question of Revolutionary Government," *French Historical Studies* 9, no. 3 (1976): 432–50.

Dorigny, Marcel. "Violence et Révolution: Les Girondins et les massacres de septembre." In Albert Soboul, ed., *Girondins et Montagnards.* Paris, 1980.

Doyle, William. *The Oxford History of the French Revolution.* Oxford, 1989.

Dupré, H. *Two Brothers in the French Revolution: Robert and Thomas Lindet.* New York, 1967.

Edmonds, W. D. "'Federalism' and Urban Revolt in France in 1793," *Journal of Modern History* 55 (March 1983): 22–53.

Fehér, Ferenc, ed. *The French Revolution and the Birth of Modernity.* Berkeley, 1990.

Forrest, Alan. "Federalism." Pages 309–25 in Colin Lucas, ed., *The French Revolution and the Creation of Modern Political Culture*, vol 2. Oxford, 1988.

———. "Le Fédéralisme de 1793: Républicanisme de province." Pages 303–11 in Bernard Cousin, ed., *Les Fédéralismes: Réalités et Représentations, 1789–1874.* Aix-en-Provence, 1995.

Forrest, Alan, and Peter Jones, eds. *Reshaping France: Town, Country and Region During the French Revolution.* Manchester, 1991.

Furet, François. *Interpreting the French Revolution*, trans. Elborg Forster. Cambridge, 1981.

Furet, François, and Mona Ozouf, eds. *A Critical Dictionary of the French Revolution*, trans. Arthur Goldhammer. Cambridge, Mass., 1989.

———. *La Gironde et les Girondins.* Paris, 1991.

Godechot, Jacques. *Les Institutions de la France depuis 1789.* Paris, 1970.

Gottschalk, Louis R. *Jean Paul Marat: A Study in Radicalism.* New York, 1927.

Gough, Hugh. *The Terror in the French Revolution.* London, 1998.

Greer, Donald. *The Incidence of the Terror During the French Revolution.* Cambridge, 1935.

Gross, Jean-Pierre. *Jacobin Egalitarianism in Practice.* Cambridge, 1996.

Guadet, J. *Les Girondins: Leur vie privée, leur vie publique*, 2 vols. Paris, 1861.

Guilhaumou, Jacques. *La Langue Politique et la Révolution française.* Paris, 1989.

———. *L'Avènement des Porte-parole de la République (1789–1792).* Paris, 1998.

Hampson, Norman. *The Life and Opinions of Maximilien Robespierre.* London, 1974.

———. *Danton.* Oxford, 1978.

Hanson, Paul R. "The Federalist Revolt: An Affirmation or Denial of Popular Sovereignty?" *French History* 6, no. 3 (September 1992): 335–55.

———. "Les Centres fédéralistes, avaient-ils un projet commun?" Pages 313–19 in Bernard Cousin, ed., *Les Fédéralismes: Réalités et Représentations, 1789–1874.* Aix-en-Provence, 1995.

———. "Monarchist Clubs and the Pamphlet Debate over Political Legitimacy in the Early Years of the French Revolution," *French Historical Studies* 21, no. 2 (spring 1998): 299–324.

———. "Revolutionary Violence, Political Legitimacy and the *Journées* of 10 August and 31 May." In Robert Aldrich and Martyn Lyons, eds., *The Sphinx in the Tuileries and Other Essays in Modern French History.* Sydney, 1999.

Hermon-Belot, Rita. "L'Abbé Fauchet." Pages 329–49 in François Furet and Mona Ozouf, eds., *La Gironde et les Girondins.* Paris, 1991.

Higonnet, Patrice. "The Social and Cultural Antecedents of Revolutionary Discontinuity: Montagnards and Girondins," *English Historical Review* 100 (July 1985): 513–44.

Hufton, Olwen. *Women and the Limits of Citizenship in the French Revolution*. Toronto, 1992.

Hunt, Lynn. *Revolution and Urban Politics in Provincial France: Troyes and Reims, 1786–1790*. Palo Alto, 1978.

———. *Politics, Culture and Class in the French Revolution*. Berkeley, 1984.

———. *The Family Romance of the French Revolution*. Berkeley, 1992.

Jaume, Lucien. *Le Discours Jacobin et la démocratie*. Paris, 1989.

Jaurès, Jean. *Histoire Socialiste de la Révolution française*, 8 vols. Paris, 1922–24.

Johnson, Hubert C. *The Midi in Revolution: A Study of Regional Political Diversity, 1789–1793*. Princeton, 1986.

Jordan, David. *The King's Trial: Louis XVI vs. the French Revolution*. Berkeley, 1979.

———. *The Revolutionary Career of Maximilien Robespierre*. Chicago, 1985.

Kates, Gary. *The "Cercle Social," the Girondins, and the French Revolution*. Princeton, 1985.

Kennedy, Emmet. *A Cultural History of the French Revolution*. New Haven, 1989.

Kennedy, Michael L. *The Jacobin Clubs in the French Revolution: The First Years*. Princeton, 1982.

———. "The Best and the Worst of Times: The Jacobin Club Network from October 1791 to June 2, 1793," *Journal of Modern History* 56, no. 4 (December 1984): 635–66.

———. *The Jacobin Clubs in the French Revolution: The Middle Years*. Princeton, 1988.

Lallié, Alfred. "Le Fédéralisme dans le département de la Loire-Inférieure," *Revue de la Révolution* 15 (May–August 1889): 6–24, 357–76, 454–73; and 16 (September–December 1889): 126–38.

Landes, Joan B. *Women and the Public Sphere in the Age of the French Revolution*. Ithaca, 1988.

Le Guin, C. A. *Roland de la Platière: A Public Servant in the Eighteenth Century*. Philadelphia, 1966.

Levy, Darline Gay, Harriet B. Applewhite, and Mary Durham Johnson, eds. *Women in Revolutionary Paris, 1789–1795*. Urbana, 1979.

Lewis, Gwynne. *The Second Vendée: The Continuity of Counterrevolution in the Department of the Gard, 1789–1815*. Oxford, 1978.

Lewis-Beck, Michael S., Anne Hildreth, and Alan B. Spitzer. "Was There a Girondist Faction in the National Convention, 1792–1793?" *French Historical Studies* 15, no. 3 (spring 1988): 519–36.

Lucas, Colin. "The Crowd and Politics Between Ancien Régime and Revolution in France," *Journal of Modern History* 60, no. 3 (September 1988): 421–57.

———. "Revolutionary Violence, the People and the Terror." Pages 57–79 in Keith M. Baker, ed., *The Terror*. Oxford, 1994.

Lucas, Colin, ed. *Rewriting the French Revolution*. Oxford, 1991.

Margadant, Ted. *Urban Rivalries in the French Revolution*. Princeton, 1992.

Mathiez, Albert. *Le 10 août 1792*. Paris, 1931.

Melzer, Sara E., and Leslie W. Rabine, eds. *Rebel Daughters: Women and the French Revolution*. Oxford, 1992.

Monnier, Raymonde. *L'Espace Public Démocratique: Essai sur l'opinion à Paris de la Révolution au Directoire*. Paris, 1994.

———. "Mouvement républicaine et fédéralisme radical à Paris au printemps 1791." Pages 51–60 in Bernard Cousin, ed., *Les Fédéralismes: Réalités et Représentations, 1789–1874*. Aix-en-Provence, 1995.

Montier, A. *Robert Lindet, député à l'Assemblée Législative et à la Convention, membre du Comité de Salut Public, Ministre des Finances: Notice Biographique.* Paris, 1899.

Ozouf, Mona. *La Fête révolutionnaire, 1789–1799.* Paris, 1976.

Palmer, R. R. *Twelve Who Ruled: The Year of the Terror in the French Revolution.* Princeton, 1941.

Patrick, Alison. "Political Divisions in the French National Convention, 1792–93," *Journal of Modern History* 41 (1969): 421–74.

———. *The Men of the First French Republic.* Baltimore, 1972.

Reinhard, Marcel. *10 août 1792: La Chute de la Monarchie, 1787–1792.* Paris, 1969.

Roberts, J. M. *The French Revolution.* Oxford, 1978.

Rudé, George. *The Crowd in the French Revolution.* London, 1959.

Sa'adah, Anne. *The Shaping of Liberal Politics in Revolutionary France: A Comparative Perspective.* Princeton, 1990.

Scott, Samuel F., and Barry Rothaus, eds. *Historical Dictionary of the French Revolution.* Westport, Conn., 1985.

Slavin, Morris. *The Making of an Insurrection: Parisian Sections and the Gironde.* Cambridge, Mass., 1986.

Soboul, Albert. *The French Revolution, 1787–1799.* London, 1972.

Soboul, Albert, ed. *Girondins et Montagnards.* Paris, 1980.

Sutherland, D. M. G. *Revolution and Counterrevolution.* Oxford, 1986.

Sydenham, Michael J. *The Girondins.* London, 1961.

———. "The Montagnards and Their Opponents: Some Considerations on a Recent Reassessment of the Conflicts in the French National Convention, 1792–93," *Journal of Modern History* 43 (1971): 287–97.

———. "The Republican Revolt of 1793: A Plea for Less Localized Studies," *French Historical Studies* 11, no. 3 (spring 1981): 120–38.

Tackett, Timothy. *Becoming a Revolutionary: The Deputies of the French National Assembly and the Emergence of a Revolutionary Culture (1789–1790).* Princeton, 1996.

Thompson, J. M. *The French Revolution.* Oxford, 1966.

Vatel, C. *Charlotte de Corday et les Girondins.* Paris, 1864–72.

Vovelle, Michel. *La Chute de la Monarchie.* Paris, 1972.

Vovelle, Michel, ed. *Paris et la Révolution.* Paris, 1989.

Waldinger, Renée, Philip Dawson, and Isser Woloch, eds. *The French Revolution and the Meaning of Citizenship.* Westport, Conn., 1993.

Wallon, Henri. *La Révolution du 31 mai et le fédéralisme en 1793,* 2 vols. Paris, 1886.

Walzer, Michael. *Regicide and Revolution: Speeches at the Trial of Louis XVI.* New York, 1992.

BORDEAUX

Bécamps, P. *La Révolution à Bordeaux: J.-B.-M. Lacombe, Président de la Commission militaire.* Bordeaux, 1953.

———. *Les Suspects à Bordeaux et dans le Département de la Gironde, 1789–1799.* Paris, 1954.

Brace, Richard M. *Bordeaux and the Gironde, 1789–1794.* Ithaca, 1947.

Butel, Paul. *Les Négociants bordelais, l'Europe et les Iles au XVIIIe siècle.* Paris, 1974.

Etienne, R. *La Révolution à Bordeaux.* Bordeaux, 1969.

Forrest, Alan. *Society and Politics in Revolutionary Bordeaux.* London, 1975.

———. "The Revolution in Bordeaux: The Significance of the Federalist Movement of 1793." In *Bordeaux et les Iles britanniques du XIIIe au XXe siècle.* Bordeaux, 1975.

———. *The Revolution in Provincial France: Acquitaine, 1789–1799*. Oxford, 1996.

Pariset, François-Georges, ed. *Bordeaux au XVIIIe siècle*. Bordeaux, 1968.

Plantadis, J. "L'Agitation autonomiste de Guienne et le mouvement fédéraliste des Girondins en Limousin," *Bulletin de la Société des Lettres, Sciences, et Arts de la Corrèze* 20, no. 2 (1908).

Trimoulier, A. *Un Missionnaire de '93: Marc-Antoine Baudot*. Paris, 1908.

Vivie, Aurélien. *Histoire de la Terreur à Bordeaux*, 2 vols. Bordeaux, 1877.

CAEN

Boivin-Champeaux, L. *Notices Historiques sur la Révolution dans le département de l'Eure*, 2 vols. Evreux, 1894.

Bonnet de la Tour, G. "Le fédéralisme normand: La bataille sans larmes (Brécourt, 13 juillet 1793)," *Le Pays d'Argentan*, no. 132 (March 1964): 3–52.

Dubreuil, Léon. "Evreux aux temps du fédéralisme," *Révolution française* 78 (1925): 244–63, 318–48.

Goodwin, A. "The Federalist Movement in Caen During the French Revolution," *Bulletin of the John Rylands Library* 42 (March 1960): 313–43.

Grall, Jeanne. "Le Fédéralisme: Eure et Calvados," *Bulletin de la Société des Antiquaires de Normandie* 55 (1959–60): 133–53.

———. "La France au lendemain du 31 mai 1793," *Bulletin de la Société des Antiquaires de Normandie* 55 (1959–60): 513–24.

———. "L'Oeuvre de Robert Lindet dans le Calvados et le problème des subsistances (août–septembre 1793)," *Bulletin de la Société des Antiquaires de Normandie* 56 (1961–62), 339–57.

Hanson, Paul R. "Les Clubs politiques de Caen pendant la Révolution française," *Annales de Normandie* 36, no. 2 (May 1986): 123–41.

———. *Provincial Politics in the French Revolution: Caen and Limoges, 1789–1794*. Baton Rouge, 1989.

Le Parquier. "Rouen et le département de la Seine-Inférieure aux mois de juin et juillet 1793," *La Normandie* 2 (November 1895): 321–33, and (December 1895): 353–63.

Mancel, George. *La Société des Carabots*. Caen, 1857.

Montier, A. "Le Département de l'Eure et ses districts en juin 1793," *Révolution française* 30 (1896): 128–55, 198–226.

Nicolle, Paul. "Le Mouvement fédéraliste dans l'Orne en 1793," *Annales Historiques de la Révolution française* 13 (1936): 481–512; 14 (1937), 215–33; and 15 (1938), 12–33, 289–313, 385–410.

Patry, Robert. *Une Ville de province: Caen pendant la Révolution de 1789*. Caen, 1983.

Perrot, Jean-Claude. *Genèse d'une ville moderne: Caen au XVIIIe siècle*, 2 vols. Paris, 1975.

Renard, Charles. *Notice sur les Carabots de Caen*. Caen, 1858.

Sauvage, René Norbert. *Rapports d'un agent du conseil exécutif sur le Calvados à l'époque du fédéralisme*. Caen, 1908.

———. "Les Souvenirs de J.-B. Renée sur la Révolution à Caen, 1789–93," *Normannia* 7 (1934): 11–39.

Sauvage, René Norbert, ed. *Le Fédéralisme en Normandie: Journal du quartier-maître du 6e bataillon bis des volontaires du Calvados*. Caen, 1909.

Vaultier, Frédéric. *Souvenirs de l'insurrection Normande, dite du Fédéralisme, en 1793*. Caen, 1858.

LYON

Benoit, Bruno, and Roland Saussac, eds. *Guide Historique de la révolution à Lyon, 1789–1799*. Lyon, 1988.

Biard, Michel. "Collot d'Herbois et la Répression à Commune-Affranchie: Mythe et Réalité." Pages 207–16 in Bernard Cousin, ed. *Les Fédéralismes: Réalités et Représentations, 1789–1874*. Aix-en-Provence, 1995.

Braconnier, Martine. "Le Fédéralisme lyonnais: Originalité et mythe d'une répression (septembre–octobre 1793)." Pages 197–205 in Bernard Cousin, ed. *Les Fédéralismes: Réalités et Représentations, 1789–1874*. Aix-en-Provence, 1995.

Brelot, Jean. "L'Insurrection fédéraliste dans le Jura en 1793 (mars–août 1793)," *Bulletin de la Fédération des Sociétés Savantes de Franche-Comté*, no. 2 (1955): 73–102.

De Francesco, Antonio. "Le Quartier lyonnais de la Croisette pendant les premières années de la Révolution (1790–1793)," *Bulletin du Centre d'histoire économique et sociale de la région lyonnaise* 4 (1979): 22–45.

Edmonds, W. D. "A Study in Popular Anti-Jacobinism: The Career of Denis Monnet," *French Historical Studies* 13, no. 2 (fall 1983): 215–51.

———. "A Jacobin Debacle: The Losing of Lyon in Spring 1793," *History* 69, no. 225 (1984): 1–14.

———. "The Rise and Fall of Popular Democracy in Lyon, 1789–1795," *Bulletin of the John Rylands Library* 67, no. 1 (1984): 408–49.

———. *Jacobinism and the Revolt of Lyon, 1789–1793*. Oxford, 1990.

Feuga, Paul. *L'Hôtel de Ville de Lyon: L'Hôtel Commun et les Municipalités lyonnaises, 1789–1795*. Lyon, 1989.

Garden, Maurice. *Lyon et les Lyonnais au XVIIIe siècle*, 2 vols. Paris, 1970.

Guigue, Georges. *Procès-verbaux des séances de la Commission Populaire de Rhône-et-Loire*. Lyon, 1899.

Herriot, E. *Lyon n'est plus*, 4 vols. Paris, 1937–40.

Longfellow, David L. "Silk Weavers and the Social Struggle in Lyon During the French Revolution, 1789–1794," *French Historical Studies* 12, no. 1 (spring 1981): 1–40.

Mansfield, Paul. "The Repression of Lyon, 1793–94: Origins, Responsibility and Significance," *French History* 2, no. 1 (March 1988): 74–101.

Riffaterre, C. *Le Mouvement antijacobin et antiparisien à Lyon et dans le Rhône-et-Loire en 1793*, 2 vols. Lyon, 1912.

Rousset, Jean. "J. E. Gilibert, Docteur de Montpellier, homme politique à Lyon pendant la Révolution," *Monspeliensis Hippocrates*, no. 17 (fall 1962): 11–27.

Wahl, Maurice. "Joseph Chalier: Etude sur la Révolution française à Lyon," *Revue Historique* 34 (1887): 1–30.

MARSEILLE

Badet, Claude, ed. *Marseille en Révolution*. Marseille, 1989.

Bertrand, Régis. "Marseille à la veille de la Révolution." Pages 17–25 in Claude Badet, ed. *Marseille en Révolution*. Marseille 1989.

Cameron, John B. "The Revolution of the Sections in Marseille: Federalism in the Department of the Bouches-du-Rhône in 1793." Ph.D. diss., University of North Carolina, Chapel Hill, 1971.

Crook, Malcolm. *Toulon in War and Revolution: From the Ancien Régime to the Restoration, 1750–1820*. Manchester, 1991.

Cubells, Monique. *Les Horizons de la liberté: Naissance de la révolution en Provence, 1787–1789*. Aix-en-Provence, 1987.

———. "Marseille entre en Révolution (1787–1789)." Pages 35–41 in Claude Badet, ed., *Marseille en Révolution*. Marseille, 1989.

Fabre, Gérard, and Véronique Autheman, eds. *Journal d'un Marseillais (Jean-Louis Laplane), 1789–1793*. Marseille, 1989.

Guibal, Georges. *Le Mouvement fédéraliste en Provence en 1793*. Paris, 1908.

Guilhaumou, Jacques. "Les Fédéralismes marseillais en 1793." Pages 105–13 in Claude Badet, ed. *Marseille en Révolution*. Marseille, 1989.

———. "Les Jacobins marseillais et la propagation des idées républicaines (1791–92)." Pages 81–85 in Claude Badet, ed., *Marseille en Révolution*. Marseille, 1989.

———. *Marseille républicaine (1791–1793)*. Paris, 1992.

Kennedy, Michael. *The Jacobin Club of Marseille, 1790–1794*. Ithaca, 1973.

Reichardt, Rolf. "Prise et démolition des 'Bastilles Marseillaises'—événement symbole révolutionnaire." Pages 53–61 in Claude Badet, ed. *Marseille en Révolution*. Marseille, 1989.

Scott, William. *Terror and Repression in Revolutionary Marseilles*. London, 1973.

Vovelle, Michel. "Le Sans-culotte marseillais," *Mesure de l'Histoire* 1 (1986): 75–95.

Index